1982

University of St. Francis
GEN 826.8 B884b
Browning, Elizabeth Barr

P9-CBH-032
00090379 5

ELIZABETH BARRETT TO MR. BOYD

Published on the Sophie Hart Fund of Wellesley College

Elizabeth Barrett to Mr Boyd

UNPUBLISHED LETTERS OF

ELIZABETH BARRETT BROWNING

TO HUGH STUART BOYD

INTRODUCED AND EDITED BY BARBARA P. McCARTHY

PUBLISHED FOR WELLESLEY COLLEGE BY

YALE UNIVERSITY PRESS · NEW HAVEN · 1955

LIBRARY
College of St. Francis
JOLIET, ILL.

TEXT OF LETTERS COPYRIGHT, 1955, BY JOHN MURRAY.
INTRODUCTION AND EDITORIAL MATERIAL
COPYRIGHT, 1955, BY YALE UNIVERSITY PRESS.
PRINTED IN THE UNITED STATES OF AMERICA BY
VAIL-BALLOU PRESS, INC., BINGHAMTON, N.Y.
ALL RIGHTS RESERVED. THIS BOOK MAY NOT BE
REPRODUCED, IN WHOLE OR IN PART, IN ANY FORM
(EXCEPT BY REVIEWERS FOR THE PUBLIC PRESS),
WITHOUT WRITTEN PERMISSION FROM THE PUBLISHERS.
LIBRARY OF CONGRESS CATALOG CARD NUMBER: 55-8706

826.8
B884b

FOREWORD

WHEN IN 1863, two years after the death of Elizabeth Barrett Browning, a certain George Stampe proposed to print her letters to Hugh Stuart Boyd, Robert Browning denounced the would-be editor as a beast and a blackguard and threatened to obtain an injunction against him. These letters, he said, were written "on the most intimate and personal subjects," [1] and their recipient, dying "old, blind, forsaken," would have been heartbroken "to let communications meant for his single ear be hawked about the world." [2] In the face of Browning's harsh words, the present editor takes comfort in the belief that Boyd, at least, would have applauded publication. The idea, in fact, occurred to him early in the correspondence, and he went so far as to secure a publisher in the person of his friend E. H. Barker, a man with, in Elizabeth's words, an "unquestionable talent for bookmaking." Although Elizabeth expressed a willingness to permit the printing of selected passages, she vetoed any general publication both at that time and again after Mr. Boyd's death, when her letters to him fell into the hands of a "complete stranger." Happily, however, we know that on principle she favored the preservation and ultimate printing of any letters of permanent interest. Discussing this question with Miss Mitford, she wrote, "Is not the natural thought when the time comes for thinking— 'Let whatever is good in me of heart and intellect live as long as the world will let it, for the use and service of the world'? Is not *that* the natural and disinterested thought, with which we should look down from Heaven?" [3]

Browning, it would seem, succeeded in reclaiming most of his wife's letters to Boyd, for two hundred and forty of them were in the possession of his son R. W. Barrett (Pen) Browning at the time of his death in 1912. At the Sotheby auction of the Browning collections the following year they were purchased by Frank Sabin of London and passed from him to Ernest Dressel North of New York and George Herbert Palmer of Cambridge, Massachusetts, who presented them in 1930 to the library of Wellesley College. Of this group of letters, sixty-seven had

1. *Dearest Isa. Robert Browning's Letters to Isabella Blagden,* ed. Edward C. McAleer (University of Texas, 1951), Letter 58, p. 149.
2. "Robert Browning, A Castigation," *Methuen's Annual* (1914), p. 49.
3. Miller, p. 212.

99630

been published in 1897 by F. G. Kenyon, who was clearly unfamiliar with the total correspondence. Commenting on the letters of the Hope End period, of which he published only three, Kenyon says, ". . . very few have been preserved, and most of those which remain are of little interest"; yet almost half (119) of the letters to Boyd in the Wellesley collection date from this early period and there is true biographical importance in the picture they present of the personality and literary pursuits of the young Elizabeth.

In addition to the letters to Boyd at Wellesley, there are twenty-one in the Huntington Library, of which twenty were published by Bennett Weaver in *PMLA,* 1950. The remaining Huntington item and single letters in the Houghton Library of Harvard University, the Cornell University Library,[4] and the Berg Collection of the New York Public Library appear here for the first time. Of Boyd's side of the correspondence nine letters dating from 1842–43 are in the library of the University of Illinois. One hundred and seventy were in existence at the time of the Sotheby auction in 1913; they were purchased together with EBB's letters to Boyd by Frank Sabin, who cannot now recall what he did with them.

The formulation of procedure in editing these letters has not been easy. One attractive possibility would have been to present, through careful selection, a continuous narrative of the changing relationship between the two correspondents. Such a plan would have meant rigorous pruning of the literary and intellectual discussions of the early letters, which are of unusual interest because they incorporate a young scholar's critical thinking and *ars poetica.* This method would have called, too, for the elimination of many of the trivia and repetitions which, notwithstanding their triviality, contribute to the picture of a living interchange between the two friends. As I continued to work with the material, I became increasingly unwilling to make such an abbreviated selection. On the other hand, since I have not wished to subject the nonspecialist to what might appear to be excessive pedantry, I have eliminated a few passages which deal with textual problems or which contain detailed criticism of Boyd's writings and of other unfamiliar works. These omissions, which are indicated by the usual three dots, are summarized in the notes, and a typescript of them has been deposited in the Wellesley College Library. As the publications of Kenyon and Weaver are readily available, it has seemed unnecessary to duplicate them here. Where Kenyon omits material, however,

---

4. I am grateful to Ferris Cronkhite, assistant professor of English at Cornell University, who very generously relinquished plans to publish this letter in order that it might be included in the present edition.

I have reprinted the complete letter, except in two instances where I cite the omitted passage in a footnote.[5] In order to clarify the sequence of the correspondence, all the known letters from EBB to Boyd have been arranged in what appears to me to be their probable chronological order (below, pp. 287–89).

The dating of the letters has presented a fascinating and at times exasperating problem. EBB frequently omits all or part of the date, and although there are some helpful postmarks, many of the letters were delivered by hand or sent through the Malvern Penny Post, which at this time did not date its mail. A few letters can be placed by the mention of some specific event, but for the most part the editor must depend on less objective evidence. Fortunately, the continuity and liveliness of the correspondence resulted in frequent backward glances, repetitions, and cross references, so that in the end an interlocking pattern has emerged into which most of the letters can be fitted with some confidence.

The transcribing of the manuscripts also has posed problems. Although EBB's small, neat handwriting is legible in a clear context, it becomes puzzling when one encounters an unfamiliar phrase or proper noun. A few of the names, indeed, have defied search and may have been incorrectly read.[6] The spelling, once the letters are deciphered, proves to be generally accurate but not always consistent. I have corrected occasional errors but have not eliminated such alternative spellings as *color, colour; judgment, judgement; tease, teaze;* nor have I modernized such spellings as *poney* or *stewart.* Ampersands, and contractions such as *wd* and *cd,* have been expanded. EBB's Greek I have left as she wrote it—"lady's Greek / Without the accents" Romney called it in *Aurora Leigh;* sometimes, perhaps when her blind correspondent was depending on a Greekless reader, the words are transliterated into English letters, with long *e* (*eta*) represented by *ee* and long *o* (*omega*) by *oo.* As for the punctuation, it is clear, vivid, and rhetorical, suggesting the pauses and emphases of oral speech, and I have tried to reproduce it faithfully. Complete accuracy is not always possible, especially with dots and dashes which, in her quick handwriting, are often indistinguishable. One frequent mark, a dash superimposed above a comma, I have interpreted sometimes as comma dash,

5. Letter 163, n. 1; 165, n. 2.

6. Some proper names in Kenyon and Weaver can now be corrected. In Kenyon, *1, 23,* for *Parker* read *Barker;* in *1,* 76 (to Mrs. Martin), for *Bury* read *Barry.* In Weaver, Letters I, V, for *Grant* read *Trant;* in Letters V, XI, for *Naby* read *Ruby;* in Letter VII for *Carron* read *Curzon;* in Letter XVIII for *the Miss Hinds* read *the Miss Heards.* Mr. Tyrus G. Harmsen, Cataloguer, has kindly checked for me the readings of the Huntington Library MSS.

sometimes as a semicolon. Two or more dashes in series have been edited to one; where dots appear in series, I have replaced them by a single dash to distinguish them from the three dots marking omission. I have taken another liberty with the text by placing uniformly in the upper right-hand corner the heading which EBB gives sometimes at the beginning, sometimes at the close of the letter. Boyd's address, when we have it, I have placed in the upper left-hand corner. Through Letter 146 the address is written on the sheet of writing paper, which was folded and sealed. Most of the subsequent letters are accompanied by separate envelopes which seem correctly matched so far as one can judge from the date and from the size and folds of the paper.

In annotating the letters I have tried to keep in mind both the general reader and the specialist. Since Greek phrases may well baffle both groups, they are given in English in the notes; unless otherwise indicated, the translation is the editor's. For abbreviations in the notes see the cue titles listed on p. x. A list of the most important works of reference on EBB can be found in a recent biography by Dorothy Hewlett, *Elizabeth Barrett Browning, a Life,* New York, 1952.

MANY FRIENDS have helped in the task of editing these letters by contributing general advice or particular information. I should like to thank them all, while I record a special debt of gratitude to President Margaret Clapp and the Trustees of Wellesley College for permission to edit this Wellesley collection and to the following libraries for permission to print single letters: the Houghton Library of Harvard University, Letter 154; the Cornell University Library, Letter 164; the Henry W. and Albert A. Berg Collection of the New York Public Library, Letter 170; the Huntington Library, Letter 172; and the Sterling Library of Yale University for permission to quote from a letter to Annie Boyd Hayes, note 3 of Letter 162. Sir John Murray and John Grey Murray have granted the necessary privileges of Browning copyright. Five scholars in the field of English literature have given me much valuable guidance—Martha Hale Shackford, Katharine C. Balderston, and Sylvia Berkman of Wellesley College, Gordon S. Haight of Yale, and Gardner Taplin of Boston University. I am grateful also to Hannah French, Research Librarian at Wellesley, for assistance in many aspects of the work, and to Jean Willcutt for her continuous interest and help at every stage in the preparation of the manuscript.

BARBARA P. MCCARTHY

Wellesley, Massachusetts
February, 1955

CONTENTS

CUE TITLES

INTRODUCTION: THE STORY OF THE
FRIENDSHIP, 1827–48

Elizabeth Barrett Barrett

IN 1827, when these letters begin, Elizabeth Barrett Barrett was twenty-one years old. For eighteen years she had lived in one of the showplaces of Herefordshire, a great oriental mansion with dome and turrets and crescented minarets, set in a park of tall trees, small lakes, bright gardens, and winding carriage roads, and ringed by a circle of low hills. Here in Hope End [1] the world was shut out, but climbing one of the hills that formed the barrier, Elizabeth could gaze on a "white ribbon of a road which unrolled itself along the green distance, and was called the London road." [2] As a child she used to fancy that she and Hope End were tied to the world by this ribbon and that an angel might some day take it up in his hand and draw them nearer. For it was not Elizabeth Barrett's natural instinct or desire to lead a life of isolation. At this period her excursions into the world had been limited to a stay of seven months at Boulogne—where the children were taken to acquire "the habit of talking French" [3]—a brief visit to Paris, and occasional family vacations in "the intoxicating gaieties of a watering place" [4] like Ramsgate. But she had dreamed of far countries and strange adventures, of dressing as a boy, for example, and going off to join Lord Byron in Greece. In the meantime, life in sequestered Hope End had gone on placidly and on the whole cheerfully.

The family was a large one, and no one who has read the childhood letters and birthday verses of the "Poet Laureate of Hope End" [5] can doubt that it was an unusually close and devoted one. The father,

1. The name was probably not intended to be pessimistic; "hope" is an Old English word for "valley."

2. Letter to Miss Mitford, January 28, 1845; unpublished: Wellesley College Library.

3. Letter to Miss Mitford, March 1844; unpublished: Wellesley College Library.

4. From "Glimpses into My Own Life and Literary Character," written at the age of fourteen; *Hitherto Unpublished Poems, 1,* 12.

5. A title conferred on her by her father (along with a ten-shilling note) for a poem on virtue written at the age of six.

Edward Barrett Moulton-Barrett, and his gentle wife, Mary Graham-Clarke, six years his senior, had true love for each other and for their children. Though commercial ventures and the business of his Jamaica estates frequently kept Mr. Barrett in London, family excursions and celebrations were shared whenever possible by both parents. So were family troubles and triumphs. When Elizabeth at fifteen developed a serious illness, both father and mother hovered over her with grave concern and for two years refused every kind of social engagement in order to be constantly with her. During the period of convalescence her mother entertained her by sketching a portrait [6] of her sitting in a high armchair with a shawl about her shoulders, a woolly nightcap framing her thin pensive face and short dark hair. A touching extract from a diary written in 1823, in the second year of her illness, records that on February 21 she walked for the first time into Mama's room and onto the balcony, and on March 2 Papa allowed her to go downstairs for the first time. Three years later, in 1826, the two parents shared together her triumph in the publication of the erudite *Essay on Mind*. A letter from her mother to Elizabeth, who was away on a brief visit, describes the arrival of the first copies at Hope End and how, after the "learned critics" (the children) had betaken themselves to bed, she and Papa "each with a precious little volume in [their] hands, drew close to the fire and conned over every word." "I wish, my beloved Ba," she wrote, "I could tell you all he said in commendation of this wondrous little book." [7]

Mrs. Barrett, with all her love and devotion, had spells of nervousness and depression and in this year of 1827 was very far from well. "A sweet, gentle nature," Elizabeth wrote in retrospect to Browning, "which the thunder a little turns from its sweetness—as when it turns milk." [8] And if their mother had periods when she withdrew from her children, their father, so gay and companionable, so proud of them, and for a man so very tender, also had another side to his nature. At times a dark mood settled on him, and he would remain morosely silent or thunder out tyrannical decrees which none in the family dared question. As he grew older, this brooding, unhappy side of his nature was to be more frequently and fully revealed.

In 1827 the Moulton-Barretts had been married twenty-two years and had had twelve children, eleven of whom were still living. Elizabeth was the eldest; when she was twenty-one her two sisters, Henrietta and

6. Huxley, facing p. 128.
7. *Catalogue of the Papers of . . . Moulton-Barrett* (Sotheby, 1937), p. 2.
8. EBB—RB, 2, 482.

Arabel, were eighteen and fourteen, Edward (Bro) was nineteen, and the other seven boys ranged in age from Sam who was fifteen to Octavius (Occy) who was only two. To all of them Elizabeth was their beloved "Ba," a name which she had bestowed very early upon herself, when she used to say "Ba [Baby] did" this or that. And Ba responded to them all with love, though the bond was especially close with Bro and Henrietta and Arabel. Of her brother she had written solemnly at fourteen, "If I ever loved any human being I love this dear Brother—the Partner of my pleasures, of my literary toils. My attachment to him is literally devoted!" [9] As children they had always shared their thoughts and their private jokes and before Bro went to school at Charterhouse had enjoyed together the study of Greek and Latin under his tutor, Mr. MacSwiney,

> While one young critic, on the classic style,
> Would sagely try to frown, and make the other smile.[10]

Now that they were older and Bro was busy with his tasks as the young squire of Hope End, his eagerness for classical learning had somewhat abated, but there continued to exist between him and his sister a gay and understanding fellowship. As for Henrietta and Arabel, the letters reveal them as affectionate, normal, attractive young women. Both seem to have had vigorous health, wit, piety, and genuine goodness. Arabel, like her mother, had a talent for painting, Henrietta was fond of music and dancing; like Bro both admired their sister's scholarship but did not emulate it.

Outside of the family circle and the relatives who came and went on brief visits, Elizabeth's world at Hope End was very limited. There were the neighbors—the Martins of Old Colwall, the Peytons of Barton Court, the sharp-tongued Commelines; there was Lady Margaret Cocks of stately Eastnor Castle, repressed and formal in her manner, with literary ambitions but meager talent; and nearer Ba's own age there was Eliza Cliffe of Mathon, warmhearted and gossipy, destined twenty years later to become fat and red and *"wear her hair in bandeaux."* [11] None of these people satisfied Elizabeth's desire for contact with a more interesting life beyond the valley of Hope End; so she turned more and more to books—both romantic novels, to which she was frankly addicted all her life, and serious study of history, philosophy and theology, the ancient classics, and English literature. Greek was her especial passion. At eight she had read the *Iliad* and *Odyssey* in Pope's translation; at nine

9. *Hitherto Unpublished Poems, 1,* 19.
10. *Works,* p. 53.
11. Huxley, p. 89.

she planted and trimmed her garden into a giant figure of Hector, son of
Priam, and dreamed of Agamemnon; she had completed an epic poem
On the Battle of Marathon when she was thirteen; and at fourteen she
wrote in her diary that the height of her ambition was to be a good
linguist. Her only instruction in Greek had come from Mr. MacSwiney,
but she continued to study Sophocles and Plato with ardor if not with
accuracy, and "read Greek as hard under the trees as some of your
Oxonians in the Bodleian." [12]

Only one friend truly shared her more learned interests—this was
Uvedale Price, country gentleman and scholar, eighty-year-old master of
Foxley Hall, a handsome estate eight miles west of Hereford. Mr. Price
(he was to become Sir Uvedale in 1828) had published a work of some
repute on the picturesque as opposed to the formal style in landscaping,
and was known besides as an amateur Greek scholar and translator of
Pausanias. The remarkable friendship between these two, almost sixty
years apart in age, had led to mutual friendly criticism. When Elizabeth,
in 1826, published the *Essay on Mind,* Mr. Price, delighted with this
compendium of erudition in verse, wrote detailed comments on both
the matter and meter; and she, in turn, read the proof sheets of his
Essay on the Modern Pronunciation of Greek and Latin, a plea for reading the ancient languages by length of syllable rather than by accent,
and offered remarks before the book was published in 1827.

Hugh Stuart Boyd

It was admiration for the *Essay on Mind* which led in this year to a
second and more important literary friendship—that with Hugh Stuart
Boyd, an eccentric, scholarly gentleman living in the neighboring village
of Malvern Wells. Mr. Boyd was of a distinguished north-of-Ireland
family with an estate at Ballycastle in County Antrim. His father, Hugh
McAuley Boyd, had been a friend of William Pitt and was well enough
known in political circles to be credited by some with the authorship
of the Junius letters, anonymous criticisms of the government which
stirred London from 1768 to 1772. When he died in 1794, his son Hugh
was only thirteen. As a boy in Hampstead he studied Greek under a tutor
with the unusual name of Spowers, who introduced him to the same
system of reading Greek by quantity that was to be championed by
Uvedale Price. The boy had a true ear and a good sense of rhythm, and
from reading aloud metrically developed an amazing verbal memory
for Greek lines, which was a source of entertainment and pride to him

12. Horne, *1,* 161.

in later years. The classics continued to interest him at Westminster and at Cambridge, where he was a pensioner at Pembroke College in 1800 and 1801. But other subjects of the curriculum had less appeal and much of his time at the university was, in fact, devoted to composing a long and incredibly dull tragedy "as a recreation from severer studies, or to speak more truly, as a substitute for severer studies." The result was that he left Cambridge without a degree. The tragedy, when submitted to the manager of Drury Lane, was pronounced "deficient in interest and effect," a comment which did not deter the author from having it published.[13]

Four years after leaving Cambridge, Boyd married Ann Lowry,[14] daughter of Wilson Lowry, well known engraver and Fellow of the Royal Society, but he never established a real home for his wife and their daughter, Ann Henrietta. Living in England on the income from his Irish estate, he moved his family and his library, as caprice or literary friendships dictated, from one furnished house to another, pursuing the career of dilettante scholar, translator, and author. The Church Fathers particularly absorbed his attention because, as he put it, they "abounded in that style of oratory which was congenial to [his] taste," [15] and he shortly published *Select Passages of the Writings of St. Chrysostom, St. Gregory Nazianzen and St. Basil.* In 1811 he contracted a serious case of ophthalmia which was to result in complete blindness, but in spite of this handicap he continued his scholarly labors by seeking out people who would read Greek to him, sometimes gaining a reader by giving instruction to a young candidate for the university. A second volume of translations, *Select Poems of Synesius and Gregory Nazianzen,* was published in 1814; in it he begs the learned reader's indulgence for errors and imperfections, since the author "has had no [other] resource than to translate some passages which were impressed upon his memory, and to get others by heart, by having them frequently read to him." The volume contains in addition to translations some very personal poems, including one entitled "Written when Afflicted by Weak Sight."

Curious motley volumes followed through the years, in which original verses mingle with translations from classical and Christian Greek poets, and with rhetorical theological discussions and personal comments. To

13. Preface to *Luceria, a Tragedy,* London, 1806.

14. "Sept. 16, 1805[.] At Dorking, Surrey, Hugh Boyd, esq. of Ballycastle, Ireland, to Miss Lowry, daughter of Wilson L., esq. of Tichfield Street," *Gentleman's Magazine,* 75 (1805), 875.

15. *The Catholic Faith: A Sermon by St. Basil, Translated from the Greek. To Which Is Added a Brief Refutation of Popery from the Writings of the Fathers* (London, 1825), p. 31.

his translation of the *Agamemnon* in 1823, for example, he appended
selections from Gregory and original poems in both English and Greek,
with the explanation that "having had the trouble of translating the
former and of composing the latter, I am not willing that they should
sink into utter oblivion, unnoticed and unknown." Compositions which
especially satisfied him were reprinted in various combinations, "corrected and enlarged." A technical work on the Greek article, which
originally appeared in Adam Clarke's *Commentary on the Scriptures,*
was reprinted in combination with an earlier essay on the Atonement
and was also made the subject of a ten-line poem in Greek entitled
εἰς τον ἐμον λογον τον περι του ἀρθρου ("To my Essay on the Article"). This
amazing self-tribute well demonstrates the mingled pompous self-
esteem and childish naiveté which characterize Boyd's writings.

His original poetry can be sufficiently illustrated by two poems inspired by a tragedy at Great Malvern in 1826, the death by lightning of
two young ladies who were members of a picnic party. The first version,
entitled "A Day of Pleasure at Malvern," was characteristically appended
to a collection of ancient epitaphs, *Tributes to the Dead* (1826). The
second was the title poem of *A Malvern Tale* (1827). After the first
publication critics protested that the author "had sent the young ladies
to Heaven, without knowing anything of their spiritual state." In the
preface to the second version, Boyd sought to justify this assumption on
the grounds of Christian charity, but he was sufficiently influenced to
change the moral of the story, as can be seen from a comparison of
the final four lines of the two poems.

> E'en so shall they, the grave's long winter past,
> Clothed in immortal spring, revive at last;
> Lift their fair heads above the withering tomb,
> And in yon Heaven's eternal summer bloom.
>
> ("A Day of Pleasure")

> Awhile they sailed on pleasure's golden tide—
> A storm arose: the lightning came: they died—
> If upon them Heaven's dart unsparing flew,
> Think that the next dread shaft may light on you.
>
> ("A Malvern Tale")

Of Boyd's verse translations it can be said without fear of exaggerated
praise that they are an improvement on his original poems; his versions
of the classical authors especially are fairly literal and succeed in keeping much of the nobility and directness of the originals. But when he

translates ecclesiastical sermons, the oratory—so "congenial to his taste"
—seems to intoxicate him and lead him into inexact and bombastic
renderings. When Basil in the oration *De Fide,* for example, says that
Moses saw the weakness of his tongue, the verb ἑώρα is expanded to "He
saw, he felt, he deplored."

The same rhetorical style permeates his own commentaries and essays.
The *Reflections on the Atoning Sacrifice of Jesus Christ* (1817) concludes
with a characteristic passage, "Alas! my mind is overpowered with excess
of brightness: it staggers, it sinks beneath such a blaze of glory. It is
time that I should return to earth. It behooves me to retire into myself;
to remember that I still am mortal; to resume the offices of faith and
hope, and to implore that blessing on the Reader, which I trust he will
implore for me." One theme dominates most of his theological writings:
the recurrent argument that the early Fathers of the church held strictly
Protestant views and that only corruption can be expected of Roman
"Catholicks" and Unitarians. "The primitive Christians were neither
Papists nor Unitarians. The church of Christ during the first three centuries was *exactly the same* as the Church of England and the Orthodox
Dissenters, in its leading doctrines; and it was *nearly the same* as the
Church of England in its discipline." [16] "Few sinners can be as guilty
in the sight of God, as they who make use of their learning to corrupt
His Holy Word, and of their influence, to deceive those who look up to
them as their spiritual guides. Of this sin the Unitarians are as guilty as
the Papists." [17] "The Popish version of passages from the New Testament
is as false as Hell, and our translation pure and unsullied as the light of
Heaven." [18]

While Boyd was absorbed in his career of curious scholarship, listening to the Fathers read aloud, chanting favorite passages from memory
as he beat out the rhythm on the table, dictating his translations and
essays, and occasionally instructing some young friend in Greek, life was
fully satisfying to him, and he wanted no roots except his attachment
to his self-appointed work and to his friends. In 1825, perhaps because of
the nearness of his old tutor Spowers, he came to the "genteel village" of
Great Malvern, then a small health resort of some sixty houses on the
slope of the Worcester Beacon,[19] and stayed with his family for a time

16. *Tributes to the Dead; in a Series of Ancient Epitaphs Translated from the
Greek* (London, 1826), p. 67.

17. *The Catholic Faith,* p. 66.

18. *Thoughts on an Illustrious Exile: Occasioned by the Persecution of the Protestants in 1815* (London, 1825), p. xii.

19. *Paterson's Roads* (18th ed. London, 1831), p. 139.

at Morison's Hotel. In Malvern, Boyd found a congenial fellow scholar in Dr. Card, the local vicar, for whose learning and oratorical gifts he expressed admiration in the prefaces of three books published in 1825 and 1826. The vicar was engaged in restoring the priory of Great Malvern, and he and Boyd discovered a common interest besides their theology—an enthusiasm for campanology and an admiration in particular for the sweet music of the ancient bells of Malvern Priory. According to a liberal local paper, the *Hereford Independent,* this Dr. Card was a stubborn reactionary who opposed Catholic emancipation and threatened to boycott tradesmen attending chapel instead of the established church; but these accusations, if true, probably did not damage him in Mr. Boyd's esteem. He decided to settle near this new friend and leased Ruby Cottage, a furnished house a mile and a half distant in Malvern Wells.

Here he found himself within a few miles of the young woman whose *Essay on Mind* with its extraordinary erudition had already excited his admiration. Elizabeth in later years came to loathe this didactic poem, "long repented of as worthy of all repentance." Even more than its "literary defectiveness" she regretted the "pertness and pedantry which did not even then belong to the character of the author." [20] But these were the very qualities which appealed to the taste of Hugh Stuart Boyd, and he set out seriously and methodically to cultivate the acquaintance of this "highly favored child of the Muses." [21] Inquiries about her and her family were followed by letters to Miss Barrett commenting on her *Essay,* by gifts of his own volumes, and by an urgent invitation to call at Ruby Cottage. The extant correspondence begins with Elizabeth's second letter, written March 11, 1827. To her the unknown scholar, with his tragic affliction of blindness, his great learning in her beloved field of Greek, and his impressive roster of publications was an exciting figure from the world beyond Hope End, and she responded quickly to his offer of friendship. This response in the early letters is wrapped in an eloquence and pretentiousness which rival Boyd's own; they are clearly the product of the young writer of the *Essay on Mind,* of the "fair author" whom a reviewer in the *Literary Gazette* had begged to "undress herself from the deep blue" in which she was attired. It is interesting to note how the stiffness relaxes and the style becomes more informal as the friendship grew which was to last through Elizabeth's marriage until Boyd's death in 1848.

20. Horne, *1,* 160.
21. Letter by Boyd, *Classical Journal* (June 1828), p. 327.

Hope End, 1827–28

During the first year of their correspondence Elizabeth and Hugh Boyd did not meet. She was grateful for his invitation to visit him and his family at Ruby Cottage, but she pleaded prettily a "deficiency in strength" or "engaged time and want of conveyance"; finally in November she was forced to admit that her father had refused permission on the ground that such a visit from a "young female" would be "overstepping the established observances of society"—this though the man in question was forty-seven, blind, and in the company of his wife and daughter. They had to be content to exchange literary works and to offer mutual criticism and share ideas, finding many points of sympathy in appreciation of each other's writings and of the classical authors. In the letters of the first year Greek is the dominant subject. Elizabeth will give up this study only when she gives up poetry, although she admits that since the elementary instruction from her brother's tutor she has been an "unassisted student" and "slovenly" enough. They discover with excitement a strong bond between them—that they are among the elite who read Greek according to quantity. Boyd begins by questions to direct Elizabeth's study. Does she read the tragedies by herself? She has read Sophocles, and Euripides' *Medea,* but not Aeschylus. He sends her his translation of the *Agamemnon,* and before many months she is quoting casually in Greek not only from the *Agamemnon* but from Aeschylus' *Choephoroe, Suppliants, Prometheus,* and *Eumenides.* Other authors from whom she quotes in Greek are Homer, Hesiod, Pindar, and Anacreon. Boyd tries to guide her into the Fathers through his *Select Passages,* but though she expresses delight and admiration for certain passages, she is not yet ready to accept a loan of Chrysostom's "Oration on Eutropius," since she is reading in quite a different direction. She is pleased, however, to borrow books from him on the Greek tragedies. Though Latin interests them both far less than Greek, they discover a common enthusiasm—in opposition to the critics—for Lucan's *Pharsalia.* Elizabeth has poetic perception enough to qualify her praise and is quite properly indignant when Boyd pronounces Lucan superior to Homer in delineation of character. In another letter she launches out against critics who prefer Vergil to Homer—she has tried on principle to like both olives and the *Aeneid,* but without success. Boyd questions her about Hebrew; she answers that she has read only a few chapters of the original Scriptures and has laid aside the study for the present.

This kind of scholarly exchange had been in progress for more than a year before Elizabeth paid her first visit to Ruby Cottage, on April 16, 1828. Leading up to it was a "long and romantic story" related in a letter which she intended for her "beloved" grandmother, Mrs. Moulton, but which bears the endorsement "Meeting with Mr. Boyd. When I had written it, I thought I would keep it." [22] On Thursday, March 13, according to this leisurely narrative, she and her two sisters set out to pay an unaccustomed visit to a cousin, Mrs. Trant, whose home was only a mile from Ruby Cottage. A hundred yards from the house they passed a lady and a gentleman walking in the road. Henrietta and Arabel, who knew him by sight, exclaimed "Mr. Boyd!" whereupon Elizabeth was thrown into such a state of excitement that she could not summon the courage to introduce herself but proceeded without any sign of recognition to Mrs. Trant's. She emerged immediately on learning that a neighbor, Lady Knowles, was preparing to set out for a call at Hope End, and hurried next door to suggest that the visit be deferred because Mrs. Barrett was not feeling well that day. These movements were reported by Mrs. Boyd to her husband, who waxed childishly indignant when told that Elizabeth had gone into the home of Sir Charles Knowles. He had accepted Mr. Barrett's absurd ruling against a visit to any man outside the family, and now he felt betrayed. The next morning Elizabeth received from him a letter of eight and a half foolscap pages, reading in part: "I suppose it was *you* who passed me this morning near Sir Charles Knowles's, and afterwards went into *his house!!* Whether it was you or not, it awakened within me feelings and reflections which for several months have been *somewhat* repressed! Mrs. Boyd is tired of this place and wishes to leave it. If I *should* do so, I shall probably write you a letter the *day before,* to tell you more fully what I think and feel!" Elizabeth's distress upon receiving these reproaches apparently gave her eloquence, for a plea to her father this time gained her permission to do as she liked.

The following Monday she set out for Malvern Wells again, with Bro driving and Henrietta and Arabel to give her moral support as far as Mrs. Trant's. The letter to her grandmother gives details of what followed. They were on the "precipitous hill" descending into Worcestershire when the pony "kicked violently and sprang madly down the tremendous descent." Elizabeth in terror clutched twice at the reins, and in three minutes they "were all precipitated upon the bank." Henrietta, who was found to have "a lump on her forehead and a strain in her ankle," was dispatched by the coach to Mrs. Trant's. Elizabeth, covered with dust and with pelisse and bonnet torn, was afraid to trust

22. The letter is published in *Hitherto Unpublished Poems,* 2, 87–93.

the pony again; so Bro fastened it to a tree and gallantly drew the carriage. At this point they again met Mr. and Mrs. Boyd walking in the road. Trembling from head to foot, Elizabeth left the carriage, Mrs. Boyd said "Miss Barrett," Mr. Boyd shook hands in silence, and they walked together to Mrs. Trant's. Elizabeth gives a picture of her new friend as he appeared to her at this moment—a "rather young looking man than otherwise, moderately tall, and slightly formed. His features are good—his face very pale with an expression of placidity and mildness. He is totally blind—and from the quenched and deadened appearance of his eyes, hopelessly so! His voice is very harmonious and gentle and low—and seems to have naturally a melancholy cadence and tone!— which is affecting when you look at his quenched and deadened eyes— totally and hopelessly blind. I did not see him smile once!" For a year she had seen Mr. Boyd in her imagination as a figure of romance, and the circumstances of this first meeting served to deepen the spell.

Minor hindrances multiplied themselves, and it was not until a month later that Elizabeth finally walked through the garden that separated Ruby Cottage from the road and entered the little door beside the bow window. Though the visit, so long anticipated, is nowhere described in detail, we know that it lasted long enough to cause a "cruel separation" between Mr. Boyd and his dinner and to awaken in his visitor some of his own excitement in the writings of the Fathers. Elizabeth that afternoon read aloud in Greek from St. Chrysostom (too swiftly for Boyd's approval) and listened to him chant the sonorous periods and descant upon the text; after this she could no longer refuse the offer of his copy but took it home and read the Saint's words to herself in both Greek and English "sufficiently loudly to startle his 'canonized bones.' " [23] But the classical writers still held first place in her affections and on her second visit, which Boyd recorded in his copy of her *Essay on Mind* as May 16, she read with him the opening of the *Oedipus*.

This second visit may have been paid not at Ruby Cottage but at Woodland Lodge, which the Boyds leased some time in May 1828. A plain double-gabled house on the farther side of Great Malvern, it faced directly on the Worcester Road, with hills rising opposite where

> Past the pane the mountain spreading,
>   Swept the sheep-bell's tinkling noise,
> While a girlish voice was reading,
>   Somewhat low for αι's and οι's.
>   ("Wine of Cyprus")

23. Letter 16, below.

Here other visits followed, and Elizabeth surprisingly was allowed to make the seven-mile trip unattended, driving the pony up the steep Wyche Road. The meetings still were less frequent than either could have wished, so they were delighted by a project which promised to bring them close together for the summer and to make the sessions of reading Greek a daily possibility. A plan had been initiated in April, probably because of Mrs. Barrett's ill health, to move the family for the summer from the valley of Hope End to the higher air of Malvern, where Mr. Barrett's mother was planning to spend the summer. To Elizabeth's great satisfaction the house finally chosen was Bradley Cottage, close to Woodland Lodge. Then suddenly in early June Mr. Barrett, who had already given his approval, sent word from London to cancel the plans, and the exchange of ideas between the two friends had to be limited, as before, to letters and occasional brief meetings. Though Mr. Boyd especially was impatient for longer study periods and proposed a more extended visit, Elizabeth was unwilling to be absent overnight while her mother was ill.

The real seriousness of this illness, however, she did not grasp and was sure that it was not likely to be "so tedious" as her own had been. All through the summer months her mother continued ailing, until in September a slight rally encouraged her doctor to sanction a "little excursion to Cheltenham." Since she took both carriages, some of her large family must have gone with her, but Elizabeth remained at Hope End. On October 1 Mrs. Barrett wrote to her daughter from Cheltenham. On October 7, in the security of home and its familiar surroundings, Elizabeth was replying when the shattering news came that her mother was dead. Elizabeth's letter, dated October 1828, was left unsigned—endorsed as "not finished or sent. I cannot burn it now." [24] On her mother's she wrote "The very last letter I ever received from *her*. One week after it was written, we possessed her no longer. It has been wet with more bitter tears than were those, the recollection of which broke heavily on her tender heart." [25] Her mother's death, she wrote Boyd, was an affliction "unforeseen and unexpected by me—and for a time, it took from me the power of thinking." Mr. Barrett received the news of his wife's death in London and hurried to Hope End. According to his daughter he was "strong in the consolation which is of God, and wonderfully well" [26]; yet he secluded his family for weeks of mourning and barred his dead wife's room for all time to visitors, even to her children. Of

24. Sotheby (1937), p. 2.
25. *Ibid.*, p. 3.
26. Letter 31, below.

the Barretts' loss, the *Hereford Journal,* usually given to flowery obituaries, carried only the stark notice, "On Tuesday the 7th inst. died Mary, the wife of E. M. Barrett, Esq. of Hope End in this county."

Hope End, 1829–30

In a few weeks her father resumed his trips to London and his normal activities, but Elizabeth found it hard to break the spell by which her mother's death bound her to Hope End. All that winter she forewent the satisfaction of her meetings with Mr. Boyd. He protested and entreated but had to content himself with sending her Greek texts to study and analyze by letter, and under the pretext of its safekeeping even bestowed upon her a large part of his classical library. By June this therapy had done its work, visits were resumed, and Boyd was once again urging her to stay for some days with him and his family at Malvern. But permission for such a visit seemed a remote prospect, although the two families were by now on terms of some intimacy. Elizabeth, it is true, had not succeeded in effecting a meeting between her father and Mr. Boyd, with their individual eccentricities, but the two exchanged gifts of game and cognac and the scholar appealed to Mr. Barrett for advice on matters of legal business. Mrs. Boyd and her daughter called at Hope End, and Ann (invited as Miss Boyd, but thereafter spoken of affectionately by her first name) paid an extended visit to the Barretts in the summer of 1829.

For the most part the years 1829 and 1830 were uneventful for Elizabeth. Her friend Sir Uvedale Price died in September of 1829, but he was past eighty and she accepted his death with composure. His place had been taken by Boyd, and visits to him were the most important events in what was, as she wrote Browning in retrospect, "a lonely life, growing green like the grass around it," a world of books and dreams, in which "domestic life only seemed to buzz gently around, like the bees about the grass." [27] Under Boyd's guidance she read Basil and Gregory, Chrysostom and Synesius, undismayed by the difficult orthography of early folios, and made reports to her director. More and more Boyd became the beloved teacher to whom she owed an undischargeable debt of gratitude for his "instruction." She read Longinus, and Euripides' *Rhesus* "regularly through," and admitted gratefully that the feat would have been "incredible and impossible" if she had not known him.[28] She is always modest about her technical grasp of grammar, but with sus-

27. EBB—RB, *1*, 43.
28. Letter 54, below.

tained reading there came a rarer and more enviable skill, the ability
to read at sight, to comprehend without translation.

To the blind scholar the progress of his pupil and her friendship had
become the central fact of his existence, and he carefully recorded the
dates of her visits in a memorandum, a portion of which, dating from
May 25 to November 8, 1830, has been preserved.[29] The very terseness
of the entries is moving. Here are sample items:

> MAY 25TH. She paid me a morning visit, and went on with the
> *Agamemnon.* She went down to v. 335, and did extremely well.

> JUNE 17TH. She came to breakfast, and spent the day with us. She
> went down to v. 571, and did extremely well.

> JULY 10TH. She paid us a long visit, but did not read any Greek.

> AUGUST 24TH. She came but read no Greek.

This record covers Elizabeth's long-projected stay as guest at the Boyds'
home; once Mr. Barrett's permission was won, he apparently made no
niggardly limitations, for the visit lasted two and a half weeks. Boyd's
notes for the first and the last day read:

> SEPT. 20TH. She came to stop with us for some days.

> OCT. 7TH. She returned home. After finishing *Agamemnon,* she read
> some passages in Chrysostom, Gregory, and Basil, which altogether was
> rather more than twelve hundred lines. She therefore read during
> her visit somewhat more than 2200 lines.

But the visit was much more than a series of Greek readings; it was a
time of happy, relaxed comradeship, days in which, Boyd said, they lived
"in clover"—a statement which Elizabeth amended to read "in
asphodel." [30] In all the letters of 1830 there is this sense of happy relaxation. Elizabeth might remember it later as a lonely life; at the time, it
found a focus in her studies, and in the teacher who was at the same
time a blind scholar and an older but childlike friend, to be helped in
his researches, to be teased gently about such subjects as bell ringing,
and to be entertained by stories and anecdotes. Only occasionally does
the outside world impinge upon their association—with mention of the
July Revolution in Paris and local indications of the vast social unrest
in rural England.

29. Published in *Harper's, 132* (1916), 531.
30. Letter 65, below.

Hope End, *1831–32*

In contrast with the tranquil mood of 1830, the letters of 1831 and 1832 show a young woman deeply disturbed in her private life and at the same time well aware of events on the social and political scene. The transition coincides with an illness which, coming upon her in the last days of 1830, confined her to the house for two months and left her with strained nerves and the tendency to a hacking cough. Scarcely was she convalescent when the security of her world was threatened. Mr. Barrett had had disastrous financial losses in Jamaica and, it was rumored, must give up Hope End. Years later the beginning of this tragedy was compressed in Elizabeth's memory into a single vivid scene. In 1842 she wrote to Miss Mitford:

> How I remember the coming of that letter to apprize him of the loss of his fortune . . . and just one shadow past on his face while he read it (I marked it at the moment) and then he broke away from the melancholy, and threw himself into the jests and laughter of his innocent boys. That was the only shadow seen by any of us, with a direct relation to those evil news! And in all the bitter bitter preparation for our removal,—there never was a word said by any one of us to Papa, or by him to us, in that relation. . . . Even now, I never say "Hope End" before him. He loved the place *so*. The circumstances of our leaving it (it was seized under a mortgage) were full of mortification to him, and to us for his sake.[31]

From the letters to Boyd it is clear that the silence upon the subject was perversely imposed by Papa and that it was vastly disturbing to his adult children, who, during a year and a half of suspense, were given no explanation of the situation and no inkling of his plans but had to conjecture their future from the gossip of tenants and servants. It is no wonder that the twenty-five-year-old Elizabeth complained, "It seems hard upon me that nothing of my childhood, except its tranquillity, should have passed away." [32]

To both Elizabeth and Boyd it was all-important, in the upheaval which threatened, that their association should not be interrupted. During her illness she had gained his promise to stay at Hope End for a visit, but now her father was unwilling to receive him. The Boyds were planning in May to leave Woodland Lodge and were free to adapt their movements to Mr. Barrett's plans—if they could discover what

31. Miller, p. 150.
32. Letter 86, below.

those plans were. But even a direct inquiry addressed through Mr. Curzon, the Barretts' minister, failed to elicit any exact information. Mrs. Boyd, who had long since tired of Malvern, did not find the same complete satisfaction as her husband in the friendship of his young pupil and despite desperate offers from Elizabeth to widen her social connections was eager to move elsewhere. While the fate of Hope End remained uncertain, however, she did not press her wishes but agreed in May that they should take a year's lease on Ruby Cottage, their former home at Malvern Wells. That same month Mrs. Barrett's sister, Aunt Bell, came to Hope End to help her nieces and nephews through the months ahead.

The first period of suspense ended for the Barretts on August 10, 1831, when London and local papers carried the advertisement that Hope End, "a chef d'oeuvre, unrivalled in this kingdom," "adapted for the accommodation of a Nobleman," would be sold at auction in London on August 25. Mr. Barrett, though he was in London, did not attend the sale, for he was ill with a violent attack of the cholera which was terrifying England in the summer of 1831. The estate was too costly (according to Elizabeth, its value, with the timber, was said to be nearly £50,000) to attract many serious purchasers, and no adequate bid was made at the sale. But curiosity seekers in great numbers obtained tickets of admission in order to view the house and grounds. More than ten years later Elizabeth could recall with bitterness how "people crowded to see it under the pretence of purchasing,—and our old serene green stilness was trodden under foot, day after day. And we had to hide, even away from our own private rooms, where we used to be safe from all the world,—and to hear in our hiding-place the trampling and the voices of strangers through the passages everywhere, and in the chambers which had been shut up for years from our own steps, sacred to death and love." [33]

As an escape from the turmoil around and within her Elizabeth withdrew to her little room to check references for Boyd and to read Greek; she even completed a translation of *Prometheus Bound* but abandoned for the time any thought of its publication. As often as she could win permission she was with Boyd at Ruby Cottage, rehearsing her troubles, reading Greek aloud, writing at dictation, and—another release from her private worries—discussing the political situation. The letters of this period contain for the first time frequent comment on the news of the day. The years 1831 and 1832 were critical ones for England, and like everyone else in the country Elizabeth followed closely the general

33. Miller, p. 151.

elections and the progress of the Reform Bill. She was a careful reader of the *Times,* which she championed as the "ablest and cleverest newspaper, of all the *are or ever-have-been* newspapers." [34] In the evening Mr. Barrett sometimes read the news aloud to the family and gave them the benefit of his political opinions; these, in sharp contrast to his own despotic temper, were ardently democratic and furnished a stimulus, no doubt, to his daughter's later liberal thinking. The family's support of Reform was more than theoretical; Bro took an active interest in the local elections, making speeches and serving on committees, and when the bill was finally passed, Mr. Barrett contributed a cow worth £20 to the Ledbury celebration. Another matter of less historic interest but very prominent both in the columns of the *Times* and in the letters to Boyd was the Pentecostal "speaking in unknown tongues" at the fashionable chapel of Edward Irving in London, which was fascinating and scandalizing religious people everywhere. Elizabeth had earlier been a great admirer of Mr. Irving's oratory and his theology, but neither she nor her father could take seriously his apocalyptic mission which began in October, 1831, and led shortly to his removal from his church and his founding of a new sect.

These current topics probably interested Boyd less than a translation of Gregory on which he was diligently at work, assisted in the task of transcribing by an old friend, Miss Henrietta Mushet. Elizabeth could give little help, as Mr. Barrett more and more curtailed the number of her visits. When Miss Mushet had trouble with her eyes in the spring of 1832, he refused categorically to allow his daughter to take dictation for a few days at Ruby Cottage: she was turning into a shadow, he insisted, and he for one would not be a party to her suicide.

This refusal may have been the factor which decided the Boyds to leave Malvern on the expiration of their lease in May, 1832. When this decision was rumored, Eliza Cliffe, realizing what it would mean to her friend, protested to the Boyds in a letter of "earnest entreaties." Elizabeth, however, as the departure grew imminent asked no questions, and Boyd, even as he had threatened four years before, made his only farewell in a note written just before leaving Malvern Wells. Their destination was Frome, but they stayed there only briefly before going on to Bath and leasing a house at Bathampton.

For over a year Elizabeth had been under serious nervous strain at Hope End. Now that her one escape—visiting her "teacher"—was removed, she seemed to lose all sense of proportion and grew hysterical over the separation, imagining even that it was a punishment inflicted

34. Letter 88, below.

by God because in her troubles she had looked for comfort less to Him than to Boyd. Her unhappiness further affected her health, so that Mr. Barrett soon transferred to Bro her task of instructing her brothers Henry and Daisy (Alfred) in Latin and forbade her all serious study. She had to forego Greek, which in any case would have reminded her too strongly of her loss, but she secretly engaged in the study of Hebrew, interspersed with such lighter interests as Madame de Stael, Manzoni, and Fanny Kemble. Her letters to Boyd grew longer and except for reports on the Reform Bill were highly personal. One rather intriguing, if baffling, episode emerges from them—a teapot tempest raging around some mysterious charge said to have been made by Mr. Boyd against Miss Mushet, his old friend and amanuensis. The clue to the story is lacking, but the incident, with its familiar pattern of petty gossip and intrigue, emphasizes the charged atmosphere at the time in Elizabeth's very little world.

Sidmouth, 1832–35

It was late July—more than two months after the Boyds' departure—before the sale of Hope End was finally completed and Mr. Barrett had to face the reality from which he had been stubbornly withdrawing. While the matter was inconclusive, he had maintained silence before his children and his friends, keeping away even from his beloved Bible meetings, and had made no plans for the future. He moved swiftly, however, as soon as the sale became an accomplished fact, departing abruptly into Devonshire, where he toured the seacoast towns. In less than a week he returned with voluble enthusiasm for the climate and a month's lease on a furnished house in Sidmouth. Then came the dreary confusion of dismantling their home of twenty-three years, packing furniture and books for storage, with Mr. Barrett resolutely cheerful through it all. Of their friends, only Lady Margaret Cocks took formal leave of them, though the cottagers on Wellington Heath, when Henrietta and Arabel made calls on "Bible business," wept and invoked blessings on the Master's head.

On August 24, while Bro and ten-year-old Sette remained with their father to help oversee the last bits of business at Hope End, the other nine Barrett brothers and sisters with Aunt Bell and five servants set out in two carriages for Sidmouth. The journey of a hundred and thirty miles was broken by a night's stop at the York Hotel in Bath three miles from Mr. Boyd, but Elizabeth could only sit at the window and think bleakly about his nearness.

The following night in her new home in Sidmouth, she was lulled to sleep by the sound of the waves. For the first time in months she slept soundly and awoke to a beautiful world of sea and cliffs, green lanes and hills, and to a sense of tranquillity long unfamiliar. After nearly two years of unhappy turmoil, Sidmouth effected in her almost overnight a miracle of better health and spirits. Her cough lessened quickly in the warm, soft air; every day brought some new delightful excursion by boat or donkey; Mr. Barrett, who soon joined them, was in a cheerful mood; and altogether, life was good. Of the family, only Aunt Bell dissented from Ba's enthusiasm for Sidmouth and soon left them, feeling, perhaps, that a visiting aunt was superfluous in their new contentment and in a house where they were all "squeezed in little rooms, two in a bed." [35]

To find furnished lodgings to fit so large a family was no easy matter, and though the house which Mr. Barrett had leased on Fortfield Terrace had served the year before as official residence of the Grand Duchess Helena of Russia, it was still small and starkly simple when compared with the magnificence of Hope End. During the three years in which they lived at Sidmouth, they moved three times [36]—in the summer of 1833 to an ugly and "ruinous house" close to the sea, in the spring of 1834 to Belle Vue, "a thatched cottage, with a green lawn, bounded by a Devonshire lane," and back for a brief time in the summer of 1835 to the "ancient house upon the beach."

Elizabeth, throughout the various changes of residence, remained at peace with herself and with a routine in which outdoor pleasures combined happily with the life of poet and scholar. Her new interest in Hebrew continued, and the first winter she set for herself the task of completing the reading of the Old Testament in the original. Quickly, too, she returned to Latin and especially to Greek, reading the *Aeneid*, Pindar, and Euripides. By mid-December she had finished a preface and notes for the translation of *Prometheus Bound,* laid aside the year before, which she planned to publish in a volume with shorter poems.

In Bathampton, meanwhile, the teacher was proving far less able than the pupil to adjust himself to their separation. His health, he felt sure, was adversely affected by the Bath climate and required a change to the air of Sidmouth. Though Mrs. Boyd and Annie were also feeling unwell, they did not consider Sidmouth a solution. The house at Bathampton had been leased for a year, and the Bath parties were attractive. A compromise was finally reached in December, by which Mr. Boyd came to live in a lodging house close to the Barretts. Elizabeth was

35. Letter 125, below.
36. See Letter 127, n. 7.

glad to have his company but found it hard to forgive his wife for permitting him to remain "so solitary, in this strange place." [37] Mrs. Boyd for her part felt that he was being kept from his family by Elizabeth's selfishness. But in the spring, when the lease on the Bathampton house was nearly up, she succumbed to her husband's wishes and came to Sidmouth, where they took for a year a house five minutes' walk from the Barretts.

During the year and a half that Mr. Boyd and Elizabeth met every day at Sidmouth the quality of their relationship underwent a change. Although Elizabeth was twenty-six when she left Hope End, in many respects the closely guarded life there had kept her a child, and she had created a romantic schoolgirl vision of Mr. Boyd as a wise and generous counselor and a great scholar, patient in affliction. Now, as she began to grow emotionally and intellectually, she inevitably found the image fading and recognized him as a rather testy pedant, a "man of slow mind," "with a child's way of looking at things." [38] Happily no break occurred in their friendship, but with the frequency of meetings at Sidmouth there came a gradual and unconscious alienation. When the Boyds moved on to another temporary home in Bath, there was this time no great agony of spirit; Elizabeth went to see her friend off and they parted quietly, his "boat upon the shore" and her "barque upon the sea." From this time on, her letters to him lack their former intensity; the hero-worship gives way to a mature sympathy and to an affection that is sometimes playful but grounded securely in grateful and often nostalgic memories.

One explanation of Elizabeth's changed regard for Mr. Boyd may perhaps be found in her growing friendship with the Reverend George Barrett Hunter, minister of the Independent chapel which the Boyds attended in Sidmouth. Mr. Hunter shared in her out-of-door excursions, inspired her by his sermons, and offered a new stimulus to theological reading, including even such unorthodox writers as the deist Anthony Collins. Soon he seems to have filled Elizabeth's need for an intellectual confidant, the role which Boyd himself had usurped from the aged Sir Uvedale Price.

The farewell at Sidmouth was Elizabeth's last meeting with Mrs. Boyd, who had on the whole been generous in her acceptance of her husband's young protégée; Elizabeth was sincerely grieved on November 2, 1834, to receive word that she had died. After her death her husband and daughter stayed on in London, where the family had moved from

37. Letter to Mrs. Boyd: Kenyon typescript in British Museum.
38. EBB—RB, 2, 258.

Bath; it could not have been an entirely happy arrangement, since Annie, though pretty and fond of society, was at the same time, it would seem, a temperamental young hypochondriac, and she and her father were never wholly congenial. The next summer Mr. Boyd's sister came to be with him and to read Shakespeare, while Annie visited the Barretts at Sidmouth.

This was to be their last summer at Sidmouth. For months it had been rumored that they were to leave, though Mr. Barrett, who had been ill much of the winter and spring, delayed decision and as usual was silent as to his plans. Elizabeth, happily, was more of a philosopher than in the Hope End days and instead of bewailing meditated a poem on the "Pleasures of Doubt." Finally in the autumn after Bro had returned from a year in Jamaica, Mr. Barrett determined to try the experiment of living in London, where business took him frequently and where George, who had taken his degree at Glasgow, would soon be studying law at the Inns of Court. A furnished house was engaged at 74 Gloucester Place. Though this move to London once again brought Elizabeth near Mr. Boyd, the prospect did not hold the enchantment that it would have had three years before. True, she promised to drink green tea with him and intended to read Plato devotedly in London, but these plans were made without heart, for in leaving Sidmouth with its beauty and its happy memories, half of her soul "stayed behind on the sea-shore." [39]

London, 1835–38

The child Elizabeth had looked longingly from Hope End at the "white ribbon" in the distance which was the London Road. Now that Elizabeth, the young woman, was at the end of the magic ribbon, she found only a city "wrapped up like a mummy, in a yellow mist." [40] She had lived all her life in open spaces and dreaded "the feeling of four red London walls closing around her for seven, eleven, or twenty-five years." [41] With her intellect she could remind herself that the city had many advantages, that "if you can't see even a leaf or a sparrow without soot on it, there are the parrots in the Zoological Gardens, and the pictures at the Royal Academy, and real live poets above all, with their heads full of the trees and birds and sunshine of paradise." [42] But in her heart she asked "Was there anybody in the world who ever loved London

39. Kenyon, *1*, 35.
40. *Ibid.*
41. *Ibid.,* p. 51.
42. *Ibid.,* p. 55.

for itself?" [43] In the fog and smoke of the city her cough returned, and "frozen to the fender" she thought enviously of the milder climate of Sidmouth. Still, in spite of a general malaise, her health the first two years in London did not interfere with normal if limited activity. She studied German with Bro and Henry the first summer and was able to attend prayer meetings and to make occasional calls on relatives and friends.

As often as she could she went to St. John's Wood to cheer Mr. Boyd, who also found the London climate unkind and was suffering from rheumatic pains. Arabel, with her gay wit and sympathy, was a welcome companion on these visits, which lacked completely the serious intensity of the study hours at Malvern. Sometimes Arabel or Henrietta or George paid a visit of kindness without Elizabeth. When Annie Boyd was married on August 1, 1837, all three Barrett sisters attended the wedding at Marylebone Church. If a writer in *Notes and Queries* for 1859 is correct, the bridegroom, Mr. Henry William Hayes, was an Irish Roman Catholic gentleman,[44] a fact which must have distressed a man of Mr. Boyd's convictions. His greatest comfort lay, no doubt, in the visits of Elizabeth, whom he cared for, she later told Robert Browning, "far more than for his own only daughter." [45] Since he was still searching out texts in the Church Fathers to refute Roman Catholic teachings, Elizabeth read Justin Martyr with him and, as she used to do at Hope End, assisted him by copying out passages relating to the Lord's Supper.

But her letters now centered on her own writings rather than on their shared studies. She was taking her poetry more and more seriously. The "Romaunt of Margret" and "The Poet's Vow" were published in the *New Monthly Magazine* in 1836, and she was at work on a "Drama of the Angels," which was to become "The Seraphim." To entertain Boyd she sent him copies of her poems, acknowledging with equal good humor his praise and his faultfinding. These must have seemed to her naive in comparison with the discerning criticism of writers whom she was coming to know in London. Soon after her arrival in the city she renewed an old friendship with her literary cousin John Kenyon and formed a new one with Mary Russell Mitford; she had gained favorable attention from the dramatist and critic Richard Hengist Horne; and among "real live poets" in London she had met and talked with Wordsworth and Landor. The days were gone when she had complained to Mr. Boyd

43. Kenyon, *1*, 42.
44. *Notes and Queries*, 7 (1859), 523.
45. EBB—RB, 2, 258.

that there was not a single literary person within twenty miles except himself and Dr. Card.

The house at Gloucester Place had originally been leased for four months, but the period lengthened to two years and a half as Mr. Barrett pursued an "eternal hunt" for a family home that would suit his fancy. Meanwhile, that third winter at Gloucester Place, Elizabeth again became seriously ill. Her lungs were weak and her cough so disabling that she began to spend much of her time in bed under the ministrations of Dr. Chambers. In the spring of 1838 Mr. Barrett's hunt came to an end with the purchase of 50 Wimpole Street in a neighborhood which Elizabeth had long particularly disliked because of its "gloominess" and its walls "like Newgate's turned inside out." [46] But she was to see little of the gloomy exterior, for after a brief sojourn with friends at 129 Crawford Street "until the ghost of paint had been sufficiently exorcised," [47] she went directly to her own room in their new home and to the life of an invalid who seldom moved further than from bed to couch. Here Miss Mitford and Mr. Kenyon came to see her, and here she continued to compose poetry, publishing in May *The Seraphim, and Other Poems.* She could no longer visit "poor Mr. Boyd," who suffered another bereavement in March in the death of his sister, but she wrote him frequent letters in which she talked intimately with him of her work and of her illness.

Torquay, 1838–41

By the summer of 1838 it was clear that Elizabeth could never recover her health in London. "The worst—what people call the worst—was apprehended" [48] for her, and Dr. Chambers insisted on a return to the milder climate of Devonshire. Mr. Barrett, after compounding difficulties and delays, finally in the fall permitted her to join her Aunt Jane and Uncle Hedley in Torquay. Her farewell to Mr. Boyd, written the night before they sailed, was filled with sadness. She prayed God to bless him, then added the hopeful note that "It may please Him for me to return and visit you again." [49] Henrietta was the only member of the family assigned to stay with the invalid in Torquay, but Bro and George were also permitted to escort her there. When the boys were ready to return to London, Ba broke down at the thought of parting

46. Kenyon, *1,* 41.
47. Miller, p. 26.
48. EBB—RB, *1,* 175.
49. Weaver, Letter XX.

from Bro. With most uncharacteristic weakness, Mr. Barrett then yielded to entreaties from Aunt Jane and allowed his eldest son to give up all share in family business matters and devote himself exclusively to his sister. Arabel at first was forced to stay in London, where she paid frequent calls on Mr. Boyd to comfort herself and him by talk of Elizabeth; after a year of pleading, she too was permitted to join the family unit in Torquay. By that time their number included Aunt Bell ("dear Bummy") and they had moved from the Hedley home in the upper part of the town to their own rented house at 1 Beacon Terrace on the warmer shore of Tor Bay. Here all activities focused on Elizabeth, with Mr. Barrett coming frequently from 50 Wimpole Street. But Torquay did not effect a miracle as Sidmouth had done, and the attacks of illness became more and more violent and prolonged.

On July 11, 1840, three months after news that her brother Sam had died in Jamaica, came the great tragedy of Elizabeth's life. The beloved Bro, "the dearest of friends and brothers in one," [50] whom she had kept in Torquay by her tears, was drowned in a boating accident on Babbicombe Bay. For weeks she lay "half conscious, half unconscious," [51] unable to shed a tear to ease her grief and remorse. Then, as the acute shock passed, she was possessed of one overpowering desire—to leave Torquay forever and to unite her broken family at 50 Wimpole Street. But she was too ill to travel, and a year passed before her physician felt that they were morally justified in risking such a move.

During the three years of illness and grief at Torquay, Elizabeth continued to compose poetry, assembling on paper whenever she had strength the fragments of poems which were constantly taking shape in her mind. Also when she had strength she wrote letters to Miss Mitford and Mr. Horne, who were encouraging the publication of her poems. There was no immediate incentive to keep alive the bond with Mr. Boyd, and though she continued to feel nostalgic gratitude and affection toward him, letters became infrequent.

London, *1841–46*

In the summer of 1841 definite plans were made for the invalid's removal to London, and Boyd—who had moved from St. John's Wood to an even more lonely life at 21 Downshire Hill, Hampstead—was stirred by the hope that this return might mean a renewal of their old fellowship. In two letters written in late August he invited her to pay

50. EBB—RB, *1,* 175.
51. *Ibid.,* p. 176.

him a visit after her return and offered to send her the folios of Gregory which she had read with him at Malvern. The simple optimism of these gestures moved Elizabeth deeply and won a smile from her at the very moment when Dr. Scully was warning her that the trip to London would be full of hazard. However, a "patent carriage with a bed in it, and set upon some hundreds of springs" [52] took her safely in September to 50 Wimpole Street, where she found waiting her as a "welcome home" the volumes of Gregory and another letter from Mr. Boyd.

The return to her family renewed Elizabeth's will to live and at this difficult moment of transition Boyd's Gregory coaxed her into resuming congenial studies which did much to improve both her mental and her physical health. Translations of three poems by Gregory sent to Mr. Dilke, the editor of the *Athenaeum,* led to a series of papers on the Greek Christian poets. Even as a young scholar Elizabeth had had far surer literary judgment than her more learned friend, and in the translations and comments written for the *Athenaeum* she shows little dependence on his pedantic scholarship. The task, however, aroused memories and made her feel once again very close to Mr. Boyd. Though she could not visit him, Arabel did—sometimes taking Flush with her for company. Greek texts were exchanged, and letters again became frequent. Those written in 1841 and the early months of 1842 are concerned largely with the Greek poets. In May, Elizabeth embarked on a survey of the English poets, a work of criticism which apparently completed the therapy that Gregory had started; by the time it was finished she had recovered her poise and serenity and was determined to write poetry the rest of her life. From this time on, correspondence with Boyd had nothing to offer her intellectually, but knowing how it comforted his loneliness, she continued to discuss with him topics as diverse as poetry and Calvinism, and debated at length with mock solemnity the merits of Wordsworth and Macpherson's Ossian.

In 1844 with the publication of two volumes of poems Elizabeth Barrett Barrett suddenly found herself a celebrity both in England and in America. In letters to Boyd she reported for his satisfaction the acclaim of her reviewers, while at the same time she accepted with seriousness his own expressions of censure and praise. One poem which was dedicated to him gave him great joy, "Wine of Cyprus," [53] in which the author relived with gratitude the hours of their study together in Malvern,

52. Kenyon, *1,* 88.

53. Robert Browning wrote Elizabeth two years later that this poem affected him perhaps the most profoundly of any that she had written.

When, betwixt the folio's turnings,
Solemn flowed the rhythmic Greek.

Her public appreciation of the Cyprian wine led to more gifts of the same divine nectar, which was sparingly tasted but acknowledged always with extravagant praise and thanks. Boyd, whose rheumatism had now become a very painful and deforming lumbago, had moved again from Hampstead to St. John's Wood, where his only companion was the maid Jane. Elizabeth, with her improving spirits and her new success as an author, felt very sorry for her old friend and very tender toward him. She would no longer allow him to call her Miss Barrett, a formality which he had always carefully preserved, and since he objected to the un-Hellenic monosyllable Ba, became his grateful and affectionate Elibet. As early as September, 1844, she was holding out hope to herself and him that she might some day again pay him a visit, and with Arabel as her emissary she fussed affectionately over such problems of comfort as a sofa with plenty of pillows and a chair with low arms.

In January, 1845, Robert Browning read Elizabeth Barrett's two green-bound volumes of poems and precipitately fell in love with them. "I love your verses with all my heart, dear Miss Barrett," he wrote her on January 10, and though the first visit did not come until four months later, it was clear from the very start of their correspondence that Elizabeth had at last found an intellectual confidant with whom she shared perfect rapport. She was at this time retranslating the *Prometheus Bound* as a "palinodia" to her earlier "frigid, rigid exercise," [54] and it was not the scholar Boyd but the poet Browning, "fast forgetting" his Greek, who gave her advice on doubtful passages and diligently compared the translation with the original text. But her old friend was neither forgotten nor neglected; and when under the goad of Browning's love she began to take tentative excursions away from Wimpole Street, one of her first calls was at the little house at 24a Grove End Road in St. John's Wood where Boyd was now living. On the first visit, June 21, 1846, they did not meet, since Boyd could not make the effort to walk downstairs nor Elizabeth to walk up. "We are both" she wrote to Browning, "perhaps rather afraid of meeting after all these years of separation." [55] So she looked at the garden while Arabel talked to him in his room. Ten days later she called again, though "so nervous —so anxious for an excuse for turning back." And at last she stood "at the door of poor Mr. Boyd's dark little room, and saw him sitting—

54. Kenyon, *1*, 244.
55. EBB—RB, *2*, 257.

as if he had not moved these seven years—these seven, heavy, changeful years." "Seeing him," she wrote Browning,

> my heart was too full for speech at first, but I stooped and kissed
> his poor bent-down forehead, which he never lifts up, his chin being
> quite buried in his breast. Presently we began to talk of Ossian and
> Cyprus wine, and I was forced, as I would not have Ossian for a
> god, to take a little of the Cyprus,—there was no help for me, no
> alternative: so I took as little as I could, while he went on proving
> to me that the Adamic fall and corruption of human nature (Mr.
> Boyd is a great theologian) were never in any instance so disgustingly
> exemplified as in the *literary controversy about Ossian.*

But he was not so absorbed in his argument as to forget his guest's
entertainment, and he appealed to her companion: "Arabel!—how
much has she taken of that wine? not half a glass?" and Arabel had
to answer placatingly, "But, Mr. Boyd, you would not have me obliged
to carry her home." [56]
This visit opened up a flood of memories of the eager young neo-
phyte and the blind scholar at Malvern, and Elizabeth wrote that
"the hours spent with you appear to me some of the happiest of my
life." [57] Nor could she keep completely silent on the new happiness
for which she was reaching: in this same letter she revealed that a
prophet but a week since had foretold that "the latter time would be
better for me than the beginning." This was, no doubt, the phrase
which led to Boyd's sharing the secret of their marriage plans. On
August 18, 1846, Elizabeth confessed to Browning,

> I wrote something in a note to Mr. Boyd some weeks ago, which
> nobody except himself would have paused to think over; but he,
> like a person in a dungeon, sounds every stone of the walls around
> him, and discerns a hollowness, detects a wooden beam,—patiently
> picks out the mortar with a pin—all this, in his rayless, companion-
> less Dark,—poor Mr. Boyd! The time before I last went to see him,
> he asked me if I were going to be a nun—there, was the first guess!
> On the next visit he put his question precisely right—*I* tried to
> evade—then promised to be frank in a little time—but being
> pressed on all sides, and drawn on by a solemn vow of secrecy, I al-
> lowed him to see the truth—and he lives such an isolated life, that
> it is prefectly safe with him, setting the oath aside. Also, he was

56. *Ibid.*, p. 282.
57. Letter 186, below.

very good and kind, and approved highly of the whole, and ex-
horted me, with ever such exhortation, to keep to my purpose, and
to allow no consideration in the world or out of the world, to make
any difference—quoting the moral philosophers as to the rights of
such questions. Is there harm in his knowing? [58]

On this point her lover reassured her, expressing utter disregard for
danger in his delight at Boyd's sympathy and approval. On her next
visit, Elizabeth had a subject to discuss with her old friend that was
of greater interest to her than Ossian. In fact, she told Browning,
"dear, poor Mr. Boyd! Talking such pure childishness, sometimes in
such pure Attic," [59] took them up exactly as if they were Ossian and
Macpherson or a criticism of Porson's. For two hours they "talked on
it," and Boyd was happy that his talented "child of the Muses" had at
last found love and, even more, that with it had come the will to
resist Mr. Barrett's tyranny.

So it happened that Hugh Stuart Boyd was the first friend to see
Mrs. Browning after her marriage on September 12, 1846. As the
bride and groom left Marylebone Church, they separated to wait for
the sailing of the boat that would take them to Italy. Elizabeth and
her maid went directly to 24a Grove End Road, where she lay on a
sofa in Boyd's sitting room while Wilson went to Wimpole Street
to ask Arabel and Henrietta to join them in St. John's Wood. "Then,"
she wrote her husband, "I was made to talk and take Cyprus wine,—
and, my sisters delaying to come, I had some bread and butter for
dinner, to keep me from looking too pale in their eyes." [60]

Italy, 1846–48

Only three letters from Elizabeth to Boyd date after her marriage. In
one written from Pisa, November 19, 1846, she assures him that of
the friends whom she loves best in England, his name stands among
the very first. "For me, the last sympathy you gave me did not touch
me least of all you have given me in the course of my life. May God
bless you, my dearest friend." [61]

Boyd died May 10, 1848, as the result of a paralytic stroke. On the
day of his death Elizabeth in Florence received word of his illness and
felt, she wrote Arabel, as if a great black shadow had fallen straight

58. EBB—RB, 2, 439–40.
59. *Ibid.*, p. 457.
60. *Ibid.*, p. 537.
61. Letter 187, below.

on her. She paid tribute to her friend's memory in three sonnets, "His Blindness," "His Death," and "Legacies." In a note printed with them she added

> To whom was inscribed, in grateful affection, my poem of "Cyprus Wine." There comes a moment in life when even gratitude and affection turn to pain, as they do now with me. This excellent and learned man, enthusiastic for the good and the beautiful, and one of the most simple and upright of human beings, passed out of his long darkness through death in the summer of 1848, Dr. Adam Clarke's daughter and biographer, Mrs. Smith (happier, in this than the absent), fulfilling a doubly filial duty as she sate by the death-bed of her father's friend and hers.[62]

The absent included both his daughter Annie and his more beloved "pupil." It would have made Boyd happy to know that "Elibet" was to be granted thirteen more years of rich life in which frail health would be compensated by pride in husband and child and by the ever increasing admiration which her contemporaries were to lavish upon her poetry.

62. *Works,* p. 338.

The Letters

To Ruby Cottage [1]
Malvern Wells

Hope End.[2] March 11, 1827

Sir,

I thanked you, in my last note, for sending me your works,—and now, having read them, I have it in my power to thank you for the pleasure you have afforded me. As you desire me to mention which of the two poems on the calamity at Malvern,[3] I prefer, I will frankly select the *first* tho' the "Malvern tale" has many lines that interest me, together with a smoothness of versification which is common in your writings. Your prologue and epilogue to St. Gregory's poems are elegant; and your preface to that translation, attractive on several accounts. I am not ungrateful to the *Elegy:* but were I to say on what page I linger longest, I think I should turn at once to your translation from the *Electra*. It is beautifully executed, to the spirit as well as the letter; and, speaking of it, I may observe with Denham,[4] that "words are not only rendered into words, but poetry into poetry." The last line [5] pleased me *least,*—if I might say so without presump-

1. Now known as The Ruby. The name Ruby Cottage appears on a contemporary plan. James Best, *A Description of Malvern, Including a Guide to the Drives, Rides, Walks and Excursions,* Malvern, 1825.

2. "Hope End, the seat of E. M. Barrett, esq. is situated about six m. from the village of Malvern, upon the right of the Ledbury road, in a retired valley in the parish of Colwall. The architecture of the mansion is in the eastern style, and many of the apartments are highly furnished. . . . In the front of the house are some fine pieces of water, and upon the banks, a variety of fine shrubs and evergreens. From the windows on one side of the house is a very large projection of rocks, which the taste of the owner has highly ornamented with a fine collection of plants." Best, *Malvern,* p. 212. The mansion was demolished in 1876, and a later house was burned in 1910. But in the midst of the ruined estate a portion of the original farm buildings is still standing, with eastern towers and minarets and a Turkish crescent.

3. The death by lightning in July 1826 of two young women who had come to Malvern for a picnic. The storm in which they were killed made such a deep impression on EBB that she described it in detail to Browning nearly twenty years later. EBB—RB, July 12, 1845. On these poems see Introduction, p. xvi.

4. Sir John Denham (1615–69). In the preface to a free translation from the *Aeneid, the Destruction of Troy* (1636) he urged the translation of not only "Language into Language, but Poesie into Poesie."

5. "τοὺς γὰρ θανόντας οὐχ ὁρῶ λυπουμένους." Sophocles *Electra* 1170.

tion! I think I should have liked the last line better, had you translated it more literally—had you written,

> Because I do not see the *dead lament!*—

instead of

> "To me the dead appear exempt from woe."

Nothing is much more odious than a *servile* translation: but, in this instance, it seems hardly possible to preserve the striking and pathetic simplicity of the original, without adopting a verbal fidelity. I trust this observation to your indulgence: and stand, of course, with regard to it, under your correction.

St. Basil writes fervently and eloquently: but do you not consider his style rather inflated?

Thank you for the trouble you have taken to explain your objection to that passage of my work, which relates to the possible extinction of England.[6] I will confess, at once, that I did the very reverse of the Heathen oracles—that I prophesied for the sake of *poetry,* instead of poetizing for the sake of *prophecy:* and *my* prophecy may deserve as much contempt as the oracular poetry does!—Yet something might be urged in my defence. I allow (to make use of your words) that there exists *"no instance* of a nation being given up to ruin and extinction, while the people continued to labour for the extension of God's glory." But I might add, as truly, that there exists *no instance* of a people *continuing* to labour for the extension of God's glory. Nevertheless I consent to give up all prophetical pretensions; and, sharing the fate of Cassandra, certainly deserve it much more than *she* did!

You must accept my thanks, and only *my thanks,* in return for your extremely kind invitation. I very seldom have it in my power to leave home, and the first time I am able to do so, must visit some friends to whom I am under a long engagement. It is therefore necessary for me to hope for other means by which, in the finer weather, I may have the advantage of your acquaintance. My health which you are good enough to enquire after, is not bad; but deficiency in strength makes me quite incapable of much exercise. I am sorry not to be able to answer your questions respecting our West Indian connections, but I know hardly anything on the subject; and I cannot ask my Father,

6. *An Essay on Mind,* 1826: eighteen lines beginning "Alas! alas! so Albion shall decay, / And all my country's glory pass away!" *Works,* p. 35.

who has been for some time absent, and whose return is still uncertain.

You ask me how I "found out your name." Perhaps I introduced a new reading into Propertius, and instead of "Certus eras, heu, heu!" [7] read *"Certe eras Hugh Hugh!"*

Believe me,
Your obliged
E. B. Barrett

I take the liberty of enclosing to you a number of the Jewish Expositor, in which there are some lines of mine—the last I have published—signed with my initials.[8]

2.

To Ruby Cottage
Malvern Wells

Hope End. Saturday evening [1827]

Sir,

I should have written before, but have been so much occupied, that, till this evening, I was forced to run the hazard of *appearing* ungrateful to the letters and verses you have honored me by sending. It is only an *appearance:* for I am naturally gratified and obliged by your good opinion. I must not say any more, as it would certainly be very impertinent in me either to praise your Greek, or disclaim your praise. Your *praise* cannot mean *flattery,* because you assure me it does not, —and therefore, when you commend more merit than exists, I attribute the kind mistake to an indulgent judgment, or perhaps to your *poetry*—your ποιησις [1]—the *creating* power of your mind.

With regard to δροσος [2] pray acquit poor Jones, who is no more guilty of advising me wrong, than *I* am of having ever seen his grammar or Lexicon. I must observe that Hederick, whose quarto lies by me just now, makes the word masculine,—and *ut Hedericus sic Schrevelius,*—with Jones (tho' he *be* a "quack") to bring up the rear.

You desire to know whether I read the tragedians, and whether I

---

7. "Eheu tu mihi certus eras / Certus eras, eheu." Propertius *Elegies* 2.24A.36–7.

8 "Is it nothing to you, all ye that pass by?" *Jewish Expositor and Friend of Israel,* January 1827. Reprinted in *Hitherto Unpublished Poems,* 2, 71–4.

1. "creation," "art of poetry."

2. "dew": feminine gender, according to Liddell and Scott.

read them by myself. As far as your question relates to Sophocles, I may answer in his words

και φημι δρασαι, κουκ απαρνουμαι το μη.[3]

but I only know Euripides by his *Medea,* and Aeschylus by his reputation. What I read, I read without assistance.

You seem rather angry with me for prefering your translation from the *Electra,* to the translation from Achilles Tatius: [4] and speak of having taken very little pains with the former. Nevertheless I must maintain that, if you had taken no pains at all, it is still a beautiful translation, and striking in many points of view. By a happy transmigrating process, you have communicated the immortal soul of Sophocles' poetry to another body, graceful enough to be worthy of it: and *such* poetry!—so different from those artificial compositions, which, like the Heathen idols are "overlaid with silver and gold" but, in whom, is no breath!

I must thank you again for the real pleasure your works have given me; and beg you to believe me, on this and several other accounts,

Your obliged
E. B. Barrett

3.

To Ruby Cottage
Malvern Wells

Hope End. April 23, 1827

Sir,

You permitted me to answer your letter "in my leisure"; and tho' I have taken that permission most literally, I am neither the less obliged to you for sending me Dr. Goodenough's satisfactory communication, or for your continued kind expressions of interest in myself. It is very good of you still to desire me to visit you. To prove that my inclinations can scarcely be in fault, I will assure you that, tho' I have relations living at Malvern,—much nearer to us than your residence,—I have not been to see them since last summer; and then only by availing myself of an accidental opportunity. They have been at Malvern nearly three years, but, before last summer, I never went to see them,—an omission they were kind enough to pardon in

3. "I affirm that I did so and make no denial." Sophocles *Antigone* 443.
4. Metrical version of a song summarized in prose, Achilles Tatius 2.1. Translated by EBB as "Song of the Rose." *Works,* p. 293.

consideration of my engaged time, and want of conveyance. You must not be harder on me than *they* are: and indeed, *I,* who lose the advantage of your conversation have much the worst of the bargain, and much the best reason to complain.

With regard to your questions,—I intend to give up *Greek,* when I give up *poetry:* and,—as Porson [1] said on a case equally decided,— "not till then". Tho' I never become a critical scholar, I may continue to enjoy that divine poetical literature, for whose sake I encountered the language. In my quotation from the Antigone, is not the prepositive article in the accusative case? And, in the line you refer me to from the beginning of the Oedipus Tyrannus,[2] does not ἐμοῦ—used with θέλοντος,—shew the genitive absolute? The expression equivalent to it in Latin, would be *me volente,* if I do not mistake. Pray believe that I could not be induced to act so unfairly as to make the answer of another person pass for my own. I have lately been giving some attention to the system of accents.

Bentley's [3] name should be venerable in our recollections, were it only on account of his research connected with the Digamma: and I certainly could have no intention of using a disrespectful expression, when I felt so much respect. I am sorry to be suspected of feeling differently; and, if I have an opportunity, shall assuredly cancel, or in some way modify, a passage that has exposed my judgment to such an imputation. Only two lines [4] of my essay refer to Bentley; the second of which can scarcely be objected to, since it comprises his own confession stated in the note. The first line, viz.

"And Bentley leaves on stilts the beaten track"

I am ready to acknowledge, sounds invidious,—and I wish it were away!—By Bentley's "stilts" however, I did not mean to intimate that his reputation as a *scholar* was supported by undue means. I had been contrasting Genius with Art; I had been lamenting the sufferings of Poetry from Criticism; and my warm feelings against Shakespeare's

1. Richard Porson (1759–1808), classical scholar, noted for his work on meter and his emendation of Greek texts.

2. "ὡς θέλοντος ἂν / ἐμοῦ προσαρκεῖν πᾶν . . ." ("Since I should be willing to give every help"). Sophocles *Oedipus Tyrannus* 11–12.

3. Richard Bentley (1662–1742), classical scholar, who discovered that many metrical peculiarities of the Homeric poems were due to the loss of the letter *digamma.* In an edition of *Paradise Lost* he tried unsuccessfully to apply to Milton the methods of classical textual criticism.

4. *Essay on Mind:* "While Bentley leaves, on stilts, the beaten track, / And peeps at glory from some ancient's back." *Works,* p. 32.

Commentators were naturally extended to Bentley,—by having full
in my mind, his anti-poetical edition of Milton, which you must admit to be the weakest work in point of criticism he ever gave to the
world.

As to the Bishop of Cloyne, if he had not what Pope allows him,
"every virtue under Heaven", he was, at least, an excellent and admirable man!—I have a sufficiently high opinion of him to believe,
that, could he have lived to observe *consequences,* he would repent,
from his soul, having ever written what involves something more
terrible than a *reductio ad absurdum.* As an Author he is responsible
for his works,—and, as a reader, I am not obliged to consider the
amiable character of a man, when I have to do with his doctrine. It
is impossible to enter on the subject here: I will only say in deprecia-
tion of that doctrine—"look at the sceptic *Hume,* who, by pursuing
Berkeley's path, has proved too surely that "it leads but to a precipice".
Locke's [5] treatise against the "Divine Right" seems to me abundantly
clear; but when Berkeley has persuaded me to give up the *ratio ultima,*
—the evidence of my senses,—I may give up my *ratio* altogether, and
be quite "passive".

Believe me
Your obliged
E. B. Barrett

4.

To Ruby Cottage
Malvern Wells

Hope End. September 1827

Sir,

I am too much obliged to you for sending me your work on the
Atonement [1] to neglect attending to the request you have thought it
worth while to make. I shall therefore speak quite frankly upon any
point on which I may venture to entertain doubts; and as such a
point can merely relate to the *manner of proving,* and not to the
truth proved, which I have the happiness of being able to join you in

5. In the *Essay on Mind* EBB dealt severely with Berkeley and paid enthusiastic
tribute to Locke.

1. *Reflections on the Atoning Sacrifice of Jesus Christ* (1817), a work containing
more rhetoric than reason.

embracing, I must, in the first place, assure you that I have read your book with sincere respect both for your ability as a disputant and your elevated feelings as a Christian. . . .[2]

With regard to the Calvinistic doctrines of predestination and irresistible grace, if I were to embrace them at all, it should be, I believe, a sub*lapsarian modification* of them,—but at present I feel unwilling to do so, even on such terms. There are great difficulties on both sides of the question, and therefore I am the more happy to agree with you, that an opinion may be entertained on either side without endangering Christian essentials.

You desire to know my views and ideas of the Atonement,—but *you*, who have filled a book with *your* "Reflections", can hardly expect *me* to comprise mine in a letter. I will however answer your question respecting my opinion of the doctrine "as a subject proposed to the head and heart". I answer it briefly tho' fully in the words of Paul—"Christ Jesus came into the world to save sinners—of whom I am chief!" Let "the head" take the general fact, "the heart" the particular application,—and head and heart will have enough to do . . .

And now I have only to repeat my thanks for the gratification and advantage received from your publication—requesting its author to

believe me

his obliged and sincere

E. B. Barrett

Thank you for the interesting little tract. My Father is sorry not to have yet had it in his power to go to the chapel—but he fully intends doing so.

5.

To Ruby Cottage

Malvern Wells

Hope End. Saturday, November 3, 1827

Sir,

When I consider the date and contents of your last letter, I feel very deeply that my delay in replying to it has been considerably longer than it should have been,—tho', I do hope, not *too* long for

2. The two passages omitted from this letter contain criticisms of Boyd's arguments.

you to pardon. I was unwilling to write without sending back your book, or to send back your book without giving it that strict attention due to its excellencies; and thus the delay has been a necessary consequence of my having been absent from home,—and of my thoughts having been harassed by illness in my family,[1]—with other engrossing circumstances.

You have extremely obliged me by lending me your *Select Translations*,—passages of which, I have repeatedly read with increasing delight and admiration: particularly the *Oration on Eutropius*,[2] which is a picture in motion,—and that *Homeric* description of a battle, contained in your extract from the 6th book of St. Chrysostom "On the Priesthood". Translation has been sometimes called the *body* weighing down the soul of original composition; but certainly in *your* case,

> "One might almost say the *body thought*" [3]—

your language has so much animation, and,—may I use the expression?,—so much *transparency*. If I may venture upon one objection, it shall regard the frequency of your inverted sentences. The objection is mentioned with diffidence, for I am thoroughly aware that language receives its *"ribs of steel"* from *inversion*,—that Milton's prose is very energetic because very inverted,—and that, in Addison's melodious compositions, the absence of inversion has proved the absence of *nerve*. With all this, I am only too convinced that the genius of our language will not admit a great *latitude* and *frequency* in inverting sentences, without putting on a constrained and artificial character; and I venture to observe to you,—under your correction,—that something of this constraint and artifice is visible here and there in your translation—ex. gr. in Page 120—"Perhaps thou art offended, because *to Philosophy I have resigned myself*",—where while you were *writing English*, you must have been *thinking Greek*. Forgive me my great freedom,—which you permitted me to take on other occasions, and which, on the present one, I dare to take, unpermitted.

You notice several plagiarisms committed *on* your saints and *by* your saints, *on* and *by* profane writers; but you do not notice one very striking imitation of Lucretius by St. Basil: I will write down the corresponding passages.

1. Illness of Mrs. Barrett's mother, Mrs. Graham-Clarke.
2. By St. Chrysostom.
3. "That one might almost say her body thought." John Donne, "The Second Anniversarie," line 246.

"So have I seen an experienced physician, who, giving
to his patient an unpalatable draught, anointed the
cup with honey." Page 244

"Nam veluti pueris absinthia toetra medentes
Quom dare conantur, prius oras pocula circum
Contingunt mellis dulci flavoque liquore
Ut puerorum aetas improvida ludificetur
Labrorum tenus; interea perpotet amarum
Absinthi laticem, deceptaque non capiatur,
Sed potius, tale a tactu recreata, valescat."
De Rerum Natura. lib 4.11.

Tasso in the first Canto (I *think*) of his *Gerusalemme liberata,* has
followed Lucretius. Your *notes* have great learning and acuteness,—
besides the still more valuable characteristic of "zeal according to
knowledge" which they everywhere discover.

And now I have spoken about your book, it remains to me to speak
about your letter: it remains to me to say that I was at once *gratified*
and *pained* by that letter,—gratified by the expression of your kind
and flattering opinion—and *pained* by finding that you could, for a
moment, suppose me prejudiced against you. Let me prove at once
the utter impossibility of such a circumstance,—and assure you, that,
if a *prejudice* on my side had prevented our *personal* intercourse, the
same prejudice must have operated on our continued *correspondence,*
—for where I objected to *visit* I should hardly be willing to *write.*
When I told you of the difficulties under which I laboured respecting
my mode of conveyance to Malvern, I spoke very truly; and at the
time I wrote my first letter,—and for some time afterwards, I did not
know but that those difficulties might be the only ones likely to interfere with our immediate personal intercourse. I have been, however, disappointed,—and my Father has represented to me, that,
whatever gratification and improvement I might receive from a personal intercourse with you, yet, as a *female,* and a *young* female, I
could not pay such a *first visit* as the one you proposed to me, without overstepping the established observances of society. I never could
persuade myself to tell you this, until now,—and have evaded the
subject as long as I *could,* and perhaps longer than I *ought.* You have
now forced the whole truth from me; for I cannot allow you to think
either that I wished to deceive *you* respecting *myself,* or that I myself was deceived respecting *you.* And now will you allow me to repeat,—and will you believe in my sincerity while I do so—that I still

"hope for some opportunity by which I may have the pleasure and advantage of Mr. Boyd's conversation"?

I must always remain
his obliged and sincere
E. B. Barrett

You were kind enough to promise to lend me the Oration on Eutropius in the original Greek. At present I am reading quite in a different direction,—but, when I am more at liberty, perhaps you will allow me to claim your promise,—if I should not in the meantime,—as I am thinking of doing,—purchase the book.[4]

6.

To Ruby Cottage
Malvern Wells

Hope End. December 1, 1827

Sir,

I have been suffering in the affliction of my family,[1]—and was unable to take an immediate advantage of the offer you obligingly made, of lending me the abstract of Porson's supplementary preface to the *Hecuba*.[2] I should now be very glad to see it,—and if you should not have repented your first kind intention, perhaps you will trust it to the servant who carries this letter. I see you are quite determined that St. Basil shall owe nothing to Lucretius—Procul profani! But tho' your defence of the saint interested and amused me, I am not yet persuaded that so extraordinary a correspondence could exist between two passages, without one's having been suggested by the other: and I think it more difficult to believe that such could be the case, than that St. Basil might have, for once, digressed from St. Gregory's line of study. I am almost afraid of you, when I take a middle course, and venture to hint that Basil may have read a *translation* of the passage in question. I am sure you never will allow this.

I *have* read the Pharsalia; [3] and am very glad that you do not join

4. Two years later EBB reports that she has read the oration twice through in Greek. See Letter 43.

1. Mrs. Barrett's mother died November 10, 1827.

2. An important statement on tragic meter in Porson's second edition of the *Hecuba*, Margate, 1817.

3. In the 19th century Lucan's *Pharsalia* was more praised by the poets than by the critics. Byron wrote in his copy that he considered it an epic of great merit; Shelley called it a poem "of wonderful genius and transcending Virgil."

in the classical *growl* against it, given vent to, by most critics—with that Cynic of Criticism, Scaliger,[4] at their head. Lucan is an ardent poet: the lightning of his spirit does not resemble Salmoneus's [5] mimic fire,—but has a real stormy grandeur which can only proceed from genius. And whether it wing the Heaven-ward sentiment, or illumine the battle-field, or "serve only to discover sights of fear",—as in Pompey's consultation of Erictho, in the 6th book,—it throws everywhere a fitful tho' vivid flame,—which *burns* as well as *flashes*. Do you recollect this 6th book in all its terror and sublimity? Do you recollect how Erictho

> Adspicit adstantem projecti corporis umbram
> Exanimes artus, invisaque claustra timentem
> Carceris antiqui—

and how

> irataque morti
> Verberat immotum vivo serpente cadaver—?

Southey has made use of the last image with striking effect in his poem of Thalaba—

> "Speak!" said the sorceress, and she snatched
> A viper from the floor,
> And, with the living reptile, lashed his neck.

In spite, however, of my admiration of Lucan, I am not prepared to go half so far as you do. I think he has too much *effort* in his *oestrus* —too much of the θελω θελω μανηναι,[6]—that his heroes speak too artificially, like orators: and the fault which you attribute to him, viz.— *want of Harmony,*—seems to me not only to belong to his *versification,* but to his design and colouring. I cannot conceal my astonishment that you should consider Lucan to be superior to Homer in the delineation of character. Homer's power of delineating character is, I believe, generally acknowledged as the most wonderful of all his wonderful powers,—nec quidquam simile aut secundum—unless we make a glorious exception in honor of our Shakespeare. The Greek epic is a grand moral *Harmonicon,*—where heroic courage and tender pathos, glory and fear, love and woe, the pride of life and the

4. Joseph Justus Scaliger (1540–1609), French classical scholar.
5. Mythological character who tried to imitate the lightning bolts of Zeus.
6. "I want, I want to go mad." *Anacreontic* 8.

desolation of death, meet together in one mighty chorus. Alexander's gold box was certainly not worthy of its contents.[7]

I should offer to send you Thomas May's *Supplementum Lucani;* [8] but you have most probably met with it—and I am sure you must think it spirited and poetical. I say confidently *"I am sure"*—for as you are no *High Church* GREEK scholar, you cannot be a High Church *Latin* one,—and are not likely to approve of Voltaire's summary criticism on Du Fresnoy's elegant *Ars Graphica*—"No Latin poetry is bearable, out of the Augustan age."

I never saw even the *outside* of the *Aethiopica,*[9] but I knew of its existence. Does not Ben Jonson make honorable mention of it, in his exquisite "Sad Shepherd"—where he speaks of

The lover's scriptures, Heliodore and Tatius—? [10]

You amused me extremely by your account of the *lava*—which,—tho' very tremendous,—cannot fortunately, do *quite* as much harm at Malvern, as at Herculaneum.

With sentiments of esteem and obligation,
I remain sincerely yours
E. B. Barrett

Have you the work containing the Dissertation on the Greek Tragedies—and if you *have,* and should not be using it, could it be trusted with me a little while?

7.

Hope End. December 15, 1827

Sir,

I feel unwilling to communicate with you until I can send my reply to your letter, and my more particular thanks for your works; but a sudden opportunity allows me to send the accompanying work,

7. Alexander the Great treasured a copy of the *Iliad,* annotated by Aristotle, in a gold box taken from the spoils of Darius.

8. Thomas May (1595–1650) translated the *Pharsalia* and composed a continuation (published in both English and Latin) carrying the narrative down to the death of Julius Caesar.

9. Greek romance of the 3d century, popularly attributed to Heliodorus, Bishop of Tricca. On May 5, 1829, EBB discusses the *Aethiopica* after reading it in Greek. See Letter 37.

10. "The Lover's Scriptures, Heliodores, or Tatii! / Longi! Eustathii! Prodromi!" Ben Jonson, *The Sad Shepherd,* I.2.

without giving me time to write a letter. You can hear from me by the post at any time,—and parcels do not find a ready conveyance always.

You must be well acquainted with the first publication of the distinguished author, whose essay on ancient pronunciation [1] I now send you. His essay *"On the Picturesque"* exacted from Dr. Parr [2] a remark —that it was "in point of *style,* the correctest production of the present time." Mr. Price has directed the powers of his highly poetical and gifted mind, for several years, to the subject upon which he has written; and has now just *printed* this dissertation,—with the idea of being thus able to collect the opinions and criticisms of learned individuals prior to *publication.* I have the happiness and advantage of his acquaintance and correspondence,—and being a most *faithful disciple* of his, am extremely solicitous to have your opinion of his theory.

If you should have the book read to you, may I be permitted to request the attention of the reader to the various *marks* which the author was obliged to introduce: as, without such attention, the whole must be unintelligible.

I shall write very soon if I possibly can—but have been much engaged. It is impossible for me, however, even to send this hurried scrawl, without expressing how much I admire your *Agamemnon.* [3] I will not forget your *poetry*—and I must by the way observe that I had some *elementary* instruction both in Greek and Latin, from the gentleman who instructed my brother before he went to the Charter House. [4] Since that time I have been an unassisted student—*"slovenly"* enough, I dare say!

Believe me, very sincerely yours

E. B. Barrett

1. Uvedale Price (1747–1829), *An Essay on the Modern Pronunciation of the Greek and Latin Languages,* Oxford, 1827. EBB had read the essay before publication and had written a detailed criticism in a letter to the author dated April 1827 (published as *The Art of Scansion,* London, 1916). Boyd, who agreed enthusiastically with Price's theories, called the attention of the learned world to them in a letter to the *Classical Journal* (June 1828), pp. 325–7.

2. Samuel Parr (1747–1825), scholar and schoolmaster. "With regard to Dr. Parr, his greatest point of originality lay in his wig. But there was powerful ponderous, uninspired eloquence in his latinity." EBB to Miss Mitford; unpublished: Wellesley College Library.

3. *The Agamemnon of Aeschylus. A Tragedy,* London, 1823. A faithful but uninspired version. In the introduction Boyd says that this was his second attempt to translate the *Agamemnon* and that it was completed in sixteen days.

4. "I never read Greek to any person except yourself and Mr. MacSwiney, my

8.

To Ruby Cottage
Malvern Wells

Hope End. December 24, 1827

Sir,

I received your parcel on Saturday; and feel extremely obliged to you for so readily giving an opinion I was so much interested in receiving. The opinion you give, really delights me,—it makes a strong point of sympathy between us,—and I could not help extracting one or two passages from your letter, without waiting for your permission, in order to send them to *Sir Uvedale Price*. He has just received a *Baronetcy*.

It is an odd coincidence,—that I made the same remark, with regard to your Greek epigram, as that which, you tell me, occurred to yourself. The epigram lost none of its harmony by being read according to the absurdly misapplied rules of accent,—for the author of the book I sent you, did me the honor of communicating his m.s. to me, some time previously to its appearance in a printed form. The subject to which he directed my mind, struck me from the first: I gave first my attention, and then my conviction and practice, to his arguments,—and the subsequent attack of a very acute and ingenious opponent, failed to shake that conviction, or change that practice!—I have therefore indulged in the delight which you yourself express,—and have been so zealous and eager about the business, that I only wonder I should so long have delayed mentioning it to you. But I have heard the question, and subject, called a *"vescata quaestio"*—a "threadbare subject"; and I knew by some experience of my own, that an argument upon it, would be interminable. Now *I* like an argument too well to object to its being interminable—but, I believe, this is not a very usual case.

I observe that all your ms. and printed Greek is without accents,— and am rather curious to know whether you omit them upon Sir Uvedale Price's view—with regard to their *application,*—or upon Dr. Gally's,[1]— with regard to their *authenticity.* Perhaps, some time, you will satisfy me upon this point.

It is certainly very hard upon me, that you should tell me what I

---

brother's tutor. . . . but then it was rather guessing and stammering and tottering through parts of Homer and extracts from Xenophon than reading." To Boyd, June 1838; Kenyon, *1,* 73.

1. Henry Gally, *A Dissertation against Pronouncing the Greek Language according to Accents,* London, 1754; *A Second Dissertation,* 1763.

might have lost, by my want of personal intercourse with you. What I *have* lost, is quite enough to regret—and too much—! therefore, for *lost,* read *deferred.*

Pray believe me, in the meanwhile,
Very sincerely yours
E. B. Barrett

9.

To Ruby Cottage
Malvern Wells

Hope End. January 12, 1828

Sir,

Sir Uvedale Price is very brief in his remarks on the musical nature of ancient accent, and does not enter into any critical discussion on its peculiarities and application. In the quotation on his title page he makes use of accents—their omission in the body of his work arises from a fear of confusing his necessary marks by their introduction,—and I never heard him desire their expulsion from editions of Greek books.

Notwithstanding all you say respecting your adoration of a great critic, and notwithstanding all the great critic said respecting the *indispensability* of accents, I cannot suspect your mind of submission to the *ipse dixit* of any man,—tho' the *ipse* should be Porson. . . .[1] I am sorry you think the new method unlikely to be generally adopted—the reasons you give for this opinion are only too convincing. If indeed some of the heads of the public schools had their *ears* about them instead of their *prejudices,* a great deal might be done—for *their pulchre!* would be followed by the *bene-recte!* of the multitude.

I never meant to charge the Muses with having blue hair. Had I even contemplated such poetical high treason,—which I assure you I would not have done for the world,—I should scarcely have the impertinence to solicit their assistance again. Your explanation of Pindar's epithet ιοπλοκαμοι,[2] is ingenious and plausible: but what can you do when you come to such an epithet as ιοβλεφαρος?[3] Can you consider that epithet to be expressive of an eyebrow wreathed with violets—or an eyebrow perfumed with the odour of violets? I think you cannot: and yet there is

1. The omitted passage contains arguments against the use of Greek accents.
2. "violet haired."
3. "with violet eyelids," "violet eyed."

certainly no tolerating a dark blue eyebrow. Perhaps in both these
cases, the *darkness* and *gloss* of the violet,—not its distinctive coloring,
—are meant to be apprehended; as in Anacreon's beautiful painting,
where he describes

Ελεφαντινον μετωπον
υπο πορφυραισι χαιταις [4]

Here the marked epithet *can* only be intended to convey the *brilliancy*
and *depth* peculiar to the colour of purple (or crimson) not the colour
itself,—the poet having taken care to state in some immediately preceding verses that the Lady's hair is quite black. If however it should still
be insisted that ιοπλοκαμος and ιοβλεφαρος express a distinct colour, I
would attempt to maintain that the ancient word which we translate
violet was probably applied by the ancients to a different flower, or to a
different species of the same flower. Virgil's *violae* were black—

Et nigrae violae sunt, et vaccinia nigra.

Ecl.X.39.

And now having done my duty as an "interminable" disputer, I am
ready to give back the golden locks to your personification, with good
will,—that she may have and hold them in right of King Apollo. I did
not intend a serious objection to the classical yellow, and I dare say
you are correct in it *to a hair.*

Your verdict upon the cause, Lucretius versus Basil, is a verdict from
which there are no means of appealing: the solution is undoubtedly a
natural one, tho' perhaps not more natural than the one I proposed
respecting a translation. But you seem quite determined to make the
Epicurean suffer with the saint—if you permit the saint to suffer at all
—and therefore I give up my prosecution. Speaking of parallelisms,
there is a curious one between Shakespeare in Macbeth, and Aeschylus
in the Choëphoroe: it is I think nearly equally striking with yours between Shakespeare and St. Chrysostom.

Could all great Neptune's ocean wash this blood
Clean from my hands?—No—

πορoι τε παντες εκ μιας οδου
βαινοντες χειρομυση φονον
καθαιροντες λουσειαν ματην.[5]—Choë. 64 Bothe

4. "Ivory brow / neath purple locks." *Anacreontic* 15.
5. "Though in one channel ran Earth's every stream, / Laving the hand defiled
from murder's stain, / It were in vain." Tr. E. D. A. Morshead.

You produce in your note two anticipations of Shakespeare's "sea of troubles" by Aeschylus in his *Prometheus* and *Persae:* but there is another anticipation of that expression, in the *Supplices,*—which I fell upon quite accidentally a day or two ago, and must mention to you. In it, the sea is coupled with an expressive and characteristic epithet— ατης δ' αβυσσον πελαγος.[6]

I am much gratified by the flattering manner in which you have received my verses, and shall certainly do myself the pleasure of acknowledging Mr. Boyd's name, in print, whenever I have an opportunity. He thinks fit to say a great deal about *vanity:* I will therefore take the liberty of wondering where he can have imagined *mine* to have been, all this time, particularly as I don't wear the *aes triplex circa pectus,*[7] and am neither willing nor able to question his sincerity. Your oriental manner of complimenting half inclines me to reply in the same style—"May you live a thousand years!" Certainly (not being Caesar) I should not put away the crown offered to me in the case of your publishing again, —but I may and must observe that the Public would not have such strong reasons for forgiving your too indulgent judgement, as *I* have for being obliged to it—and that the poetical merit would probably be considered as much a *dream* as the "wit and vivacity".

You are not likely to wish, this time, that my letter were "much longer": nevertheless I must lengthen it by thanking you for your explanation of the idiom, which is very calculated to be useful to me. I understood distinctly the meaning of the passage,[8]—but took the two negatives together in order to enforce the negation, and never should have thought of putting μη with δρασαι. So much for my *slovenly* mode of translating! I wish to explain that your questions had not the property of "teazing" which you attribute to them,—tho' the person to whom they were addressed, is of the *"irritabile"* as well as of the *"mutabile* genus". Waiving every privilege of the latter, I beg to be considered

Most respectfully and sincerely yours
E. B. Barrett

I had almost forgotten some items in your letter. To the question, "Am I not right?" I answer in the negative. I know very little Hebrew and have indeed only read a few chapters in the original scriptures. I have even laid aside the study, for *the present*—as Hebrew roots require a

---

6. "A bottomless sea of ruin." *Suppliants* 470.
7. Horace *Odes* 1.3.9.
8. Sophocles *Antigone* 443. See Letter 5.

great deal of ground to grow in, and my time is continually engaged
either in writing, or in reading that I *may write.*

I am glad to hear you say that you converse in a *slovenly* manner—
by which I understand that you don't think it worth your while to follow the example of some persons, who not only talk *in print* but talk
as if they were correcting the press. I never could bear an Elzevir edition [9]
of familiar conversation—and prefer, a thousand times, the freedom
and animation of nature—errata and all!

My brothers know Mr. Chapman, but are unacquainted with his
family.

10.

To Ruby Cottage
Malvern Wells

                                              Hope End. March 3, 1828
Dear Sir,

Your reproach made me smile—and makes me promise that if you will
forgive my having remained so δηρον [1] in formality, you shall never be
"frozen again". I like good epigrams,—and I particularly like two of
yours—not the *first,* in spite of my sincere condolence with you and the
Lincoln Cathedral! It seems to me to want unity—it looks too many
ways—and I admire an *epigrammatic squint* as little as I do a physical
one. But there is a great deal of point in the direction of your artillery
against Bishop Tomline,[2]—whose family is not of our acquaintance and
shall not hear any *report* thro' my means: such treachery would be an
ungrateful return to you for trusting and amusing and pleasing me at
the same time! I am delighted with the ingenuity of the Greek epigram
—and am glad to understand from it, that Lemprière [3] has Professor
Anthon's νεαροι λογοι,[4]—of which, having some imperfect humanity
about him, he certainly stood in need.

Poor Bothe and Schütz! and the οἱ περι [5] in Germany! the magnanimi
and the sagacessimi as they call each other, after the manner of modest

9. Seventeenth-century editions famous for elegance of design and type.
1. "long."
2. Sir George Pretyman (Tomline) (1750–1827), bishop of Winchester. The epigram
may have dealt with the much discussed fact that Marmaduke Tomline, who had
seen him only once, left him a large estate on condition that he take his name.
3. John L. Lemprière, *Bibliotheca classica,* re-edited by E. H. Barker from the
American edition by Charles Anthon, 1828.
4. "new words."
5. "those around them," "their circle."

critics! After all I recollect an excellent "German Sausage" in a note
to your Agamemnon—and not a word against Schütz *there,* tho', in the
letter before me, you cut him up as unmercifully as he could have cut
up Aeschylus! I know Mr. Knible has not Blomfield's edition, which I
will get from London by the first opportunity,—and, in the meantime,
won't you allow me to make use of Bothe? I hope you will! When I am
able to discharge him I will do so effectually, by remembering as little
as possible of the "abomination" and as much as possible of the "execra-
tion"—and by settling the former, PONDERE *fixa suo* [6] (like Lucan's oak)
in the dustiest corner of my bookcase.

I have reconsidered Io [7]—and attentively considered your pathetic
"Ιω Ιω," [8] without being in the least inclined to acknowledge your right
to an *Io triumphe!* and yet I quite agree with you in admiring the night
visions, the geographical descriptions, and several other passages full of
animation and power. I can do this with perfect truth, as I read the scene
in an unconnected state—but I cannot help continuing to think that
when a mind, winged by the noble preceding scenes, lights upon the
place of the *gadfly,* there is something comparatively low and terrestrial
in its sensations. If you tell me that this scene is on a level in sublimity
with the preceding scenes, I shall only be astonished—but if you allow
it to be a tone lower in moral elevation, you must also allow that it
occasions a corresponding change of feeling in the mind of the reader,
—in which case he must feel, as in all cases of suddenly suspended
enthusiasm—that he is fastened to a *dead* weight. I appeal against you,
to the character of the very passages you select. *Can* you actually attend
to geographical descriptions and to one eyed one toothed hags with your
head and heart full of Prometheus? [9] As to the Phorcides,[10] there is surely
a long story about them in Hesiod. I have not the Theogony in my
possession and therefore cannot speak decidedly, but I have some uncertain recollections on the subject which you will know more about
than I do. And even if these favorite κυκνομορφοι of yours (How do you

6. *Pharsalia* 1.139.

7. Horned girl pursued by a gadfly, character in Aeschylus' *Prometheus.* EBB later
published two translations of this play, one in 1833 and another "in expiation of a
sin of my youth" in 1850.

8. "Io Io": Greek exclamation.

9. "[The readers] are impatient at Io's long narrations; not because those narrations
are otherwise than beautiful, but because they would hear Prometheus speak again:
they are impatient even at Prometheus's prophetic replies to Io, because they would
hear him speak only of Prometheus." EBB, introduction to *Prometheus,* 1833; *Works,*
p. 139.

10. Hesiod *Theogony* 270–3. Not a "long story."

understand that expression? Bothe says *cygneo* COLORE, which I think it can't be!) Even if these κυκνομορφοι μονοδοντες [11] had not been noticed by Hesiod, I should rather have heard nothing of them anywhere, than have heard of them in the Prometheus! . . .[12]

You have given a beautiful translation of the most beautiful and original passage in Virgil's poetry,—the episode of Eurydice: [13] but you never mention him, and I wonder if you feel as coldly, respecting him, as I do. I have tried hard to like olives and the Aeneid upon principle,— and I could succeed on neither point against nature. That is to say I could not turn *Scaligeric* or *Mantuamaniacal* in any degree,—but I am far from being insensible to his elegance, his purity of feeling and majestic diction. Critics who think it necessary to compare Virgil and Homer (they may as well compare the mouse with the mountain!) after delivering up the praise of judgement to Virgil, are graciously pleased to leave the *fire* with Homer: as if Homer's fire were more astonishing than his judgement—or Virgil's judgement less often deficient than his fire! There cannot be (to my mind) a more palpable instance of this deficiency in judgement than a circumstance which everybody thinks it a bounden duty to applaud vehemently—I mean the silence of Dido in the 6th book.[14] Did you ever hear of any *"silent woman"* except Ben Jonson's [15]—who turns out to be a gentleman, in the last act? And can you conceive a woman's being silent under Dido's circumstances? If indeed she had been meditating a violent attack upon Aeneas or upon herself, she might be allowed a limited dumbness—as in the case of Dejanira [16] a short time preceding her suicide—or in that of Jocasta, whose moment's silence (she had been speaking immediately before) terribly alarmed the Chorus.

δεδοιχ' ὁπως
Μη 'κ της σιωπης τησδ' αναρρηξῃ κακα [17]—Oedip. Tyr.

But Dido meditated nothing but a walk with Sychaeus—and, being quite at leisure to abuse the pious Aeneas as he deserved, only proves by her unnatural and unprecedented conduct, that she was really *dead*.

11. "swan-formed single-toothed."
12. The omitted passage takes exception to a critical note in Boyd's *Agamemnon*.
13. *Georgics* 4.
14. *Aeneid* 6.469 ff. Dido in the Lower World refused to answer Aeneas and "fled back to the shady grove, where Sychaeus, her lord of former days, responds to her sorrows and gives her love for love."
15. *Epicoene or the Silent Woman.*
16. Sophocles *Trachiniae* 813.
17. "I fear lest from this silence evil break forth." *Oedipus* 1074-5.

The silence of Ajax Telamon in the 11th Odyssey,[18] is on the other hand, highly natural—highly characteristic of the sullenness and moroseness of that proud warrior: and certainly in this instance, Homer has not only all the originality but all the judgement on his side. I have been writing on at random, without considering that perhaps, after all, you may be a thorough *Virgilianus*—that you may be as fond of Dido's silence "as a Scotchman of Scotland, or as Miss Barrett of the Modern Greeks". In that case I recommend myself to mercy, which, however, I can scarcely extend to *you* on the latter question. Really, when you call the Greeks "savage monsters" and profess a total want of interest in their emancipation from the Turkish yoke,[19] I wonder Aeschylus does not let loose his Furies upon you. They must be *snoring* VERY hard! [20] I do not know how horrible the story may be which you are unwilling to tell me; but I *have* heard of many atrocities practiced by the Greeks— and not one narration has had the effect of shaking from my mind, the strong interest with which it regards their cause. Indeed, the more barbarous the atrocities, the more earnest is my desire for the emancipation of the criminals. If they are *darkened* by subjection, there is another reason for removing the obstacle to light! If the "iron has entered into the *soul*", there is another reason for striking away the iron! The bravery of the Greeks, their eagerness for glory and contempt of death, the quickness of their apprehensions, and the pride with which, in spite of imperfect knowledge, they advert to their ancestral dignity, are I believe, unquestioned and unquestionable! When Lord Elgin committed his profanation ("Quod non fecerunt *Goti,* Hoc fecerunt Scoti") [21] many of the people shed tears,—and a rumour was abroad, which sufficiently proved the state of public feeling in Greece, that the statues on being removed from their bases, emitted a moaning sound. The Greeks are Greeks by name and soil and descent: the antique cast lives on their countenances—and their language (tho' *quantum mutata ab illa!*) has degenerated wonderfully *less* than analogical cases would lead us to suppose. You cannot think how delighted I was the other day, to discover the *Trochaic Tetrameter* in a part of the patriot Riga's [22] spirited war

18. *Odyssey* 11.563.

19. Greek War of Independence, 1821–29. Boyd's and EBB's reactions are typical of the extremes of aroused British sentiment.

20. In Aeschylus' *Eumenides* the ghost of Clytemnestra finds the Furies asleep and snoring instead of pursuing Orestes.

21. Lord Byron inscribed these words on the Parthenon as protest against the removal of the "Elgin marbles" from Athens.

22. Rhigas Pheraios (1751–98) was both poet and hero of an earlier attempt to win Greek independence. Cf. EBB, "Riga's Last Song," *Works*, p. 58.

song. The following lines, put into *one,* and read, in the Romaic manner, according to accent, have exactly the old cadence.

$$\Sigma\pi\alpha\rho\tau\alpha, \Sigma\pi\alpha\rho\tau\alpha, \tau\iota \kappa o\iota\mu\alpha\sigma\theta\epsilon$$
$$\text{`}\Upsilon\pi\nu o\nu \lambda\eta\theta\alpha\rho\gamma o\nu \beta\alpha\theta\upsilon\nu; \text{ [23]}$$

Anyone, altho' as totally ignorant of Modern Greek as I am, may make out the greater part of this song. Besides, I have a regard for the very earth and air—and would not have tyrants breathe where poets sang,—or slaves tread in the footsteps of heroes!

So you do *not* hold the divine right of kings! Then, when you told me that Lady Olivia Sparrow [24] *annihilated* you on the subject, I suppose you only meant that her Ladyship made *nothing* of you! I am glad to understand this. I should not like to hear of the annihilation (from any cause whatever) of the Malvern Demodocus

$$\tau o\nu \pi\epsilon\rho\iota \text{M}o\upsilon\sigma\text{'} \epsilon\phi\iota\lambda\eta\sigma\epsilon, \delta\iota\delta o\upsilon \delta\text{'}\alpha\gamma\alpha\theta o\nu \tau\epsilon \kappa\alpha\kappa o\nu \tau\epsilon$$
$$o\phi\theta\alpha\lambda\mu\omega\nu \mu\epsilon\nu \alpha\mu\epsilon\rho\sigma\epsilon, \delta\iota\delta o\upsilon \delta\text{'} \dot{\eta}\delta\epsilon\iota\alpha\nu \alpha o\iota\delta\eta\nu \text{ [25]}$$

and, without meaning disrespect to you, I certainly never knew a person less fitted for being "passively obedient", than you appear to me to be. With regard to Berkeley, I neither doubt his conscientiousness, nor am surprised at his conclusions—for,—rejecting, as he did, the testimony of his eyes and ears,—he could not be expected to receive that of his reason!

What a world of closely written words I am going to burden you with! and yet, I assure you, their writer,—notwithstanding her opinion stated a page or two back, and notwithstanding her loquacious letters,—is often uncommonly afflicted by *Virgilian* DIDOISM,—when she is off paper, and out of reach of exciting influences. But this will seem incredible—!

You have too much *universal information,* to need being assured from the best authority, that I remain

Very sincerely yours

E. B. Barrett

I will follow your prescription for a *Hugh memory.*

23. "Sparta, Sparta, why do you rest / in sleep profound and deep?"
24. The "formidable" sister of Lord Gosford and "a great light among the Evangelicals"; E. C. Mayne, *The Life of Lady Byron* (New York, 1929), p. 243.
25. "whom the Muse loved, and gave both good and ill, / She deprived him of his eyes, but gave him sweet song." *Odyssey* 8.63–4.

11.

To Ruby Cottage
Malvern Wells

Hope End. Saturday, March 15 [1828]

Dear Sir,

I received your letter [1] last night—and if an "untoward event" (as the King's speech says of Navarino!) [2] had not prevented my having the carriage, I should have *been with you* THIS MORNING! As long as my selfish gratifications only, had to suffer, I *could,* and *did,* wait for the expected reward of my patience; but there is no enduring to expose my own sincerity to suspicion, and above all, to pain *your* feelings, for the sake of a formality. Having felt and expressed this, warmly,—and being permitted to *"do as I like",* I will be at Ruby Cottage on the earliest day I can,—ready to receive your *"at home"* or to submit to your *"not at home",* just as you may be inclined to be *forgiving* or the contrary. I do hope you may *not* leave Malvern, and that this interview may be the first of many agreeable ones. It will give me great pleasure to be introduced to Mrs. and Miss Boyd—and, with regard to yourself, I need not say how sincerely glad I shall be to *lose* my *unknown* correspondent, upon the *one* condition (the *only* one I could admit!) of *gaining* a personal friend. And so, you intended to leave me a letter (full of reproaches, of course!) as a legacy? *That* would have been *very hard*-hearted—and *totally undeserved!* You say I might have asked some of our mutual acquaintances to have introduced me to you. I *might* and *would* have done so, if I had met you in company with them: but how could I take the liberty of asking persons with whom I am not *very intimate,* at whose house I have only called four or five times, to go with me a mile off, for the purpose of making such an introduction? I assure you that, until within this fortnight, I had not seen any individual of the family you allude to, for *six months.*

I am grieved that you should seem hurt at my having passed *you* on Thursday, and having gone into Sir Charles Knowles's house. If you knew how strong an impulse almost made me stop the carriage, when I heard of your being so near—and how my courage failed at the idea of

1. See *Hitherto Unpublished Poems, 2,* 88, and Introduction, p. xx.

2. An unplanned battle (October 20, 1827) in which British ships annihilated the Turkish fleet. At the opening of Parliament, January 29, 1828, the King called it an "untoward event" which it was hoped would not destroy the harmonious relations between His Majesty's government and the Sultan.

99630

LIBRARY
College of St. Francis
JOLIET, ILL.

introducing myself *there,* you would not blame my inclinations. I went
to Malvern to see our relation Mrs. Trant, who, meeting me in the
garden, said, that Lady Knowles's carriage was at the door,—on the
point of setting out to Hope End. My mother has been lately suffering
from indisposition: and as, on that morning, she was not in a state to
receive visitors, without being the worse for the exertion, I went in a
hurry to beg they would *defer* their drive our way.

I hope to be at Ruby Cottage almost as soon as this note,—but as I
may possibly be delayed, it shall go. Pray don't be very solemn, and
critical, and awful, with me at first. I am not half so brave in conversation as on paper—and you may *Dido* me, in a moment!

Thank you for the longest letter you ever wrote in your life, and
which you did me the honor of addressing to *me!* It amused me particularly! I might arrest you on several charges of High Treason if I had
time, just now. But I have not—and must,—for this morning,—leave
the modern Greeks to fight their own battles out, and even Homer (proh
pudor!) to be drowned in *coniac!*

> Believe me
> Very sincerely yours
> E. B. Barrett

I never *did* read the *Dialogues* on matter and spirit.

Do you know Hume's "Sceptical solution of sceptical doubts"? etc. etc.
I think you cannot!

How can you libel your poetical tastes as you do? Do you wish to
make game of my credulity? Exercise the *interminable argumentatives* as
you *will*—you will never make me say "I believe Mr. Boyd prefers *sound* to *sense*"—unless indeed I could add, "Credo, quia *impos-
sibile!"* [3]

Thank you for the interesting prolegomena. I like Mr. Barker,[4] so
far, very much! This scribble of mine does not pretend to answer your
letter as a whole—but only that IRRESISTIBLE *part* dated Thursday! I
am ashamed of sending such a disjointed hurried scrawl!

---

3. Tertullian's "rule of faith."

4. Edmund Henry Barker (1788–1839), indefatigable scholar and editor, friend of
Boyd and later correspondent of EBB, who had recently re-edited Lemprière's
Bibliotheca classica. "I have heaps of his valuable letters written in red and black ink
within and without. I did not know him personally. I mean the author of the Parriana, and a most multifarious editor, and one of the most learned men, particularly
in Latin matters, in England." EBB to Miss Mitford; unpublished: Wellesley College
Library.

12.

Spring Cottage [1] [1828]

My dear Sir,

I cannot say how much I am obliged to you for your kind constructions upon my very *ordinary* actions. You do not seem to recollect that what you call *good temper,* was the natural selfish course of my inclinations. Your letter did certainly make me feel uncomfortable—but it did *not* make me feel that you were exacting, or harsh. When I returned home last Thursday, I was sure that I had been, at least, *risking* an imputation entirely foreign to my real feelings towards you. I was rallied by my family on account of my irrepressible fears respecting the probability of your recognizing me on the road—but I was *right* after all.

As to this day's occurrence,[2] I will not have you think it *ominous.* My sister who unfortunately is the greatest sufferer, was *not* coming to visit *you!* She is not seriously injured, I thank God—but it seems uncertain whether she will or not leave Malvern tonight. In the case of her remaining, *I* may remain—and tomorrow morning, will try my fate again at Ruby Cottage. I hope you and your family will accept my sincerest thanks for the interest you express towards me. I am not hurt,—only *shaken,* and frightened and agitated a good deal—and ready to dare as much again in *so excellent a cause.* The experience I have had today is worth something! I used to think that the *shaking of a carriage* did me harm—and now I find that even the shaking *out of one,* has done none! At any rate my pleasure at seeing you will make the recollection of this day anything but unpleasant to my mind!

While I am writing, it is resolved that my sister should go home *now:* therefore I am afraid I shall not see you tomorrow. If I should not happen to do so *soon,* "do not let anyone or anything prejudice you against me". I hope, *that* caution is as unnecessary from *my* pen as it was from *yours!*

The only circumstance likely to delay my visit to you is a doubt (really a most unfounded one) respecting the dexterity of my brother's

1. Home of the Barretts' cousin, Mrs. Trant.
2. An accident caused by a runaway pony frustrated Elizabeth's first attempt to visit Mr. Boyd. See Introduction, p. xx.

driving. If my parents should not like to trust him again, I must only wait a little while longer till I can enlist another.

> Pray believe me
> Most truly yours
> E. B. Barrett

You will forgive this abominable writing—

13.

Hope End. Wednesday [1828]

My dear Sir,

In Homer's own style, I granted one half of your request, and gave the other half to the winds! [1] That is to say, I read your postscript *first,* and read the rest of your letter *immediately.* When you desired me *not* to do so, I wonder what you fancied me made of!!

I am very grateful to you for your kind interest and enquiries respecting myself and those dear to me. My Mother is tolerably well. She was a good deal alarmed at our long absence—but after her first agitation on seeing us was over, I made her smile by my account of my interview with you on the road. It was not like the rest of our intercourse—*out of the* COMMON WAY! I have the happiness of being able to say that my sister is much better. She was more hurt than I at first thought she was, tho' not at all *seriously* so,—and she is likely to be quite *unstiffened* in a day or two. As for me, now that my nerves have recovered a little, I am *miraculously* well. Papa accuses me of having contrived the whole upset for the sake of dramatic effect, and of taking care to fall lightly myself. I am afraid Mr. Trant's accusation was too just—that the immediate cause of the accident was my want of presence of mind in seizing the reins—but really I had nothing to do with the *running away.* My brother is acquitted on all sides. I shall however never get permission to visit you, till I can be *chaperoned* by a dragchain and a safer horse. You may depend on my coming as soon as possible. I hope that we may have a great deal of personal intercourse this summer, and that the Agamemnon may be a party concerned. How very kind you are to interest yourself so perseveringly in my improvement!

I have a great deal to say about Homer and will write in a day or two if I should not be able to see you quite so soon. If you would

1. *Iliad* 16.250.

continue your penance of Monday evening, I think we should agree at the end of a week!

I was not *sure* that the lady whom I had the pleasure of meeting with you, was Mrs. Boyd, till I had sent away my note from Spring Cottage. May I offer my best compliments to her, while I beg you to believe me

Most sincerely yours
E. B. Barrett

Thank you for your medical advice *postscriptum*. I will try the remedy you are kind enough to mention for my headaches, the *notoriety* of which surprises me. But you seem informed on all points. My eyes are not *very* strong,—but they don't inconvenience me to any unpleasant extent—they only make me like to read in the *dark*. I am sometimes stared at, on account of my drawn curtains, and dusky room—and *distant* candle, at night.

I forgot to say that I received your letter, which was waiting for me at home. It does not require an answer. When I read your first letter, upon which it is a commentary, I said that I should have felt, *myself,* very much as *you* did. You had a *right* to expect from me something better, than my *passing you* might seem to imply! But you have found *now* that my intentions and feelings towards you were *not* in fault, however appearances might belie them.

14.

Hope End. Wednesday [1828]

My dear Sir,

You must allow me to thank you rather by my *feelings* than my *words,* for the present I have just received. I hate affectation of any kind, and hate more particularly, an affectation of *modesty,*—but I know too well, that you have considerably over-rated my actual merit. Knowing this, it is a real satisfaction to me to think, that, do what you will, you *cannot* over-rate my gratitude and sincerity towards yourself. It is not necessary to say that I will highly value your book, or that I will doubly value the *first page*—since I see *what* is written there, and recollect by *whom,* it was written! The writing surprises me, because it is yours—and the kindness *hardly* surprises me—*because it is* YOURS!

As far as concerns Homer, you make *me* sorry that I should have written what I did. Some of my *illnatured* friends might tell you that

I rather like to be "contradicted",—and rather *dislike* perpetual smooth-sailing thro' sympathies. However this may be, my actions shall prove my desires respecting your acquaintance. I meant to have been with you today or tomorrow—but my Father's uncertainties about going to London, make me disinclined to leave home just now, even for a few hours, for fear I should find him gone, on my return.

I send you three notices of my poem,[1] which I am ashamed of sending in their "tattered and torn" condition. They are the only ones I have *seen,* tho' I have heard of one or two others, of a rather favorable character. The flat contradiction between the Eclectic Review and Literary Gazette, with respect to *Akenside,* will amuse you,—and did not increase my veneration for my critics. I was put out of humour for at least ten minutes, by the charge of my having imitated *Darwin.*[2] I never could *bear* Darwin! I have tried his Botanic Garden four or five times, and never could get thro' above twenty pages!

You are too indulgent, in the paper which has so much delighted me—but your animated remarks are likewise so *animating,* that if I were to begin speaking of them now, I should keep your messenger longer than he might like to be kept. I think your *criticisms* unquestionably just, in general. If I were to tell you I thought so in *every instance,* I should not be *myself,*—and I like you to be assured of my identity, when I subscribe myself

Most sincerely yours
E. B. Barrett

Will you read Irving's[3] Prefatory Discourse, in the book I send you?

15.

To Ruby Cottage

Hope End. Saturday night [1828]

My dear Sir,

I have an opportunity of sending a few lines to you tomorrow morning, and therefore will write them now, in order to relieve my mind,—

1. *Essay on Mind.*

2. Erasmus Darwin (1731–1802), grandfather of Charles Darwin. His *Botanic Garden* discourses in heroic couplets on the theories of Linnaeus.

3. Edward Irving (1792–1834), *The Coming of the Messiah in Glory and Majesty,* trans. from the Spanish Jesuit Lacunza, 1827. The study of Lacunza's work led Irving to a study of unfulfilled prophecies, centering in conferences at the home of Henry Drummond in Albury, and to a revival in his church of Pentecostal speaking in "unknown tongues." See letters of 1831.

which is afraid of your attributing my *alibi* to some wrong motive. The horse was harnessed to the carriage today, when in consequence of the treachery of my driver and the weather, I was sent back again to my *Patience*—the shadow of her former self, thro' frequent disappointments! If I were philosophical enough to be amused by my own misfortunes, I could not help being amused by the variety and abundance and *extempore readiness* of these obstacles, which have sometimes made me think of your *omen*. Twice during the present week, I have been on the very *point* of getting into the carriage; and, every day, for the last ten days, has been successively fixed upon for the purpose. The *Furies* seem to have taken upon themselves, the office of the *Fates*—but will certainly have exhausted all their malice in their attack on this *first* visit, and must allow me to pay every other, upon which I venture to calculate, without opposition. I only hope that you may not have taken my proposal of proving "my desire of your acquaintance, by my actions", quite as literally as I, at first, wished you to do. When I *can* please myself, you may be sure of my not *displeasing* myself—the interpretation of which is, that when I *can* visit you, I will not *delay* doing so. I have been supplying the place of your conversation as well as I could, by reading over again, the book, you made me so proud, by sending. You know how much delighted I was with this book, from the first—and it is impossible to speak of having read it again, without thanking you for *more* delight. Your translation is certainly very eloquent, and never throws cold water on the fire of your authors. You do not let us see them thro' a *mist,*—but give us the open sky,—παντα δε τ' ειδεται αστρα! [1]— What a quotation to venture upon, in a note to you! As however it is too short to require a great deal of "wading", on your part,—it shall remain where it is. *I* remain,—with my best compliments to Mrs. Boyd,—

Most sincerely yours
E. B. Barrett

16.

[1828]

My dear Sir,

When I adjourned from the kindness of your conversation [1] to the kindness of your letter, I should have instantly written to thank you for both, if you had not given me something to do in the way of read-

---

1. "And all the stars are seen." *Iliad* 8.559.
1. The first visit was paid Wednesday, April 16, 1828.

ing. I like your article against the Unitarians particularly. . . .[2] What am I to say of the *ultimus Romanorum,* where you mention my name in so flattering a manner? When you shewed it to me the other day, you surprised me *out of my voice:* and even if I could have talked quite as fast as usual on the subject, I should have been obliged to have left a great deal unsaid. You certainly have a fault—which *I* must be the first to forgive!

It is in general very *humbling* to be *over-praised.* But is there not sometimes a pleasure, not only in *being* over-praised but in *knowing* ourselves to be over-praised? that is when we are more anxious about friendship than justice—and are inclined to value the fault of the judgment on account of its discovering the leaning of the feelings? In *this* way, I hope I may be allowed to be *pleased,* while I think of all your kind expressions—written and spoken!

My diplomacy is being exercised about the house at Malvern,—and if I were to sacrifice willingly my individual advantage to the public interests, I should do what no politician of this enlightened age would think of doing. After all, my hopes rest on the *promising bad* accounts of the houses between yours and Mrs. Trant's. In whatever way the business may be ultimately settled, you will be no prophet— for I think I shall often be at Malvern this summer,—and I am *sure* I shall never be there without going to see *you*—the *ergo* is tremendous! I should not be inconsiderate and unfeeling enough to mention it to you, before you can possibly have recovered [from] the visitation of Wednesday, and that cruel separation between yourself and your dinner which I was the means of effecting. You see what the *omen* meant!

I have been reading St. Chrysostom in Greek and in your English, sufficiently loudly to startle his "canonized bones": [3] and if my sending back your Greek copy depend,—as your kindness says it must,— on my having felt no pleasure from what I read, I am afraid you are reduced to receive my thanks instead of the book. *Being of a very martial disposition,* I have been more particularly delighted (again) with the description of the battle,[4]—tho' you did not select it for its harmony, and will be shocked at the barbarity of the preference. *Preference* is *not* a right word to use. The different characters of the

2. In the omitted passage EBB comments on Boyd's article and on three epigrams which he had sent her to read.

3. *Hamlet,* I.4.47.

4. Chrysostom, "On the Priesthood," 6. EBB had already admired this passage in Boyd's translation. See Letter 5.

passages prevent the propriety of their comparison; but I meant to say that I was more *moved* by the battle—that I dwelt upon it longer than on the other passages. Its *imitative* harmony is electrifying, stunning, and overwhelming! . . .[5]

Besides this, I have been reading several parts of your translation, exactly as you desired me to do—slowly, and out loud: and I have admired the particular cadences and the general rhythm, all the way. Can you forgive my insolence if I say *tu quoque* or rather CHRYSOSTOMUS *quoque,*—and remark to you a *"confusion of metaphor"* in the last sentence of the eloquent discourse on prayer—where prayer is described as being implanted in the soul, spreading its luxuriant foliage, and *laughing unhurt* [6] etc. etc.? I *have* observed your orthodoxy about accents. You know Payne Knight [7] was one of the Dissenters from that doctrine—and never printed a line of Greek (did he?) which was guilty of an accent.

I have just heard from Sir U. Price. He is full of *the* subject, as usual: and has been much pleased by receiving the sanction of no less an authority than *Hermann's.* . . .[8]

Monday morning

I did not receive your letter till last night.

When I had written *that,* I kept my pen in my hand without moving it, for several minutes,—and now I must write down the question I have been asking myself during this pause—*"What can I write?"* It is a difficult question to answer—and *Davus sum, non Oedipus.*[9] I cannot regulate my expressions towards you by any expressions I ever had occasion to use towards any other person—for the course of your conduct towards me, the course of your most persevering and disinterested kindness,—is wholly unexampled and unparalleled in my experience. Would you believe me, if I were to say that,—notwith-

---

5. The omitted passage contains detailed criticisms of Chrysostom and of Boyd's translation.

6. "Fifth Oration on the Incomprehensible," *Select Passages of the Writings of St. Chrysostom, St. Gregory Nazianzen and St. Basil* (London, 1813), p. 31. The "laughing unhurt" is a flourish of Boyd's not found in Chrysostom.

7. Richard Payne Knight (1750–1824), numismatist and classical scholar.

8. Gottfried Hermann (1772–1848), classical scholar, authority on meter. The omitted passage cites praise by Hermann of Sir Uvedale's essay on the pronunciation of Greek and Latin and lists objections raised by a "determined adversary."

9. Proverb, e.g. Terence *Andria* 1.2.23. Davus, a slave's name, stands for a plain, uninspired man.

standing the gratifying character of your enclosure, the means by
which I came in possession of it, the circumstance of being indebted
for it to *you,* gratified me still more? I dare say you would *not:* and yet
it is the simple truth.

> I remain, with much regard,
> Gratefully and sincerely yours
> E. B. Barrett

17.

Hope End. Saturday morning [1828]

My dear Sir,

I was provoked when I came home on Thursday, to find that my
unusual *absenteeism,* had prevented my taking advantage of the opportunity, and replying immediately to your letter. Certainly it *was*
"very kind in you to take so much trouble"—and the less *disinterested* your motive was, the more reason I have for being obliged to
it. It was also very kind in Mrs. Boyd to allow us to profit from her
local knowledge. We had however nearly concluded the business before your letter arrived, and have now quite determined upon taking
Bradley Cottage at Great Malvern. Give me credit for being extremely pleased!

I am forced to write in a great hurry this morning, that I may not
miss an opportunity of returning twó of your books. With regard to
the Classical Journal,[1] *you,* of course, do not like the new construction of the passage in *Romans. I* do not either. I think it is (with all
its ingenuity) *very forced.* Bear with my conceit, in thinking anything
about the matter!

I like Hermann now and then—tho' perhaps he has more prolixity
and *mysticism* than he might have had. There seems nothing *new,* and
something not *quite correct* in the Article on the Theology of the
Ancient Greeks—but I am too hurried to explain what I mean—or
what the objector meant by his term "physical experiment".

Do not imagine that I could think of being ceremonious with *you.*

---

1. March 1828. Two of the articles to which EBB refers, "A Critical Dissertation on
Romans viii. 28–31" and "The Theology of the Primitive Greeks," are unsigned.
Hermann's "De differentia prosae et poeticae orationis" was originally written in
1794. EBB does not mention an article by Boyd entitled "Classical Criticism," pp.
8–11, in which he refutes Unitarians by a philological argument drawn from the
Alcestis.

If you would trust Gregory with me a little while, and direct me to what you consider his finest passages, I should be delighted. I am anxious to be acquainted with one whom you once distinguished by calling "your favorite, of all Greek writers,—and consequently of all writers whatever". Forgive me my incoherency this morning,—and believe me ever

Yours most sincerely
E. B. Barrett

18.

To Ruby Cottage
Malvern Wells

Hope End. May 1, 1828

My dear Sir,

My Father did *not* take the parcel on Saturday. It was too late after all, and did not leave this place till Sunday morning. A Catholic servant of ours (you will think we have a great deal to do with Catholics!) who attends Mrs. Wakeman's chapel,[1] and afterwards invariably goes on to Spring Cottage, took it with him. Mrs. Trant happened to be from home. On Monday she was *here,* and told me that she had sent the parcel to you that morning. Therefore I am inclined to lay the blame on *her servant's* negligence,—tho' I am not the less sorry that *any* cause should have prevented your receiving your books immediately.

Does not Catullus, somewhere, in the character of the "pessimus omnium poetarum", address his "optimus omnium patronorum"?[2] If I were half as good a poet as Catullus, I might afford to be quite as much modest,—but,—that, unfortunately, not being the case,—the "optimus patronorum" is reduced to receive my thanks without an antithesis. For I won't commit suicide by applying the *pessimus* to myself. Better judges may do so, if they like,—tho' I am tempted to observe that they could not so apply it, without bad grammar,—or render it grammatical, without bad manners! Really the adjective in question should have no *feminine: should* it? I believe I am writ-

1. In her home at Little Malvern, next to the Little Malvern Church. "The living is in the gift of Mrs. Wakeman, who is a Roman Catholic, and therefore incapable of presenting; she has, however, the nomination of the living, and the presentation is made by the Right Hon. the Earl Somers." Best, *Malvern,* p. 175.

2. Catullus 49, addressed to Cicero.

ing nonsense merely for one reason,—namely, that if I were to write
seriously and feelingly, and assure you how deeply I am sensible to
all the interest and kindness expressed and proved in different ways
by your letter, I should make sad work of it! I will certainly "do my
lesson" according to your desire, and will go to say it, not when I
can *"conveniently"* but when I can *possibly* do so. We are now expecting some relatives, who have agreed upon staying here a few days.
You must never think that I calculate coldly my *own conveniences*
when there is a possibility of satisfying my *inclinations* by visiting you,
—you must lay it down as a canon as infallible as any of Porson's,—
that whenever our personal intercourse has been long interrupted, the
interruption has annoyed *me*. You do not often do me *justice;* on this
subject it is my *interest* to exact *bare justice* from you! To go back to
the lesson, pray be as little awful as you can help being—make as many
allowances as you *can,*—and do not give me over to the secular arm to
be *"caned"!* There is no new copy of my poem [3] in the house—but I
send enclosed, a note to Mr. Duncan containing the direction you advised me to give. Why should I annoy you, by repeated thanks? You
know how much obliged to you, I must necessarily feel.

I have been for some time desirous of noticing the one or two points
of your valued criticisms, upon which I venture to entertain doubts. I
may as well do so now. In page 26, *prejudice* and *eyes* do make an
imperfect rhyme [4]—but I think that imperfect rhymes relieve the ear
from a monotonous impression. They are sanctioned by the practice
of the most uniformly correct poets—by the *frequent* practice of Pope
himself.

In page 30, there are *two* opinions against me. The masterless
steeds [5] could not be expected to do otherwise than *"kick"*—but the
passionless brow should certainly have been smoother,—and the physical dress had no business to stick in anybody's throat! Upon the whole
I will confess to you that tho' this structure was once very pleasing
to my ear, what you have said at different times respecting it, has
diminished the pleasure by changing the course of my associations. And
yet *my ear* (like every person's ear) having a right divine of its own,

3. *Essay on Mind.*
4. "But when the sun of blinding prejudice / Glares in our faces, it deceives our
eyes." *Works,* p. 36 (EBB's references are to the 1826 edition of *Essay on Mind*). The
matter of "imperfect rhymes" was a battle which the poet was to fight frequently with
her critics.
5. *Works,* p. 37. The "passionless brow" and "physical dress" (p. 41) occur in a later
passage; like the "masterless steeds" they offend by substituting an anapest for an
iambus.

and being unwilling to submit to *authority*, asserts its independence by modifying its concession. I think that the structure is occasionally admissible for the sake of expression. I think that *I* have used it much too frequently, and not in general for the sake of expression.

Page 54. My "ideas" have been abused by most of my critics. Placing the accent on the last syllable of "nothing", would certainly be a *thing* not to be endured! Sir U. Price said, that, to scan the line, the word must be read *"idee"*—but I have no *idea* of doing *this* either! I am not going to be disingenuous enough to attempt a defence of what I am convinced is indefensible, upon any just metrical principle. When, however, I wrote the objectionable lines,[6] I meant the last syllable of the word in question to be pronounced exactly as *"dear"* is pronounced, in

"Dear as the ruddy drops that warm my heart"

or

"Oh Name, for ever sad, for ever dear!"

where the separate sound of the two vowels is distinguishable, while the metre continues uninjured.

Saturday morning

In page 71, "But Nature's glorious masterpiece is *here*", *here* refers to the "crowded cities". I dislike a noise and confusion very much: but the sight of a great multitude, always appears to my mind, calculated to excite the most affecting and sublime contemplations.

Perhaps you will indulge me some day, and gratify my curiosity, by saying a great deal "about craniology".[7] If you ever had a *leaning* to the science, you must have been confirmed by hearing that Thurtell[8] had the organ of benevolence very strongly developed. A Craniologist once told me that a young man whose head and forehead were naturally and smoothly formed, suddenly devoted himself to hard study, and that after a short lapse of time, he appeared before his friends

6. "All is idea and nothing real springs / But God and Reason!—(not the right of kings?)" *Works*, p. 43.

7. Boyd's remarks on craniology were probably inspired by "And though we may not reasonably deem / How poets' craniums can be turned by steam—" *Works*, p. 33.

8. John Thurtell, hanged for murder January 9, 1824. His spirited defense made him a popular hero and he became the subject of several ballads. "Organ of benevolence" refers to the popular phrenological conception that the brain is divided into separate areas (organs), each of which governs an aspect of character.

with the most satisfactory development of organs, signified by the most deforming protuberances. The story was told to *me*, with a grave face, as an unquestionable fact,—and *I*, in my candour, am willing to acknowledge it to be a *"knock 'em down* argument"—for I am quite sure that the gentleman's studies must have been chiefly directed to the noble science of boxing!! You say "there is an art still more wonderful" than craniology, which you *"know to be true"*. This is very mysterious! What *can* you mean? Do you mean the *black art?*

Two of the lines on Jeffrey (the second couplet) [9] I would wish omitted. Otherwise, I do not believe, I have said too much. His style is not *chaste*—it is forced and ambitious, but it is striking and brilliant.

Two of the lines on Locke, [10] I would wish omitted. He is neither "first in my heart nor noblest in my song",—and I cannot conceive why I should have said so. Sometimes people are led by the heat of composition, to say more than they are willing to assent to, afterwards. I may however observe in my own defence that this is not a common fault with *me*—that it can be justly attributed to only four lines out of my whole volume! With respect to Irving, [11] I would not recall a single word of what is written. As a Preacher, he affected me more than anyone I ever heard; and as a writer he seems to me to abound with passages highly oratorical and splendid. Nevertheless I quite agree with you, about the account of the *dietings* at Albury Park in the book which you would not read, and *ought* to have read! I *wish* you had!

Page 73. You tell me I am "unquestionably positively decidedly wrong" in what I have said about Artists! [12] Dugald Stewart reverses the motto of Sir U. Price's book, [13]—and (I continue to think so!) with

---

9. "Who justly judges, rightfully discerns, / With wisdom teaches and with candour learns." *Works,* p. 33.

10. "Oh! ever thus, immortal Locke, belong / First to my heart, as noblest in my song." *Works,* p. 46.

11. "Thus reason oft the aid of fancy seeks / And strikes Pierian chords—when Irving speaks!" *Works,* p. 46.

12. "The artist lingers in the moonlit glade, / And light and shade, with him, are—light and shade." *Works,* p. 48.

13. "Quam multa vident pictores in umbris, et in eminentia, quae nos non videmus!" (Cicero): motto on title-page of Price's *Essay on the Picturesque.* Stewart, protesting that the artist has limited vision, would prefer to read "Quae multa videmus nos quae pictores non vident." Dugald Stewart (1753–1828), "On the Beautiful," *Philosophical Essays,* ed. William Hamilton (Edinburgh, 1855), p. 240.

great justice and feeling. Surely poets *do* see more in nature than artists do! Surely you cannot disagree with me in this! I do not mean to shut artists from the Eden of ideal beauty, where the voice of God is speaking to the soul of Man! The great artist *does* see more than the actual light and shade *before* him—more than the hills and valleys *around* him—more than the clouds and sunshine *above* him: but still he sees only *light and shade,* only *hill and valley,* only *cloud and sunshine!* He only deals with *matter,* under whatever beautiful combination, his genius may enable him to view it. With the poet, on the other hand, matter is not an *object* but a *medium.* He looks *thro'* nature that he may look *beyond* nature! He binds together the moral and the natural with golden bands,—rendering what is beautiful in nature, more hallowed, by associating it with what is elevated in intellect,—and rendering intellectual conceptions more distinct and definite by a reference to material objects. How the artist particularizes! How he dwells upon coloring and grouping and foregrounds and distances! How the Poet generalizes! How he delights in abstractions —in depth and height and silence and space!! I suppose I should make an *honorable* exception in favor of Mr. Bowles,[14] whose censure of Pope would have been just, if Pope had been a painter,—or if the world were likely to gain by Pope's poetry resembling Mr. Bowles's!

Ought I to have added a note explaining and qualifying what I said of Lord Byron? Then if I ever have an opportunity, I will do so. At the time I wrote the passages relating to him,[15] I could not find it in my heart to leave a word upon paper, calculated to reflect upon his memory. Were not his errors of faith and his errors of conduct sufficiently known? By the allusions of my book, I thought I had guarded myself from any possible suspicion of extending my admiration to that faith and conduct. I thought I might please my feelings by keeping silent upon those points, above his grave. Whenever there is anything in character or conduct, to *condemn,* it will never want *condemners!* Justice will do her part,—and, afterwards, Calumny and Malice and Insult will do theirs! Poor Lord Byron was

14. William Lisle Bowles (1762–1850). His hostile edition of Pope and his proposition that images drawn from nature are per se more poetic than those drawn from art aroused a storm of criticism, e.g. from Lord Byron.

15. *Works,* pp. 32, 50. In the first passage Byron is praised as the "Mont Blanc of intellect"; in the second a eulogy of Greece leads into a Theocritean lament for "The pilgrim bard, who lived and died for thee." The original edition of the *Essay* also contained two shorter poems on the death of Byron.

cruelly used, in life and death, by unfeeling relatives, false friends, and open enemies—by a world which can never understand what is not cold and heartless as itself! *He* was not by nature cold and heart-less—but his affections were turned into bitterness. You know how his wife introduced a medical spy into his room, when he was writing the Siege of Corinth, in order to obtain proofs of his *insanity!!!* I saw *her* once!

I think that, humanly speaking, Lord Byron's extraordinary sensibility of heart and mind was his bane. He could not stand unhurt in that burning fiery furnace—for "the likeness of the Son of God" was not in the fire! Religious knowledge he had none—but every real poet must have *natural devotion*—and *he* was a real poet! I think he had more devotional *feeling* than Sir Walter Scott has! A relative of mine was in St. Peter's at Rome as Lord Byron entered it,—and saw him throw himself, in a transport of enthusiasm, on the earth before a cross, and kiss the feet of the Crucified. You see—the *knowledge* was not there—but the *feeling* was there! In his last moments, he said "Not *my* will—not *my* will!—" Perhaps it may have pleased Him who remembers that we are but dust, to have touched and turned the evil heart of unbelief,—to have had mercy, and not sacrificed! I like to dwell upon this consoling possibility.

The subject makes me think of the circumstance you mentioned in your letter. It is the madness and folly of man to disregard his immortal part, even while it is entering its eternal state, for the sake of his perishable part, even while it is perishing. I *have* prayed, and *will* pray for the poor sufferer!

Saturday, eight o'clock

Our dinner hour was rather later than usual today, and I am ashamed to say, we have only just left the table. I find your parcel waiting for me in my room, and hear that your messenger is in eminent danger of being benighted. Therefore my quick way of reading, which you are so severe upon, has done me some service, in looking over the magazine and your letter,—and my quick way of *writing* must also be in request. Thank you again and again for everything for which I am indebted to you—for the Review, and your *astonishing* references to Gregory. I wish you had sent me your memory at the same time. The Review is a very satisfactory one to *my* vanity,—and I am going to take it down to Papa, to please *his*, too.

I hope I shall see you *very soon,* tho' I am sure not *quite as* soon as I could wish—but then I am unreasonable!

Believe me

Your grateful and sincere friend

E. B. Barrett

My best compliments to Mrs. and Miss Boyd.

19.

[1828]

My dear Sir,

They have this moment sent up stairs to me, to know whether I have anything to send to Malvern. Having just received your letter, and recollecting that you wished to read Sir Uvedale Price's sheet of remarks, I must not neglect the opportunity, tho' it has offered itself so suddenly that I shall not be able to say half of what I have to say. Upon the sheet in question, Sir Uvedale marked the passages he liked best in my book,—and the two letters which I likewise send you, contain his defence of one or two of his criticisms. I did not think them *just,*—and said so with unreserve. Tell me whether you consider him to have been right or not. The line I quoted from Lucretius, is

Carmine Pierio rationem exponere nostram.[1]

The line from The Dunciad, is

"On Dulness' lap the sacred head reposed"—

but this is not a solitary instance of such an elision. With respect to *illustrate* I was unquestionably wrong—and only wonder that *you* did not attack me about it,—that you, were not *inimical* to it.

Thank you for your letter, and for the extract from Lord Byron's. Neither of you could persuade me that in "imagination passion and invention", he is Pope's inferior: tho' I do agree that no one should willingly imitate *him*—or *Pope!* Is it not a bad thing to imitate the best authors? Is not an imperfect original, at any time better than the most excellent copy? By the bye, I believe I told you the other day that the juvenile poem, with whose dulness you are so unnecessarily

1. *De rerum natura* 1.946; 4.21. In a letter to Sir Uvedale, EBB had defended the expression "Aonian song" (*Essay on Mind, Works,* p. 49) by citing as a parallel "Carmine Pierio."

afflicting yourself, and which is so *un*original throughout, was not *intentionally plagiaristic*. When I came home, and looked thro' the preface, in order to form some idea of what you were going to endure, I found that I pleaded guilty occasionally with regard to *the intention*.[2] I had really forgotten the full extent of my iniquity!

I have a great deal to say about Gregory, but no time now, to say it in. How can you think that *I* require to be stimulated about the house! The fact is I have no influence in any way, as the business stands. I am *afraid* of the consequences of Mrs. Trant's provoking emigration,—tho' I have heard *nothing against* the fulfilment of the first plan. Grandmama is *sure* to come. We have not yet heard, upon what day.

In the greatest hurry, believe me, my dear friend,

Most sincerely yours
E. B. B.

20.

Hope End. May 28, 1828

My dear Sir,

You must have thought the letter which took no notice of yours, and its accompanying papers, a very odd and ungrateful one—but I could not thank you for what I had not received,—nor could I possibly know, that, while I was writing *to* you, a packet *from* you was on its road to me, and that I should receive it an hour after I had sent away my letter. How *could* I? *I* am quite ignorant of the "four arts" which are "more wonderful than craniology".

With regard to the first sentence of your letter,—and it is impossible to help noticing *that*, first,—I may assure you, that, if *wishing* were as efficient *now* as in the classic days of Fortunatus and black puddings, I should certainly have known you all my life. Judging from the intercourse I have had with you, I may say that the accomplishment of such a wish would not only have tended to increase my *knowledge*, but my *happiness*—and perhaps, according to your suggestion, my *vanity*,—in an equal degree. It is natural and reasonable that you should begin to have some self-reproaches and misgivings as to the probable result of your *orientalisms*: and the letter which crossed yours,—in which my "modesty and diffidence" took upon themselves to

2. "I confess that I have chosen Homer for a model, and perhaps I have attempted to imitate his style too often and too closely." Preface to "The Battle of Marathon," 1819.

I am sorry to hear of Mrs. Boyd's indisposition; but perhaps it is better on every account,—except on *that,*—that the pleasure my Mother anticipates in seeing her, should be deferred for a little while longer. For the last few days, my dear Mother has herself, not been so well as usual. Mr. Carden however who saw her yesterday, does not give us cause of alarm but rather of comfort, in his opinion: and in a short time, when the weather has become more settled, I trust she is likely to be better able to derive pleasure from Mrs. Boyd's visit. Besides, Hope End begs to be seen for the first time, in *sunshine*—for the sake of its vanity!

Pray do not *think* of sending your letters to Mrs. Trant's. You may *direct* them to *me* at her house, if you like, and I can receive them as usual, from thence. I have always plenty of means of having *my* letters conveyed to you, without applying to the general Post.

There is a great deal *written,* of my new poem,[6] tho' it is not in a state yet to be *read* by anybody. When it *is,* I should extremely like to submit it to you. I do not like your advice, *at all!* When I published last, I did not know any person whose opinion I considered very valuable, and therefore did not communicate with any person, out of my own family, on the subject. *Now,* I cannot see why I should throw away my privileges, for fear people should suspect me of abusing them.

In the event of Bradley Cottage being let, we certainly shall *not* take Spring Cottage, and therefore we certainly *shall* be nearer to you than I contemplated at one time.[7]

Believe me ever
Your sincere friend
E. B. Barrett

Perhaps you had better send your letters to me by the general post, till Grandmama comes.

21.

To Woodland Lodge
 Malvern

Hope End. Saturday morning
June 6, 1828

My dear Sir,

I ought to have thanked you before now for the note and letter and

6. Probably "The Development of Genius"; *Hitherto Unpublished Poems, 2,* 99–133.

7. The Boyds must already have moved to Woodland Lodge, Great Malvern, since Spring Cottage (occupied shortly before by the Trants) was close to Ruby Cottage.

the edition of Gregory,[1] which I received last week. At the beginning of the present week I had an opportunity of sending a letter,—but to say the truth, was too much out of humour to write. The fact is this. In consequence of a communication from London, we had actually *taken* Bradley Cottage, when another subsequent communication, speaking of the continued uncertainty and tediousness of my Father's business, directed us to dispose of the house if we could,—as another week or fortnight might pass, before a removal to Malvern became practicable. You may imagine how provoked I was! I have been besides continually disappointed about receiving a book which I mean to send you,—but, having just read your last letter I cannot wait for anything before I reply to it. I cannot wait for anything before I thank you,—and warmly thank you,—for the great and gratifying kindness you shew me with regard to my staying in your house. It would delight me to do so,— and *that,* I believe, I once told you—*unnecessarily* told you, for you must have known, long ago, the only feeling I could entertain on the subject. I told you at the same time,—and *not unnecessarily,*—the reason which prevents my doing so at present. When *I* was ill, my Father and Mother, during *two years,* scarcely ever left me to go anywhere, not even to dine in the neighbourhood,—tho' I was in *immediate danger* for only a *few months.*[2] Ought *I* to do less for *them?* My Mother's case is not likely to be so tedious as mine was,—and when she is once in a satisfactorily progressive state, I shall not mind leaving home,—even if she should not be *quite well.* In the meantime "the most useless person in the house" as I am generally and too justly called, must stay where she is, and only *dream* of her visit to you. Of course when Grandmama is at Malvern, I shall be able to stay with *her* for a few days at a time—but then *that* is a different thing. *That* will be paying a necessary attention— it will not be for the mere sake of amusing myself,—and no one can say to me, "You go *there,*—why should you not come *here*"? If on the contrary, I were to stay with *you,* this would naturally be said. I could not avoid giving offence to several persons who have been kind enough to invite me to their houses during the last six months,—or else I should be obliged to leave my Mother in her reduced state, for the purpose of mixing in society. Certainly I could not go to you without going to

1. A 1690 folio containing the orations and letters (now in the Wellesley College Library), which Boyd subsequently presented to EBB as a gift. The signature H. S. Boyd with the date 1804 appears on the inside cover; under it EBB has written "qui hunc librum Elizabethae B. Barrett amicissime dedidit. A.D. 1829." The volume passed back and forth between them and was one of the gifts which Boyd bequeathed to EBB. See "Legacies," *Works,* p. 339.

2. To R. H. Horne EBB wrote (October 5, 1843) in an unelaborated parenthesis, "At fifteen I nearly died." Horne, *1,* 162.

the spirit of his times,—but whether it is conformable to the dignity of his philosophy. Lord Bacon's mind was not like *clay, impressible:* it was like *granite,* which is *impressive*—it was not calculated *to be formed* by an age, but to *form* an age. He went *before* his age in philosophical research: why should he be only *equal* with his age, in the moral scale? He shook off the chains of false opinions and prejudices: why should he *keep* chains of a yet baser metal? Why should the knees which were stiff to Aristotle, become so supple and obedient before James the first? I do not understand how the law of *moral rectitude*—the law impressed on the soul of man when man was created in the similitude of his Maker— can be called properly, an *ex-post-facto* law.

I think besides, that Lord Bacon does not merely *conform* to the spirit of his times—he is not, in an ordinary degree, adulatory and subservient. It was not *necessary* for him to have incorporated the basest and most disgusting of dedicatory prefaces with the noblest and most elevating of philosophic works. The volume containing that preface and that work, should hold the place of a Death's head, in the chambers of contemplative men,—as a memento of what is more humbling than death!

If Bacon is "not to be *less* respected" on account of his subserviency, —it follows that, *without* the subserviency he would not have been more respectable,—the moral of which is at least questionable. It appears to me that if Mr. Barker's plea,—the plea of *humanity*,—is admitted,—an amnesty of all evil in act and will, must be the result. *That* plea swallows up all condemnation; and is disarming to the moralist and satirist. Juvenal must not stab—nor Persius scoff—nor Horace rally! *For* there is no tendency to corruption, and no consummation of corruption, which is not *human,*—and the stronger the humanity, the deeper the corruption! Lucan was *human,* in his adulation of Nero,—and Nero was human, when he put Lucan to death. You know, your craniological bulwark Thurtell's, organ of benevolence, did not interfere with his *humanity*—and neither judge nor jury considered his being *human,* any just and legal obstacle to his being *hanged.* I think that *they* were about as right, with regard to Thurtell, as Mr. Barker is *wrong,* with regard to Bacon.

I have begged you to thank Mr. Barker for me—but whom can I employ to thank *you?* I wish you could know by intuition, how very deeply I feel all your kindness—for if your knowledge of my real feelings be dependent upon my describing them faithfully, you will certainly think me ungrateful and unfeeling, all your life. Cannot your *powder of projection* [3] help you to this knowledge—enabling you to collect the real

3. Powder which assisted the alchemist to change base metal into gold.

feeling from the imperfect expression? And yet, *not* by *transmutation.* Your letter about the occult sciences amused me extremely. My guesses were not so far wide of the mark after all—which encourages me to hazard another—Are you Gregory Nazianzen, with the *aurum potabile* at your elbow? *That* would account for the coincidence you mentioned to me,—and would relieve me from the labour of wondering so much, at the familiarity of your memory, with his works. Gregory himself *might* have mistaken page 37 for page 38, in his invectives against Julian, if he had not looked at the book for 17 years—so that solitary mistake of yours, does not interfere with my speculation.

I am obliged to come abruptly to a close,—or I shall not be able to send this, tonight. Whoever your "second Daniel" is, he can know nothing of his profession, if he ever should look at *my* handwriting, and not judge from it, that its writer *is,* and must continue to be

Your grateful and sincere friend
E. B. Barrett

The weather really appears settled now. Will you give my kind remembrances to Mrs. Boyd, and say that we are pleased at the continued sunshine, on *every account.* The party in London is as uncertain as ever.

23.

To Woodland Lodge
   Malvern

Hope End. Saturday [1828]

My dear Sir,

I believe I shall be able to pay you my visitation on Monday,—or on any other day during the coming week which may be more convenient to yourself and Mrs. Boyd. If my coming on Monday should be likely to inconvenience either of you, I hope you will say so at once—as it will be *quite* the same to me and the carriage, to leave home on any subsequent morning. Perhaps you will write a line to tell me what I am to do,—and if you send it by tomorrow's post to Mrs. Trant's, I can receive it in the evening.

We hope Miss Boyd has not forgotten her promise of riding here soon! Will she do so on Wednesday, to dinner?

I am writing in such a hurry, that I have not a moment to express how much surprised I was to find out that *you* like Terence! Is not *that* an inconsistency?

Believe me
Your sincere friend
E. B. Barrett

If you *can* receive me on Monday, perhaps Miss Boyd will return with me in the evening, and sleep here—and spend the next day with us. She will give us all great pleasure, by agreeing to this proposal.

24.

Hope End. Friday [1828]

My dear friend,

I did not think I should be able to send a letter to you till Sunday,— but, as an opportunity is likely to offer itself this evening, I cannot help taking advantage of it. I will *not* keep Miss Muschett's poem,[1]—notwithstanding your kind permission. If you received it from the author, you really should not give it away,—and, if you did not, I am still as able as you to procure another copy. My general impression of the poem is this,—that it is very elegantly and feelingly and pleasingly written—but it is deficient in harmony, and the ideas seem to me much diluted by a *wordiness* in the expression. This wordiness not only enfeebles, but *obscures* whole passages. *Diffuseness,* as well as *conciseness,* sometimes produces obscurity—there is ice at the south pole as well as at the north! I do not like the word *style* in the third stanza—it is not appropriate or poetical or dignified. I like the 20th and 21st stanzas best. I should like the 12th, very much, if it were not for the concluding lines,—and I may observe the same of the 8th, which begins beautifully, but ends in a rather weak commonplace manner. The *"silent* heart", for the *pulseless* heart is a beautiful expression,—and, I think, original,—for Wolfe's [2] poems were, I believe, published subsequently to Miss Muschett's stanzas. Sir Uvedale Price once pointed out to me, two lines of an exquisitely pathetic little poem,—"To Mary",—by Wolfe, author of the Elegy on Sir John Moore. Sir Uvedale thought them very original and striking; and *I,* who thought the same, will submit them to your judgment.

Still would I press thy *silent heart*—
And *where thy smiles have been!*

Is there not a touching beauty in this manner of adverting to the lips, without naming them?

I hope that Miss Muschett's present opinion upon the Greek question is a newly formed one,—and that she did not write her 13th stanza,

1. Probably Henrietta Mushet, an old friend of Boyd with whom he later had a misunderstanding. See Letters 116 ff. The poem seems not to have survived.
2. Charles Wolfe (1791–1823).

merely that she might write poetically. It is a bad thing to employ in composition a different mind from the ordinary mind,—because, with that habit, it is impossible to be a natural writer: and when a writer ceases to be natural, he must cease to be poetical.

You see, I return the Classical Journal! If you will reflect a little, you will perceive that,—without any superabundant *modesty,*—I could not very well or becomingly, make the use which you permitted me to make of your letter,[3]—tho' I am anything but *ungrateful (that* word is not prohibited!) for the honor of being *laudata a laudato.* "The hint towards the correction of a passage in Aeschylus" in page 185 of the Journal, will certainly enrage you. You will observe that the critic adopts *your* correction without acknowledgement, and supports it by quoting "an author *whom Aeschylus was very fond of imitating."* [4]

Speaking of imitations, when you mentioned to me that poem by Shelley,[5] which you met with in the Examiner, its quaint form put me strongly in mind of something I had read somewhere—but I would not tell you so at the time, on account of the extreme indistinctness of my recollection. The recollection, however, became less indistinct, when I thought it over afterwards. Is not the prototype of Shelley's poem to be found in Anacreon's ode, beginning 'Η γη μελαινα πινει [6]—, where, because the trees drink the earth, and the sea drinks the rivers, and the sun drinks the sea, and the moon drinks the sun, the poet considers it quite allowable to drink too?

Will you tell me whether you believe Dr. Dunbar or the writer of the *Adversaria literaria* (vide page 268 of the Journal!) to be right, in the interpretation of the epithet χερσαιον as applied to κυμα by Aeschylus? [7] I *hope* you will say the Professor. The meaning which *he* attaches to the word is unquestionably the most poetical and expressive—whether it be philologically correct, or not.

Your indignation about Irving's scholarship, prevented my telling you

3. In a letter to the *Classical Journal* (June 1828), pp. 325–7, commending Sir Uvedale Price's book, Boyd spoke of "Miss Barrett, a highly-favored child of the Muses, whose beautiful poem, entitled *An Essay on Mind,* written at the age of eighteen, would be generally admired, if generally known."

4. The note quoted a line from the *Odyssey* in support of a "new" emendation in the text of *Prometheus.* Boyd promptly insisted on the priority of his own conjecture, noting that he too had supported it by a reference to Homer. *Classical Journal* (September 1828), p. 138.

5. "Love's Philosophy," 1819.

6. "The dark earth drinks." *Anacreontic* 21.

7. A note on *Seven Against Thebes,* line 64, discussing the exact meaning of the words "land wave" as applied to an army.

what I was going to tell you respecting his Aeschylean application of the verb *to see* to *sounds*. You will recollect the expression in his Orations. Blackwood's Edinburgh Magazine has an elaborately abusive article on Irving,[8] which animadverts something in the following way on this expression—"We have heard of pigs seeing the wind, but we believe that Mr. Irving is the first who ever *saw a voice*". The accomplished critic need not have looked into Aeschylus for the purpose of "seasoning his admiration",—for the first chapter of the Revelations might have satisfied him in a moment. St. John says "And I turned to *see the voice* that spake unto me!"

I would write a longer letter,—but I am told that if I attempt to do so, I shall lose my chance of sending this today—and I do not like to detain the Classical Journal from you any longer. Yesterday I was tantalized by being taken within two miles of you without being enabled to see you, for which, I was naturally and vainly sorry. You cannot blame my *will*. I wish I could tell you how deeply I felt the happiness and advantage of those *Horae Atticae* I passed with you,—and yet how can I do so,— and at the same time attend to your *request?* A Poet once constructed a long poem without the letter *t*. That must have been very difficult—but it would have been still more difficult for me to speak of last Monday, without using the three proscribed words—*"gratitude—grateful—gratefully"!!*

Believe me always
Your very sincere friend
E. B. Barrett

My kind remembrances to Mrs. and Miss Boyd—I fear Miss Sibree has left Malvern. There is no *decision* from London—tho' we had a letter today.

25.

Hope End. Monday morning [1828]

My dear friend,

Henrietta is going to ride to Malvern Wells,—but she cannot go farther, on account of the convenience of the lady who accompanies her. I shall however be able to send this as far as Mrs. Trant's,—and to write to you till the horses are ready. It will be impossible in so short a time to speak to you as I feel, of some parts of your last letter—and yet, why

8. A review of "The Oracles of God, Four Orations," *Blackwood's Edinburgh Magazine, 14* (1823), 145–62.

should I complain? With *any* allowance of *time,* the difficulty would be equal. *At last,* after waiting my patience fairly to an end, I am able to send you the little volume [1] which, I said so long ago, I would send,—towards which, you have shewn so much indulgence and patience,—and with regard to which you have so forcibly exemplified the sentence from Gregory Nazianzen, quoted on the first page. Then let it be a memorial, not of my *friendship,*—I hope *that* requires *none,*—but of your own disinterested kindness,—which is the only thing you are capable of forgetting.

The accompanying pamphlet was sent to me two days ago. I have not read it yet, and know nothing more of it, than its subject. This may interest you,—but if you are not curious about the opinions and arguments of Dr. Adam Clarke's [2] Antagonist, pray do not let the circumstance of my enclosing the book to you, induce you to annoy yourself even with the *third* part of *three pages.*

I do not at all agree with you in what you say of the Elegy on Sir John Moore—(nobody should call it an ode!) unless it be in your general dislike to that kind of metre. I do not like it *generally:* but the whole effect of Wolfe's poem is so grand and striking that I cannot *feel* a criticism. I would rather have written that elegy, and the pathetic little poem, a passage of which I quoted to you, than almost all Moore's lyrics. I am surprised that you should not very much admire the passage I quoted, and that you should find fault with its grammatical construction. Such an ellipsis appears to me by no means uncommon in poetry.

In great haste, believe me
Your always sincere friend
E. B. Barrett

Pray give our kind remembrances to Mrs. and Miss Boyd. Nothing satisfactory from London.

I must open my letter again, to ask you whether you will be indulgent enough to let me see your *elegy.* If you feel any objection, forget the request.

1. Probably Thomas May, *Supplementum Lucani.* See Letters 6, 34.
2. Adam Clarke (1762–1832), Wesleyan preacher and theological writer, friend and relative of Boyd.

26.

To Woodland Lodge
  Great Malvern

Hope End. Saturday night [1828]

My dear Sir,

It is late for me to be writing,—but I have this moment received your elegy, and I do not wish our servant to go tomorrow (which he will do early in the morning) without taking a few lines from me on the subject. I agree with you in your judgment of this elegy as exactly as I did, in your judgment of Wolfe's poetry—for it has *particularly pleased* me. . . .[1] Your poem is addressed to the heart; and a calculating criticism from the head proves the latter's bad judgment—I hope nothing *worse!* I will not however complain of *my* bad judgment, in venturing to criticise, since it is at least kept in countenance by *yours,* in determining to underrate.

Most probably I have been writing tonight, what critics generally write—i.e. positive nonsense; but what can a person be expected to do, in such a hurry? I am hoping to be able to visit you on Tuesday,—if not more than *half* of the usual obstacles, should come in the way.

With my kind regards to Mrs. and Miss Boyd, I remain

Your ever faithful and sincere friend
E. B. Barrett

I have not gone *thro'* the Parriana [2] yet. I have been extremely amused by your most *characteristic* letters, published by Mr. Barker.

Mama is going on tolerably well.

27.

To Great Malvern

Hope End. Wednesday [1828]

My dear friend,

You are *too* kind to send me a copy of your work on the Atonement, when so few remain,—but if my valuing the gift can render me in any degree worthy of it, it has not been quite thrown away. I once wrote a

1. The omitted passage contains a criticism of Boyd's elegy.

2. E. H. Barker, *Parriana, or Notices of the Rev. Samuel Parr, L.L.D.,* 2 vols. 1828–29. Condemned with justice by reviewers as "a motley pyramid, ill arranged" and a "burlesque upon minute biography." Among the miscellaneous matters included were four letters from Boyd to Barker on the subject of bells.

letter [1] in which I frankly told you the opinion I ventured to entertain with regard to this production,—and I will not teaze you with any more *"it may be doubted's"*. As a doctrinal work, I do question its probable utility—its *general* utility—and yet I could not help being delighted with the acuteness and fervour, pervading the line of argument and style of composition. I never closed a volume of yours with greater respect for the talents of its writer, than was excited in my mind by a perusal of the little volume in question—which is now placed in the good company recommended to it, by your note.

I have finished the *Parriana*—but not the work on Junius.[2] The former volume is interesting,—displaying, nevertheless, an unquestionable talent for *bookmaking.* . . .[3]

If you should go *thro'* the book, you will discover that there was not a mere *campanological* sympathy between yourself and Dr. Parr. *You* are fond of *cats. He* was fond of *a* cat, which used to sit upon his shoulder. Whether his taste was universally extended, like yours,—or yours particularly applied, like *his,* I have no means of knowing CATegorically.

I cannot hope to see you this week,—and whether I may see you in the ensuing one depends entirely on my beloved Mother's health. She has been very, very unwell,—and tho' she is again better, my thoughts continue harassed and restless, on her account. Long may *yours* be more tranquil,—more unagitated by solicitude respecting those nearest and dearest to you! My best regards to Mrs. and Miss Boyd,—and

Believe me ever

Your sincere friend

E. B. Barrett

28.

To Malvern

Hope End. Wednesday [1828]

My dear friend,

I was going to write a few lines to Mrs. Boyd for the purpose of begging herself and Miss Boyd to dine with us today at half *past three,* instead of

1. Letter 4, September, 1827.

2. E. H. Barker, "The Claims of Sir Philip Francis, K. B. to the Authorship of Junius' Letters, Disproved," *The Pamphleteer,* ed. A. J. Valpy, 27 (1826), 415–30. Junius was the name used by an anonymous polemicist who published letters attacking the government in the London *Public Advertiser* from 1768 to 1772. Their authenticity was much debated. Most frequently assigned to Sir Philip Francis, they were also attributed to Boyd's father. See L. D. Campbell, *The Miscellaneous Works of Hugh Boyd, The Author of the Letters of Junius,* 2 vols. London, 1800.

3. The omitted passage is a criticism of the *Parriana.*

drinking tea with us at *six*. I hope they will be able to do *both*—and that they will consent to receive our request thro' your medium, as I wish to thank you for the kind expressions of your note yesterday. Lady Mary Shepherd [1] is not a *friend* of mine,—but, on the contrary, a very slight acquaintance. She is staying for a short time at Malvern Wells on account of the ill health of one of her daughters,—and called here for the first time a few days ago. When she proposed to me to go with me to your house, I felt pleased,—because I felt sure that she would at least amuse you. Her talents are mathematical and metaphysical,—but her conversation is very able, and brilliant, and entertaining. I cannot fix a day for our visit, tho' I hope on every account that it may not be a distant one. In the meantime you must believe me when I assure you of the deep value attached by me to every expression of your regard, and of the truth with which I remain

Your sincere friend
E. B. Barrett

29.

Hope End. Thursday morning [1828]

My dear Sir,

I send you what I amused my Father by calling *"my experimental simplicity"*. You should have had these Hymns long ago, if you had happened to be more a child, and less a critic,—or if I had agreed in opinion, respecting them, with one of my little brothers, who was heard to pay me the following rather equivocal compliment—"Really I never thought *Ba* could write so well".[1]

I believe I never asked you whether you cared or not, about *pastoral* poetry,—and whether, setting aside Theocritus and Virgil, (I would omit the last name if I *dared*) you deeply sympathize with shepherds and

---

1. Lady Mary Shepherd (1777–1847). "Lady Mary *is* a singular woman. I think gratefully of her from some passages of kindness which passed from her to me, when I wanted kindness most, and the saddest of domestic losses was nearer than I thought or *would* think. I believe her to be a *kind woman*—a better if not a higher name than a great metaphysician. Have you seen her books on the External Associate and Cause and Effect?" To Miss Mitford, September 27, 1837; Miller, p. 54 (last sentence omitted in Miller). Lady Mary's visit had already been proposed in a brief note. Weaver, Letter IV.

1. These may be three "Hymns Sung on the Occasion of the Annual Sermon for the Benefit of the Sabbath School–By the Children." One verse is quoted in a catalogue of Henry Sotheran and Co. (London, 1915), p. 20: "Almighty God—our feebleness / Implores thy gracious care— / Upon thy smile an angel lives— / And *that,* a *child* may share."

shepherd*esses*—*asses,* in the modern long run of making love and hay.
I am perfectly intolerant of them all, except of Ben Jonson's Sad Shepherd and Fletcher's Faithful Shepherdess—and would grant nothing,
even to Tasso and Guarini, but the mere dull immortality, which, I
suppose, no one can withhold from them—*"vivete*—et VALETE!"

Here is a good burlesque of the modern Shenstonian pastoral! The
first stanza is by Gally Knight [2] author of "Eastern Sketches" etc. etc.:
and the second, which appears to me the best of the two, is a supplement
affixed by Sir Uvedale Price. Neither have been published.

> Coughing in a shady grove
> Late my Juliana!
> Lozenges I gave my love—
> Ipecacuanna!

> Full half a score, th' imprudent maid,
> From out my box, did pick—
> Then, sighing tenderly, she said—
> My Damon! I am sick!

My brother declares that, whenever he goes to Malvern, I am sure to
make him wait for something,—if he is unfortunate or imprudent
enough to apprise me of his intention. I must spare him this morning.
Give our best remembrances to Mrs. Boyd,—and our acknowledgements
for her *very* kind proposal respecting Henrietta and the ball. I thought
it would not be found possible to return the answer she would like to
return—but at any rate she will be at the library in the *morning.*

Believe me
Your always sincere friend
E. B. Barrett

30.

Hope End. Friday [1828]

My dear Sir,

As you desired me to let you know the result of the London plan, I
will not delay doing so. Mama has determined upon not going at
present,—for tho' she was referred to her own judgment, yet,—the com-
parative deprivation of air and exercise during the fine weather, and

2. Henry Gally Knight (1786–1846). Sotheby lists a copy of his *Eastern Sketches*
with these verses by Knight and Price copied on the flyleaf in EBB's hand.

the positive and necessary deprivation of the society of her children, being reasonably dwelt upon,—she cannot keep to her first resolve. Her present one pleases and satisfies me, selfish feelings apart. For the last few days she has been comfortable. This is all we can expect just now, and we must thank God for this!

I so much out-staid the Berkeleian *idea of daylight* on Monday evening, that I was obliged to trust to the *idea of moonlight* for the purpose of getting home,—and, as it had even more *vivacity* than the Bishop would think necessary to constitute *reality,* my drive was anything but dark,—and as little *gloomy* as possible, considering that my *late idea of the direction of the poney's head had* become *inverted.* On getting home I anticipated a reproach, and asked—"Am I going to be very much abused"?—notwithstanding which, I encountered none,—and was assured that no one could have supposed my discretion capable of bringing me home before *twelve,*—when I was with *you,* and had the carriage quite to myself. So you see how unexpectedly trustworthy I proved myself to be!

I have been much amused by your Pope Joan of Arc! [1] The knowledge of bare facts has no more intellectual dignity, than has the knowledge of consecutive simple alphabetic sounds. The dignity of wisdom, as of eloquence, is formed from the *combination,*—from reasoning *by* and *upon* that combination. I have Miller's four thick octavos, entitled the *Philosophy of Modern History.* [2] Now *some people* who do not like "Modern History", like the "philosophy" of *anything,*—and the first volume, containing the philosophic theory without the historical references, is the only one which has been thumbed and dog-eared. I was once asked on a point relating to the treatises for the "Diffusion of Useful Knowledge". My Father overheard the question, and interrupted the questioner, by exclaiming—"Oh! don't ask *her!* She knows nothing about it! She is an enemy to all useful knowledge whatever!" I certainly think, and you perhaps may agree with me, that what is generally

1. "A Popish antagonist . . . may ask what right Protestants have to complain of their still printing and circulating the Rhemish notes, when Protestants circulate such groundless and malicious stories, as those about Joan of Arc. . . . The cases are not parallel. Whether a young woman ever was Pope, is a question which cannot be positively decided. . . . [it is] ascertained fact that the Rhemish translators corrupted the word of God." Boyd, *Thoughts on an Illustrious Exile* (London, 1825), p. xiii n.

2. George Miller (1764–1848), "Enlightened Miller of our modern days!" praised at some length in *Essay on Mind, Works,* p. 36. A footnote in the original edition referred readers to the *Philosophy of Modern History* (Dublin, 1816–28) in order to "judge the reality of the merit."

called *useful knowledge,* is not often *elevating* knowledge, and is not *always,* even *useful.*

On opening your book to look for Joan of Arc, I came upon your translation of the beautiful episode in the Georgics [3]—the finest and most original passage in Virgil's poetry, I *maintain!* Did I not once tell you how much I admired this translation? [4] I believe I did—but I must say it over again. I must say besides that this translation appears to me *now,* superior to the version from Sophocles,[5] which I formerly thought, and still think, so beautiful. The translation from the Georgics is undeniably *superior* in beauty,—and I am aware that I did not at first dwell upon it sufficiently. The harmony is various and expressive, yet unbroken—not a tone of the original's energy and pathos wants a corresponding tone,—and the diction is warm, graceful, and flowing. Altogether it is an highly finished performance. The monosyllables in the following line finely preserve the *imitative harmony.*

"She, cold and mute, moves on in that dim boat"—[6]

Speaking of *boats* puts me in mind of your censure on Lord Byron's nautical professionality. When I did not agree with you on that subject, I was only *consistent,* tho' I did not know it at the time. I did not, at the time recollect having, myself, written the following *"vulgarity"*—

Man! hast thou seen the *gallant* vessel sweep,
Borrowing *her* moonlight etc. etc.[7]

I was going to tell you that Sir Uvedale Price proposes to spend a few days here on *Friday,*—but I have just learnt Mama's intention of visiting Cheltenham, in which case, he of course will not come. I am sorry on every account,—and I should have liked you to have had an opportunity of knowing him to be something more than a *"pleasant agreeable man".* At any rate, you will probably have this opportunity in November.

I have written a much longer letter than I intended,—but I find it difficult,—from bad habit and other causes,—to write *briefly* when I am writing to *you.* To make amends, I have sent you no *queries,*—so there is no necessity for you to trouble yourself in any way about replying. Pray do not think of it!

3. Orpheus and Eurydice episode, *Georgics* 4.
4. Letter 10.
5. Letter 1.
6. "Illa quidem Stygia nabat iam frigida cumba." *Georgics* 4.506.
7. *Essay on Mind; Works,* p. 51.

Saturday

You see I had nearly finished a letter to you when I received your note. You must forgive my detention of your messenger, for I have been obliged to get a letter ready for London,—and have been engaged with my brother, who has just parted from us in an *heart-broken state*. Mr. Carden was here this morning, and has given so favorable a report of our dear invalid, that we are rendered happy and thankful on her account. He sanctions her little excursion to Cheltenham,—and as the separation from her will not be a very long one, I am inclined to consider it with pleasure,—as a probable means of increasing her strength and power of enjoyment.

I have no Pindar,—except Dalzel's *dislocation*, which you will not condescend to receive. Keep the Sophocles and Euripides as long as you please—after *my* good example! With our kind regards to Mrs. Boyd,— and Miss Boyd,

believe me
Your very sincere friend
E. B. Barrett

Will you tell Miss Boyd that my sister's silkworms have monopolized nearly all my franks. I send her what I have remaining—and she promised to tolerate duplicates. Mr. Hutchinson's autograph is the only one at all valuable.

Mama takes both the carriages to Cheltenham—so you must not be angry if I *cannot* go to see you soon. Nothing *decisive* from my Father!

31.

To Woodland Lodge
Malvern

Hope End. Wednesday morning [1828]

My always kind and dear friend will not have reproached me for not replying more immediately to his letter. I did not receive it until more than a week subsequent to its date,—for, on its arrival, I was not well or in a state to read, and therefore, instead of its being given to me, it was put away with my other letters, by which means it became mislaid. When I did read it, while I deeply felt its kindness, I was still inclined to defer my reply. I could not trust myself to write calmly; and to have written otherwise than *calmly*, would have shewn a want of consideration to- wards feelings which have already sympathized with mine.

I believe I can write calmly *now*. Therefore I will write to thank yourself, dear Mr. Boyd, and to thank your family, for your kind sympathy in the deepest affliction of my life.[1] The affliction was unforeseen and unexpected by me—and for a time, it took from me the power of thinking. Oh Mr. Boyd! Are we not of the earth earthy,—and must we not cling with the strong clinging of natural affection to that which is of earth,—to that which is resolvable to earth? Perhaps I have done it too much, and too long—and God has reproved me, by cutting asunder one of the dearest and tenderest and holiest ties that can bind finite beings to finite beings. God's will be done! His will—not our will—is just and merciful and to be fulfilled.

Now I can consider all the details of this calamity, and can understand all the mercy involved in it by Him who in the midst of judgment remembers mercy. I can understand that by this dispensation, He has intended blessing both unto *her* who has departed, and unto us who remain. It is good for *us* to be afflicted,—and *she* is happier than *we* could be if she were restored to us. *She* is freed from disease and weakness,— and we are no longer *too happy*. I can even understand why *one* consolation was denied to me—why I was not permitted to behold her last smile, and to receive her last embrace! Blessed be God for permitting me to understand this!

I am not regardless of those earthly consolations of which you speak, and with so much in Heaven to trust in, and on earth to love, I could not be ungrateful enough to shut my heart against happiness. You say "Many have been bereaved of their Mother in their infancy". I have only to look around me, to know indeed that *many have! Who* can supply to *them* what *she* was? But I cannot speak of these things.

I have the comfort of seeing my dearest Father strong in the consolation which is of God, and wonderfully well. I shewed your letter to him, and he very deeply felt the kindness of its expressions. So you will not allow me to consider you as an *old friend? I* never could calculate friendship by *weeks* and *days!* I could not leave my family and my home at present, even to see *you*. Do you think I would, to see anyone else?

We are all well and very composed. Give our kindest regards and acknowledgments to Mrs. Boyd and Miss Boyd—and believe me, my dear friend,

Most gratefully and earnestly yours
E. B. Barrett

1. Mrs. Barrett died in Cheltenham on October 7. *Hereford Journal,* October 15, 1828. On the monument in the church in Ledbury, erected after Mr. Barrett's death, the date is wrongly given as October 1.

I have not told you after all, how soothing it was to me to receive your letter, and to be assured of your *unaltered regard*—unaltered, while so much around me is *altered forever!*

32.

To Malvern

Hope End. Saturday [1828]

My dear friend,

Whenever you *think* that your letters can, under any circumstances, be otherwise than welcome to me, do let it occur to you that you are *thinking wrong*. Circumstances cannot change the *nature*—and unless *my* nature should be materially changed, it must continue to give me pleasure to read, whatever your time and inclination may enable you to write.

My Father is, thank God, well and composed—and so are we all. I will prove to you how much better *I* am, by telling you that I have been reading in your Gregory this morning. I never can lose again what I have lost—and I never can forget what I have lost. Her voice is still sounding in my ears—her image is in my heart—and *they* are to be loved, however unreal they may be! But my Father's fortitude has assisted mine. After all, *his* is the great affliction—and *he* has taught me to use exertion,—and God has enabled me to do so successfully.

I was *going* to answer Mr. Barker's letter when this change came, since which I have received another letter from him. I am afraid that my silence may appear a want of attention,—and yet I really cannot, just now, force myself to write letters upon subjects and to persons, respecting which and whom, my mind with its present feelings cannot help being indifferent. If you should be writing to him soon, will you mention to him, the *cause* of my silence?—I dare say he will forgive my not writing for some time longer, when he knows the cause.

You should have had a longer reply to your note,—but I have been interrupted by Papa,—and obliged to talk instead of write. Now I will not venture upon detaining your messenger, who, I hope, did not bring back the books before you had done with them entirely.

Give my kind regards to Mrs. Boyd—and always

believe me

Your sincere friend

E. B. Barrett

33.

To Malvern

Hope End. Tuesday morning
November 18 [1828]

As Papa has given me some game, for the purpose of sending it to you, I think, dear Mr. Boyd, that you may like to hear at the same time, of our being better. I assure you, I feel myself every day, less nervous and more tranquil,—and better able to *think* as I used to do. I never knew before how much the heart could bear—I know *now,*—and I also know how *little* it can bear, in its *own strength*. Both these kinds of knowledge are useful: they are worth the painful experience by which they are bought, tho' every tender remembrance and vain anticipation be called upon to "count the cost". Forgive my intruding my feelings on you so selfishly, and so naturally, and so uselessly!

When my poor father received his melancholy summons, Grandmama was very anxious to leave London at the same time,—but he would not hear of it,—dreading the effect of agitation and fatigue upon her already weak frame. As it was, the sudden unexpected intelligence caused her to be very unwell for several days. She will not come to Malvern *this winter*. I hope she will, *in the spring*—but I have recently suffered too much from a much too sanguine disposition, to trust to it again, and so soon. I have mentioned this subject to you, because I think you were interested about her coming. Do not mention it to *me*. I would rather not think of it, on many accounts—for it is very painfully associated in my recollections!

If you can conveniently lend me Dr. Kidd's work [1] which I once saw at your house, *will* you? It shall be taken care of, and not detained for six months, *"meo more"*. I really might return your Gregory today, but I suppose that my messenger will have enough to carry without a folio, and that I may trespass on your long-suffering, a very little while longer. Give my kind regards to Mrs. Boyd,—and to Miss Boyd if she should have returned to you. At any rate, I hope that she is well and happy,— and that *you* are likewise, and have Mr. Segur to read Greek to you every evening!

Your ever sincere friend,
E. B. B.

1. This may be John Kidd (1775–1851), physician, writer of works on mineralogy and geology, or James Kidd (1761–1834), Presbyterian clergyman, author of religious dissertations and sermons.

Hope End. Saturday. 18—

My dear friend,

Whenever you think that your letters can, under any circumstances, be otherwise than welcome to me, do let it occur to you that you are thinking wrong. Circumstances cannot change the nature — & unless my nature should be materially changed, it must continue to give me pleasure to read, whatever your time & inclination may enable you to write.

My father is, thank God, well & composed — & so are we all. I will prove to you how much better I am, by telling you that I have been reading in your Gregory this morning. I never can lose again what I have lost — & I never can forget what I have lost. Her voice is still sounding in my ears — her image is in my heart — & they are to be loved, however unreal they may be — But my father's fortitude has assisted mine. After all, this is the great affliction — & He has taught me to use cicatrice — & God has enabled me to do so successfully —

Letter 32, signed E. B. Barrett.
Written shortly after her mother's death.

34.

To Woodland Lodge
Malvern

Hope End. January 10, 1829

I return "Master Boyd's" letter to him, with my thanks for his allow-ing me to read it. Some parts of it do not seem to me applicable, even if I make the broadest allowances for *humour* on his correspondent's side, and *good-humour* on his own—but altogether, it amused me and made me smile. I hope I have not kept it too long. I would have written be-fore, if I had not been dependent on my brother's calling at Woodland Lodge,—and if there had been anything which required an earlier an-swer in the accompanying letter. The only question it contained, was answered by me, lately. It is unnecessary for me to say that I would *rather* talk to you than write to you—and *that* makes me wish you were nearer. Under any circumstances I could not do otherwise than receive pleasure from seeing yourself and your family,—and if you were nearer, I might see you *here*. I assure you, I have been nowhere yet, out of our own grounds. It is natural, I think, that I should be unwilling, yet, to do so; it is natural, I am sure, that I should visit *you*, when I can visit anybody.

In the meantime, do not write again—for it has become quite evident to me that you are tired of it. Haec hactenus!

I was glad to hear from you, of Miss Boyd's looking so well,—and I hope to hear from my brother, a continued good report of you all.

My kind regards to Mrs. Boyd, and Miss Boyd.

Ever yours very sincerely
E. B. Barrett

Sir Uvedale Price has had a letter from Mr. Charles Butler,—Southey's Papistical opponent,[1]—assenting *in toto* to the accentual reformation. Perhaps you may be interested in hearing this—for tho' Mr. Butler be of no classical notoriety, that I know of—he is universally estimated as a man of acute and vigorous intellect.

January 15

I open my letter for the purpose of speaking of your note, which I received yesterday evening. *I* don't wonder that *you* should wonder at not having had an answer from me, in the course of three weeks. Did

1. Southey's *Book of the Church* (1824) was answered by Butler in his *Book of the Roman Catholic Church* (1825), followed in its turn by Southey's *Vindiciae ecclesiae anglicae*, 1826.

you conjecture that I was wearied of *writing much,*—or, (according to a somewhat different, tho',—perhaps, not always inapplicable collocation) —*much wearied* of writing?

You will find by the contents of this letter, why it was not written before,—and by its date, that I intended it to go to you, before. My brother was actually on the road; but the rain came on, before he reached the entrance gate,—and forced him to return. Now, I do not know whether, after all, I shall be able to send my letter by him,—for he is likely to be prevented from going to Malvern at present, on account of the unexpected arrival here, of Mr. Clarke,[2] (of Kinnersley Castle) yesterday.

You see my transgression was not voluntary. Forgive and forget it!

I was very glad to find that you liked May.[3] I thought you would,— and yet I had in my head, an anathema of yours against modern Latin and Greek poetry. What you write, you shouldn't refuse to read.

35.

To Great Malvern

Hope End. Monday
February 2, 1829

Dear Mr. Boyd,

. . .[1] I am tempted to express an earnest hope that you have put no unjust construction upon my relinquishment of epistolary claims, the other day. After I had sent away my letter, it occurred to me that you might make such a misconstruction, in consequence of my not having laid the *natural emphasis* upon my own regrets. My reason for not doing so, could only be *one,*—and shall not be concealed from you: it was a fear, that, in your desire to oblige me, you might inconvenience and annoy yourself—and *that* were an obligation which I could not submit to owe, even to *you,* to whom I owe so many. You told me you were "*not wearied* of writing to me". I am sure you were *not,* as you said so. But then your new dislike of dictation must have operated, in a degree at least, on every correspondence;—perhaps, without your being sensible of it—and you said so much about your preferring *talking* to *writing,* when I had previously spoken of my inability to visit you just at present,

2. EBB's uncle John Altham Graham-Clarke.
3. Thomas May, *Supplementum Lucani.* See Letters 6, 25.
1. The omitted passage is a comment on Barker's edition of Cicero, which EBB returned to the editor through Mr. Boyd.

—that I could not help supposing that you would *prefer* not writing at all. To this supposed and not unnatural preference, I make a sacrifice,—which,—tho' a real *sacrifice*,—is made, I do assure you, with willingness and entire good-humour. After all the kind and long and frequent letters, I have received from you,—you would have a right to think it hard, if I could not think of your convenience.

I will explain to you when we meet, *why* I cannot visit you at the present time and under present circumstances, with*out visiting other* people,—and *then* you will make allowances for my unwillingness to leave home just now. It is scarcely four months, since I lost what was dearest and kindest,—and it is impossible, sometimes, to help thinking bitterly! I may assure you, that if I could have seen you whenever I *wished,* and wished *earnestly,* not seventeen weeks, or seventeen hours, should have passed since our last meeting. I shall *find* and *make* some opportunities of enquiring about you and *Mr. Segur*—now and then. May God bless you!

Give my best regards to Mrs. Boyd and to Miss Boyd—and think of me as

Your ever sincere friend
E. B. Barrett

36.

To Great Malvern

Hope End. Thursday [1829]

Dear Mr. Boyd,

I received your letter on Saturday night,—but, tho' Papa gave it to me, the moment he came into the house, it was so late that I had not time to prepare an answer before Sunday,—or I would have done so. Our servants go to Malvern very early on Sunday morning.

I need not say that I shall be glad and proud to take the charge of any of your books,—your *materia classica,*—which you may like to confide to my keeping. But you really amuse me by your dislike of having "all your favorite books in one place". What are you afraid of? Of a second "Battle of the books",—or of a "general conflagration"? If of the latter, it is but fair to remind you that my room is situated at the very top of the house,—*Atticè,* you know,—while yours is on the ground floor,—whence, in the case of fire, all your valuable possessions may be easily taken out DORICÈ! I don't wish, however, to persuade you not to trust me with your books. The trust will give me pleasure.

I believe, I am not apt to complain,—and yet I do feel inclined to complain of your expression,—"if you should ever come to see me again". You never told me that you desired me not to go and see you again,— and, *until you do so,* you must allow me to consider your *"if"* as alto- gether unreasonable, and out of place. If I had had such an intention as the one you indirectly attributed to me, I should have been *capricious,* —and if I could have had that intention without intimating it to you, I should have been *disingenuous.* I hope I am neither. It will give me the most real pleasure to see you again,—and when we have once broken the ice, of staying at home, I will take advantage of the very first opportunity in order to go to Malvern. With regard to conveyances and opportunities, you know I am not otherwise than dependent—and you should not be hard upon me, and make me responsible for circum- stances. It *must* not be very long before I see you.

Give my kind regards to Mrs. and Miss Boyd—and ever believe me

Your sincere friend

E. B. Barrett

37.

Hope End. May 5, 1829

My dear Mr. Boyd,

I am far from considering you to be otherwise than perspicuous in your general style and manner of expressing yourself: but if you expressed yourself perspicuously in this *particular* instance, I can only say that I was *particularly* stupid in misunderstanding you. At any rate, I thank you (how often I have to thank you!) for a book which I do indeed truly value.

Lord Bacon says that "a little philosophy turns the mind to atheism"; (or,—he might have added,—to what is equivalent to atheism); but that "depth in philosophy bringeth it back to religion": which ob- servation discovers much "depth in philosophy". For all possible mis- apprehensions respecting the nature of things, arise from *partial* views of things,—whether they be things in Heaven or things in earth. There- fore I am always inclined to hope sanguinely and to wait patiently, when a mind affected by scepticism, is acute and inquisitive and pos- sessed of that degree of restlessness and energy which is obvious and remarkable in the mind of your philosopher. If he lives long enough, the very light of nature may be a means in the Divine Hands, of con- ducting him to the light of revelation: the very result of learning may prove to him the necessity of being taught of God. In the meantime there can be no ground for the apprehension you suggest. He and his family are about to leave the neighbourhood,—a circumstance which you must not mention, until you hear it from other authority than mine. He was here the day before yesterday, to hear Mr. Curzon,[1] but arrived too late.

I return Heliodorus,[2]—and *keep* many pleasant recollections of him. . . .[3]

You desire to know whether "there is anything in your essay or post-script, with which I do not agree." You desire to know whether there is any additional or superabundant presumption in my composition, with which you were not acquainted. I will satisfy you,—or try to do so. I never learnt anything about the rule in question, of the Greek Article,—except what I learnt from *you*—first, from your notes to the Agamemnon, and Select Passages; and secondly, and more fully and clearly, from your essay in Dr. Clarke's commentary.[4] And therefore notwithstanding my intimate and profound knowledge of Greek syntax, and my singular exactness in the grammatical construction of sentences,—which has not escaped your observation,—it is *not* very probable or very possible that I should be able to find fault with you *in ipso articulo;* even if you were not as immaculate as I believe you to be. . . .[5]

You cannot think how much you amused me and made me laugh with your campanology. When you spoke of the variance and discord at Malvern, and of your efforts to restore harmony, I could not think what was coming. I am glad it was only the man to improve the bells! To tell you the truth I don't quite understand this very strong taste of yours,—and yet I assure you I like to hear you *discourse* upon it,—having no kind of antipathy to any kind of bell, except Bel and

1. Nonconformist clergyman, mentioned in the *Hereford Journal* in accounts of Ledbury and Hereford Bible meetings.

2. *Aethiopica*, unfamiliar to EBB as late as December 1, 1827 (Letter 6). Heliodorus is included in *Greek Christian Poets* (1842), *Works*, pp. 608–9, and is mentioned in "Wine of Cyprus" among the authors read with Boyd— "And we both praised Heliodorus / For his secret of pure lies,— / Who forged first his linked stories / In the heat of lady's eyes."

3. The omitted passage contains a detailed criticism (generally favorable) which shows careful study of the Greek text.

4. "Essay on the Greek Article" in Adam Clarke, *Commentary on the Whole Books of Scripture,* 8 vols. 1810–26.

5. In the omitted passage EBB suggests an exception to one of Boyd's rules on the use of the Greek article.

the Dragon.[6] Gray's idea of Paradise was "to lie upon a sofa and read eternal new romances by Crebillon". Yours would probably be,— "to sit in the belfry during an eternal succession of New Year's Days". Therefore I congratulate you upon the tenor,[7]—and heartily hope for your sake, that there may be marriages enough at Malvern this summer, to enable you to hear it every hour every day. But by the time this long letter is *dinged* into your ears, you will be tired of it and me. Bro, who went today to dine with the Trants, behaved very shabbily in not waiting for it—and I don't mean to speak to him when he comes home.

> Believe me dear Mr. Boyd,
> Your ever sincere friend
> E. B. Barrett

38.

To Great Malvern

Hope End. May 16, 1829

My dear Mr. Boyd,

I have actually and absolutely finished the seven hundred and thirty one lines of Gregory Nazianzen's poem *In laudem virginitatis*.[1] It will be impossible for me to forget the exact number, as long as I live! I began the poem with the very best intentions of being pleased and interested. At the end of two hundred lines, my Patience became restless and uncomfortable, but took courage and toiled on; and then grew feverish and spasmodically affected,—and finally sank under accumulations of dullness and dryness and heaviness and tediousness and lengthiness, between the 400th and 500th lines. The Coroner's verdict is, wilful murder, against H. S. Boyd, Esq. The next two hundred and thirty one lines were read *posthumously,* as far as regards Patience—and yet, out of the 231, it is right to except about fifty which are beautiful. Is it possible that you can admire the composition really

6. See Vulgate, Daniel 14 (Apocrypha).

7. "The most musical and most ancient" of the Malvern bells. Henry Card, *Dissertation on the Antiquities of the Priory of Great Malvern,* London, 1834.

1. Cf. "Wine of Cyprus": "Do you mind that deed of Ate / Which you bound me to so fast,—/ Reading "De Virginitate," / From the first line to the last? / How I said at ending solemn, / As I turned and looked at you, / That Saint Simeon on the column / Had had somewhat less to do?" In *Greek Christian Poets* EBB grants that the poem has graphic touches but condemns it as "dull enough generally to suit the fairest spinster's view of that melancholy subject." *Works,* p. 606.

and seriously, or was it an act of *malice prepense,* to make me read it?
What have I done to deserve such an infliction? The work has no reasoning, and no imagination, saving a flash now and then to produce
"darkness visible" [2]—"a little gloomy light, much like a shade".[3] It has
no profundity and no vivacity, no descriptiveness and no sentiment,
no boldness of conception and no variety of expression. There is abuse
for you! When I wrote last, I had not finished it, and I was determined not to let you see my opinion, until I had seen the utmost extent of my suffering. I admit that the poem has beautiful *lines,*—considering them separately . . .[4] At line 460, there is this expression,
θερμον ετι ζειουσα κονις,[5] which is like Gray's "Even in their ashes live
their wonted fires".[6] Perhaps Gray went out of *"Paradise"* for the purpose of reading Gregory's Panegyric upon single life. Of course, I will
look thro' the other poems.

I have an advantage over you. I have heard a piano and harp and
organ, without receiving the adjacent ideas of wood wire and harshness. You have an advantage over me. I never heard any scientific bell-
ringing,—and have not the most remote knowledge of the meaning
of grandsire trebles, triple Bobs Majores, and triple Bobs Maximi. If
it were not for you and Dr. Parr, I should doubt the application of
those classical epithets to the unclassically sounding monosyllables
before them—but, as it is,—I stand in their presence with as much
silent reverence, as the Papists do before the chair of St. Peter,—a
relic sedulously preserved at Rome,—and upon which was discovered,
a few years ago, the following inscription in Arabic characters, "There
is no God but God, and Mahomet is his prophet". Supposing that I
ever go to see you again, I certainly will not go on Whit Monday,—
because I would not be in your way for the world,—and would not
have you out of the way, for little less! And now to be serious. I am
very fond of music, and can hear the harp piano and organ "thumbed"
"strummed" and "thumped", in the execution of a fine composition,
for two or three hours together, with great satisfaction. I think that
when the human voice "marries immortal verse" to the sounds produced by these instruments, aural *sensations* become purified and elevated into *sentiments.* Bells of the finest tone "please the ear"—they

2. Milton, *Paradise Lost,* Bk. 1, 63.

3. "A little glooming light." Spenser, *Faerie Queene,* 1, 14, 5.

4. Omitted are two passages of Gregory's poem, "the only beautiful [ones] of any
length."

5. "ashes still seething hot" (of Julian's dead body).

6. "E'en in our Ashes live our wonted Fires." "Elegy Written in a Country
Churchyard."

do not "move the heart"—at least not mine; yours may be more loco-
motive. Therefore I have two objections to your planting the palm in
the churchyard. 1st. No bells can play Handel. 2d. No bells can ac-
company poetry. Did you ever hear of any words being set to any set
of bells, except the immortal words "Ding Dong"?

I dare say I am wrong in all this,—and if I am, what a pity it is
that Collins was wrong too! Imagine his ode on the Passions,[7] with the
scene changed to the belfry! Give the Passions "rope enough"—and
what an effect the "long pull and strong pull" would produce! He
could not indeed make *"Madness* rule the hour",—unless the bells
were *cracked,* which would frighten "Music, Heavenly Maid", out of
her wits. But he need not dismiss any other personage. Anger's "rude
clash", and Despair's "low solemn sounds", would do very well,—and
Hope might "call on Echo still"—and I should admire Melancholy's
"tones *by distance made more sweet",* above all the rest.

"Thy numbers, Jealousy, to naught were fixed",—

so Jealousy would be very clever and scientific at *ringing changes,*—and
Fear might ring an alarm bell,—and Joy and Cheerfulness a dinner bell.
Do you approve of my disposition of the dramatis personae,—or are you
thinking of sending me a *cap and bells* by the first conveyance?

I had a very obliging letter from Mr. Barker yesterday, to tell me
that he had lent my poems to the Bishop of Limerick [8] who was indulgent in his opinion of them, and intended to send me his sermons.
I mention this to you, because I cannot feel gratified by the circumstance, without remembering to whom I must feel grateful. Directly
and indirectly, I owe you far too much to pay—and if I do not often
speak of my obligations to you, it is not that I do not often think of
them,—but that you have seemed to desire me to be silent. Do you
suppose that you have banished them from my memory and my feelings? Neither you, nor I, could effect *that.*

I have been anxious and provoked (as usual) about going to see
you; and earnestly wish and hope to be able to accomplish it soon.
You will not be angry at what I have said about Gregory,—and at my
nonsense about the bells. You know, you are not so easily *"offended"*
as *I* am!

Ever your sincere friend
E. B. Barrett

7. "The Passions: an Ode for Music." The quotations in this paragraph are all
taken or adapted from Collins' poem.

8. John Jebb (1755–1833). The sermons were sent, and EBB found them "very well
and classically written." See Weaver, Letter II.

My best regards to Mrs. and Miss Boyd. I hope they are quite well. Good accounts from London,—and Papa still there. He does not say a *word* of returning.

39.

Hope End. Friday
June 26 [1829]

My dear Sir,

Your letter has pained and gratified me in *several* ways,—and affected me in *every* way. I wish I could answer it in the only proper manner, by instantly going to see its writer,—but I shall not be able to do this during the present week. We are expecting our relations Mr. and Mrs. Hedley; [1] and it will not be considered right for me to be out of the way. Besides, I cannot have the carriage either today or tomorrow. That you should receive any pleasure from having me with you,—and that you should feel any regret at my leaving you, are circumstances upon which I am *pleased* to dwell,—and *proud* to be permitted to dwell. Certainly I hoped you were a little sorry when I left you on Monday—but I did not think you were half as sorry as *I* was. It is the only subject, upon which, *I* could be glad that *you* should be sorry.

I never could forget to think of, what you forgot to mention—the deprivation, to which you so pathetically allude. As you not only allude to it,—but, for the first time, dwell on your feelings respecting it, I may venture to say to you, what *I* have thought on the same subject. The common effect of any peculiar and distinguishing affliction is an active and passive selfishness—an inordinate egotism, and an indifference to the welfare of others. I have often been forcibly struck by your total exemption from this contracting influence of suffering. Your mind must be of a very uncommon cast. I have often observed, in speaking of you and thinking of you, how seldom you obtrude your state of deprivation upon the attention of others—and with how much simplicity and dignity you allude to it, when you have occasion to do so. And tho', in any case, I must have deeply felt the singular kindness I have received from you, my feeling is naturally rendered more deep and earnest, by a consideration of the circumstances under which that kindness has been offered. I hope you will forgive my having said so much on this subject.

With respect to any individuals who may have been deficient in consideration and feeling towards you, I would say with Dante "Be-

1. Mrs. Hedley was Jane Graham-Clarke, sister of Mrs. Barrett.

hold them—and pass on!—" [2] They are not worthy of a second observation. Is it thro' a superabundant *charity*, that you have suffered
them to annoy you? Are *you pained,* because *they* are *degraded?* I can
find no other reason. You cannot be reasonably *surprised,* when there
is darkness at night,—or ice in winter,—or "unkindness and selfishness in the human heart"! I admit all your powerful reasons,—all
your irresistible claim—I need no other inducement for staying with
you, but your *wish,*—even if it were not so strongly seconded—by my
own. I *think,*—I am almost *sure,* that I shall be able ultimately to stay
with you—but you know I cannot do everything I like, or everything
when I like. I only *rule* in my own room—where there are no *subjects* to be ill-governed—except the literary inanimate. At any rate I
must see you very soon—and the next time I go to your door, it shall
not be with visitors of Madresfield. In a letter by today's post, Papa
says "I sympathize with you about the *interruption*". I wish he said
something satisfactory respecting the period of his return—but he is
not yet able to do so. . . .[3]

                                                                Saturday
  I hope Mrs. Boyd did not suffer from her kindness in driving thro'
the heat to see us yesterday—and that the *supplementary* sunshine in
the garden, did not bring Miss Boyd's and Miss Sibree's patience to a
finis. My sin of omission, when you were at the Wells, it is impossible
to help lamenting,—and yet, considering the five miles and the *pea-
cock,* perhaps I ought not lament it. Mrs. Boyd was so kind as to ask
me to return to Malvern with her. I was obliged to resist *that* temptation; but I thought I should be able to visit you in the course of next
week. *Now* I am obliged to ask you not to expect me. Perhaps I *may*
be able to go—but they have reminded me, that, while our relations
are staying here, my having the carriage *may* not be possible. It cannot be necessary to say, how little likely I am to delay my visit *volun-
tarily,* a day, or an hour.
  Here is another question which I am desirous of asking you, and
which I will mention at once, before I speak of Mr. Harn.[4] You do
not care much about Latin, I know—but you may tell me which of the

  2. *Inferno,* Bk. 3, 51.
  3. The omitted passage contains an unfavorable criticism of Gregory's "Against the
Arians."
  4. The name (three times repeated) seems clearly to be spelled Harn; it would be
tempting to read Horn (or Horne).

Latin *prose* writers you *prefer*—setting aside St. Bernard St. Cyprian and Lactantius,—and keeping to the *orthodox classics*— Do you like Tacitus? Can you enjoy Sallust—? Can you bear Livy? Erasmus's student says somewhere, "Decem annos consumpsi in legendo Cicerone",[5] —and the Greek echo answers *OVE!* Am I to "write you down an *ass*" [6] by this rule?

Mr. Barker was very kind in procuring Mr. Harn's opinion,—and Mr. Harn's opinion was, of course, very gratifying to me. And yet I may assure you, that I received *much* more gratification from your last letter,—particularly from that part of it, upon which I can scarcely trust myself to speak—where *you* speak of having received comfort from my acquaintance and correspondence. Could you say anything capable of gratifying me in any equal degree? I am *sure* you could not! It is inconsiderate and arbitrary in you to desire the exclusion of the word *gratitude* from my letters—but you cannot command its exclusion from another place. *That* is one of the few things which I would not attempt, in order to please you—it being as impossible to withdraw from you my *gratitude,* as to withhold my *regard.*

> Ever your sincere friend
> E. B. Barrett

40.

To Great Malvern

> Thursday evening [1829]

My dear Mr. Boyd,

I received your letter yesterday, and was in hopes, notwithstanding the obstinate clouds, to be able to answer it this morning by going to see you. Every day since Saturday, I have been hoping to see you, —and today, the horses were actually ordered. What can I do? I can neither arrest a deluge, nor persuade anybody here (except myself) that being wet thro', is a very comfortable and pleasant thing!—a *desiderandum!*

I meant to have taken with me today the following extract from the learned Abbè Barthelemi's introduction to his "Voyage of Anacharsis".[1] It consists of his opposition to a few of the charges generally and principally brought against Homer—and pleased me very much

5. "The Ciceronian," *Colloquies,* 1528.
6. *Much Ado about Nothing,* IV.2.78.
1. Jean Jacques Barthelemi (1716–95), *Voyage du jeune Anacharsis en Grèce.*

when I read it for the first time a few days ago. Don't criticise my translation, which sounds to my own ear, as stiff as buckram, or the grounds at Croome.[2] No one can succeed at translation, without having the talent *for* it and the habit *of* it, neither of which I have.

"Plato imagined that he did not find sufficient dignity in the grief of Achilles nor in that of Priam, when the former rolls himself in the dust after the death of Patroclus—when the latter assumes a lowly demeanor in order to obtain the body of his son. But what a strange dignity is that which would destroy sentiment! For my own part, I admire Homer for having, like Nature, placed weakness by the side of strength, and the abyss by the side of the elevation. I admire him yet more, for having displayed to me the best of fathers in the most powerful of kings, and the tenderest of friends in the most fiery of heroes.

I have heard Homer blamed for the violent language which he permits his heroes to use in the midst both of their counsels and their combats. I have then cast my eyes upon children, who are nearer to Nature than we—upon the populace, which is constituted like children—upon savages, who are merely a *populace*—and I have observed among them all, that anger, previous to discovering itself by effects, announces its presence by ostentation by insolence and by outrage.

I have heard Homer reproached for having painted in their simplicity, the manners of the times which preceded him. I smiled at the criticism—and was silent!"

Tell Miss Boyd that the Malvern dinner party is not given up in spite of the wind and rain. Tho' I send you the Abbè Barthelemi's criticism on the critics, and write a letter besides, you shall see me as soon as ever I can see the sun, and the prudent people here cannot feel the rain! If the rain continues much longer, and Proteus does not drive us [out] of the valleys, *videre altos montes* (in which case we may float in the Malvern direction) there is nothing for us but drowning—and then you may moralize and Deucalionize on the Worcestershire Beacon![3]

> Believe me—till then
> Yours affectionately
> E. B. Barrett

2. Croome d'Abitat, mansion of the Earl of Coventry, with grounds laid out by the designer of Kew Gardens.
3. Highest of the Malvern Hills.

41.

To Great Malvern

Hope End. Saturday [1829]

My dear Mr. Boyd,

I have looked over, not read the *Parriana,*[1] and I now send you as you told me to do, a list of the passages which seem to me most likely to interest you. Read first the two which I have marked first,— because you are quoted in them. The error of the press that has oc- casioned the omission of two or three lines in one of these quotations, is *not* corrected in the *addenda.* I have supplied them in my own copy in my own handwriting. I also send you your verses on Miss Tessy Owen. The following lines

> Perhaps what thou hast been, she now may be,—
> A guardian angel watching soothing *thee—*

seem to me very beautiful, and I hope, very true. And yet why should *that* be hoped? Those who are gone, *can* see the earth no more, since they can feel sorrow no more! They could not look upon us without mourning for us—without mourning for our remaining, as *we* have mourned for their departing! and who would desire *that?*

Ever yours, dear Mr. Boyd!—with much regard!

E. B. Barrett

. . .[2] Will you give my love to Mrs. and Miss Boyd,—and ask the latter to come here on *Tuesday week* to spend a few days with us,— or as *many* as she can spare to us? I shall be very much pleased if she can and will. I should have ventured to make this request before,—but when you had company, I knew asking such a thing would be quite vain,—and, since Miss Roys went away, we have been prevented by different circumstances from doing as we wished. *Good-bye* once more.

E. B. B.

42.

Monday [1829]

My dear Mr. Boyd,

I have waited for two things in order to write to you,—for another

1. Vol. 2, published 1829. Cf. Letters 26, 27.

2. Omitted is a list of passages from the *Parriana.* On one dealing with the authen- ticity of Ossian, EBB asks, "About Ossian: Do you care about it?" Apparently Boyd had not yet developed his later strong interest in this subject.

number of the Gleaner, and for an opportunity of returning your book. Otherwise I would have thanked you before now for sending me the verses which amused me and the criticism which surprised me so much. The verses are clever, and particularly happy towards the end. I don't like one line where there is an unusual transposition. I think that inversions, which give a rigid and studied appearance to the diction, should be avoided in familiar compositions,—and that the language should be natural where the thoughts are unelevated. I hope you have not published these verses in the streets of Askalon! Let me entreat you not to do it, if you have not already. If I had not thought that some circumstances were altogether unworthy of one angry reflection of *yours,* I would not have talked to you about them. It was very wrong of me, *I believe.*

The last line which went from me to you was written in such a hurry that I quite forgot to tell you that the stanzas in the Gleaner, called the *Hour of Prayer,* were contributed by Lady Margaret Cocks.[1] You cannot imagine how you astonished me by saying what you did of my poem. I was resigned to the opinion that you would dislike and condemn it on account of the measure and the *t-h*'s; and this made me less in a hurry about procuring and sending it to you. The measure is my own *transposition* of a measure, invented I believe by Barry Cornwall,[2] which the Edinburgh Reviewers *hallucinated* from their usual orbit of defective poetical taste, in order to praise. You who move in a very different orbit, yet surprised me by liking the measure, —because I have been used to fancy that you were apt to *dis*like new measures, to which your ear was unaccustomed and your associations untrained!

I send you the July Gleaner, and my unapplied wisdom in it. I also send an old magazine containing some stanzas of mine,[3] written, when I was fourteen, upon the palm which I wanted to give you the other day, and about which you sent me such a cold-blooded message. Pray observe how differently I felt—how I made my verses "lash" and "flash" and "crash"—(don't say anything about *trash*)—and filled them with *O*'s enough to furnish a parallel scene to the last in Tom Thumb.[4] Do not think of reading these things till you feel quite in-

1. Daughter of John Somers (Cocks), Viscount Eastnor and first Earl Somers, whose home, Eastnor Castle, was close to Hope End.

2. Pen name of Bryan Waller Procter (1787–1874).

3. "Thoughts Awakened by Contemplating a Piece of the Palm Which Grows on the Summit of the Athenian Acropolis." *Hitherto Unpublished Poems, 2, 31.*

4. Henry Fielding, *Tom Thumb. A Tragedy,* 1730.

clined; and if you should not be inclined to write to me, pray do not. Tell Mrs. Boyd with my love, that *Ann* is quite well, growing fatter I think every day,—and I am sure, giving a great deal of pleasure. My hopes lead me to dwell on the idea that Papa will not go after all,— at least not for some time.

Believe me dear Mr. Boyd,
Your ever sincere friend
E. B. Barrett

I have written in your book as you desired, and what you desired.

43.

To Woodland Lodge
Great Malvern

Thursday morning [1829]

My dear Mr. Boyd,

I am very much obliged to you for taking so much trouble about my elegy, and am still more pleased by the opinion which you in-dulgently express respecting the greater part of it. You are quite right with regard to the want of variety in the pauses on the first page. I had observed that the exordium was sluggish and inanimate,—but I did not observe the *cause,* until you spoke about the pauses, which I will at-tend to better, another time. I have seldom been satisfied with the beginnings of any of the short poems of my writing,—and compare myself to a lame horse belonging to a neighbour of ours, which requires to be warmed by exercise before it can go well. I never shewed this elegy to anyone except you—not even to Papa. As to printing it in a maga-zine, you know it can be printed in my own book,—and that will do as well.

You will think me very idle when I tell you that the *Apologetic* [1] is not finished yet. But the Oration on Eutropius,[2] *is,*—I have read it twice,—and I have besides, been reading a little of Longinus's treatise every day, of which I had previously read only one or two chapters. His style is very rough unflowing and inharmonious,—but the Sun plays on the rocks—and the brilliancy of his imaginative powers daz-zles you so much, as almost to prevent your perceiving the roughness

1. By St. Gregory.

2. By St. John Chrysostom. See Letter 5 (November 3, 1827) for comment on Boyd's translation.

and cragginess. I *hope* he is considered difficult—for I am obliged to look at the Latin every five minutes. . . .[3]

I return Mr. Barker's letter. I shewed it to Papa,—but he seems to think that he can do nothing about it. I think that he does not know many persons likely to be much interested in a work of the kind,—and I am sure *I* do not. There is not a literary person of whom I ever heard, within 20 miles of this house—excepting yourself and Dr. Card.[4] I was thinking the other day (why should I say *the other day?*) whether it would have been possible, in the case of my never having known you, for me to have known half as much Greek as I do now—half as much as I do now, in consequence of your kindness in directing me to different authors,—besides the kindness of giving me direct instruction! I need not say that my conclusion was a negative one—nor that

I remain, dear Mr. Boyd

Your ever sincere friend and grateful

E. B. Barrett

44.

To Great Malvern

Wednesday [1829]

My dear Mr. Boyd,

I received your letter yesterday, and acknowledged it by a few lines which I *thought* I had an opportunity of sending to Malvern; but before they were finished, the opportunity went away in the shape of Mr. Trant's gig—and now I shall begin again. Even now I can write only a few lines. I wished to go thro' the orations to which you referred me, and to look over the Treatise *On reading the works of the Gentiles*,[1] before post time, that I might be able to write about them to you. I find it to be in vain—the post is going,—so I am forced to delay writing about *them,* tho' I cannot delay writing on other subjects.

You have probably heard that *before* my last letter to you was written, it was all over at Foxley—Sir Uvedale Price was no more.[2]

3. The passage omitted contains a criticism of the "Oration on Eutropius."

4. Henry Card (1779–1844), vicar of the Priory at Great Malvern. His learning was much admired by Boyd, who dedicated to him his *Tributes to the Dead,* London, 1826.

1. By St. Basil.

2. Sir Uvedale died on September 14, 1829. The editor of the *Hereford Journal* (September 16) paid tribute to "his learning, his sagacity, his exquisite taste, his indefatigable ardour," confident that "the obituary of 1829 will not record a name more gifted or more dear!"

They knew about it here, but put off telling me what was likely to
give so much pain,—and on this account I did not hear till my letter
to you was gone. His very advanced age, and the little probability
there could have been of his retaining, with life, those faculties which
make life worth regard, are consoling circumstances. There is indeed
much that calls for consolation. Literature and his literary and personal friends have lost much—his poor daughter has lost everything.
I had a letter from her and from his son yesterday, and I have the
satisfaction of knowing that they are as resigned as human nature can
be under such a blow. Among my many causes of deep regret, is the
thought, that I can now no longer hope to make you known to each
other. I *think* you would have liked him,—and I *know* that he would
have liked *you*. But upon this, there is no use dwelling.

Somebody has just interrupted me by announcing a second opportunity of sending to Malvern, and thro' Mr. Trant again—so I will
conclude abruptly. I must tell you, tho', of Papa's coming home suddenly and unexpectedly last Sunday. Can you imagine a *part* of the
surprise and happiness? He has brought your coins which I have in
my possession. As it is some time, since you told me to keep them for
you, you may have changed your mind about it,—in which case, let me
know,—that I may deliver them up to you immediately.

With regard to our visitor, your word *endure* was surely a misprint
for *indulge*. I have been indulged instead of being *enduring*,—and I
think that, in your heart, you cannot do otherwise than know this.
Even if there were nothing to like and love *abstract*edly, there would
be *relative*ly,—and besides you cannot think how much good she does
me in offering an irresistible inducement for staying down stairs and
walking out. What a scribble this is, and what a hurry it is scribbled
in!

Give my love to Mrs. Boyd—and believe me dear Mr. Boyd

Your ever sincere friend

E. B. Barrett

45.

Hope End. Wednesday [1829]

My dear Mr. Boyd,

I will write today because I am afraid I *may* [sic] have an opportunity of sending a letter to you tomorrow, and of returning your
Basil [1] at the same time. I have now read the oration[s] on Barlaam

1. Cf. "Wine of Cyprus": "And your Basil, you upraised him / To the height of
speakers old."

and Gordius, and the treatise on reading the books of the Gentiles. The *homily on the Faith* I had read by your desire, before your last letter reached me.

When you say that the Benedictine editor, judging from the *style*, attributes the *Oration on Barlaam,* to Chrysostom, I conclude that he had no other except this internal evidence, by which to judge. I wish I knew how you had settled the question in your own mind, before I said anything!—and then if I found that you agreed with the Benedictine editor, I would say nothing. As I know nothing about your opinion, and you desire me to say what I think, I will confess, at the risk of being very wrong indeed, that I have read the whole oration out loud, and listened for Chrysostom all the way, and could not hear the sound of his cadences. Was he absent, or was I deaf? Something here and there reminded me of Gregory's worst manner—I mean the long conceits about the Martyr's hand, and the way of applying the scriptural quotation, "He teacheth my hands to war and my fingers to fight." But I have since thought that this ingenious misapplication of scriptural phraseology is not peculiar to Gregory,—that Basil is nearly as much given to it as he,—and, besides, the general style and construction and modulation of the sentences are certainly not Gregory's. I believe I do not upon the whole, particularly admire this oration. . . .[2]

I think the Homily *De Fide* is very fine; finer *as a whole* than anything which I have read of Gregory's on the same subject—considering it *partially,* (take the word *partially* in the right sense) not nearly so fine as some things in the Theological Orations. I read your translation[3] over again, immediately after I had read the original, and admired it *more* than I did when I read it previously. This is a sure proof —is it not?—of the translator's fidelity and congeniality. Fidelity in translation, without congeniality, would have produced what *was* Basil but *unlike* Basil—congeniality without fidelity, would have produced what was *like* Basil but *not* Basil. . . .[4]

As I know the benevolence and philanthropy of your mind, I believe it will give you pleasure (in spite of your having no personal acquaintance with the inhabitants of Ledbury) to hear that the Church bells are rung there no longer.

Yours ever, my dear Mr. Boyd,—truly and affectionately,—

E. B. Barrett

2. The passage omitted contains a criticism of the orations on Barlaam and Gordius.
3. *The Catholic Faith: A Sermon by St. Basil,* London, 1825.
4. The passage omitted contains a criticism of "On reading the works of the Gentiles."

Finished on Thursday

I forgot to say that I did *not* think the *Oration on Barlaam* written in *Basil's* usual style—tho' the style did not seem to me *Chrysostomic*. Is it absolutely necessary to attribute the composition to Basil, if it is not attributed to Chrysostom? I hope not! When I say that the *style* did not seem to me Chrysostomic, I refer merely to the modulation of the cadences. Where the author speaks of the propriety of dancing on the graves of the saints, and when he compares the soul of the martyr to stone and iron, he *is* Chrysostomic. But I cannot get over the absence of the Chrysostomic cadences. I hope you like my word *Chrysostomic* because I find I have repeated it four or five times in not many more lines!

46.

Saturday night—*past eleven* [1829]

My dear Mr. Boyd,

You are wrong in two things—first, in supposing that anything had been said to Papa about Mr. Roberry's capacity for bell-hanging, or honesty towards the Malvern parish—and secondly, in apprehending that Papa was likely to exert any influence at Ledbury or anywhere else, about *bells*. He is one of the uninitiated, of the profane on this subject—one of those whose amiable motives for being indifferent respecting campanology, you once investigated and pointed out to me. If your friend Mr. Roberry were to spoil the Ledbury bells for ringing *Bobs* for ever and ever, Papa would not say a word, or move a step, in an attempt at vengeance. You will sleep tranquilly after this!

I admire your zeal for science; but, to speak seriously, I admire still more the forgiving and disinterested spirit of your letter. Whatever doubt there may be about the authorship of the oration in Basil, there *could* be none about the authorship of this letter, were it unsigned.

Your sincere friend,
E. B. Barrett

47.

Hope End. Tuesday evening [1829]

My dear Mr. Boyd,

I return Dr. Clarke's commentary on the Romans,—and, with it, Miss Boyd's [1] cloak which she was kind enough to lend me and which

1. This must be Mr. Boyd's sister, since his daughter is now referred to as Annie.

I am quite ashamed of not having returned before. I calculated upon opportunities which never arrived; and when I lost all patience and was going to send it today, the rain prevented my good intentions. Do tell her this, and give her my best love at the same time.

I admire the 9th hymn of Synesius, and I should think that it must be a very good translation.[2] Some translations are of such a character that you *dare* say so of them, even without conferring them with their originals. The expression

> "Death insatiate
> Feeds on the ghostly nations"[3]

is very fine. . . .[4]

Gregory Nazianzen's address to his soul[5] is beautiful in his Greek and also beautiful in your English . . .

With regard to your treatise on Geology,[6] I will say nothing about the science of it, for fear you should laugh at me, in which case I could not have even the satisfaction of complaining of your injustice. I assure you I have read it quite thro', and more than once. . . . I enter a solemn and serious protest against the *yea* at page 6!—Let your candour judge whether it has not a ludicrous effect in the following sentence—"the bones of animals have been preserved, which are as small as those of a rat; *yea!!* as small as those of a field mouse!!!" I like your *yea* abstractedly, very much indeed; but I do not like it in company with rats and mice. Its introduction is correct and effective in poetry and in poetical prose,—anywhere where a warm and elevated diction is not out of place. Where a warm and elevated diction *is* out of place, your *"yea"* has no business to be,—and I wish you would tell it so.

Your sincere friend
E. B. Barrett

---

2. *Select Poems of Synesius and Gregory Nazianzen*, 1814. In *Greek Christian Poets* EBB included a version of this same hymn, which she calls "closer if less graceful and polished than Mr. Boyd's." *Works*, pp. 610–11.

3. "ψυχῶν ὅθι μυρία Θάνατος νέμεν ἔθνεα." ("Where Death pastured myriad tribes of souls.") EBB translates "Where Shepherd-Death did tend and keep / A thousand nations like to sheep."

4. The three passages omitted from this letter contain detailed criticism of Boyd's translations.

5. For EBB's translation of this poem see Letter 156 and *Works*, pp. 606–7.

6. Published in four installments in the *Imperial Magazine*, *1* (1819), 775–80, 849–57, 912–18, 1031–43.

Wednesday morning

Give my love to Mrs. Boyd,—and forgive my impertinence. I intended to send you my elegy on the death of Sir Uvedale Price,[7] and to ask for your criticisms,—but I believe it will not be possible for me to copy it out in time. There is no occasion for you to answer this letter, if you feel *in the least* disinclined to write today. I have not finished the Apologetick.

Thursday

It rained yesterday—and I did not like sending the cloak thro' the rain, for fear of doing more harm than good, in every way.

48.

To Great Malvern

Hope End. Thursday morning [1829]

My dear Mr. Boyd,

One of the first things that Papa said to me when we met at dinner yesterday, was—"Where did you go to, immediately after the meeting? I looked for you on every side,—as I wished to walk with you to visit Mr. Boyd. I should certainly have gone to see him, if I could have found you". Upon hearing this, I believe I looked nearly *half* as much pleased as I felt. Often and earnestly and naturally as I have wished Papa to call upon you, I never once asked him to do so, —because, from my knowledge of his habits and usual inclinations, there appeared to me no kind of probability of hearing any other than a negative answer. And I should have been pained by hearing *that*, for many reasons,—or rather, for every reason. Now, you see, you may expect a visit from him, unless indeed you walk out at the back door when he is entering at the front,—as I often do, to get away from disagreeable visitors. His feelings of esteem and obligation with respect to you, I have heard him express more than once or twice or thrice, and strongly,—and I hope and believe that you will like the character of his mind and conversation.

We did not arrive at home yesterday until seven,—and anticipated, all the way, arriving in time for a scolding, and *not* in time for dinner. Fortunately however, Papa adjourned from the meeting to the farm, and stayed there until half past seven, so that we were at home

7. "To the Memory of Sir Uvedale Price, Bart."; *Works,* p. 70.

even before him. It will interest you to be told that we were at dinner when the clock struck nine. "Hear it not Duncan!" [1]

Perhaps you know by this time that the collection at the door of
the Bible meeting,[2] was £31, and that it was expected to be only
£20. Dr. Card consulted a clergyman so lately as yesterday morning
about the propriety of himself attending the meeting. How he must
have been hanging like Mahomet's coffin between earth and Heaven
—or rather between High Church-ism and the Duchess of Kent— [3]
for *Heaven* could have had little to do with his uncertainties! Mr.
Forethall's conduct has been much and justly commended. Of the
five guineas which were offered to him for the use of his room, he returned one guinea.

As I wish this note to go by today's post, I will not keep it to make
it as long as I should like to do. Give my love to Mrs. Boyd and Annie,—
and believe me ever, dear Mr. Boyd,

Yours affectionately

E. B. Barrett

I hope Miss Gibbons was not tired by, and did not suffer from, the
running walk she was kind enough to take with me.

49.

[1829]

My dear Mr. Boyd,

I am going to write only a few lines to tell you of the recovery of the
books—of their having been safely restored to us on our way home yesterday, by a man working in the road. He had rescued them from a
strolling Pedlar who would have carried them past the columns of
Hercules by this time, if our knight had not observed, "Them books
belongs to some young ladies whom I knows", and given him a six-
pence into the bargain. So the "persuasive words and more persuasive
bribe" prevented my receiving the full reward of my carelessness,—but
indeed, as it was, the retribution was severe enough, tho' *you* were not.

1. *Macbeth,* II.1.63.

2. The *Hereford Journal* reports a Bible meeting in the Herefordshire Hall on
Friday, October 16, 1829, which was attended by a "most respectable assemblage of
company." The speech expressing thanks to the magistrates was "seconded by E. M.
Barrett, esq. in a most eloquent address," and the collection at the door amounted
to £31 6s. 11d.

3. The Duchess of Kent had marked Dr. Card's church "for an object of her benefi-
cent liberality, soon after her arrival at Malvern." Card, *Priory of Great Malvern.*

51.

To Woodland Lodge
Great Malvern

Monday [1829]

My dear friend,

. . .[1] If you have your Greek epitaph on a cat, written out, do send it to me CAT*aspeusmenoos*.[2] When I was reading to you last, I thought several times of putting you in mind respecting it,—but after all, when the time for doing so came, I forgot. Pray do not *you* forget!

I forgot to tell you in my last note, what I was going to say when the interruption came—I mean, about Miss Smith's book.[3] I saw it for only five minutes,—and therefore was able to look over, only in a cursory way, the verses on the Malvern accident. There appeared to me certainly and obviously a resemblance between them and your poem on the same subject. I have been told that one of Miss Smith's poems has the following title,—"On the death of a child—*by particular desire*". If this is a fact, I have no "particular desire" to look at Miss Smith's poems more particularly!

I have been reading over again Plato's Phaedon,—a daring effort in this snowy weather, considering "the coldness of the style". The reasoning seems to me very inconsecutive and inconclusive,—built upon ingenious subtle brittle analogies which can have nothing to do with proofs. But the style is a veil of golden tissue, like that which over-hung the countenance of Moore's Veiled Prophet [4]—and let no one upraise it! The little that Plato has effected, in his endeavour to penetrate spiritual mysteries without the light of "The Spirit", is a proof a fortiori and a fortissima, of the impossibility of any other mind effecting anything, without that Light. Do you recollect the chapters on natural philosophy? How splendid they are!

I have been reading Chrysostom too. You never called his orations a commentary, that I recollect. I called them so, of course improperly (since you say so) but I do not clearly understand how. The work seems to me as right down a commentary as any that ever was written. Do you

1. The passage omitted comments on three poems by Boyd.
2. "swiftly."
3. Elizabeth Smith, *Poems on Malvern and Other Subjects,* Worcester, 1829. Listed *London Catalogue 1816–1851;* not in the British Museum.
4. Thomas Moore, "The Veiled Prophet of Khorassan," *Lalla Rookh,* New York, 1817.

observe that the most difficult clause in the most difficult chapter of Romans is not noticed by Chrysostom—"Whom he did predestinate, them he also called." Chrysostom's construction of the disputed passages, has too much High Church Arminianism to please me at all,—and is I think less able, less clear, less satisfactory than Dr. Adam Clarke's.

You cannot expect this to be read to you intelligibly, as it is written so illegibly; and you could not expect it to be written legibly if you knew that it was written half way between the fender and the grate, and within hearing of Arabel's soliloquies. Unfortunately, she has discovered that my room is the warmest in the house,—and, not being able to make me talk,—in a true woman's style she is talking herself.

Will you think me very stupid,—for wishing you (by the rule of the season) a great many happy Christmases and New Years,—and for super-adding (by the rule of human selfishness) "at Malvern"? Well! you may think me very stupid for doing so—only believe me

Your sincere friend

E. B. Barrett

52.

To Great Malvern

Hope End. Monday [1830]

My dear friend,

I am very much obliged to you for your epitaph. Your *felis* is *felix,*— and amused and pleased me really and extremely. There was, however, one thing which I expected to find and did not—I mean the introduction of your favorite euphony the *me-ou.* The lines which I like best, are, the first line about the "he cat a-mewing", and the fifth about "the rat" and "mouse". These are admirable,—but indeed the whole is very cleverly and playfully put together, and could not fail at making a "Sir Gravity" smile. You told me never to read anything of yours to anybody, because I read so badly. Notwithstanding this, I did transgress on Saturday by reading your *feline* epitaph to Bro, because I thought it sounded better when read in *our* way, than Carthusianly, as he would have read it. And as I really read very slowly (for *me!*) and distinctly, and made every cat and rat and mouse audible (which fact was satisfactorily proved by Bro's laughing in the right places) you need not bewail yourself nor be severe upon me. As to the "first cat",—when is there to be a *last?* You are a hard person to *deal* with! but I think it is very good!

Mrs. Mushet wrote me a long letter to ask me to lend her a *thousand pounds* for two or three years, in order to relieve the embarrassment of a friend of hers, a young man who cannot continue at College without some pecuniary assistance.[1] She enclosed letters from his late and present tutors, and sent the whole packet thro' you, because she had mislaid my address "given to her by a late visitor at Malvern"—Miss Gibbons, of course! I am sorry that, before taking so much trouble, Mrs. Mushet did not inform herself better as to circumstances,—as to my being wholly dependent, and not having, very often, even a thousand pence at my own disposal. She seems to be a benevolent woman.

I have finished looking thro' the orations on the Romans, and extremely admire a great part of what I have read, tho' the exposition of the *most* difficult texts did not satisfy me. The peroration of the last oration seemed to me very eloquent animated and striking,—too much drawn out, of course,—but not *wire-drawn*—that is, not drawn out to hardness and thinness.

Don't let it be known to Mrs. Mushet, that I have mentioned the object of her letter.

Your sincere friend
E. B. Barrett

I send you at the other side of this sheet two very juvenile productions of mine.[2] Perhaps they may amuse you when you have nothing better to think about (or, rather, when you don't feel inclined to think about anything better),—and I *trust* to you, not to have them read to you until then. I did not know till very lately that I had them in my *own possession*. The first was written when I was seven years old,—the second when I was nine. I don't in the least understand the meaning of my verb "to whelp"—If you *could* have the benefit of the original orthography!!

> By the side of a hill hollow,
> There's the dire abode of Sorrow.
> Where lurking Mischief hides itself
> In dark holes, and Murders *whelp*—

1. EBB was to receive other requests for scholarship aid; in one case the "young geniuses" (unnamed) proved to be the applicant's son and prospective son-in-law. To Miss Mitford, March 6, 1840; unpublished letter: Wellesley College Library.

2. Published in *Hitherto Unpublished Poems, 1,* 76, 87. The original copy of the first poem (owned by Arthur A. Houghton, Jr.) is signed Miss B. B.; it is accompanied by a childish drawing of a castle and is labeled on the back, "For the benefit of the Public."

Theft in black robes is standing here—
Passion and Pride *is* reeling near—
And Man is ever known to sin,
And Virtue's path does not begin.

On putting up the clock at Hope End

Hark! What deep tones proceed from yonder tower,
For tell-tale Echo's voice betrays the sound!
A Clock—the minstrel of the parting hour—
While breathing zephyrs gently sport around.

New is the note amidst these varied shades,—
Sweet Nature's songsters startle at the tone:
Cynthia appears, and Day's gay habit fades,—
But still the clock maintains its drowsy moan.

Oh! may its warning never cease to bring
A useful lesson to our listening ear—
That hoary Time is ever on the wing
To teach the value of each passing year.

For *him* who rear'd in Albion's rocky clime,
Constantinople's minarets and dome,—
May rich rewards, borne on the wings of Time,
For ever chain him to his lovely home!

E. B. B.

53.

Hope End. Saturday [1830]

My dear Mr. Boyd,

I am not sure that I am doing right in sending you the letter,—but as you wish to have it read to you, I cannot hesitate. Do not let the subject be mentioned out of your own house,—for that would not be fair towards Mrs. Mushet,—nor would it be pleasant to me to think that I had "published in Gath" what was written to me in confidence. I believe I *ought* to have been silent about it altogether, but I did not like to conceal from you anything which you might feel curious to know,—and the great packet seemed a sufficient stimulus for a little curiosity. You see I am apologizing to my conscience for unintentionally causing your ebullitions poetical and prosaic, against poor Mrs. Mushet.

I maintain that her act, granting it to be ill-judged, and knowing it to be unusual, still is a benevolent act, inasmuch as its motive and end are clearly distinct from any selfish interest and advantage. And I am quite sure that to some minds, (and why not to hers?) the making such an application as she made, would be infinitely more painful, more difficult, and involving a greater effort and sacrifice, than the lending or giving of a thousand pounds, *could*. Therefore (now we come to the *ergo*) it seems to me that people ought not to call an act like Mrs. Mushet's, "sovereign impudence",—and that no *Hekeebolos* [1] has a right to shoot at her in consequence of it, with his poetical *cross*-bow.

The enclosed letters, I have returned. They were from Mr. Robert's late master at Winchester, and his present tutor at the university, in answer to letters of Mrs. Mushet's, and merely speak generally as to his good conduct, abilities, and embarrassed circumstances. No light is thrown by them on his particular situation with regard to his family, or on the motives ostensible or supposed, of his family's conduct towards him. On these points Mrs. Mushet should certainly dilate more than she has done to me, if she wishes to be successful in making similar applications to others—but I did not tell her so, for fear she should suspect me of hinting at my own curiosity.

You have almost made your epitaph a *cat o' NINE tails*. I like the additional lines very much indeed, and think you have brought in the me-ou extremely well, and produced a good effect by the neighbouring *mew*. Do send the whole to the Classical Journal,—or have it printed somewhere.

Now I will end this scribble and fold it up, that it may be ready to take advantage of the conveyance which has been *promised,* today.

Your ever sincere friend
E. B. Barrett

54.

Wednesday [1830]

My dear friend,

Unfortunately or fortunately (which shall I say?) I cannot give you an opportunity of criticizing my answer to Mrs. Mushet, as I did not take any copy of it. I, and Arabel, who had the impertinent curiosity to look over me while I was writing, have been trying hard to recollect what I wrote, for your benefit—but it is all in vain—we have not been able to

1. "Far darter": Homeric epithet of Apollo.

make out more than a few words, between us. It was not a long letter—
it stated *facts* almost barely. One circumstance you seem to have neglected to observe,—namely, Mrs. Mushet's intention of paying five per
cent upon the loan. I don't pretend to understand much about this kind
of thing; but would not such an interest be something considerable for
her to give,—and not *"all gammon"*?

I have more reason to thank you for the epigram than she would have,
(if I were to send it *"by permission"*) but I am not sure that I have a
much higher opinion of its *justice* than she would have. I certainly agree
with you about the mystery. It is quite *Eleusinian,*—and a very injudicious accompaniment to such an application.

As soon as we escape from this snow prison, I do hope I shall have
the happiness of seeing you; but the present weather is not practicable—
at least, it would not be thought so generally, whatever *I* might think.
The next time I go to see you, it will be for a visit of the usual length;
and then, when I have proved that I *can* come away at the right time, I
may venture like a good politician on the *Great Question*.[1] Besides, there
seems to be a doubt just now, if Mrs. Boyd and Ann are or are not
going to Miss Cockburn's.

Chrysostom has been staggering me lately by his commentary on those
passages of the Epistles to the Corinthians, which relate to the Lord's
supper. I have felt every now and then, that he *must* hold transubstantiation,—and then I look at your pencil marks upon those very
passages, and recollect your opinion of his holding no such doctrine—
and then I am in perplexity, and wonder how you can possibly reconcile
some of his expressions with your opinion! [2]

Today I finished Longinus's treatise, and Euripides's *Rhesus*. I read
them *regularly* thro', which would have been incredible and impossible,
if I had not known you. It is doubtful with me whether Longinus should
be called the philosopher or the poet among critics. If the philosopher—
he is not of the schools but of Nature: if the poet—the very reverse of
the character which he most unjustly attributes to Euripides, may be
attributed to himself—he is a poet, not *tees sunthesioos* but *tou nou* [3]—
his style is very rough. As to *Rhesus,* I know what Porson says about its
not being a genuine work. Tho', as a whole, it is worth its weight in lead,
yet it has beautiful passages—one somniferous one, which I will quote to

1. The question (whether she might stay with the Boyds for a few days) was
eventually put and favorably answered. See Letter 64.

2. In *Select Passages* Boyd had translated and interpreted selections from Chrysostom and other Fathers to prove that they did not believe in transubstantiation.

3. "not *of composition* but *of intellect.*"

you the very next time you *orationize* me about getting up late in the morning.

Your sincere friend
E. B. Barrett

Did it ever strike you that the first few scenes of the *Rhesus,* appear to be by a different hand?—that they are marked by evident imitations of Aeschylus's metaphorical daring?

I have had an opportunity of writing this postscript by the snow coming on so violently as to prevent anyone's going to Ledbury; so that, not being able to send my letter, I was able to open and write in it. I am *so* anxious for the snow to go! Hughes, in his preface to Chrysostom's Priesthood, says hyper-pathetically—*Dolui—vehementer dolui— expectavi—diu expectavi!* If *I* were to say the same thing; instead of exaggerating my feeling, I should fall short of it—I should be *hypo,* instead of *hyper.* Good-bye, once more!

55.

To Woodland Lodge
Great Malvern

Hope End. Friday
[January 29, 1830] [1]

My dear friend,

Do you think that I did not remember the appendix to your Select Passages? I have re-read it attentively according to your recommendation; and after all, I cannot feel convinced that the extracts from Chrysostom contain any doctrine clearly and decidedly opposed to that of transubstantiation—rather on the contrary. The extracts from Irenaeus are very satisfactory, and I dare say you will say something that will satisfy me with regard even to Chrysostom, when I see you, if this obstinate weather should ever fall into a *"melting* mood" and let me see you again. Perhaps Chrysostom held something like *con*substantiation,—but, as you observe, it will be better to *talk over* the pros and *cons* of this question.

So you think I have been wasting time in reading Rhesus, and would not be "condemned" to do such a thing yourself? No one could condemn you to do it,—but I wonder you never submitted to it as to a voluntary penance. It would not be worse than moderate castigation, or saying fifty Ave Marias in a white sheet—at least, not to an Athenian, like you, who has not occasion to wander up and down a lexicon, like me and other

1. Dated by the *Times* epigram on Shee.

Barbarians. After all, it won't do me much harm to have been exercised in this way, even over Rhesus, which I would certainly rather have read than not. As soon as I had read what you wrote about my poem, I began to write. I will have it done for the spring; but we need not trouble Mr. Barker respecting it—and indeed, when I found that your kindness had induced you to write to him, the motive pleased me far more than the act. A parcel has been lying in this room, three months, containing his collection of Hall's works, and Berger, and my answer to the curious and memorable application on the subject of Sir Uvedale Price's letters,[2]— and waiting for some opportunity of private conveyance to Mr. Barker, who must have strong doubts either as to my honesty or vitality. I might pay the carriage, and send it immediately,—but then the books might not go safely.

Thank you for both the epigrams—the *"last* not least"—and the *"dux femina facti"*.[3] Be an Oedipus, and tell me why your nature is very analogous to caper sauce. You can,—if you think a little, and know yourself at all. As you like epigrams, and are not likely to have met with one which I met with yesterday in the Times newspaper, and thought ingenious, I will write it down. The subject is Mr. Shee's election to the office of President, in the room of Sir Thomas Lawrence,[4]— a circumstance unexpected by any person,—Mr. Shee being better known by his "Rhymes on Art" than by his practice in art.

> "Pictoribus atque poetis,
> Quidlibet audendi"—
>
> Lo! Painting crowns her sister Poesy—
> The world is all astonished! So is *She.*

I am glad to hear that the other sister art is doing well in the Ledbury belfry,—that the ringing of the Ledbury bells has produced no "bella, horrida bella" [5] among the inhabitants,—that the bells themselves are not "bella detestata matribus" [6]—or patribus, or filiis! I wish the wonderful wind would set in, which, according to Bro, is to make these bells audible to our ears, that I might be among the admirers of Mr. Roberry's skill, and less ignorant of his art—but I would rather have such a wind

2. Barker later suggested publishing EBB's letters to Boyd. See Letter 61 and n. 1.
3. *Aeneid* 1.364.
4. Sir Thomas Lawrence, President of the Royal Academy, died January 7, 1830. The election of Martin A. Shee, portrait-painter, author of *Rhymes on Art* (1805), was reported in the *Times,* January 28. Mr. Shee was knighted shortly afterward.
5. *Aeneid* 6.86.
6. "bellaque matribus / Detestata." Horace *Odes* 1.1.23–4.

to set in between us and Malvern that I might hear—not the bells—but something better worth attending to. Nay—fond as I am of your hills which bound our horizon, I would cheerfully sign a warrant for their annihilation, and that of a good deal more ground, in order to bring Woodland Lodge and Hope End a good deal nearer together. Now I am so conscious of having written libels against your Muse of the belfry, and our spirit of scenic beauty, that in the case of your taste being very much shocked, I do beg you to refer what I have said to a *lapsus* linguae—not extraordinary in this slippery weather. We have all been tumbling about in a corresponding manner, on the ice and off it,—and my pen, wishing to be in the fashion, *"cadit* in silentium".

Your ever sincere friend
E. B. Barrett

56.

To Woodland Lodge
Great Malvern

February 2, 1830

My dear friend,

Papa is at the farm and I shall not see him till the evening,—but as at this moment I have received your letter, I will at this moment begin to answer it. I can write what *I* have to say, and then I shall be ready to write what Papa has to say, with the probability of being able to send the whole by return of post. When I first began to read your account of your legal dilemma, I felt in a fright for you, for fear you should be apprehending an attack upon your folios,—a piece of premature sympathy for which I am glad to find, there was no occasion. But it is bad enough for you to be annoyed in any way by landlords' debts and creditors' attorneys—"bad's the *best!"* [1]

With regard to the caper sauce, it is no wonder that you did not make it out! I found out my mistake after I had sent away my letter, but *that* would do neither of us any good. There is the effect of being anti—instead of archimageirical! [2] I meant *mint sauce,* in which there is a proportion,—is there not?—both of the saccharine and the acid: but what *you* mean by your *riddle,* [3] I do not in the least understand. In propounding it you confounded me, and unless you *com*pound with me by an explana-

1. Beaumont and Fletcher, *Rollo,* IV.2.
2. Word coined from Greek roots to mean "first in the art of cooking."
3. See Letter 57 and n. 1.

tion, I must be *sphinxed* (constricta) to death with curiosity. I should
have thought that considering the *ba-r-ba*-rity of my name, I was more
likely to put you in mind of sheep, than other members of Mr. Barrett's
family possibly could.

By your expression, when you tell me to send Mr. Barker's parcel
"without delay" I am afraid you think I have delayed sending it too
long. If there is any rudeness in the delay, I am sorry for it. It was un-
intentional,—for, from month to month, I have been calculating on
opportunities which never came,—and Mr. Barker did expressly tell
me that I was to take an *opportunity* of returning the books,—that
some acquaintance might be going to London etc. etc. So I thought that
it was safer and better to take him at his word. However, as you say there
is no risk when a parcel is booked, booked it shall be to Mr. Valpy's.[4] I
did not read Boyer thro'. I did not like the style,—and of the matter,
there is more than enough—the work is heavy and elaborate—at least,
so it seemed to me! and leans much more than half its weight upon
authorities! I do not like a writer's mind to be carried about like a
Chinese Lady, because it cannot walk alone!

It is very unfeeling in me to go on writing all this nonsense about mint
sauce, and sheep, and Chinese ladies, when you are expecting to be
executed, but—

The last sentence was in progress just after dinner, when Bro happen-
ing to come into my room, we found out between us that my chimney was
on fire, roaring like Niagara. I was down stairs out of the reach of this
sheet of paper in one moment as you may suppose,—and in a few more,
Papa and a crowd of assistants were doing what they could in my room.
The result you will be glad to hear: the fire was extinguished before it
reached your books. After the fire scene, I was able to speak to Papa about
your business. He does not know whether Mr. Best is or is not related
to the celebrated person whom you have designated so properly as the
Knight of the Gauntlet,[5]—but he does know his *respectability,* which is
unquestionable. Papa is of opinion that before taking any notice of Mr.
Best's letter, you should *write* (not *speak*) to your landlord, and inform
him of the communication which you received from Worcester. Unless
your landlord sanctions the proposed disposal of the rent, or is made a
bankrupt, you must pay it to *him* and to no other,—otherwise he may
force you to pay it *over again.* On this account Papa thinks you should
be very guarded, and have his answer about your paying your rent into

4. A. J. Valpy (1787–1854), editor and printer, founder of the *Classical Journal,*
friend of E. H. Barker and co-editor with him of classical editions.
5. Probably Thomas Best, mayor of Worcester.

the hands of Mr. Best, in *writing*. It is impossible for Papa to know whether it is probable that your landlord's furniture should be seized, unless he knew more of the circumstances. He advises you to learn as much as you can from your landlord himself, and to make him *write* everything. Your great danger seems to Papa to be, their cheating you into a double payment of the rent.

Now, having given Papa's legal opinion, I shall give my private one as to Mr. James Best being related to the Knight of the Gauntlet. *I* think he is his brother. The sentence which was interrupted by the conflagra-tion, was going on to say that I hoped Mrs. Boyd would read the last part of this letter first,—in order that the mint sauce, sheep, and Chinese ladies, might not keep you in suspense, waiting for all the information which Papa could give you touching James Best Esq.—Attorney—Wor-cester!

Your ever sincere friend
E. B. B.

57.

To Woodland Lodge
   Malvern

Saturday night [1830]

My dear friend,

It was certainly very stupid in me not to guess your riddle.[1] You need not have excepted me from the rest of "Mr. Barrett's family"; for till I was eight years old, I never sinned in the way of *ego*tism, but always said "Ba will do this",—and rather too often "Ba won't do that."

I compared your translation with the original, and found it not merely *line for line*—but word for word. I like it very much,—particularly the latter part. There are two things in it, which I do *not,* however, like very much, or at all. I do not like the additional syllable in any blank verse, except the blank verse of a *dramatic* poem, in which licences of every kind are more admissible than in other kinds of composition. And I do not like the contraction *I'll.* You cannot think how I dislike the whole family of such contractions, the I'ds and I'ms and he's and she's,— when they are used in any measure more dignified than the octosyllabic. Campbell uses them sometimes,—and he ought to know better. I am sure you would have done better in this respect, if you had not been com-

1. The riddle seems to have been: Q. Why do Mr. Barrett's family (except for Elizabeth) resemble sheep? A. Because they're always saying "Ba."

posing after dinner—that very un-Aonian time!! You will receive my criticism after tea, and will be sure to admit its justice. . . .[2]

Your ever sincere friend
E. B. Barrett

58.

[1830]

My dear Mr. Boyd,

I am quite well now, and am going to see you very soon, perhaps on Saturday. I would say *certainly* on Saturday or on some previous day; but I heard from Papa today, and he wishes me not to pay you a visit till we have ascertained at what time the Worcester dentist will be at liberty to receive my companions. I know the parcel which you describe, and will bring it with me. It appears to me a short eternity since I saw you last, so that I shall have even more pleasure than usual in going to Malvern—tho' that looks hyperbolical, to my eyes, while I am writing.

I was just thinking of dismissing the parcel of Mr. Barker's books, booked, when Papa's intention of leaving us became known to me. By him I sent the parcel, but I was not well or in the humour to write, and therefore sent it without a letter. I hope my letter written since, may overtake the parcel, or I shall be considered a Goth or Esquimeau or one of the Antipodes to any and every kind of civilization. Of course I would not send the epistolary antiquity which was written last October.

With regard to the visibility of the manuscript you are so kindly interesting yourself about, I will answer for it in a little time. Papa should have taken the papers to London, if I had been as well as usual some time previous to his setting out,—and now they must follow him when they are in a state to do so. Your objection to the other house, amused me. I should like to see (tho' not to ascend) the number of steps which is too great for you to remember!!

Papa desires that Bro should go with us, as an escort to the Worcester party, and poor Bro has been in no state for anything of the kind today, but I hope he will be convalescent by Saturday. Otherwise, I must, you see, wait for him.

Believe me
Your ever sincere friend
E. B. Barrett

2. The omitted passage contains an inquiry about a quotation, perhaps from one of the Greek Fathers, and a paragraph on bells, copied from the *Times*.

59.

Hope End. Monday [1830]

My dear Mr. Boyd,

Your books and formes are perfectly safe from any heat or brightness of sunshine in any part of my room, for the sun never thinks of looking in upon me till the evening. Perhaps he knows how much I hate *morning visits.* You may be sure that I will take care of all your deposits. The most valuable one, Ann, was going to Malvern today with Arabel and me,—but the rain anticipated us,—and now we can only hope for tomorrow and finer weather. If it is not fine *then,* I shall be very very sorry,—because Miss Price's coming and staying will prevent my going to see you for some time longer—at least, longer than I like. Ann's being quite well, is proved satisfactorily by her good looks and good spirits,—and Mrs. Boyd (tell her, with my love) shall soon judge of both. She and Arabel will certainly spend an *hour* at Malvern, in a day or two,—if not tomorrow, and if not in my company. You cannot know how much pleasure it gives me, to have her here.

I have been extremely amused in the churchyard, and in a different way from what I expected. I expected to read something about *bells,*—when you told me that in reading the chapter you directed me to, I should find out the reason of your directing me to that particular part. The parody is very clever indeed, and made me laugh in spite of my allegiance to Homer. I suppose you think that it is all over with *him*—*hic jacet* in the churchyard—but you should recollect that a churchyard cannot and ought not to shake our faith in *immortality.*

I have often observed that the sublimer a composition is, the easier is its transit into burlesque, by the road of parody—in which road, there is more dirt than stones.

Talking of profane jests on sacred subjects, did you ever see the epigram [1] on the Latin gerunds—

> When Dido's spouse to Dido would not come,
> She wept in silence, and was di . . do . . dum.?

It has been so generally admired, that if you answer *no,* to my question *"did you ever?"* I must say *"did you never!!!"* with many notes of admiration.

Your sincere friend
E. B. Barrett

1. Generally attributed to Porson.

60.

Sunday [1830]

My dear Mr. Boyd,

I am very much obliged to you for taking the trouble of writing the note which I have just received. I have been extremely uncomfortable, ever since yesterday, at the idea of having displeased you,—and it was a real relief to me to find that I did not do so as much as I feared. At the same time, you must let me exculpate Miss Price. She was *not "selfish"* in keeping me with her against my will, as you have heard. I did *not* tell her of my wish to go and see you,—but, as the gratification of that wish would, in the opinion of some of our party, have appeared a neglect of her,—and as I could not, at any rate, have remained long with you, I decided upon practicing a severe kind of self-denial yesterday, and of rewarding myself for it by visiting you on Friday. I was thinking all the time I was at Malvern, of my own *costs,*—but, to speak sincerely, it never once struck my vanity that *you* were likely to be annoyed. Without any vanity, tho' with a little reflection, I might have remembered, that people are sometimes and naturally annoyed by a *want* of attention,—even when the attention is of little real value to them.

Ann was quite right and kind in telling me exactly what she did tell me.

I will remember Ion.[1] Give my love to Mrs. Boyd, and believe me to remain

Your sincere friend
E. B. Barrett

61.

Wednesday [1830]

My dear Mr. Boyd,

I will tell you exactly what I think about your verses; and then however severe you may be upon my correctness, you will have no reason to be dissatisfied with my sincerity. I will say at once, I do not think that the sheet, *if published as it is,* could be considered worthy of you,—and yet there are some things in it, which I should be sorry not to give people an opportunity of admiring. . . .[1]

1. A play by Euripides, *ca.* 424 B.C.
1. The passage omitted contains criticism of Boyd's poems.

I am afraid of teazing you on another subject, and yet I believe I must ask you in the case of your writing to Mr. Barker before I see you, to tell him not to print the letters in the way you at first suggested.[2] Do not think it affectation in me. You would not,—if you knew how hard I have been trying to accustom and reconcile myself to what you seemed to wish. I wish that you had wished almost anything else. Let him print, if you desire it, whatever passages relate to works of yours,—or even an *extract* or two relating to other subjects, if you desire *that,*—but do not let him print the letters entire, and with only a few trifling omissions. I cannot reconcile myself to the idea of it. They were written for *you*—and if they pleased you at the time, could their writer wish for more, *now* or *then?* Could the commendation of hundreds of other readers, (supposing for a moment such an improbable supposition) make her prouder and happier? You know little indeed about her, if you think it could.

As you desire it, I will try to go to see you next week.

How sorry I shall be to see Mrs. Boyd tomorrow! considering what she is going to take away,—but I suppose there is no help for it!

Believe me ever
Your sincere friend
E. B. Barrett

62.

To Great Malvern

Hope End. Tuesday
August 2 [1] [1830]

My dear Mr. Boyd,

Your letter was marked "too late", and I did not receive it until yesterday. *It is a long time since I have been as annoyed and irritated as I was the other day by*—not being able to go and see you. I was up at twenty minutes after four, and finished the lessons by eight, when unfortunately Papa's presentiments sank lower than the thermometer and just as he was setting out for Gloucester, and I for Malvern, he sentenced me to stay at home for fear of being wet thro'. I suppose he thought of the scriptural account of the cloud as large as a man's hand overspreading the whole Heaven,[2]—for nothing else could have alarmed

2. Barker, an avid editor, did not easily give up the project to publish EBB's letters to Boyd. See Letter 132.

1. Misdated for August 3, which was the first Tuesday in August 1830.

2. 1 Kings 18:44.

him on Saturday. I am very anxious about going to see you and will do it as soon as I possibly can,—as *that* is one of the subjects on which *I* cannot "bear delay".

The very moment you spoke of having been "irritated and annoyed" I guessed the cause of it. Was not I very penetrating? If I am right in my guess, do not attribute more blame than is attributable, until you hear the other side of the question.

I was surprised (and pleased of course) by your liking the verses which I sent you. You appear to me quite correct in your criticism on the second line,—but I don't understand your objection to the line about the *consumption of breath*. How should I, when you do not mention it? But you will, when we meet next, and, in the meantime, I kiss the *shadow* of the rod.

Miss Cliffe [3] arrived here on Saturday and is likely to remain a fortnight I suppose—or at least, as long as Mrs. Cliffe thinks it necessary to be at Cheltenham. Her being here shall not be allowed to prevent my going to Malvern,—but you know, when visitors are in the house, the poney cannot be quite as disengaged as usual—nor I, quite as much at liberty. I shall use my liberty, when I get it, better than the French people are likely to do theirs. Are you interested in the cannonading which has been going on in Paris,[4]—and does Napoleon's son inherit your sympathies as well as his father's crown? I hope that the king will not pay for his madness, the price which poor Louis the 16th paid for his weakness! Any price less than life, he certainly deserves to pay. The French nation is not an interesting nation,—and yet no English ear ought to like hearing its chain clanking over our sea.

I am anxious to see the additions and omissions,—and offer up my orisons to any Fate who will spin silk instead of worsted, that you may be made Poet Laureate in the next reign. Perhaps this prospect prevents your wishing my poem [5] to be published. You think it better that a person, with whom you have unfortunately had something to do, should not be known as so very disloyal a scribe. You are quite right,—and I would not for the world, that my sackbut should interfere with your sack. Besides, it would be ungracious and ungrateful in Malvern—un-

3. Eliza Cliffe of Mathon, near Hope End.
4. July revolution of 1830, in which Louis Philippe was installed as "citizen king."
5. Sotheby lists an autograph poem, "The Reply of Malvern to the Address of H. S. Boyd, Esq. on the occasion of the Arrival of the young Princess Victoria." Victoria, a rather delicate child of eleven, was spending the summer at Malvern with her mother, the Duchess of Kent.

gracious and ungrateful in the extreme! to attack the Princess's longevity,—and no compliment to her own air and water!

All your ruptures and interruptions and pauses à la Sterne, produced
their proper effect. But tho' I have, of course, a womanly proportion
of curiosity, yet I believe there is a stronger motive even than *that*, for
my wishing to go to see you. I am more anxious to see you than to know
why my verses should not be published,—or what Mr. Spowers [6] did,
said, wrote, or thought,—or even what was the occult cause of my feeling less comfortable than usual when I was in the act of being scorched.

I do know what annoyed and irritated you, on—was it on *Thursday?*

I was told yesterday that my handwriting is easier to read than any
handwriting extant or upon record,—so there certainly can be no difficulty about reading this letter, tho' it seems to me rather more scribbled
than usual. Give my love to Mrs. Boyd and Annie—and tell them that I
would write to them, if I did not hear our *wheelbarrow* (which is to
storm the post today) rolling round to the door. So I must conclude
and seal now, or I shall have no other opportunity of sending, in time.

Your ever sincere friend
E. B. Barrett

63.

Hope End. August 13 [1830]

My dear Mr. Boyd,

Thank you for letting us know about Dr. Adam Clarke,—but I am
afraid it is all in vain. Papa has heard him twice in London,—and I,
who should so very much like to take advantage of his being at Worcester, am very sorry to find it impossible to do so. I am writing this in a
great hurry that Bro may leave it at Malvern. I forgot, when I saw you
last, to tell you how delighted Mr. Owen was with your epigram on the
Tom Cat. He is a man of some talent, and *would* be, I believe, a good
classic if other avocation did not compel him to neglect that line of
study. Bro is calling out to me to "abbreviate my sentences", therefore
believe me dear Mr. Boyd

Your sincere friend
E. B. B.

The *"therefore"* in the last line is out of place.

6. In the preface to his *Agamemnon* Boyd speaks of "my learned and much
esteemed friend, Mr. Spowers of Hampstead . . . the instructor of my youth and my
initiator in those studies which have been the amusement of my riper years."

64.

To Great Malvern

Hope End. Friday morning
[October 8, 1830] [1]

My dearest friend,

I cannot let today pass without saying something of what I shall think
of on everyday for so long—of the last happy fortnight—or nearly three
weeks. Did I not once tell you of the old charge against me, about my
never *enjoying the present moment,*—and must I not say that *you* have
taught me that the present moment *may* be enjoyed? Surely I must,—
and in my measurement of happiness, I do not make *false quantities* as
I do, you know, in Greek. Thank you for this lesson in philosophy tho'
it has soon ceased to be practised—for now that the teacher is at a distance, now that the pleasure of being with you, like the pain of going
away, is over,—I find myself enjoying the past and dreaming of the
future, in my own usual style. You will guess (will you not?) *how* I am
enjoying the past,—and *how* I am dreaming of the future—and you will
believe—I am sure you will,—in all that I say, and in more than I *say*.
I forgot to tell you, tho' I began to think it before I left your house,—
that upon consideration it seemed to me scarcely politic and advisable
to apply to Papa again as soon as your kindness proposed. It is really far
better to wait a little,—and you will assuredly *see* him before long. I
was received most graciously, and had done everything right both in
staying and returning. "Well", he said with a good-humoured smile,—
"so you have *condescended* to come back at last." And when I told him
how happy I had been, the reply was—"I do not doubt *that*. I am only
afraid that you will find it impossible to tolerate us, after Mr. Boyd." I
was determined to talk of what is natural (and can anything be more
natural than certain feelings?) before saying a word of the supernatural.
Papa seems resolved on considering the ghost a hoax,—and expects more
from the vigils of Mr. D'Orlier on the spot with a brace of pistols, than
from any possible searching for bones. I find that the field has been for
years called haunted; and that in the course of last week, two men,
besides the present sufferer, had seen the appearance, and that they all
agree in describing the face and dress in every minute particular. The
bonnet had large bows; the face was of an ashy paleness, surrounded by

1. Dated by visit to Boyd from September 20 to October 7, during which he kept
a daily memorandum of his guest's reading of 2200 lines of Greek. See George S.
Hellman, "Some Unpublished Papers of Robert and Elizabeth Barrett Browning,"
Harper's Monthly, 132 (1916), 531.

long black frizzed hair; and the drapery white and confined by a white satin girdle reaching to the feet. Each of the two men who first saw this figure was much terrified,—and indeed from the effect of terror, one of them was confined to his bed for several days. It leapt, he said, upon his back,—and when he shook it off, and looked behind, it seemed to lie and spread upon the road, and cover it all over with whiteness, like a sheet of moonshine. On Wednesday night, no appearance took place and nothing has since been seen,—tho' the unfortunate man who was last terrified, persists in saying—"I must meet her twice more". You shall hear whatever I do: but Mr. D'Orlier watches every night near the bridge,—and as long as he does this, Papa declares that neither you nor I will hear anything further.

I just escaped a bevy of people who called here on Wednesday. Henrietta Bro and Sam dine today at the Cliffes, and Henrietta sleeps there. Mr. Barker's parcel contained two of his books for children,[2] and the Cl[*remainder of word torn away*]—book,—accompanied by a short note which is so characteristic of him, that I have a great mind to send it to your "odoriferous hands" according to his own expression. At any rate your critical and poetical tastes must be gratified by an extract from an effusion contained in one of the little books which were sent to me by *the editor.*

> The ice it was most hard indeed
> As hard as it could be;
> It made my little head to bleed,
> And almost killëd me.
> I own that I most fondly tried,
> Which was a naughty thing,
> A boy, that on his legs did slide,
> Down on his back to fling.
> But I, alas! was rightly paid,
> Indeed in my own *coin;*
> For soon upon the ice I *laid*
> All wounded and *forlorn.*

I always used to think that children might be allowed the privilege of at least reading good grammar, even if good sense should be considered above their capacities. "But I, alas!", you see, was quite wrong all the time.

2. We can now restore to Mr. Barker "the authorship of a few books for children of some popularity in their day," which the biographer in *DNB* thought could "hardly be accepted by those who are familiar with his recognized volumes."

I found here a note from Lady Margaret, containing an invitation to Eastnor for next Friday,—but I will not go if I can help it.

Give my best love to Mrs. Boyd and Annie—and let me be remembered to Miss Gibbons. I hope they will enjoy themselves tonight! May God bless you! I think of you very very often,—and remain

Ever yours affectionately and gratefully
E. B. Barrett

I hope the heaviness went off very soon,—and that it now exists as little *physically* as it does *intellectually*.

65.

Monday [October 11, 1830]

My dearest friend,

I think that we did not live in *clover,* as you say, but in *asphodel* which certainly sounds much more classical. Do you know (what I have just thought of) that asphodel is the common yellow and not very pretty flower which grows about our meadows, and that an expression of Homer has been thus translated—

the stern Achilles
Stalked thro' a mead of daffodilies? [1]

So that, after all, you don't let our dignity down *so* much,—in speaking as you do,—and we may quite as well stalk thro' clover as daffodilies— may we not? I wish that *my* trouble in repeating words, was the only thing which I thought of, and you had reason to regret. But "si tibi cura mei", what must have been my "cura tui" in this respect! I was certainly *troubled* in thinking of what you sometimes endured,—and this was my only trouble worth mentioning. Is it allowable to hope that the rapidity or indistinctness or the obstacle whatever it may be, to your understand- ing me readily when I read, can be corrected or removed? The correction and removal can scarcely be among impossibilities—utter impossibilities, such as Lord Byron having no pre-eminent genius, and I no regard for you!

I have heard no more about the ghost—excepting that now she has not merely a "local habitation" but a "name"; for she is said and devoutly believed to be, Lady Tempest, who was the proprietress of this house before Papa bought it. I hope she may keep to the bridge, and not show any other local attachments. Mr. D'Orlier, in consequence of hearing or

1. *Odyssey* 11.538–9.

fancying that he heard some noise in the hedge—near the fatal spot, fired both his pistols into it, a night or two ago. Fortunately for him, no coroner's inquest ensued.

How many orisons did you make, that the Duchess of Kent might be inflicted on Papa? She and Prince Leopold and Sir John Conroy [2] were here yesterday when we were at chapel,—and upon Papa being announced to be from home, Sir John Conroy left his card and his compliments, the Duchess rode thro' the yard, under the clock, and after having seen everything that was least worth seeing, went back to Malvern. Papa seems to be much gratified that their Royal Highnesses—did not ride over the grass,—and asked with a little expression of anxiety, what Sir John Conroy could mean by leaving his card. I suggested (out of spitefulness) that he clearly meant—Papa to return the visit. Papa certainly ought to do so,—and still more certainly will not.

What did you do to the Quaker on Friday night—dip him in Helicon,[3] —that he should be *wet* enough to go to the ball?

You acknowledge the weather to be colder now,—do you not? Either the weather is, generally,—or our climate is particularly,—for I have been inclined to shiver, ever since my return home. Henrietta and I are going to Eastnor on Friday; but I have refused to stay longer than Saturday morning.

Have I really delayed till the last, to thank you for your kind letter? And yet, *"thank you for it"*, is not less feelingly said. Papa makes me talk of you, till I am quite tired!

Ever yours very affectionately
E. B. Barrett

66.

To Great Malvern

Friday night [1830]

My dear Mr. Boyd,

Papa says that you may keep what you mentioned to me as long as you like, if it is English,—but that if it is Irish, he does not understand

---

2. The Duchess of Kent was the sister of Prince Leopold; Sir John Conroy was her secretary. The *Hereford Journal* for October 6 records the Prince's arrival in Malvern "about four o'clock in the afternoon of Friday last at the Foley Arms." The paper ignores the royal visitation at Hope End but does note similar visits, e.g. (September 22, 1830): "Her Royal Highness and the Princess Victoria honoured John Biddulph, Esq. of Ledbury with their company, and spent some time in viewing their grounds."

3. I.e. the springs of inspiration on Mt. Helicon.

how business is transacted in Ireland, sufficiently well to pass any opinion upon it.

I hope you did not think me unkind or disobliging this morning in seeming to hesitate at first about making the application for Payne Knight's work,[1] to Sir Robert Price.[2] I have been uncomfortable since about it—I mean about my hesitation. Do not write to Mr. Barker just at present, unless you have particular occasion for doing so,—and as soon as ever Sir Robert Price returns from London which he is sure to do very soon, on the prorogation of Parliament, I will write to him and ask him to lend me the book in question. He has always seemed inclined to oblige me, and I dare say he will lend me the book,—and I can prevent any and every unpleasantness, by begging him not to do so in the case of his feeling the slightest objection, or reluctance in the matter. In that case, you can take advantage of Mr. Barker's offer! Now mind you do not write to him now,—for, not only have I no *objection* to write to Sir Robert Price, but I am quite and decidedly resolved on doing so,—and *will* have my own way.

It was very nearly dark when we got home,—and yet no vote of censure was passed upon us,—as no questions were asked, and therefore, by a happy consequence, no answers returned. Besides the circumstance of leaving Malvern late, we were detained on the road longer than we usually are, principally by the poney, which had lost its taste for moving forwards; and also by Mrs. Trant, whom we found fasting upon oysters, and in a lower deep than the lowest deep of anxiety about *me*— the deeper, as she has for so many months found it, and still continues to find it, utterly impossible to go four miles to see me. So we stayed a few minutes at South Lodge,[3]—and then on descending into our own valleys, were intercepted again by Mr. Peyton.[4] He had a long account to give us of the incendiaries [5]—and as we and they were *near home,* we stopped to listen to it. The night before last, a workman of his, the same Abbotts who was honored by the ghostly visitation, announced to him, when he was in his slippers, (you see how long Mr. Peyton's details must have detained us) that six men had just entered his rickyard. So Mr. Peyton instantly went out, slippers and all, with two loaded pistols and a regiment of servants, to the supposed scene of action,—previously stationing two of his little boys at the front door, loaded with two

1. *Homer,* ed. Richard Payne Knight, 1808.
2. Son of Sir Uvedale.
3. House where the Trants were then living in Malvern Wells.
4. Nicholas Peyton of Barton Court.
5. Rick burning was a common form of protest in the social disorders and terrors of 1830.

loaded guns—(the boys and the guns were equally likely I should think
to *go off!*) and Mrs. Peyton in a garret, with her hand on the alarm bell!
Did you ever hear anything so awful? And must it not be rather provoking to people who undertake to tell the story, that nobody was in
the rickyard after all,—and that tho' the whole household sate up all
night, not an enemy was heard or seen? Should not you be inclined to
suspect that Abbotts saw only the *ghosts* of the incendiaries? Do not
reproach me for leading you along "passages which lead to nothing"—
for these passages did lead to something! At least Mr. Peyton's passage
from his house to his rickyard, led to his catching a violent cold, the
effects of which were quite perceptible, when I had the fortune, good
or bad, of meeting with him this morning.

I hear that Papa did relieve the beggars with whom he was parleying
when I left home. He was working his machine all today!!! and Mr.
Martin [6] has lowered his rents for two months, till the danger is over!
I wonder which of them, the over-brave or the over-cowardly, will escape. Perhaps neither.

Arabel having come into the room, has just observed, "Your writing
is rather difficult to read backwards",— and as this letter is besides to
be read at the Post Office, it may as well be ended before it has talked
any more scandal.

Ever believe me
Yours very affectionately
E. B. Barrett

[*In Arabel's handwriting*] I never read her letter backwards or forwards.

Saturday morning

Papa said at breakfast today, "Are you going to Malvern today Ba?"
To this of course I said *No!* "What! not going to Malvern! I thought
you always went there every fine day. You *ought to go, by rights.*"

67.

Hope End. Wednesday [1830]

My dearest friend,

If it had not been for Annie, who asked me to wait one day longer,
that my parcel might take under its cover some letters from her, I
would have sent the *right* number of the Christian Examiner yesterday.

6. James Martin of Old Colwall. Many of EBB's published letters were written to his
wife.

It is *right* in more ways than one—by my saying which, you will guess that I have read the short but satisfactory review of your work. But indeed without my saying anything, you would guess that I could not have helped cutting the leaves for that purpose, even at the risk of being turned, like some Heroine of Ovid's, into a crow, for peeping!

Thank you for sending me your epitaph on Payne Knight. Among your other guesses you must have anticipated my liking it very much, and if you did, were quite as right as the Christian Examiner. It has a great deal of point and cleverness—and I like it even better now than I did on reading it for the first time. Do you know I am far more inclined to criticize the epistolary winding up of what you sent (though it may wind *you* into a passion to hear me say so) than the epigrammatic *prolegomena?* I hope there is no harm in wishing that your style on *this one occasion* had resembled Foster's! [1] Did you ever read any part of his Essays? They are powerful and original but I did not speak of their writer on those accounts. I spoke of him, because if he had had the writing of the two sentences which compose your *letter* (which I assure you I do not wish) each of them would have filled a sheet as large as this! Talking of the style of letters, Papa had an anonymous one yesterday, very calligraphical and orthographical, to inform him that he was surrounded by a "sett of roges", and that there was one man among them who was "a roge impartikler"—and that they were all "agloring" in the discharge of a certain workman, who, being of "a gode carickter", should have been "inkuridged" instead of discharged. Papa suspects the workman with the "gode carickter", of *"inkuridging"* the writing of this letter. He cannot write himself.

Annie is in high spirits, and not complaining of headache,—and her cough is much better. Give my love to Mrs. Boyd. I might go on writing, but perhaps, as I have nothing particular to say, you might not like to go on reading. "So", as Papa's correspondent says, "no more at present from"

Yours ever affectionately
E. B. Barrett

Thursday morning

Since finishing my letter, I have heard (thro' a letter from Miss Clarke) that a gentleman whose name is unnamed, accidentally mentioned to her, your father, as an "intimate friend of his, the cleverest and most agreeable man he ever knew, and the certain author of Junius's

1. John Foster (1770–1843), author of *Essays, in a Series of Letters to a Friend*, 1805.

letters".² I have besides heard that Annie and I are going to Malvern on Saturday, which of course I, for one, am very sorry for. She *waltzed* herself last night into a headache—but it soon seemed to go off.

And now I will put a second finis to this scribble, which does not seem to have quite taken your *hints of brevity*.

68.

Hope End. Friday [1830]

My dear friend,

I wish to send you the passage from Cyril, which Dr. Milner ¹ quotes (by a translation) in his End of Controversy; and also to thank you for many happy recollections. I will do the easiest thing first.

Dr. Milner omits the former part of that translation which you attacked, and writes thus—"Since Christ himself affirms thus of the bread—*This is my body,*—who is so daring as to doubt of it? And since he affirms,—*This is my blood,*—who will deny that it is his blood? At Cana of Galilee, he, by an act of his will, turned water into wine, which resembles blood; and is he not then to be credited when he changes wine into blood? Therefore, full of certainty, let us receive the body and blood of Christ—for, under the form of bread, is given to thee his body, and under the form of wine, his blood." No mention is made of your remarks, directly or indirectly. If you should like to have the book, you have only to let me know.

And now that I have finished your business, how am I to begin my own? Won't your columns before Carlton Palace,² speak for *me* also? or must I seem to forget myself into their marble? ³ You are aware of my deficiency in the *parts of speech*—and in that part of speech which is capable of expressing a great deal of gratitude for a great deal of happiness, I am particularly deficient. Forgive my deficiency here, as you have

2. Anonymous letters directed against the Ministers 1768–72. Generally attributed to Sir Philip Francis; but see L. D. Campbell, *The Miscellaneous Works of Hugh Boyd, the Author of Junius,* 1800.

1. John Milner (1752–1826), Roman Catholic bishop whose learning Boyd later attacked in *The Fathers not Papists: or Six Discourses of the Most Eloquent Fathers of the Church,* London and Sidmouth, 1834.

2. Referring to some incidental poems published with his *Agamemnon,* Boyd admitted in the preface, "If the question be put to them, which was put to the Ionic columns in front of Carlton House—'What do you do here?' I fear the same answer must be given—'We really do not know.'"

3. "Forget thyself to marble." Milton, *Il Penseroso,* 1, line 42.

forgiven it in many other things! And let me assure you, that, if my Memory were as good as yours or Porson's, the recollection of the last few days could not last longer than it must do now!

Your grateful and attached friend
E. B. Barrett

69.

To Great Malvern

January 9 [1831]

My dearest friend,

I cannot send a note to Woodland Lodge, without thanking you for yours, which I have this moment received. As Maddox is going imme-diately, I can scarcely do more than thank you,—but I will write again when I have done as you desire, and I will do that, as *soon* as possible. Of course I received your letter about Bentley,—and answered it—did I not? At least I intended to do so, in spite of all its severity. I cannot conclude this, without saying that your expression *"I hope you will soon be better and able to come and see us",* made me experience a movement of pleasure which I had not experienced for some time.[1] It made me feel that *one* happiness at least, that of your society, was not removed from me—I thank God for that. I can value it, even if I am not worthy of it—and indeed there never were or could be any, out of my own immediate family, towards whom I have felt as I have and must ever feel towards *you*. If Bro were in the way I would ask him now about the digamma, and satisfy you on one point. I do not ask *you* to write *if you should be disinclined,* but I hope Mrs. Boyd or Annie will not let me be without a note, for any length of time.

May God bless you, dear Mr. Boyd. Remember me in your prayers— You are never forgotten in mine!

Yours affectionately
E. B. Barrett

There seems to be no necessity for sending back the Homer *now*. And if I do, how can I consult it for you? Sir Robert will, I am sure, allow me to keep it as long as either of us can wish.

This letter is more illegible than my most illegible letters. I am tired of writing—being not strong enough to be *long* in tiring.

Bro has just come in. He pronounced the digamma at the Charter-

1. EBB was confined to the house by illness for two months at the end of 1830 and beginning of 1831.

house, as *w,* not *v;* and never pronounced it in the *middle* of words.

Ten days ago, I was thinking of writing to ask you whether you would prefer seeing the passage in my poem, which relates to you, before it is printed. Perhaps there may be something, in your opinion, to be omitted or added.

70.

To Great Malvern

Friday morning [1831]

My dear Mr. Boyd,

. . .[1] Of course your corrections of my verses shall be adopted. How I wish the whole poem had the same advantage.

No! You did not send back the Edinburgh Review; but give yourself no more trouble about it, than if you had. You will lend me Phalaris [2] (will you not?) at some future time—I have read it *once* thro',—yet, as there are many things in the book which I should like to read oftener than once, I do not feel quite satisfied, and would bespeak a second loan, when you have so completely done with it, as to be thinking of consigning it to your boxes. It is certainly a wonderful work,—and less wonderful in the extent and depth of its learning, than in the felicity and aptitude and vivacity of that learning's application. Bentley's learning is not a stiff heavy scholastic thing,—but (with deference to you) *"plays a* tune" instead of "waking" one. His style is manly and unaffected and clear. It has no grace or harmony—and is not inviolate *always* as to grammar. . . .[3]

I am dreaming, dear Mr. Boyd, about having a favorable answer to the petition which I sent you the other day—a dream very unlike one which I had lately, about reading Vitruvius—and which seemed to have been dreamt from a consideration rather of your inclinations than mine.

I had a note from Mr. Curzon a fortnight ago, to say that Papa wished him to see and talk to me. So I did see him,—and since then, he has very

1. The omitted passage reports on the spelling of "double letters" in Knight's *Homer.*

2. Richard Bentley, *A Dissertation upon the Epistles of Phalaris* (1699), an argument attacking the genuineness of the Phalaris letters. Bentley's famous controversy with Charles Boyle on this subject gave rise to Jonathan Swift's *Battle of the Books.* For fuller comment on Bentley see Letter 3.

3. The omitted passage reports on Knight's treatment of the *digamma* in his *Homer* and quotes a Latin tribute to Sir Uvedale Price written in the editor's hand on the first page.

kindly come of his own accord, for Papa's sake more than mine, and for Christ's sake more than Papa's.[4] He told me that he wished very much to know you, and would walk from Ledbury to Malvern to see you, willingly and at any time, if I would introduce him and you would receive him. Therefore the making of this new acquaintance depends upon yourself; and in spite of the want of congeniality on subjects of taste and literature, his piety and keenness of mind may render it a valuable one, and better worth having in every way, I should think, than Mr. Wood's.

Arabel, another new acquaintance of yours, says that you will think her extremely *"impudent"* in being persuaded by me to go to see you, without any invitation from yourself. So, if you *do* put on the black cap, condemn the guilty person—who is guilty of a little *envy* just now, besides the other offence.

Yours affectionately
E. B. Barrett

Do you observe (page 217) that Bentley writes the first verse of the Iliad as he imagines it to have been written anciently,—and yet *without the digamma?*

Arabel will take the Phalaris with her on Monday, as it is too wet for her to go today. I hope you will not want it tonight.

71.

Monday morning [1831]

I was told the other day that I was "very kind" to eat my dinner,— and now you tell me that I am "very kind" to ask you to stay here for "so long a period". Really there is no end of my disinterested beneficence! But I am afraid that the last act does not deserve quite so many thanks as the previous one, and that it may be found on the examination of Henrietta or Arabel as witnesses, that I never said, in talking of this subject, "How pleased *Mr. Boyd* will be to come", but "How pleased *I* shall be if he will come". Therefore take back your laurels. It was natural for you to write a little *nonsense of course,* such as the words I have just commented upon,—but it was neither natural nor necessary for you to go out of the way as you have done more than once, to talk of my making *"returns"* for the kindness you have shewn me. If

4. This need for spiritual help may be connected with the death of Mr. Barrett's mother, about January 15, 1831 (buried January 18).

I were so happy as to be able to render you any real service,—in *that* case which is improbable I fear to occur,—even in *that* case, you never could make a correct use of a word most strangely misapplied in your note. By no services, could I, or *would* I, make *"returns"* for your kindness to me (—if by "returns" is meant something to cancel obligations—) for like the stain on Lady Macbeth's hand, not all great ocean's waters could wash out *that* from my memory.

And now with regard to your coming here. You cannot think how delighted I am with your half promise to come here,—tho' Hesiod is not right in this case, when he calls *half* better than the *whole*.[1] But if *you* will not *"speak* positively", *I* will *think* positively; and it will be "very *un*kind" in you, and very hard upon me, if you should ever think of disappointing me. Arabel would not tell me her opinion of the probability of your coming, before your letter arrived, for fear I should be disappointed afterwards—so there is a good example of considerate conduct, for you to imitate! Papa is as little likely as I, to object to your adopting Foster's style in the length of the *period* of your visit—and everything else shall be settled and talked over, just as you like when I see you. In return for Mrs. Boyd's encouraging prophecy that I shall not be able to do that *for months,* tell her my conviction and hope to the contrary. My best love to her and Annie respecting whom I am so glad to hear good news—And now I have time only to thank you for the pleasure you have given me,—and to assure you of my being

Ever yours affectionately
E. B. Barrett

72.

To Great Malvern

Hope End. Tuesday
[February 8, 1831][1]

My dearest friend,

I must begin my letter by telling you what a fright the beginning of yours gave me—i.e. "I am sorry that when I gave the promise of going to your house—"! I could not think what was coming, and dreaded lest it should not be *you,*—in which case, you never could have expected (with any kind of modesty) to hear from *me* again, in spite of the acrostic and epigram. Could whole hecatombs of verses, supposing you took

1. Hesiod *Works and Days* 40.
1. Dated by mention of Hope's death.

the trouble to write them, propitiate me? No indeed! So "think of *that!*" (You know you sometimes direct *my* thoughts to particular subjects!—) But as the acrostic came in such far better company than you led me to suspect, I cannot delay a moment longer, thanking you for dedicating its elegance and harmony to me. If one fault (the fault of inappropriateness) is obvious, *I* at least ought not to complain of it—and you have my best wishes for more disinterested critics to lay whatever blame they may be inclined to lay, rather on your good nature than on your bad taste. The epigram sounds nearly as well in English as in Greek. It has been truly said that, *laudari a viro laudato* is a pleasure; but there is a *greater* pleasure—and it cannot but be very *very* pleasant to enjoy the greater and the less at one moment!

I am glad that you did *not* think of making "conditions" before promising to come here,—for my philosophy could not have helped yielding to them,—and then I might have been Sangrado-d [2] into a far worse *condition* than I am in now. Your charge against me is a grave one, and is enough to make *me* grave, as I did not expect it from *you*— et tu Brute—then fall Caesar! So I give up the argument,—(which, you once told me, a woman never would do if she could help it),—and after clean orthodox sprinkling of dust and ashes, do acknowledge myself at the feet of you, my ghostly confessor, to be guilty of the mortal sin of recovering my health and strength without the aid of Physician, Surgeon, or Apothecary. Well! I am very sorry for it, of course—but what can I do now? Can you suggest any remedy? Think of *that*. I went down stairs twice today, and have begun to look as well as I usually do,—and indeed drove down to our last gate this morning, without being in any way, the worse for it. Think of *that*. As I had not been out of the house for nearly two months before, I enjoyed it very much,—and as it rained nearly all the way, am likely to profit from it. There are however some misgivings in my mind, as to whether or not I shall be able to go to Malvern this week. If possible I will,—for, besides other motives, I am anxious to talk to you and to hear you talk about coming here—to "enter into the details" as they say in the House of Commons.

By the way, I saw in the paper yesterday, a notice of the death of Mr. Hope the celebrated author of Anastasius.[3] Did you ever read that book? I never did, the whole,—because Papa's censorship would not let me,—but from what I have heard respecting it, it must be a won-

2. The humbug physician in Le Sage's *Gil Blas.*

3. Thomas Hope died Thursday, February 3, 1831. *Anastasius or Memoirs of a Greek,* when first published, was attributed to Byron; Hope was thought a too "respectable and decorous gentleman" to be its author.

derful production. Your fragment of your translation of the Agamemnon has of course interested me very much,—and not the less so, from the circumstance of its being so strikingly inferior to the one you afterwards finished and published. I mean to return it to you, myself. As you send back Foster's essay without any remark, I suppose you don't "think (much) of *that*".

Ever yours affectionately
E. B. Barrett

On the death of Thomas Hope Esq.

Lamenting age!—whom Genius could not save
From heavier ills than those Pandora gave!—
When all that wrings the heart and clouds the mind
Escapeth thus—nor Hope remains behind!

On the same

Afflicted Genius veils her drooping head—
For what averts despair, when Hope is dead?

Wednesday
Will you give my love to Mrs. Boyd and Annie,—and thank the former for her note. The birds are singing this morning, as if not only the snow, but the winter had gone. I did not receive your letter until yesterday,—for, not expecting to hear from you, I did not send to Ledbury on Monday which is not a day for London letters.

73.

[1831]

My dearest friend,
    In spite of all the happiness I shall have in seeing Papa today, I am disappointed—for it has now become impossible for me to spend two days with you next week, as you had proposed, and as I could not help agreeing to do. A note saying this, was actually written. Well! it cannot be helped. Certainly *Papa* will not help it,—for he would not like to part with me or any of us, so soon—not until we had tired him a little!
    How could you think of sending me Heyne's Homer? Tho' it was much too kind in you, yet you may be forgiven by very lenient judges,

in consideration of the pleasure you gave me with the books. Shall I not value them always? Saying "yes", is saying only that I must always be

Yours affectionately
E. B. Barrett

I mean to contrive to see you soon some way or other,—tho' I am afraid not quite in the *best* way!

Friday

This note was written to go yesterday but was left behind,—and it is opened today that I may tell of Papa's being come. Mr. Curzon had arrived only a short time before him,—so that I had no opportunity of talking to him (Mr. C.) about you, as much as I wished. But he told me that he meant to go to see you soon. Do you observe how wrong you were?

74.

March 8, 1831

My dear Mr. Boyd,

All the commencement of the 20th book [of the *Iliad*] is retained by Knight . . .[1] Further on, Mr. Knight omits 44 lines, from line 112—an *episodium molestum,* as he calls it,—considering *that* an excuse for *molesting* it! I will not molest *you* any longer now, as I am to do so in a different way tomorrow.

Yours affectionately
E. B. Barrett

75.

Hope End. Monday morning [1831]

My dearest friend,

Tho' your *two* epigrams are certainly very good, yet they are *too* bad —and if you will reconcile this contradiction, I will—*not* transcribe them into your book or any book. . . .[1] How could you write anything so *untrue* as that second epigram? Acknowledge it to be untrue, and I will acknowledge, as I do at this moment, all its cleverness. I think it is

1. The omitted passage reports on the text of Knight's *Homer*.
1. The omitted passage contains a criticism of Boyd's epigrams.

very clever. With regard to the supposed incorrectness of the word "be-side", I have looked in Johnson and found that Addison justifies your manner of using it for *"besides." Besides,* since "thou wearest thy wit at thy *side"* [2] (as Pedro says to Benedick) it would be a shame to put you *"beside* your wit" by carping at an incorrectness,—supposing it could be proved to be an incorrectness!

When we were at chapel yesterday, Mr. Curzon said to me, "I suppose it is not necessary to send a herald to Malvern, to announce my next visit to Mr. Boyd". He is thinking of going to see you next Wednesday. Papa was regretting the other day that he did not question him last Thursday, and find out exactly what he thinks of you!

If it should be fine on Thursday, and no obstacle occurs, Arabel and I will be at Malvern.

Ever believe me
Yours affectionately
E. B. Barrett

Papa thinks that Ministers will try the fate of the new bill,[3] thro' another division, and be satisfied with the smallest majority. If they fail, he does not doubt their intention of immediately dissolving parliament. He says, "All London is quite *mad* about it."

76.

Hope End. April 1 [1831]

My dear Mr. Boyd,

I think I may as well, and perhaps better, write a few words to tell you that the scene in the garden, which we were talking about, was the produce of somebody's inventive genius. I have to say also, what I forgot to mention yesterday, that a vote of three thousand, six hundred pounds, has been made or is thought of being made in the House of Commons to Mr. Babbage,[1] for his *thinking* machine. They intend to erect a house

---

2. "Dost thou wear thy wit by thy side?" *Much Ado about Nothing,* V.1.126.

3. A bill for reform of Parliament had resulted on March 22 in a division (302 to 301), and a revised measure was now pending. Mr. Barrett's political forecast proved correct: the bill was defeated (299 to 291) on April 19, and on April 23 the King dissolved Parliament. It is clear from the *Times* that London was "quite *mad* about it," especially about the fact that many opponents represented the rotten boroughs which the bill was intended to disenfranchise.

1. Charles Babbage (1792–1871), inventor of elaborate machines for calculating and printing numerical tables. From 1823 to 1842 the government put £17,000 into the project, which was finally abandoned. EBB's account is based on the *Times* report of March 29.

for it, and to apply it to the purposes of the government,—and the expenses of the erection and purchase, are estimated at 12,000 pounds. I thought you might like to hear something of this.

I detailed as well as I could your port wine and roast goose logic, for the benefit of Papa who very much approves of your side of the question and thinks your manner of defending it "very fair". Indeed we all agreed that you *roasted* your antagonist,—tho' his likeness to your illustration ends there!

Now I was going to end this note,—but I can't do so without telling you that you annoyed me a little yesterday,—and that thinking of what you said, has annoyed me *more*. How you could possibly think that I would say one thing to Mr. Curzon, and another to *you* (and that other not the truth!) would be a wonder to me, if it were not in some measure solved by the assurance which it brings with it, that up to this present time you can have known nothing at all about me. And this knowledge is nearly as disagreeable as your charge. If I had wished to do what you charged me with, you might have doubted whether my folly or my disingenuousness was the greater—and now *I* may doubt whether that supposed folly and disingenuousness, or your ignorance of me, is the greater. Happily *something* is greater than either,—and *that* makes me forgive your charge yesterday (on condition that you never think of such a thing again, except when you are in sackcloth and ashes) and remain, besides,

Yours very affectionately
E. B. Barrett

77·

Hope End. Friday
[April, 1831] [1]

My dear friend,

. . .[2] I forgot to tell you that Moore in his Life of Lord Byron, states respecting the *Devil's Walk* that tho' it is commonly attributed to Porson, it is in fact by Coleridge. Are you incredulous? or is your interest in the composition "fallen, fallen, fallen, fallen",[3] like Darius?

1. The reference to Moore's *Life of Byron* (1830) dates this letter soon after one to Mr. Boyd (Kenyon, *1*, 8) in which EBB speaks of reading Moore's book. From the earlier letter it is apparent that the Boyds were planning to move soon, a fact which may explain Mrs. Boyd's absence from Malvern.

2. The omitted passage reports Chrysostom's reading of two Biblical texts.

3. John Dryden, *Alexander's Feast*, Stanza 4.

Moore's book was lent to me for a few days by Mrs. Ricardo [4] who is now in London,—or I would have sent it to you, that you might read at least some parts. It is a thick quarto; but I read it with so much interest, that it was finished on the day after it was begun,—and I could scarcely dine, or drink tea, or go to sleep, in the meantime.

I had not an opportunity on Monday to speak to you on several points which I put off mentioning till the last. Mrs. Boyd told me that you *might* have your letters read to you even now; and therefore I thought I would send you the information which you desired me to collect from your own folios. As to my continuing to write to you for the next three weeks, it may be convenient to you to receive my letters—and it may not,—you may like to hear from me as usual, and you may not. My not asking, has occasioned the evil of my not knowing; but if you do not answer this note, I shall know what to do, or rather, what not to do! At any rate you will receive two assurances upon trust—1st that there are not many things in the world, which I like better than writing to you—and 2dly that, your doing exactly as you prefer, is one of those things.

Is there anything that I can do for you in the way of writing, or in any other way? If there is, I shall think it kind in you to let me know. I will send Mr. Barker's Demosthenes soon.

> Believe me dear Mr. Boyd
> Your ever sincere friend
> E. B. Barrett

Only think of my forgetting the brandy. Perhaps you consider *that,* equivalent to forgetting yourself—but I hope you do not. Bro is in the very Attic of admiration!

I have written or intended to write, particularly *at large* and perspicuously today,—out of compassion to unpracticed and unmicroscopic eyes.

4. Probably the wife of Osman Ricardo (1795–1881), eldest son of the political economist, David Ricardo. His home was at Broomesbarrow Place near Ledbury. David Ricardo was a nephew of Mrs. Boyd's stepmother, Rebekkah Delvalle Lowry. *Imperial Magazine,* 7 (1825), 126.

78.

To Woodland Lodge
  Great Malvern

Wednesday [1831]

My dearest friend,

As Mrs. Boyd says that you wish me to write soon and be as explicit as I can, I will write to you immediately: but as to being *explicit,* how can I attempt to explain what I do not understand? [1] I might as well try to explain Lycophron, whom, you know, I never even tried to understand! I will tell you what I have *heard,* but I ought to tell you first, that upon *anything* I have heard, it is impossible to rely— much less upon *everything.*

The land surveyors or measurers or whatever they may be, are said to have said that the fat gentleman with the rings, will return from London in the course of a few days—for what purpose nobody knows. The fat gentleman himself is said to have said that *"the place is to be sold"*—and that *he* was appointed by a counsellor to take possession. It is reported that he even desired a neighbouring farmer who is sometimes employed here, to plough our hopyard. The farmer would not do it, without Papa's own order, and applied to him for it. His answer was *"Do as you please",*—and this not being considered sufficiently distinct, the fat gentleman's intended ploughing is still unperformed. None of Papa's people are employed in the fields as they usually are at the present season. They are all threshing out the grain, and getting in the wood, *for sale.* But Papa is so often given to *selling,* that no conclusion, one way or the other, can be drawn from this. His spirits are very good,—but our knowledge of his extraordinary power of self-command, prevents our trusting even to *them.* You will easily judge what a state of bewilderment we are in. Every day I expect to hear something decisive,—and every night comes, without my having heard it. Today, however, I have heard what is indeed a consolation—that "wherever we are you mean to be near us". Shall I cut that sentence out of Mrs. Boyd's note, and use it as a "frontlet to my brows"? [2] I have a great mind to do so. You cannot think how it has relieved me. Going away while you were remaining at Malvern, would have been doubly and triply going away. And yet—(you know unreasonable peo-

1. With this letter begins a period of unhappy tension, as the family (never taken into their father's confidence) hear rumors that Hope End is to be sold.
2. Perhaps an echo of *King Lear,* I.4.208.

ple like me, are never satisfied) I am inclined to grumble about Annie's news to Arabel,—that you "have *settled* not to remain at Malvern". I am sure I never *could* like the structure of those words,—until we ourselves were actually packed up. And at present we are in neither bundles nor boxes. Perhaps, after all, all the stories we have heard, with and against our wills, may prove to be *stories,*—the awful fat gentleman may remove his shadow from us,—the landmarks, some of which, Georgie [3] pulled up two days ago, in a fit of indignation, may be never reinstated,—and you may be settled in the Turkish room in May! And then how should I like to hear of your settling not to remain at Malvern? Why I should think you in a conspiracy with the fat gentleman to make me wish the landmarks back again.

Thursday

Mr. Curzon dined here yesterday, and slept here—and talked a great deal about you. He called your essay on the Greek article "a very masterly performance"; yourself "a most interesting companion", and afterwards, "a most valuable companion to a minister". But Papa enquired about your degree of piety; and then his answer was, "Ask Miss Barrett. She knows more about Mr. Boyd than I do"! "Oh!" Papa said "who would ask *her?* Why she swears by Mr. Boyd." "Never mind"—Mr. Curzon answered. "She knows more about him than I do." And he would not say anything further then,—but he had told me previously what made him doubt with respect to you. I will tell you when I see you next. It is a mere misunderstanding arising from something which you said, and, I am quite sure, did not mean to apply in the manner he supposed—not anything about science or poetry!

If we do leave this place, it is most probable that we shall go somewhere near London, on account of Papa's business there,—certainly *not to London,*—not improbably to Brighton. Papa has a house at Epsom,—but I believe it is let on a long lease—happily for those who might otherwise be forced to live in it. Now I have told you everything. Should I have the happiness, when driven from this neighbourhood, to find you in some other,—don't let us be seven miles off again, and obliged to write, instead of talking.

Ever affectionately yours
E. B. B.

3. George, the fourth Barrett brother, was fifteen at this time.

I have just heard that Papa "is very ill, *not expected to live*",—and that "all the servants are discharged except Mrs. Robinson,[4] because no one else will go with the family to the West Indies." Mr. Babbage is nothing to some of our inventive neighbours.

79.

To Woodland Lodge
   Great Malvern

Wednesday, May 4, 1831

My dearest friend,

When Eliza first told me of having written to you, much as I felt the kindness of her motive, I regretted her having done it. I was fearful that you had given me as much time as you could conveniently, and that you might be annoyed by being spoken to about extending it. I am much obliged to you for giving me another week—and I think it very kind and considerate in you to suffer "willingly" the uncertainty so long. At the end of that time, if nothing conclusive happens, you may depend on my speaking. I myself see the necessity of doing so— for, as to giving up having you here, in the case of there being the slightest chance of no insurmountable obstacle intervening, you cannot suppose that I should or would or could think of such a thing.

If Eliza had not written the other day, I think I myself would have written to you this morning and sent my letter by a private messenger, that you might be able to send me an answer as to whether you would let me put off the question *beyond tonight,* or whether you would still wish me to ask it. My reason for doing this would have been what I heard yesterday afternoon,—which has made me apprehend that we shall know too soon about the mystery. Did I tell you the report of Kenrick, at whose house the fat gentleman lodged, being appointed land stewart? Well! that report must be certainly true! Kenrick had a letter from this principal last Friday, which he shewed yesterday to Daly. The letter desired that he, Kenrick, would immediately begin to plough the fields,—that he would take an exact account of the live stock at present in the pastures,—and that he would make Daly attend to the garden. There was besides some allusion to the house,—as if it were considered no longer inhabited! After this, and after hearing that the 12th of May is a *moving day,* I

4. The housekeeper ("Minny"), who was still with the family at the time of EBB's marriage.

would certainly, I think, have asked you to wait for a day or two more —as that day or two may decide so much. The writer of the letter is to be here in a few days!

Last Saturday we were talking about my aunt Miss Clarke [1]—as to the probability of her being in London or not. Henrietta said she was probably there,—and I maintained that it was very unlikely that she should have left Fenham. Papa was perfectly silent. The next morning, he sent a letter to London directed to her at George's Hotel Albemarle Street! So you see, he knew all about it, all the time. There is nothing but mysteries!

Arabel sends you the cup.[2] À propos to "presumption", are you aware that my eloquent and intellectual cousin Dominick Trant is a candidate with Mr. Knowles [3] for the representation of Shaftesbury? Papa is so angry, and anxious for his defeat! When will people know what they are fit for? Not until they cease to be ———. If Mr. Trant had called upon you, your *judgment* would have been able to fill up that hiatus; but as it is, your ingenuity must do it. Sir Thomas Butler [4] has come forward for Carlow. I hope he will do us more credit.

Of course I will go again to see you, my dearest friend, if it is possible. But circumstances are not in my power,—and what may be the event of the next hour, it makes me even sick to think of! Are not the probabilities against my ever going to Malvern again? and if you do not go where we do, are they not against our ever meeting again? I may see Mrs. Boyd and Annie—but how can I hope to see *you?* You know, Papa will not let me travel to any distance to visit my nearest relatives,—and whatever my own feelings may be, *he* would rather give such a permission on their account, than on yours! The future, present, and past, all make me turn from them—but why should I write what you can scarcely have pleasure in reading?

Ever yours affectionately
E. B. Barrett

1. Arabella Graham-Clarke ("Bummy"). The family home was Fenham Manse in Newcastle-upon-Tyne.

2. Decorated with a design of the orbits copied from an engraving. Boyd had teased Arabel about the "presumption" of her undertaking and had offered to wager fifty guineas to two that it would prove a failure. Weaver, Letter X.

3. Francis Charles Knowles, son of Sir Charles, whose home was close to Ruby Cottage. The defeat of Knowles and Trant is recorded in the *Times*, May 7. This was Knowles' second unsuccessful attempt within the year to win the Shaftesbury seat. See *The History of the Shaftesbury Election of 1830*, an anonymous play by play account compiled by his friends.

4. Husband of EBB's aunt, Frances Graham-Clarke.

Our best love to Mrs. Boyd and Annie. Did Annie give you a message from Arabel about writing some verses for her album?

I forgot to say that Kenrick began on Monday to plough the fields. Pray, do not tell *anyone* the particulars you hear from me.

80.

Hope End. Friday [1831]

My dearest friend,

I cannot bear you to continue to think what you seemed to think yesterday, that I have less regard for you than I ever have had. You certainly must have employed a curious and most illogical process of reasoning, to arrive at such a conclusion. Assure yourself that if I had not cared for *you* I should not have cared, for one moment, about sending back your book; and I wonder this is not obvious to you without my saying it. The fact was simply this—I was pleased two years ago by what I considered a mark of your friendship when you gave me the two books you had used at Westminster [1]—and when last Friday you sent for the Terence, I considered *that* a withdrawing of one mark of the friendship I had so much valued—as if you had said—"*I* care less than I did, about *her* caring for me." This was the feeling and the only feeling, I do solemnly assure you, that passed over my mind—and the circumstance of my being very much out of spirits and doubtful as to the probability of our ever meeting again as happily as we have done,—made it leave a stronger and more obvious impression as it went, than might otherwise have been the case. I hope you will forgive me for writing anything on this subject or any other, that may have displeased you in the very slightest degree. If you had even behaved ill and unkindly to me, I am not sure whether I *could* have cared less for you—and never, not even on Friday, did I attribute to you anything but that possible change of feeling which must have been too involuntary, for me to *blame,*—to whatever extent I might have been pained by it! And now are you convinced? I hope you are. I cannot bear to think that what may be the last period of our *near* communication, should be clouded, in a way unknown to the first.

Yours ever and very affectionately

E. B. Barrett

My best love to Mrs. Boyd and Annie.

1. The records of Westminster School show that a Boyd (Christian name not recorded) was living in "Grants" in March 1797.

81.

To Woodland Lodge
Great Malvern

Wednesday, half past two [1831]

My dearest friend,

I did not mean to write at all today, much less so late,—but I feel clearly now that I shall sleep the better tonight for having written. Do let me hear the result of the visit to Cheltenham—and pray do not take any decisive step after you have received Mr. Curzon's reply, without my knowing something about it. Papa's manner in speaking of you last night proved to a certainty that he was not displeased by your application. Yesterday he put his own men into the Hope End part of the hop-field, which some people think a good sign,—tho' others, merely, that he has decided upon appropriating to himself the present year's crops which he has had a right from the beginning to do. But this morning he sent for 32 gallons of beer, for somebody (he said to the messenger) who was coming to stay here and could not drink cider. Who can the somebody be? Miss Clarke, or Mrs. Hedley, or *you?*

I cannot help thinking that something is doing for the release of the estate, and that we shall not go after all. But if *you* go, what is my pleasure in staying, reduced to? Is it not possible for you to stay? I know you wish it to be possible,—and Dr. Garlike's [1] opinion must quite relieve Mrs. Boyd's mind with respect to Annie.

If you *would* try the Wells for *one* year—May Place, or Ruby Cottage as you seemed to prefer it! When Lady Margaret Cocks returns, she will no longer be obliged to visit or to forbear visiting as another person wishes [2]—she will be much more her own mistress in this respect, and I will do my very best to bring her to see you. And this would be making an opening for Mrs. Boyd and Annie into quite another kind of society. Mrs. Berrington too, is *sure* to call upon them —and thro' her, Mrs. Hornyhold,—and thus they will have in different ways more agreeable people than the Malvern people to associate

1. A list of homes on the road from Great Malvern to Malvern Wells (Best, *Malvern*) names in order "Melton House, on the left, the genteel residence of Bennet Garlike, esq. M. D., Firs House, embosomed in wood, the property of Thomas Hornyhold, esq., Ruby Cottage to the right, Essington's Hotel to the left, Gloucester House and Regent Lodge, May Place to the left." *The Visitors' Guide to Malvern* (n.d.) places the Berrington residence near Little Malvern church.

2. Lady Margaret's mother died February 9, 1831.

with. Besides, Annie could manage her garden and ride her poney much more happily and independently than she could do, in the midst of, or at least in the neighbourhood of those crowded houses, where nothing can be at ease, but depravity. And if Hope End is inhabited as it now is, will it not always be open to her whenever the other side of the hill begins to tire her? And whenever she and Mrs. Boyd *like* to be tired of both sides of the hill, then, you know, the same Hope End is open to *you*—not once or twice but always!

Now cannot you talk of and manage this—or at any rate try it for one year more? Have you not been very well at Malvern? Is it not possible that a change to a less bracing air may have an injurious influence on your nerves? Did you ever hear of the extraordinary longevity for which people who have lived long at Malvern, are celebrated? And (for a final question) are not such places as Bath and Cheltenham generally considered little calculated for the permanent good of girls of Annie's age. I wish you could hear all I have heard of *both places,* from sensible women and men.

I have said nothing of myself—it is vain to say anything. I am *very* unhappy at the idea of your going away—but you all know this as well as I do. Pray send to Mathon, as soon as ever you hear,—and beg Eliza not to lose a moment in sending to me.

May God bless you! In the greatest hurry, believe me

Your affectionate
E. B. Barrett

82.

To Woodland Lodge
    Great Malvern

Hope End. Thursday [1831]

My dearest friend,

I am sorry that you were disappointed by my letter saying nothing of Papa—but by your letter, I have been more disappointed than it is possible for you to have been by mine! Am I to understand that in the case of your not hearing from Mr. Curzon at the end of this week, it is your intention to take the house at Charlton, without waiting even till the *nineteenth,* as you told me you might do? Do you not know how apt Papa is to delay answers to questions respecting his own affairs? You are wrong if you think that he would be unwilling to receive you here in the case of his remaining at Hope End,—or that, in another case, he could dislike your being near us. He can have no very strong personal feeling about either, as he does not know you: but for *my* sake, I know what his wish must be. I am sure I am wrong in thinking and feeling so much *merely* for myself—but I cannot help it. And I must suggest one thing to you, tho' to you it may seem of no consequence. Supposing Papa were to write to you next Monday or Tuesday or Wednesday, to regret his inability to answer your question before, on account of the suspense in which he himself has been held. If after writing such a letter, he were to hear that before receiving it, you had precluded yourself from either coming here or living near us, what would his inference be? Not surely that your wish for doing either could have been very strong.

I will not tell you *now* what I myself think about the *degree* of your desire to live near us—but I know you too well not to know your manner of writing and speaking when you desire anything very much. I dare say you will go to Charlton, and that you will be very happy there. I hope you may—earnestly I hope it. If you make other friends there, may they care for you as sincerely as I have done,—but *not as much!* For *that* is a thing to be "regretted" by *you,*—and would be a cause of unavailing pain to *them.* You are right in saying that all things are for the best—but *that* is only saying that it is best to suffer distress of mind sometimes. That I have suffered it lately in different ways, until my body could scarcely bear the struggle within, God knows—and that I am to suffer still and longer, God has willed.

With your letter today I had one very short one from Miss Trepsack,[1] written in a way that leaves no doubt of her being well-informed about Papa's misfortune. It speaks of Miss Clarke's coming here next Monday or Tuesday. I am sorry for *that.* She will only come to be made unhappy, and will not relieve *us* in any way. For my own part, I would rather bear it all, alone—all, that it pleases God, I should bear!

Thank Mrs. Boyd for her note. But what can she mean by saying that she does not desire more acquaintances, and would like to know as few people as possible? In that case, must not all places be alike to her? And must it not be pleasanter, considering our lovely country, to live in solitude at Malvern than at Charlton? I cannot write any more now. I would give up all the pleasure and advantage I have derived from your society, for *this*—that you had gone away three years

1. "Treppy," friend of all the Barretts and constant companion of Mr. Barrett's mother until her death in January 1831. For a warm appreciation of her see EBB—RB, 2, 200.

ago instead of now. Will you be *very* angry at my saying so? There is little reason indeed for your being angry.

Give my love to Mrs. Boyd and Annie. Arabel sent her orbits to you this morning.

Ever yours affectionately
E. B. Barrett

83.

Thursday night [May 12, 1831] [1]

My dearest friend,

Arabel has just been saying that you will certainly think me mad for writing so many letters. I write now merely to let you know of Papa having written today to Mr. Curzon. The letter has not gone; and it is possible that Mr. Curzon may not be at home tomorrow in time to send you its contents by the post. Therefore my intelligence may reach you before it—and help to keep your patience alive a little while longer.

After having sent away my letter to you Friday, I was half sorry for having done so. Have you ever observed this in me—that tho' I can restrain myself and mask myself as well as anybody else, in conversation, yet as soon as I begin to *write,*—out everything comes, foolish or otherwise, just as it enters my head? That is the effect of writing so much, and of encouraging myself in writing naturally. You will suggest another word instead of the last—and you are welcome to do so, if you will promise to forgive any word that *may* have happened to annoy you (for I don't remember what was written) in my last letter. I would not willingly annoy you *ever*—much less *now!*

Papa's spirits have been very bad for the last two days,—and nothing else has a brighter aspect—except my imagination, which has trimmed its lamp since the news about the letter to Mr. Curzon. And this news arrived so late as five o'clock. Well! I won't teaze you any more now, this being the third epoch of your sufferings today, including Arabel's parabolas.

Ever affectionately yours
E. B. Barrett

Tell Annie with my love, that she shall have her property back again. Arabel desires me to remind you about sending the verses for her album.

1. The postscript dates this letter May 12, the only Thursday during the Worcester elections (May 6–13).

Twelve o'clock

As Lane is going to Worcester tomorrow morning, to vote for the Reform Candidates, he shall leave this in his way.

84.

To Woodland Lodge
Great Malvern

Hope End. May 14, 1831

My dearest friend,

I suppose I shall have time to write a few lines to you before your post passes Chances Pitch—and I cannot help writing them tho' they must be indeed few. Eliza has brought Mr. Curzon's letter for me to see, and the news of your intending to remain another year at Malvern. How I wish that the last had come without the first! How happy I should have been then! But, as you say, even that which grieves us must be best for us! Is it absolutely necessary for you to take the house at the Wells for a year certain? Could it not be taken for a *less time,* that in the case of our going to any place which is likely to suit you, you could join us there—perhaps at the end of the summer, when Mrs. Boyd begins to be afraid of the cold for Annie? You see how very considerate and disinterested I am! It has *certainly* given me pleasure and *very* great pleasure to find that you are *not* going to that abominable Charlton or Bath,—and however unaccountable it may seem, I would certainly rather know of your being at Malvern than anywhere else, *except where we are.* How long we are to remain here seems to be uncertain indeed, but we may, you know, remain some time longer—and I am daring enough to hope for the happiness of paying you more than one visit at Ruby Cottage.

Things are bad enough certainly—but they might be worse for *me*—for instance, if you had gone to Charlton, where, in any case, I should have had scarcely one chance of ever seeing you again. As to the impossibility of your coming here, that was anticipated and must be borne. I can only say and feel that if you *had* come, it would have made me *too happy,*—and that being so is good for nobody.

There is not time to write any more. What a relief it has been to me even under our present circumstances, to hear of your change of plan, I have said once before, and feel every moment!

Give my best love to Mrs. Boyd and Annie. Why does not Annie

write? Arabel is quite offended. Will not *you* write, when you can?
May God bless you my dearest friend!

Yours ever affectionately
E. B. Barrett

Saturday evening

The postman went round the other way, so that this letter has come
back to me from Chances Pitch. Arabel desires me to say that our engraving of the orbits is divided in two, and that therefore she supposed you intended her to do only half. She wishes to know whether
Mrs. Boyd examined the ellipse of the cup very attentively,—as she
traced it from a figure in a mathematical book. She dictates—*"therefore it must be right"*—and afterwards—*"but upon my word he'll think
me dreadfully obstinate."*

I believe Miss Clarke really comes next Tuesday. I wish it were not
so! It would be better for *her,* if it were not—and by ourselves, a certain degree of pain must be felt, whatever comforters approach us. For
more reasons than one, I am very anxious to know when and where we
are going. Most probably, Papa does not know, himself, but the *place*
will not, I think, be far from London, on account of the business which
necessarily keeps him there a great part of the year. The certainty of
our leaving Hope End, tho' not of our leaving it *immediately,* is evident from Mr. Curzon's letter. Papa might not like to receive the visit
of any person out of his own family, in the present state of circumstances—even if he did not intend leaving this house for a few weeks!
And he *may* be uncertain at present whether he must move very soon
—and he *may* remain longer than he at present thinks possible. All
these mights and mays help, with other considerations, to make me
feel pleased at your going to Ruby Cottage. When do you move?

85.

To Woodland Lodge
   Great Malvern

Monday evening [1831]

My dearest friend,

Thank you for your kind letter, and the good news about your
going to Ruby Cottage on Wednesday. I decided upon telling Papa

about it today at *dinner;* because at dinner I sit with my back to the light, and some people are Lavaters.[1] "Papa, I have heard from Mr. Boyd, and he is going to Ruby Cottage." "Where?" "To Ruby Cottage—the house at the Wells, where he used to live before." "Really! How long do they mean to stay there?" "I believe, a year." "A *year!* will they stay a *year?*" "I believe so." He did not say a word more,—nor of course did I—but we all are of opinion that he seemed very much pleased when I first mentioned your having taken Ruby Cottage—and that his manner throughout was expressive of eagerness. Before I could observe anything about it aloud, as soon as we came out of the dining room, Henrietta said to me "How pleased Papa seemed to be at Mr. Boyd's going to the Wells!" And it certainly *was* the case, whatever the motive was! I think it is clear that he felt, as he ought to have felt, more gratified than otherwise by your application thro' Mr. Curzon,—and I cannot understand how Mrs. Boyd or any of you could imagine that he *disliked* the idea of living near you. As to the non-expression of his "hopes" and "regrets", if you knew him, you would argue nothing from *that.* I feel sure in my own convictions, that he himself does not up to the present moment, know with any certainty *where* we are to go—and the *when* may be equally uncertain. If I *could* hope that the uncertainty extended to the circumstance of going at all—! but I cannot venture to hope it! I suppose Miss Clarke will arrive tomorrow. You know we deal in *suppositions* just now! Treppy in her letter last week said, "I *suppose* Bell will leave London next Monday for Hope End." On Sunday a letter came from Bell to Papa, containing most probably something more than a "suppose" on the subject—but Papa is dumb. He would *not* speak even today at dinner, when Henrietta began to "wonder" whether she would come tomorrow. I wonder when we shall cease to wonder!

You may depend on my going to see you as often as I possibly can —and indeed the distance to Ruby Cottage is nothing! How long will the distance between us and Ruby Cottage, be nothing? I can't bear to think of it—so I *won't!* at least not now. If our aunt arrives before Sunday, shall I be able to go to you before Sunday? That is doubtful! but you will forgive its being so!

Three letters went from this house to you, last Thursday,—and as you received only two of them, my *apologetick* on Friday must have appeared to you positive insanity. Indeed if *compos mentis* may be translated "of a *composed* mind", I certainly was far from being compos

1. Johann Kaspar Lavater (1741–1801), writer of works on physiognomy.

mentis. Do you not mean to let Mr. Curzon know of your change of plan? Otherwise, he may imagine that you have no wish to meet him again "in the flesh"—at least not at Ruby Cottage.

With regard to my staying at your house, it is very kind in you to wish it, but I have misgivings about it, which I will tell you of when we meet.

Tuesday

Papa said this morning at breakfast—"Do you think that Bell will come before dinner?" So you see, it is certain that she will come. I am writing on the verge of post time!

Ever affectionately yours
E. B. Barrett

I send you a parody [2] on a poem *you* once parodied. It may amuse you.

86.

To Ruby Cottage
Malvern Wells

Hope End. Thursday
May 19 [1831]

My dearest friend,

You may like to hear from me now, as you will be expecting to hear that, through my aunt, we have been let into all the mysteries. What will you say when I tell you of our knowing no more on the subject than when I wrote to you last? She is, either from a promise to Papa or a judgment of her own, *hermetically sealed*—and all I can extract is—"How can you suspect *me* of having any information? Why should you make yourself uneasy my dear, till your Papa tells you himself? Why should you not trust him with doing what is best? You may depend upon his doing it. If nobody has been to look at the house, how can it be going to be sold?" and similar questions and answers which mean nothing but, "I won't be questioned",—and "I can't answer". It seems hard upon me that nothing of my childhood, except its tranquillity, should have passed away.

Minny learnt from her maid who is a degree more communicative,

2. "Lygon's Retreat or The Colonel's Political Funeral . . . A Parody on 'The Burial of Sir John Moore,' by a Madresfield freeholder."

that Brighton *has been* thought of as a place of residence,—but that *now* everything is uncertain. So, you see, I *was* right in what I said. One thing however is satisfactorily certain—*we are not going to Jamaica.* The possibility, not the probability of it, haunted me, I scarcely know why—but when I mentioned it, my aunt said at once with openness and decision, "How can you be so foolish as to let such an idea once enter your mind! Such a family as this, to be taken to Jamaica! and when there is not and cannot be a necessity for it."!

I thought of you yesterday, when you may have been moving to Ruby Cottage,—and I shall have particular pleasure in directing this letter there, tho' directing *myself* there would be a pleasure still more particular. Miss Clarke has seen the Knowles's since she saw us. She found them in a small dismal-looking house, regretting Malvern in chorus—poor Sir Charles the choryphoeus, on account of his health.

I believe there is nothing more to tell you, and I acknowledge that I have told you nothing. Then why did I write at all? As I can't get people to answer my questions, I won't answer my own. My best love to Mrs. Boyd and Annie.

Ever yours affectionately
E. B. Barrett

One o'clock

I am so happy I can hardly write. That is something quite new,—is it not? *Promise me* that you will not to *any one person,* say one word of what I am now going to tell you,—and now listen!! My aunt has not until this morning, had any conversation with Papa on THE *subject.* She has come up into my room to say, in consequence of one which has just taken place, that Papa has received a letter lately, and answered it, and that he is at present in the hope and expectation of retaining Hope End in his possession. I know you will be glad! Thank God for His great mercies! She has begged us not to change our manner before Papa,—as in the case of his suspecting her of repeating to us his communications, they would cease from that moment. So I must entreat you not to mention what I have told you. I could not help telling *you.* This is the 19th,—is it not? the day, I thought, would have been made so sorrowful by your going away. And now, how happy it is!

Thank Mrs. Boyd for her note which I have this instant received. Is not Papa's pleasure at your going to the Wells, explained now?

87.

Hope End. Monday
[May 30, 1831] [1]

I have just sent a poem of mine on the King, to the Times Newspaper,
—and if they put it in, I will send it to you in company with my
prophecy that you won't like it. But its loyalty will at any rate be
worthy of your notice,—and I never wrote anything half so historical
in all my life. I have seen Mr. Curzon, and delivered your message, before Papa. Mr. Curzon looked surprised on hearing of your "where-
abouts",—but his only remark was, "Well—I must contrive to pay
Mr. Boyd a visit, in spite of my engagements, before I go to London"
—or something to that effect. He has to attend several Bible meetings
next week, and goes to London the week after. So you will probably
see him in the course of the *present* week,—but he dines here on
Thursday.

They have been changing clergymen at Cradley. The Dean of St.
Asaph wished to nominate one, and the congregation was anxious
about another—*so* anxious, that they sent up a petition to the Dean
praying him to yield the point to them. The Dean threw down the
petition, and said *Pooh.* "Mr. Dean" observed the bearer of it—"that
is not the way in which King William treats petitions!" The Dean not
only read, but granted, what he had thrown down a moment before!!
Papa asked the teller of this story, why Mr. Davis was the popular
candidate. "Why Sir" was the answer, "ye see the other parson does
not speak well. He *draps* his voice at the end of his *sentiments.*" (sentences)

Have you heard that Mr. Knowles is elected after all—by Miss
Emma Pocock, to whom he was married [2] a few days ago? It was in
our newspaper yesterday.

We are going to send the carriage to Ledbury today,—and if it can
be mended in time, and if it does not *snow*, we shall be at Ruby Cottage tomorrow. Last night Papa talked of nobody and nothing but
you and Ruby Cottage. They are waiting for my note,—so I must drap
my pen at the end of this sentiment. I *drapped* the ink before! My

1. Dated from the poem "Kings," published in the *Times,* May 31, 1831. Reprinted,
B. McCarthy, "Another Unnoticed Poem by E. B. B.," *Notes and Queries, 196* (1951),
409–10.
2. May 26, 1831.

love to Mrs. Boyd and Annie who I hope received a letter from Hope End, tho' two days after the post for which it' was intended—but that was not *my* fault.

Yours affectionately
E. B. Barrett

88.

To Ruby Cottage
Malvern Wells

Hope End. Wednesday
June 1, 1831

My dearest friend,

Papa has read both your letters, and is of opinion that Mr. Seager [1] is quite ignorant on the subject,—and that if Mr. Spowers was ever a democrat, a more complete revolution has lately befallen him than *we* have to anticipate. He says that this is proved not only by Mr. Spowers's opposition to the bill,—tho' no democrat *could* oppose that bill,—but by the undemocratical arguments by which he opposes it. Papa exclaimed "How is it possible that any even moderately con- stitutional friend of the people and liberty, could *think it of little importance how or by whom the representatives of the people are chosen!* Why Mr. Spowers according to his own principle, would think it of little importance, if the king were to nominate them all,—and then we should be living under a despotic government."!!

Papa thinks you wrong for having said that "we have nothing to do with consequences and have only to consider whether the thing be just and right in itself." He says that we *have* to do with *both* the consequence and the justice of the measure. In our government, the king is actually represented, the aristocracy is actually represented, and the people is only virtually represented. Now is this just? or should the people too be actually represented? And if they should, is not the "cry of the people" a cry to be attended to? At any rate, *must* not the cry of the people be attended to, when all power emanates and ought to emanate from the people? I recollect many years ago when I read one whole volume of Blackstone through, I also read a little treatise by a Mr. Hawkins an *infinite* Tory, entitled "Reform in Parliament, the ruin of Parliament",[2]—and I distinctly recollect that

---

1. John Seager (1776–1849), clergyman and classical scholar.

2. Henry Hawkins, "Reform of Parliament the Ruin of Parliament," *The Pamphle- teer*, ed. A. J. Valpy, *1*, 1813.

the very argument made use of by your democratical friend Mr. Spowers, was the Tory Mr. Hawkins's leading argument. You know I know little or nothing about it—but this is a fact indicative of no liberality in Mr. Spowers,—and you ought not to find fault with anyone for finding fault with him on account of this. If he wears the enemy's colours, he must expect to be taken for an enemy.

You know I know little or nothing about it—but I do like a nation to be free,—and I do like to belong to a free nation. And if the meaning of freedom is not, that the majority of the nation, called *the people,* should have a proportionate weight and influence in the government of the nation, I confess I do not understand what freedom means.

Papa said a great deal with regard to the *consequences* of the measure,—but to tell you the truth, he spoke so very technically and deeply that I did not understand him clearly enough to be able to *report* him. He finds fault with you for expressing to Mr. Spowers, or feeling in your own mind, any fear about any "venerable institutions"; and I had to rescue you from the obloquy of being a "half and half reformer". Papa thinks that the universities may be "learned" without being "wise"—and that they have not been wise in their present decision.

Mr. Seager abuses the Times Newspaper. Is he aware that it is the very ablest and cleverest newspaper, of all the *are or ever-have-been* newspapers?

We got home in very good time yesterday,—in better time than I shall be in today, if I do not finish this letter. Did I tell you yesterday —no I did not! that Bro dined at Ledbury politically, to celebrate the victory of our Hereford reform hero Mr. Hoskins? [3] He did not come home until one,—when I, by a miracle, was asleep; but he told us this morning of his having met a select party of a hundred people, —and that your unpatriotic avaricious friends the bell-ringers would not ring, because Mr. Hoskins would not give them two guineas. Won't

3. Kedgwyn Hoskins, esq. His election, with Sir Robert Price, was the occasion for a great Reform demonstration in Hereford in which both successful candidates were "carried in procession through the principal streets of the city, greeted by the loud huzzas of the people, and cheered from the windows of the houses, which were filled with respectable spectators." *Hereford Journal,* May 11, 1831. This newspaper, on June 8, 1831, gives the date of the Ledbury dinner as "Tuesday, the 31st ult." and names "E. Barrett, jun; esq." among the members of the committee. "Many gentlemen delighted the company by their songs; and the conviviality of the evening terminated only as the clock struck twelve. . . . It is delightful to find how private virtues in this case have called forth universal approbation."

you send them a *maliso*N instead of a *benison*—that their bells may be "out of tune and harsh" in secula seculorum?

Ever affectionately yours
E. B. Barrett

When Mr. Curzon goes to see you, I hope you will take care not to repeat to him a word of my knowing or *not* knowing anything. And let me hear when Annie's time for going away, is fixed. My best love to her and Mrs. Boyd.

89.

To Ruby Cottage
Malvern Wells

Hope End. June 24, 1831

Sir,

When I announce myself as about to give you a brief account of the much abused and misrepresented race of the Thoughts, too well am I aware that my doing so might require an apology,—were I not addressing myself to *you.* Too well am I aware that upon such an announcement, some young readers might immediately begin to yawn soporifically, some old readers, to sigh dolorifically, and many would-be young and must-be old female ones, to steal a frightened glance at their mirror—with a "Dear me! I have been avoiding these people all my life! and now that they should thrust themselves upon me in this manner! How very impertinent and provoking!" But *your* nature and habits are well known to me. I cannot doubt *your* willingness to hear, and hear leniently, a Thought upon Thoughts. . . .[1]

My dearest friend,

You know you need not read this long letter from your allegorical correspondent, *thro',* if you should feel any disinclinations upon the subject. Pray *don't,* if you *do.* I shall not be in the very least degree offended by such omission,—nor, if you put it into the fire,—by such a *com*mission. As I conclude that Mrs. Boyd has returned, I will send my love to her.

Yours affectionately
E. B. Barrett

1. A long essay follows, subsequently published in the *Athenaeum* (July 23, 1836) and reprinted in *Hitherto Unpublished Poems, 2,* 157–65.

I got home yesterday *before eight,*—and Bro observed that the poney looked as "fresh" as when he went out of the stable.

90.

Hope End. Sunday evening
[July 17, 1831] [1]

Were you very angry with me for forgetting to tell Mr. Spowers about the newspaper? If you were, you have your revenge: for I was very angry with myself, and would have turned back as soon as I thought of my forgetfulness, if I had not also thought that by the time I had driven two miles, you would most probably have employed somebody else to deliver the message. It is not a usual fault in me, to forget anything you tell me.

I have both written and spoken to Eliza Cliffe about the chapel, and she and Mrs. Cliffe will go. As for ourselves, we are all going, if it should be fine externally and internally. There was no letter yesterday, and is none today—and no advertisement.[2] Now if you were a professor of Lagado, how many "sunbeams" could you extract from these "cucumbers"? [3]

I *thunderstruck* Bro and all of them with the Homer; [4] and I am thinking of raising a supply for the Greeks by making a show of it— admittance half a crown. Don't you think that I should soon have the Grecian boundaries extended and fixed,—and make Prince Leopold wish in his heart that he had taken the first crown offered to him, instead of the second? [5]

I know I did not say half I ought to have said to you yesterday,— I mean, not half I felt. I will not try to say it now. But even at the risk of appearing ungrateful, I must say one thing—that I am *sorry* you should have thought of making me so costly a present. Was it not quite uncalled for, and unnecessary? Was it likely that I should require a present of any kind from you—particularly after you had

1. Dated by mention of Wolf's *Homer* (presented Saturday, July 16).
2. Of the sale of Hope End.
3. One of the "projects" of the scientific academy in *Gulliver's Travels.*
4. *Homeri et Homeridarum Opera,* ed. F. A. Wolf, Leipzig, 1806. Sotheby lists Vol. *1* autographed by EBB "from my dear friend, Mr. Boyd, Malvern Wells, July 16, 1834 [sic]." The item sold for £1, with the purchaser unrecorded.
5. Leopold refused the crown of Greece on February 3, 1830, and was elected King of the Belgians on June 4, 1831.

made me so many? And even if it were, do you not know that if you had given me something not valuable in itself, it would have been *at least* as valuable to *me,* as Wolf's Homer,—had Wolf's Homer been given to me by some other person? Therefore you would have acted more politically and prudently if you had kept your costly presents for people, to whom your presents are not valuable *unless* they are costly.

After all these wise reflections, you must know very well how proud I am about the cause of them,—and how much I shall value it, both per *se* and pro *te.* And after all my "sorrow", I am *pleased,*—in associating the most beautiful book I ever saw, with the kindest and most valued friend I ever had.

Yours affectionately
E. B. Barrett

Give my love to Mrs. Boyd.

91.

Tuesday morning, August 23, 1831

My dearest friend,

I send Keats's poems for Miss Boyd,—and will at the same time tell you, that if Dominick goes to see you, which he certainly will do, you must not blame me. I did not say one word about you to him, on my way home yesterday,—but his first words to me were "I had intended to do myself the pleasure of calling upon Mr. Boyd today, if—" I forget what subject the "if" introduced. He is *"anxious to consult you about the Greek historians".* I took your part so far as to observe that you had not paid much attention to historical subjects: but nothing will save you—depend upon it! So I advise you to be as philosophical, if not as historical,—and certainly as *grave,* as you can!

Dr. and Mrs. Card, Mrs. and Miss Wall and Miss Wall's uncle, provided with a ticket of admission from Bentley of Worcester,[1] made a *party of pleasure* to this place yesterday. As the ticket was not a proper one, they were not allowed to go farther than the dining room, —and Bro who was a good deal excited, said to Lane in a voice, meant to be audible, that if Lane did not instantly see them out of the

1. Hope End was advertised in London and local papers on August 10, "to be sold at auction at Garraway's Coffee-House, 'change-alley, Cornhill, London on Thursday, the 25th of August 1831 at Twelve. . . . To be viewed by tickets." Mr. Bentley, Worcester, is listed among those from whom particulars may be had.

house, he himself would do so. Accordingly they went out of the house,—and had the moderation to be satisfied by walking along the walks, and looking in at the windows of the tent-room and drawing room where my aunt was sitting. I conclude that they *were* satisfied and pleased, as there was a good deal of very loud laughing and talking, —Miss Wall the coryphoeus! Not long ago I saw a letter from her to Eliza Cliffe in which she professed a strong feeling of "compassion" for "those poor girls". She is happy in her manner of illustrating it,— and of acting, at the same time, consistently with the delicacy and good feeling and womanly kindness which I ever attributed to her! Her acquaintance with us, slight as it has been, places all this in a stronger and more creditable point of view.

You know how little I care about the conduct of people for *whom* I don't care,—but still it is very painful to be exposed to such intrusions—to live as we have lived lately and have been never used to live—so *very* painful, that I should long ago have wished myself away, even from Hope End—if it were not for *you!* Well! I suppose both the pain and consolation will soon be over. I mean, this particular kind of pain—and every kind of consolation.

> Ever affectionately yours
> E. B. Barrett

Since coming to an end of this note, Bro has received one from our dear Papa, who, in addition to his other troubles, has had a violent attack of cholera.[2] He is weak and low in consequence of it—and is going out of London for two days, to regain his strength by changing the air. Oh if it had been the will of God to have taken *him* from us! What should we have done *then?* It is certainly wrong and sinful to repine, when there might be so much greater reason for sorrow: and as long as he is left to us, I should not have talked of losing every kind of consolation—*earthly* consolation, of course I meant!

May God bless you with joy as long as joy will last,—and with *all* consolation afterwards!

Papa says nothing about Hope End.

2. A serious cholera epidemic began in May, 1831. The pages of the *Times* are filled with reports of outbreaks and casualties.

92.

August 24 [1831]

My dearest friend,

Tho' you entirely "acquit Dr. Card", I am very sure that what *he* did, you are the very last person in the world to have done. Recollect the circumstances, well-known to everybody, under which Hope End is advertised,—and the other circumstance of Papa's daughters being there. Now would any *very* considerate and feeling person have taken advantage of the advertisement and joined a party of pleasure,—remember, a *mere* party of pleasure,—to go there and remind them of their distresses? Oh no! I never supposed otherwise than that the Walls were the sole movers and instigators of the measure. Everything you know "after its kind",—which is true of creeping things as well as of leviathans! It is amusing that Mrs. Cliffe should have told me only last Sunday a long story about "dear Millicent" who when her uncle asked her to ride over to Hope End on account of its being advertised, refused at once—"She would not do such a thing on any account"—and Mrs. Cliffe estimated her amiability accordingly. I wonder what the estimation will be now!

I did not understand until today that this estate is valued at £32,000, *without* the timber which is considerable,—so that altogether the sum is nearly £50,000. It is not probable—is it?—that any man would purchase to such an amount without examining his purchase,—and only one gentleman has been here with that apparent object. *He* seemed to think more of disturbing us than of examining the premises, and would look only into the lower rooms, tho' Lane asked him to go up stairs. By the way, his conduct was a contrast to that of some other people. He walked as lightly as he could that his footsteps might not be heard by us, and seemed unwilling to see even as many rooms as he did see, for fear of "disturbing or distressing Mr. Barrett's family".

I have found—ferreted out, Mr. Kidd [1] for you. Thank you for your letter. You cannot think how pleased I was to see the signature—which does not mean that I was pleased to get to the end of the letter—because I saw the signature first.

Yours affectionately
E. B. Barrett

1. Borrowed over two years before. See Letter 33 and Weaver, Letter VIII.

93.

To Ruby Cottage
Malvern Wells

Wednesday, September 6 [1] [1831]

I am going to write one line, *upon business*. I quite forgot to give you on Monday, the direction of Mr. Henry Bohn, 4 York Street, Covent Garden, London, which you may perhaps like to have, and which, if you do not have it now, will be of the less use to you. He has advertised in the Times, a catalogue,[2] just published, of very rare and valuable books, Aldine editions, etc., and states in the advertisement that he will send it gratis to any gentleman who will give his name and pay the postage. Now I meant on Monday to ask you whether I should write for you or not— and I won't mean to put off asking you, because this weather is so very rainy-looking, and *may* be very obstinate.

We had a satisfactory letter from our dear Papa yesterday. He has perfectly recovered from all the effects of his late attack, and writes in better spirits than usual,—and without making any direct reference to *the* business, or saying one word about his return. On the contrary, he speaks of intending to write to *me*. Therefore he can't be coming, and we can't be going, *immediately!* My aunt thinks decidedly that he is making some new exertion—but I will not trust myself with hoping for anything beyond a respite.

Tell Mrs. Boyd with my love, that I had intended to send her some partridges today, and that on another day, I shall be more successful. You know your pheasants cannot have the honour of being shot at, until the first of October.

Ever yours affectionately
E. B. Barrett

1. Misdated for September 7; September 6 was a Tuesday.
2. "I found Mr. Bohn's parcel directed to *E. M. Barrett, Esq.* on my return home yesterday. . . . Mr. Bohn seems to have some valuable books: but you beat his whole catalogue in the antiquity of your Gregories." Weaver, Letter V.

94.

To Ruby Cottage
Malvern Wells

Hope End. Saturday
[October 22, 1831] [1]

My dearest friend,

I got home very well, and had no trouble in being absolved from all my sins of the last few days. So, you see, I stole "the sheep" without "being hanged"! I sent away the letter with a seal large enough to be taken for the Lord Chancellor's,—and do not doubt about its striking the editor with sufficient awe and admiration, for you to have every chance of being prosecuted for libel. I have just heard from Sam, who has seen an evening paper, that Parliament is prorogued, and by the King in person, and until the 22d of November. This is quite satisfactory—is it not?—and calculated to make the anti-reformers *almost* as uncomfortable as if they were in the neighbourhood of rope and lamppost, and out of sight of the police!

Such an account as I have heard of Mr. Knowles! He is branded for ever in my opinion,—and will be in yours, when what has reached me reaches you. Can you believe that the whole weight of the Shaftesbury expenses falls upon poor Dominick,—and that it should fall entirely upon him, was the evident and only cause of Mr. Knowles' forcing him into the business? Mr. Knowles will not, or cannot, pay *his own part* of those expenses!! Dominick acknowledges that Mr. Knowles completely deceived and cheated him,—but does not wish people to know, to what extent. Well! not satisfied with being sleight of hand and slight of conscience with respect to Dominick, he went down to Poole a short time ago and offered himself as a reform candidate. When finding that the interests of the place were in the power of two anti-reformers, in order to get in, he prefixed *anti* to his old political designation, and had the assurance to write to Dominick to tell him that he had become a *moderate* reformer. The newspapers wondered what could be the politics of Mr. Knowles who stood now on one side, and now on another,— and the people of Poole had good sense enough to turn him out. But is not this even more intolerable in the eyes of Heaven and Earth, than could be dreamt of from his philosophy?

1. Dated from the proroguing of Parliament (Thursday, October 20), after the House of Lords rejected on October 8 a new reform bill passed by the Commons September 21.

I was very happy in being with you last Monday and Tuesday and Wednesday,—and the more so, as it was a happiness which my Fancy had half resigned for ever! There has been no letter from Papa since I left home. It is supposed here, that the next will be final! Whatever it may be, and whatever may be its consequences, neither it nor they nor any other thing can make me less than I have been and am,

Your attached friend
E. B. Barrett

I forgot to ask you to speak to Miss Boyd about my Battle of Marathon. If she is kind enough to think it worth her acceptance, I certainly will not receive it back again.

Do my dear Mrs. Boyd let me hear everything about everybody, and when I may hope to see you. As the boy is going I can't write a word more. Have you *heard?*

Yours affectionately
E. B. B.

95.

Hope End. Tuesday
November 15 [1831]

As you have such a regard for the bishops, you will be glad to hear that Mr. Martin has written a letter [1] to the Bishop of Hereford, severe enough, and containing a *charge* about the state of the surrounding parishes with regard to clergymen. A copy is sent to the Times—therefore don't forget to have his signature ferreted for! No anonymousness! no initials! but *James Martin* at full length. He will have the whole church militant in this part of the world upon him, Mrs. Cliffe as well as his correspondent,—and will be more unpopular than even *you* were, in your imaginary zenith. You know I have not seen the letter—only heard of it. The spirit of it is likely to be far from the right spirit, and rather *magistraterial* than theologian—and yet I am sure you will be more glad than otherwise at its having been written. So much for the mint sauce! You are exactly in Mr. Tone's humour just now,—who used to bless everybody generally, and—do the contrary—to the bishops particularly!

1. The *Times*, November 17, 1831. A vigorous protest against the Bishop's assigning of parishes to "pluralists" with no intention of residing in the community. The rector of Colwall, recently deceased, had not visited his parish in over twenty years. For Martin see above, Letter 66, n. 6.

I got home very well yesterday, in spite of the wind which blew my bonnet into an hexagonal shape—is not that the word? Occyta ² ran down stairs with a face much brighter than the daylight was *then,* and gave me such a flattering reception that I forgot all about you for three or four minutes. Afterwards he sate on my knee until *one* of us was tired,—my gratitude won't let me say which,—and began to tell me all about my squirrel running away, and how he could not stand at my door all day as its guard, because Minny *would* make him do his lessons. In short he is the dearest thing of the kind that ever was or will be.

No letter from Papa by today's post! I hear that he has been written to about his sheep and cows which have hitherto remained in the park and are now to be turned out. He must send some answer—and *what* answer? Well! there is no use in thinking of it.

A better account of the cholera than of the reform bill in today's paper. Suppose it should be thrown out again! Would not the Marquis of Londonderry ³ have reason to rejoice if he were only thrown *at,* as a consequence? If such a catastrophe were to occur, nolo episcopari would be more sincerely said than it ever was before. But surely Ministers cannot be quite so lineally descended from the saviours of the capitol, as for us to be justified in *supposing* any such thing. I have been reading an article in the Quarterly Review this morning *about* the administration, where of course bill the second, is prophetically considered as dead and buried, and Lord Grey turned out. Nothing beats the insolence of the writer except his own folly! All the excitement of the people attributed not to the rejection of the reform bill by the Lords, but to the stirring up, with a long pole, of those *"beastises"* vulgarly called the people, by the king's government! If nothing had been said about a second reform bill we should have been perfectly quiet by this time,—and now we are only waiting for its rejection, in order to become so. Therefore you see you may keep up your spirits!

Did you know that Dr. Whately ⁴ is the new Archbishop of Dublin? *I* did not until this morning, and am most particularly particularly sorry for it, as I am sure you will be. You will recollect that he wrote against evangelical religion, and clenched his arguments by translating Plutarch's treatise on superstition,—implying of course that Plutarch knew

2. Octavius, the youngest of the Barretts, was six in 1831.

3. Charles William Stewart, third Marquis of Londonderry (1778–1854), uncompromising opponent of Reform. In October he was twice attacked by "immense and riotous mobs"; the second time he was stoned by the crowd and knocked from his horse.

4. Richard Whately (1787–1863), one of the so-called "noetics" or intellectuals.

more about Christianity than he did!! And yet this man is now the Archbishop of Dublin! And he means too to be an active archbishop; and has told his friend Dr. Willis (Mrs. Martin's brother in law) that whatever may be the Archbishop of Canterbury's intentions, *he* will instantly commence a reform of the church in Ireland! What kind of reform will it be? An ejection of evangelical preachers,—and persecution of dissenting ministers?

I have written more than I quite intended,—*not* that I intend now to make you answer what you may be disinclined to answer—so don't think of *that!* I miss the squirrel and you very much indeed; but I am modest enough to believe in the possibility of its being better for both of you that I should.

May God bless you my dearest friend—

Ever yours affectionately
E. B. Barrett

96.

To Ruby Cottage
Malvern Wells

Hope End. December 1, 1831

My dearest friend,

I think I had better tell you about the t's and s's, without waiting for the *opportunity* of forgetting them again. You know my Isocrates is a bad edition. In it, there is sometimes a double tau and sometimes a double sigma quite ad libitum. . . .[1]

I have found that passage in the Apologetick, which I hunted for in vain yesterday,[2]—at least I think I have found it. You will be able to decide whether it is the right one or not, when I see you next. *To d'eu nikato.*[3] I hope the seeing next, may be seeing soon. No letter today, and no Papa!—and we thought that one of them was certain to arrive! But I dare say you will excuse my sending you all the groans of Testy and Sensitive; and will prefer a very good and true story about the unknown

1. The omitted passage reports on spelling in texts of Isocrates and Xenophon.
2. Boyd was working on translations of Gregory in 1831–32, and EBB on her visits read passages aloud to him. Sometimes these passages are marked in the margin of the Wellesley folio as "read with Mr. Boyd at Ruby Cottage" or "at Malvern Wells," with the date or sometimes only the month given. Specific dates recorded are, in 1831: September 19, November 12, November 13, November 22; in 1832: January 13, January 19, April 30.
3. "Let the good prevail." Refrain from Aeschylus, *Agamemnon.*

tongues.[4] Now listen. Archdeacon Probin [5] or Probbin (I am not sure of the spelling) is the father of those inspired twins, respecting whom, you will recollect, Papa wrote to me. The Archdeacon has been lately in some little difficulty as to his temporal affairs,—and in the midst of it, up came the two children. "Papa!—never mind about your business—don't think about it! The Spirit says that the world is coming to an end." Therefore the archdeacon, being a believer in inspiration, didn't mind about his business—didn't think about his business—and—lost his estate!! As soon as he had heard of the loss, up came the children again —"Papa! we have made a mistake. The Spirit says that the world is *not* coming to an end"! If I had been the archdeacon, I would have requested them to deliver their future prophecies in the unknown tongue. Would not *you?*

Ever yours affectionately
E. B. Barrett

Best love to Mrs. Boyd and Annie.

97.

To Ruby Cottage
Malvern Wells

Hope End. Saturday [1831]

I am going to tell you what you wished to hear about the reform bill and the unknown tongues; at least all that Papa has told me about either of them. He thinks that the King and his ministers are certainly honest men,—that the next bill [1] will be equally efficient with the last—that it will pass—and that, in the improbable case of its being rejected,

4. In October, 1831, Edward Irving's eloquent apocalyptic sermons inspired members of the congregation of his new Regent Square church to speak out in "unknown tongues." The phenomenon spread quickly, and stirred outraged protests. Many of the Barretts' friends were among Irving's followers. "Did I ever tell you how many of Irving's disciples are friends of mine—even relatives—cousins? Oh I assure you I have apostles prophets and angels belonging to me! But they are not strict in the manner you describe. At least I know that one mature angel, above forty—and I mention the age that you should not attribute the act to any heterodox flightiness of youth—that one real mature angel borrowed Pickwick from this very house, not long ago, 'for the purpose of relaxation.' Books such as angels read—should you have said so of Pickwick before you heard my story?" EBB to Miss Mitford; unpublished letter: Wellesley College Library.

5. John Probyn (1796–1843), Archdeacon of Llandaff.

1. Introduced December 12 by Lord John Russell.

a revolution must ensue. The bishop of Bath and Wells [2] has come over to the right side of the question,—and Lord Harrowby [3] is coming. Mr. O'Connell [4] and Mr. Hunt [5] have shown no principle, on this, as on other subjects,—and Lord London-don-don-derry (as Occyta calls him) is mad. The bishops, as a body, are supposed to be less mad than they were,—and the *compos mentis may* be proved by their next vote. Altogether, Papa's view of politics, walks on the sunshiny side of the street. I advise yours to cross over.

Now with regard to the unknown tongues—Four thousand persons are assembled every Sunday at Mr. Irving's chapel,—two thousand sitting, and two thousand standing; and after his fervent extempore prayer, he folds his arms in his black gown, and exclaims in his majestic manner, and deep solemn voice, "I wait, until it please the Holy Ghost to speak unto us by the mouth of his servants". Then comes the unknown tongue: the most terrific sound, Papa says, that he ever heard or expects to hear. "Believe it, or do not believe it—you must be awed by it." He was present at the first exhibition [6]—women shrieked and fainted, and there was a general rush towards the doors. Papa jumped upon a bench, and shouted to everyone who would hear him, that the danger of the pressure in rushing out, was greater than any danger they could meet with in remaining; and while he spoke, he thought that there was real danger— he mistook the voice of the exhibitor for the roar of flames. You may

2. George Henry Law (1761–1845), Bishop of Bath and Wells 1824–45, who had voted against the recent reform bill. Early in December he addressed to his clergy "A pastoral letter on the present aspect of the times," on which the *Times* (December 8) commented that "we should have supposed, from his sentiments on Reform that he had given [the Bill] his support."

3. Dudley Ryder, first Earl of Harrowby (1762–1847), who favored the principle of reform but had voted against the recent Bill. On December 8 the *Times* expressed a belief that "the noble Earl has not misspent the opportunity afforded him since the late prorogation for ascertaining the prevalent voice and feelings of the nation, on whose interests he is a second time about to decide."

4. Daniel O'Connell (1775–1847), Irish member of Parliament, favored "repeal of the union," and supported parliamentary reform only as a necessary preliminary to repeal. He is as controversial a figure in EBB's letters as elsewhere: she and her father distrusted and disliked him, while he was a hero to her brother Stormie, to the Martins, and to Miss Mitford.

5. Henry Hunt (1773–1835), radical politician, advocated universal suffrage. He felt the people had been deluded by the press into clamoring for a bill which offered far too little reform.

6. An account in the *Times* of October 19 corroborates Mr. Barrett's description: the whole congregation rose from their seats in affright, people screamed, rushed to the door, stood on benches, some supposing that a murder had been committed. An editorial on October 26 names Miss Carsdale as one of the "exhibitors."

imagine what a voice it was. All London was and is, in a state of excitement. Everybody acquits Mr. Irving of being intentionally deceptive,—and some people acquit the exhibitors—but there is not so much unanimity in the latter decision. Mr. Nisbet the bookseller, an intelligent and pious man and one who *used* to be a thick and thin follower of Irving, said to Papa—"I would not be too confident in *them*. I call Miss Emma Carsdale *a light character*." Papa recollecting that Mr. Nisbet was a starch stiff presbyterian, and that "a light character" with him might be a heavy character with anybody else, begged for an explanation. Mr. Nisbet told him that Miss Emma and another inspirée, had been heard talking and laughing very loud just before service, and arranging how they would disobey their husbands, whenever they happened to marry, by speaking in the unknown tongue, whether the aforesaid husbands liked it or not. Miss Emma is not however, on all occasions, so self-willed. She dined at Albury's, Mr. Drummond's,[7] in company with Mr. MacNeil,[8]—who is not a believer in spite of all that I told you,—and several of the faithful. On a sudden, symptoms of the tongues came on, Pythian contortions and agitations of her body, which always precede an oracle. But Mr. MacNeil would not stand this. He fixed his eyes upon hers, exclaiming in the most imperious tone "I command you to be silent. Speak if you dare." The young lady was quiet in a moment.

Papa heard "a very fine sermon" from him, on the subject of the tongues. Mr. Irving was alluded to in it, in an affecting manner—as "one whom he loved with the love of a brother". Did you ever hear, or are you hearing now for the first time, that Mrs. Irving dreams dreams, and sees visions? Visions are all the fashion in Mr. Irving's chapel,—where one man has seen a "handwriting on the wall", and another, the "ghost of a skull". I have not read Wesley's treatise, because I talked to Papa, or rather heard him talk, the whole of yesterday. He is looking quite well—a little thin, *I* fancy—but everybody else calls that, fancy indeed. It is clear enough that nothing has been done. Nothing has been said to me—except an inference of Miss Clarke's, about the non-probability of our moving immediately. Of our moving sooner or later, there can be no doubt whatever. Papa enquired after you, even before he enquired after Mr. Curzon,—and indeed made a great many minute

7. Henry Drummond (1786–1860), one of the founders of the Irvingite church; his home at Albury, Surrey, was for many years the center of conferences on the unfulfilled scriptures.

8. Hugh McNeile (1795–1879), rector at Albury 1822–34; he at first followed Irving but very soon rejected his doctrines and criticized them in three sermons on "Miracles," 1831–32.

interrogations about you. He wore a thick mask of high spirits yesterday. He must feel bitterly—and when I think *only* of him,—and I certainly *ought* to do so always,—I cannot wish his time of trial here to be much prolonged.

Is Mrs. Boyd's headache gone? I hope so. Give my love to her and Annie—and tell yourself that whenever I write a long letter or any kind of letter to you, I don't mean to saddle you with the *necessity* of answering it. Whenever I take it into my wise head, that you write to me because you can't help yourself—then all my pleasure in reading what you write, comes to an end. This scribble must come to an end at any rate. In a great hurry,

Ever yours affectionately
E. B. B.

Think of my forgetting to tell you, that Papa certainly does *not* believe in the tongues.

98.

To Ruby Cottage
Malvern Wells

Hope End. Saturday night
[January 14, 1832]

I send you a list of those letters of Gregory which you have marked. . . .[1]

I admire every letter which you have marked,—and I hope you will return my compliment. I have done as you desired, as well as I could,—but your ferret was in a hurry today—and (to vary the metaphor) my sieve has holes in it, and has let through several letters, I dare say, which don't deserve to lie among the chaff. But the enumeration of those with your mark attached to them, is certainly accurate—and *that* is the point of consequence.

I had a letter from our dear dear Papa yesterday, beginning "My beloved Ba, cum multis aliis"—written as if he were *determined* to be in good spirits. He says that he has "tasted so much happiness" with us lately, that it is but fair for him to feel a little of its contrary now. We are to hear tomorrow on what day he returns. Now if he does not return on Tuesday, I think I will not go to you on Monday when Henrietta

1. EBB lists with occasional comment fifteen letters all marked with asterisks in the Gregory folio, and adds nine more which Boyd had "undeservedly" overlooked.

may want the poney, but on another day when I can have it without inconveniencing anybody. Therefore don't expect me. You can't think how much I was pleased by your seeming to wish me to go to see you again before Papa's return.

Did I tell you, or not,—for your cholera panic interrupted me,—that I had sent the verses [2] I spoke of, to the Times? They were in today's paper,—with a motto from Lucretius, which I assure you was enough in itself to give anybody an attack of the *real Asiatic*.[3] Don't be afraid,—the paper is not going your way!

I had intended to answer Mrs. Boyd's and Annie's *very* kind letters,—but you and Papa have taken to yourselves all my time today. Good-bye must be said now,—as it is nearly twelve—so good-bye, my dearest friend!

Yours affectionately
E. B. Barrett

99.

To Ruby Cottage
Malvern Wells

Hope End. Thursday [1832]

My dearest friend,

Altho' I have begun to write upon this *hala polleen*,[1] I am not going to write a long letter which would exact (or seem to do so) a long reading, and take you away from Gregory. Either a long or a short letter, however, I must write to you today—and that is the *long and the short* of it. If you were as cold as I was yesterday on our way home, you would take away the towel and the coat and even the screen, and enter upon a *holy* alliance with the fire, as you know, my shoes do sometimes. We met the Miss Berringtons,—and one of them told me that she had heard of your being "metal most attractive" [2] and wondered why she had never seen you. "Does he never walk out? I have seen *Miss* Boyd, but I never saw *him*." Now your principle of general benevolence will certainly make you "lift up" or "elevate" that green curtain of yours,

2. "The Pestilence (nec requies erat ulla mali—Lucretius)," a poem of twelve stanzas signed EBB, published Friday, January 13, 1832. Printed from a MS copy (without the Lucretius motto), *Hitherto Unpublished Poems, 2,* 176–8.

3. Most violent form of cholera.

1. "vast sea."

2. *Hamlet,* III.2.118.

and come more in front of the stage, and gratify people who are moderately curious.

I have been thinking that when you have finished your translation, there could be no harm in *trying* whether Mr. Nisbet would or would not buy the copyright. . . .[3] I protest against the Methodists' Magazine,[4] again and again and again and again,—and never shall be consoled if you are obstinate about it. . . .

I hope there is not a very great deal of harm in my envying Miss Mushet for her occupation,—because if there is, I have "sinned damnably", as a clergyman told Papa, *he* had done, in holding an opinion favourable to Catholic emancipation. I don't mean to imply—"equal the fault"! I can't help mine,—nor could I help being very very sorry indeed at going away from Ruby Cottage yesterday. It seems to me likely enough that by force of feeling so much pain of different kinds, my nature will become more capable of feeling it acutely than of feeling pleasure acutely. But perhaps it may seem otherwise to me, when I see you again! There was a letter today from Papa to Bro who would not read the whole to us,—and the part which he did read, mentioned his return as remaining an uncertainty,—and not a word of business! Best love to Mrs. Boyd and Annie—and my regards to Miss Mushet. May God bless you my dearest friend! Can I ever cease to be

Your affectionate
E. B. Barrett

Mr. Curzon has not come yet. I don't think I ever told you Mr. Martin's high compliment to the Commelines. But I can't now—for Bro is waiting!

100.

Friday night [January 1832] [1]

My dearest friend,

I have been reading thro' your oration again,—and something has come into my head about that *chronicon* business which puzzled me so

3. This and the following omitted passage offer advice on the publishing of his translation, suggesting pamphlet form.

4. Boyd's translations were published, despite these protests, in the *Wesleyan-Methodist Magazine*, December 1832, May 1833. See Letter 125.

1. Dated from the "chronicon" passage in Gregory (*Oration* 38.13). In the margin of the Gregory folio EBB recorded, "Read the two preceding columns with Mr. Boyd, Thursday, January 19, 1832."

much the other day. . . .² the general idea seems to me tolerably obvious. Yet it may be *"but* seeming", like many things of more consequence to me—and in that case you will set me right some time before I have lived all the days of man,—and I will kiss the rod as in allegiance bound to do. Mind! not your walking club!

Mr. Curzon very kindly walked here yesterday at three o'clock, and back again in the dark at ten. He told me to tell you that his long absence had much increased his business and engagements here,—otherwise he would have gone to see you immediately. He intends to do so as soon as time will let him. I wish you could have heard him talk about Miss Gibbons whom he "admires more than ever", and acquits of even *believing* in the tongues.

Now I am going to tell you Mr. Martin's compliment to the Commelines,—but first of all, I must tell you something about *them.* Some of them are very amusing sensible sharp-minded people,—and as they don't spare their pricks in making remarks on their neighbours, they are considered not altogether as good-natured as they might be. A short time ago, at a very large and formal dinner-party at Eastnor Castle, Mr. Martin said, "I can't help liking those Commelines, tho' I know I shall be damned for it." The compliment was of course repeated to Miss Commeline who told Bro that her family considered it the very highest they could under any circumstances receive.

Well! I suppose I must not waste your time any more—or I "shall be d———d for it." If you had Mr. Martin's good habit, I am sure I should!

Yours affectionately
E. B. Barrett

101.

To Ruby Cottage
Malvern Wells

Hope End. Saturday night [1832]

I was very glad to find that black swan, a letter from *you,* ready to meet me here, tho' I had learnt the table of contents at Ruby Cottage. I believe I did not thank you for asking me again to your house, when I said that I could not go. If I did not thank you then, I must do so now instead.

2. The omitted passage proposes an exegesis of the Greek text.

You desired me some time ago to look at Chrysostom's commentary on the latter part of the chapter of Romans. I did not forget to look at it, but I have had no opportunity since of telling you what I saw. Chrysostom as far as I can understand him, seems to be perfectly orthodox, in his exposition of the texts in question.

Papa says that Mr. Irving did lately in his presence, address the whole of his congregation of four thousand, in this manner—"You are saved! I do not say that you are in a salvable state, but that you are saved." In a few minutes afterwards, he exclaimed with all the inconsistency which must always characterize error—"Repent, and turn unto the Lord, or you will be damned."! "Follow the leader" is a hard game to play at, with Mr. Irving,—and I think and hope Mr. Bulteel [1] will be tired, before it is half over. Do you recollect the little Calvinistic book which Mr. Curzon lent to you and to me? He sent that very book to Mr. Bulteel, as a book he was likely to be particularly pleased with.

I do not object to the *rhyme,* in your epigram.

May God bless you!
Ever yours affectionately
E. B. Barrett

102.

To Ruby Cottage
Malvern Wells

Hope End. Saturday night [1832]

My dear Mr. Boyd,

I am going to ask only one question. While I was with you this morning, Papa was taking a great fancy to my translation,[1]—and this evening he wishes me to write to Mr. Barker to enquire from him whether his friend Mr. Valpy will publish it in a future number of the *Classical library,*—where, consistently with the plan of the work, a translation of Aeschylus will of course appear. I want to know what you think about it. I do not ask *you* to write to me, but Mrs. Boyd or Annie

1. Henry Bellenden Bulteel (1800–66), theologian converted to Irving's ideas in 1832.

1. *Prometheus,* published by A. J. Valpy, London, 1833. In a letter from Sidmouth to Mrs. Martin December 14, 1832 (Kenyon, *1,* 16) EBB speaks of having completed the preface and notes. But it would seem from this letter that the translation was made at Hope End. It was, she wrote Horne in 1843, "written in twelve days, and should have been thrown into the fire afterwards,—the only means of giving it a little warmth." Horne, *1, 162.*

might be so kind as to write down some short message from you. I forgot to tell you one thing today. Papa, who knows Mr. Nisbet and the character of his publications, thinks that he won't do for your publisher.

Yours affectionately
E. B. Barrett

Of course I will not write until I hear your advice.

103.

To Ruby Cottage
Malvern Wells

Saturday night [April 1832]

I like your blank verse translation very much indeed,—but after all, I am quite obstinate in thinking that what is lyrical in Greek should be lyrical in English—and that in losing the sudden transition from one measure to another, you lose a great deal of what is animated expressive and beautiful. That is my creed,—and one not founded, I do assure you, upon any prejudice in favour of my own translation which I have sent to the tomb of the Capulets, and without a *resurgam* by way of epitaph.

I was pleased to receive your letter,—as, you know, I am apt to be on such occasions. What made you expect to hear from me this week? Your letter is dated Thursday, and I was with you on Tuesday,—and you did not ask me to write immediately. The other thing which you did ask me to do, I have done. I leave Arabel to speak for herself. Both you and I appear to *me* to have acted wrong, or at least with what the Westminster Review elegantly terms, *unwisdom*. When *you* mean to repent I don't know,—but *I* began to do so last Tuesday.

Yes! I liked the article [1] in the Times which you like,—at least if you mean the one in which poor Lord Grey is looked upon with a prophetic eye as an "archangel ruined".[2] Papa thought it was extravagant,—but I thought nothing of the kind. After all the bill will pass—

Whigs or no Whigs, their votes will turn to *Grey*—

1. On Tuesday, April 3, 1832, the *Times*, in its leading article, predicted the "downfall of Lord Grey" if the Reform Bill should fail to pass because of failure to create new Peers: "Surely none less than Milton could present to us, in its entire amplitude, that awful ruin which awaits the destroyer of the temple his own hands had raised, and his own lips had consecrated."

2. Milton, *Paradise Lost*, Bk. *1*, line 593.

See if it will not be so. If it will not, I would as soon be in the cholera hospital as in Downing Street. The king will make new peers, or the people will unmake old ones—and either way, our end will be answered.

I am in hopes that our affairs must come to a crisis before very long. My aunt's going away to Kinnersley in such a very sudden manner, without giving herself time even to write and tell them of her intention,—and her deciding upon returning in four days, prove to me that something is impending. She said to me with tears in her eyes, that nothing should induce her to remain a day longer away from us,—and that if I would consent to go with her, she would remain away only two days. But *that,* I could not and would not do. I dread one thing—the probability of Papa going to London again—and when the cholera is there. And yet there may be no cause for this dread. If he goes, it may not be to London,—and he may not go alone. My aunt left us, out of spirits and unwilling to leave us, even for so short a time. She had *intended* to spend some *weeks* with her brother,—and there certainly must be a reason for this sudden movement of hers.

The poney's feet are not very well, and I have been warned not to make any use of him for a week,—which week will not be at an end until Wednesday. The Miss Mushets will be disappointed in hearing Mr. Curzon tomorrow,—but Mr. Preace is to be the substitute, and is reported "a good preacher". I did not receive your letter until today—!

Ever yours affectionately
E. B. Barrett

104.

Hope End. Monday [1832]

I believe I ought to have written to you before to thank you for lending Synesius to me,—but I thought I should have seen you long before now, and did not think that you would expect to hear from me. The rain prevented Mrs. Cliffe from taking me with her to Malvern this morning. Tomorrow she is engaged at home,—but on Wednesday she has promised to call for me. In the meantime I will write.

I have gone thro' the whole of Synesius,—and notwithstanding his occasional diffuseness and self-repetition,—which seem to be haunting faults among writers of the first centuries,—he does *make you feel* that he is a poet. Your Gregory is not as despotic: *he* will *let* you *think* so of him,—but he does not *make* you *feel* it. Synesius is certainly a better poet and Platonist than a Christian,—and deserves the warning prologue of Franciscus Portus. But I can't write any more about him or anybody else. Only, for fear of forgetting to mention it to you when I see you again, I will observe here, that the finest part of the 9th hymn [1] is a mere paraphrase of the fine passage [2] in Gregory's oration on the nativity, which relates to the gifts of the magi. You will recollect what I mean— and Synesius's verses form so beautiful and striking an illustration of it, that I think you should, either in your preface or in a note, refer to them.

I was planning to send a messenger over to you with the reform news, if I had not seen Miss Henrietta Mushet—and it appeared from her account that you knew it before I did. They will be obliged to make peers after all.

I hear nothing which I can tell you—and feel nothing pleasant which I can tell you—therefore it is surely better that I should come to an end.

Ever yours affectionately
E. B. Barrett

105.

Hope End. Thursday [1832]

My dearest friend,

After all we have found it impossible to do as we intended and wished, about going to Malvern today or tomorrow. The Wyche [1] is a steep fatiguing road, and the poney is considered not quite well enough to attempt it. Therefore it must be given up—and we must send our kind love to Annie and our kind remembrances to the Miss Mushets—instead of ourselves. I hope and think that dear Annie will have a pleasant visit—but not *too* pleasant.

These are the lines from Anacreon,

Makarizomen se tettix,
Hote dendreoon ep' akroon

1. Translated by EBB in *Greek Christian Poets,* with the comment that it has a "thought in it from Gregory's prose, which belongs to Synesius by right of conquest." *Works,* p. 611.

2. *Oration* 38.613. In a marginal comment in the Gregory folio EBB quotes from the Synesius hymn, with cross-reference to a similar passage in the oration against Julian.

1. Or Wytche, "a deep artificial cut made through the solid rock," until 1836 "traversed by a narrow road inaccessible to carriages." *Visitors' Guide to Malvern.*

Oligeen droson pepookoos,
Basileus hopoos, aeideis—[2]

And there is a lightness and delicacy in them, which Synesius does not preserve in his copy. When I was turning over Anacreon's leaves, I came to that pretty ingenious ode, beginning

Ee Tantalou pot' estee.[3]

Did I ever observe to you, or did you ever observe to me, that it is a dilation of Romeo's idea, "Would that I were a glove upon that hand."? [4]

I have looked over the first Pythian again. The finest passage in it, is *longer* than Synesius's ninth hymn.

I gave your message to Arabel almost immediately,—and of course she thinks you more "impudent" than ever.

Ever yours affectionately
E. B. Barrett

It seems to me that I have said nothing to you today—My love to Mrs. Boyd.

106.

Saturday night [1832]

If I do not write tonight, I may have no means of sending a letter on Monday, and you may not hear about the preface until you hear *me*—which may be on Tuesday or Wednesday. This is a list of *may bes,* and now I come to the *must bes.* I am very glad to receive your letter, and to understand from it that you forgive Scholefield [1] and me for our impertinence in reminding you of your birthday. If you had been a woman, we would not have done such a thing for the world,—but you know you are not as bad as *that!!* and indeed notwithstanding your dislike to birthdays, you must excuse my saying that I hope you will see a great many of them.

2. "We deem thee blessed, O cricket, when on the tree tops, having drunk a little dew, like a king, thou singest." *Anacreontic* 32. Imitated (at length) in Synesius' First Hymn.

3. "The daughter of Tantalus once stood." *Anacreontic* 22. The poem contains the lines "Would I might be a robe that you might always wear me!" and "Would I might become a sandal—only tread upon me with your feet!"

4. *Romeo and Juliet,* II.2.24.

1. *Aeschylus,* ed. J. Scholefield, Cambridge, 1830.

I have gone thro' Wolf's prefaces [2] with your object in view. Another time, instead of beginning at the beginning of any business, I will try how beginning at the end answers: for just at, or just before, the very last page of the very last preface, there is the remark about brackets. He says that in this business of including passages supposed spurious, within brackets, he has followed in every particular the judgment of the ancients,—and has affixed the *atrocem notam* (quite the right expression) to no verse which has not been remarked upon, or entirely rejected by the best Greek critics.

In page 60 there is a little, but nothing that you would consider valuable, about the hiatus; and an acknowledgement of the authority of the digamma—as "a doctissimis Britannis repertum".

If I were you, I would not mind this general reference to the judgment of the ancients, by Wolf. Aristarchus was an ancient. The system of mutilating Homer, whether it was introduced by ancients or moderns, is quite monstrous,—and cries out, like a naughty child, for a little of your flogging. When Coriolanus said that he "would rather be a dog and bay the moon",[3] he did not mean Homer's moon.

I will take the extracts to you, and you may read them whenever you like,—but I must say over again that *I* should like you not to do it, until you have quite done with every line of your own work.

Ever yours affectionately
E. B. Barrett

When I had Payne Knight here, I took the trouble of counting the number of lines he has thought proper to leave out of *his* Homer. If I made no mistake, about 2500 lines are left out of his Iliad, and 1926, out of his Odyssey. Is not this *atrox*?

107.

Hope End. Saturday evening [1832]
My dear Mr. Boyd,

. . .[1] I have not any complete edition of either Hesiod or Theocritus; and would not write to you by today's post, that I might have time to borrow them. Mr. Deane however, to whom I sent, is without either.

2. F. A. Wolf, *Prolegomena ad Homerum* (1795), the famous work on the "Homeric question" which argued that the *Iliad* was compiled from separate short poems.

3. Brutus in *Julius Caesar*, IV.3.27.

1. In the omitted passage EBB lists instances of hiatus in the texts of Theocritus and Hesiod.

Dalzel gives very copious extracts,—and these I have examined,—but I cannot find in them, ανηρ in the right position. I will try to procure the book somewhere else,—and if I succeed, you shall hear again from me.

Yours affectionately
E. B. B.

108.

To Ruby Cottage
   Malvern Wells

Hope End. Wednesday
[April 1832]

I enclose a note directed to you. It was in the parcel containing Dr. Clarke's commentary,—and as you never opened the parcel last year, you did not, of course, find the note. I forgot to give it to you until now— a forgetfulness you will readily forgive, as by this time it is likely to contain as little news as this letter of mine.

Do not be angry with me. I have not asked Papa. I have thought about it, and spoken about it, and Henrietta and Arabel think with me that it would be quite a vain attempt. Suppose Papa were to be displeased at my teazing him so much on the same subject. In that case, it might be *worse* than vain. He was not pleased on Monday at my having left home on such a day, and told me that I would certainly kill myself—and *then* I might be satisfied. That was not a good time to ask the question— was it?—and indeed there seems to be little chance of a good time coming. I would not mind running the risk of being scolded,—but the risk of being prevented from passing some hours with you very soon again, I do not like to run. The poney's feet are a great deal better,— and I hope you will make up your mind about the additional Greek lines, that we may begin as soon as ever I get into your room—when the air of your head is most rarified. I shall like to be able to say, "Mr. Boyd can repeat eight thousand Greek lines" [1]!!

There is another thing which I should like to be able to say—how much your seeming to wish me to spend two or three days at Ruby Cottage, gratified me—It gave me as much pleasure as any thing could give me *now*, or is likely to give me,—and for this I ought to thank you,

---

1. Over three years before, Boyd had sent EBB "the numerals of his memory." See Weaver, Letter VIII. A document in EBB's hand, dated May 1, 1832, gives a new accounting: acting obviously as amanuensis for Boyd, she lists "Number of Lines Which I Can Repeat"—a total of 8000, 3280 of Greek prose and 4720 of Greek verse.

and do thank you. May God bless you. It is not injurious to everybody *to be happy!* To *me,* it must be so,—or my spirits would not have been permitted to be so broken down and rooted up on every side.

Your ever affectionate friend
E. B. Barrett

My love to Mrs. Boyd.

109.

To Ruby Cottage
Malvern Wells

Hope End. Monday [1832]

My dear Mr. Boyd,

I need not tell you how much I have wished and wish to go to you today, and to do everything you require. I told Papa last night of my wish and yours, and begged him and argued with him as long as I had any chance of being heard. It was all in vain! He said—I will tell you exactly, that you may not be *more* angry than you are sure to be at any rate,— that he would willingly oblige you, but that he could not be a party to anything likely to fatigue me in any way just now—that I was turning into a shadow, thinner and thinner every day, and that he knew perfectly well what would be the end of it—meaning, I suppose, the end of *me.* I assured him of the fact of my doing much less with you than by myself,—and of there being no mental exertion necessary on my part to write what you dictated. But he was sure of my being fatigued, in the case of my going to you—and as to my fatiguing myself at home, I might commit suicide if I pleased, but he would not be party to it, by consenting to your proposal. I am disappointed—far far more disappointed than *you* are—for I dare say Miss H. Mushet's eyes will soon be better,—and then you will have a more agreeable and satisfactory secretary, tho' not a more willing and anxious one than I could be. You know how much pleasure it gives me to write to your dictation,— to write even a letter—besides the pleasure of doing what you wish. Perhaps Papa *may* relent—but he seems to be in a panic about me all at once, because he thinks or fancies that I am looking thinner and worse than usual. If I am, it is not wonderful,—and certainly not attributable to mental exertion.

Whenever I can go to you, I am ready to write all the time I stay,—if you will let me—and a good deal can be done you know, in five hours.

Yours affectionately
E. B. Barrett

110.

[*To* Mrs. Boyd
  Ruby Cottage
    Malvern Wells]

Hope End. Tuesday [1832]

The rain today, my dear Mrs. Boyd, must bear the blame of my not appearing at Malvern,—and my intention yesterday of appearing there today, must bear the blame of my not sending the letter which was actually written and directed to you.

What can Annie mean in her note to Arabel on Sunday,—and what could she mean by saying what you report of her conversation with you on Friday? What have I done or said, or not done or said, that my affection for her should be considered "lost in what I feel for Eliza Cliffe"? Can she mention any coolness of manner or un-affectionate expression which fell from me when she was here? If she can,—entreat her to do so, —that I may explain what can require only explaining. But I know she cannot—she will not try to do it—it is impossible! Was it not necessary for me to sit near Eliza when she was painting, and when so few days might remain on which she would be able to do so? Am I no longer to call her "an affectionate girl", because Annie has interlined those words? Am I to be ungrateful and insensible to all the attention and kindness and sympathy she has offered me, when I most wanted all? I am not speaking or thinking or feeling about her *words!*

With regard to myself, I solemnly assure you that, as far as my memory can be trusted, this is the first time I have ever been charged, directly or indirectly, with variableness of feeling. Among those who have known me best and longest, the *tenacity* and *obstinacy* of my feelings, have often been observed—and if the observation were not a true one, I should be happier now. With regard to you, where or when have I ever charged you directly or indirectly, with discovering a want of feeling towards me or any of us? I have no kind of recollection of having ever done it. If I had, I should feel, at this moment, very sorry—but, as it is, I feel simply that you are mistaken about it. Assure yourself, that I never thought of even *implying* such a charge.

Pray say no more about Hastings or Brighton. I do not like to hear it— and besides it is unnecessary. You say quite truly that nothing can be more uncertain than our going to the latter place. If, as you once suggested, we were to be taken to Jamaica, I should care less about *that,* than I should have done a fortnight ago.

I assure you, I am well aware that you feel for me and all of us, compassionately and kindly—and I gratefully thank you for the very kind expressions contained in your last note. Give my best love to dear Annie, in spite of her injustice—and believe me yourself, my dear Mrs. Boyd,

Ever affectionately yours
E. B. Barrett

111.

To Ruby Cottage
Malvern Wells

Hope End. Friday [1832]

What Eliza meant and did, she meant and did kindly and like herself—but I am sorry that anyone should have addressed you on the subject of living near us, with "earnest entreaties". Either you wished it—and then they would have been unnecessary,—or you did not—and then they would have been vain. I think I said before her, that if *you* did not wish it at all, *I* did not wish it. I would have done anything, and made any sacrifice to obtain the end of your living near us—I would do anything—I would make any sacrifice now, to obtain that end—but you will forgive me for saying, that a concession wrung from Mr. Boyd by the entreaties of another person, could not have much value in my eyes.

Before I received your letter I had thought of taking Bothe's edition with me, the next time I went to see you, because I found in it the fragment for which we looked in vain, in Scholefield's. In spite of Bothe's opinion which estimates it as being more worthy of Clemens than of Aeschylus, I think it is very fine.

I mean to write out the ms notes here, and by that means save all the turning over of leaves which would waste a good deal of time at Ruby Cottage. I am glad that you told me to do it for you.

Ever yours affectionately
E. B. Barrett

112.

To Ruby Cottage
Malvern Wells

Saturday morning [May 12, 1832] [1]

I cannot go to Malvern today—but it will be the same thing. I will go on Monday; and I could not, I believe, go both today and Monday, even if you wished it.

Papa's speculation about the king seems to have fallen to the ground already. As a popular king he is no more! The bill is considered to be safer than ever it was, tho' the people will have to thank for its safety, not any of the house of Brunswick, but themselves. The non-payment of taxes, is an irresistible engine, and will be put into action everywhere. None will be paid at Ledbury,—where they call William the fourth the Duke of Clarence, and are about to establish a Political Union. There are reports that an anti-Grey administration cannot be made up, in which case, peers must be made after all. And perhaps the address of the Commons to the king, which was to be resolved upon last night, may produce some effect. The poor king—I cannot help being sorry for him. His error was not duplicity but weakness—and those Dalilahs, the Queen and the Duchess of Kent and his sisters,[2] deserve to be thrown to the Philistines, instead of him. It is stated that after Lord Grey's departure, he was very much affected. Lord Grey's conduct has been worthy of his cause.

This is all that you will care to hear about. I shall be with you on Monday—and altho' I shall be with you on Monday, I shall be glad when next week is over—I have asked no questions and shall ask none. I have struggled for a long time with the stream—and now—let it flow on. There is no use in struggling with it—and in a little while it will be of little consequence, even to *me,* if it flowed or not.

Ever yours affectionately
E. B. Barrett

1. Dated by political references. The final Reform Bill was still meeting with difficulty in the House of Lords; when the King refused Lord Grey's advice to create peers in "such a number as might ensure the success of the bill," the ministry resigned, Wednesday, May 9. The Duke of Wellington tried without success to form a new government, and on May 15 advised the King to recall Lord Grey.

2. The *Times* (May 14, 1833) speaks of the King as influenced by "domestic importunity" and "female solicitations, or even tears."

113.

To Post Office
Frome, Somersetshire [1]

Hope End. May 17, 1832

I am grateful to you my dearest friend, for writing to me, and for writing so kindly. I fancied that you would write—and I felt rather more comfortable than I had felt when I had read your letter—the last letter I shall ever receive with your signature, from our Malvern— Even now it seems to me like a dream. It seems to me scarcely possible that if I were to go there, I should find nothing but even more painful recollections than I find here, that I shall never go there again to see you, and that perhaps I may never again see you or read to you or write for you or hear you repeat Greek, anywhere. Forgive me for saying so—I say *perhaps,* at the same time. I have had the dread upon my mind for three years, that you would go at last,—and the feeling, that if you once went away, we should meet no more. The dread is gone—but the feeling remains with the reality. And yet you desire me to hope that it may be otherwise. God grant that it may. I try to hope that it may—and if I did not succeed sometimes, I should be less able to bear this present pain.

Your letter was read by me with many tears. They would have been bitterer, if it had not been read. I thank you for looking back with pleasure to our past intercourse—and for retaining throughout it, as I believe you have really done, some degree of regard for me. Is there nothing else to thank you for? Ought I not to thank you for all the knowledge I have derived from you, for all the happy hours I have spent with you, and for all the patience and indulgence and confidence I have met with from you, as your pupil and your friend? Oh Mr. Boyd! I thought it would all end in some way like this way. I *deserved* it to end so—because when under the pressure of those heavy afflictions with which God has been pleased to afflict me since the commencement of our intimacy,—I often looked too much for comfort to you—instead of looking higher than you. No help that is merely human, is stronger than a reed—and it is rightly ordered that the reed should pierce. But recollect, always recollect, that altho' I have deserved to be pained on your account, I have not deserved to be pained by *you.* I have not deserved— and I think, never can deserve, that you should forget me or neglect to

1. On the expiration of their year's lease of Ruby Cottage (see Letter 84), the Boyds left Malvern, with their next residence still undetermined.

write to me, or withdraw your friendship from me. And therefore I entreat you, never never, as long as you live, to do so. Tho' you cannot save me from other griefs, you can save me from that, and I have a right to expect that you should save me from it. I have a right—because I know well that while you may become acquainted with many persons who are superior to me in most things, and happier than I am, in all, yet you will never never have another friend whose regard for you can be stronger or truer or more incapable of change than mine. I have said, "stronger truer and more incapable of change", because I was speaking of *possibilities*—if I had been speaking of *probabilities,* I would have said, *as* strong, *as* true, and *as* incapable of change!

When you observe that you never had a single quarrel with me, you observe besides that you have not often spoken to me crossly or peevishly. Often! You *never* did,—and I believe I assured you so before. Do you think, if you had, that I should not have perceived it or recollected it? that the pain of hearing you speak crossly to me, would not have forced me to perceive and recollect it? Indeed it would. You have found fault with me sometimes, and justly,—but you never spoke unkindly to me in your life, except in my dreams. Therefore do not, because your nature will not let you be cross to anybody else, be cross to yourself! And do not call yourself "grateful" to *me* about anything. If ever I was useful to you for a little time, and in little things, was I not pleasing myself? If you wish me to be pleased now, you will sometimes give me something to do for you; and tho' that something must be done at a distance from you, I shall be pleased in doing it.

I am glad I am not obliged to live last Monday over again. I guessed then that you thought of going the next day or the day after,—and if I had had courage to talk to you about it, I would have begged you to write as soon as ever the journey was at an end, and say how you bore it. Perhaps you may think of doing so, which will be kind. Pray write as often as you can and as fully,—and tell me of everything which you do and think of, and about all your new acquaintances. You know you cannot say now as you used to do, in your letters—"but we will talk of this". Therefore you ought to talk to me upon paper as you used to at Ruby Cottage,—if it is not *very* disagreeable to you. This is a dull letter.

I should congratulate you upon Lord Grey's return to office, which was reported currently at Ledbury yesterday. It is a proud triumph for the minister and the people, and a glorious proof of the omnipotence of public opinion. You see, no anti-Grey government *dared* to form itself—and after all the success of the base intrigues, Tories could do

nothing with their *pulverem Olympicum* except bite it. The bishop of
Lichfield and Coventry does not seem to have suffered so much from
the populace as your informer reported,—tho' all the bishops are in
bodily fear. If you had been at Malvern yesterday, I would have sent an
express to you about the reported changes. I suppose you passed thro'
Ledbury on Tuesday, and went within a mile and a half of this house!!
Well!—it is all over now! I have heard nothing more on the subject of
our leaving Hope End,—but I earnestly hope that we may go soon. You
praised me once for feeling *naturally,* because I desired to stay here under
any circumstances as long as I could. You were at Malvern *then. Now* it
is my turn to feel *un*naturally,—and in the apprehension of these events,
I have felt so, for some months. My paper is at an end. I cannot conclude
this letter as I have done others by saying "I shall see you soon"—but I
can still say, May God bless you! Do you remember the day when we
met first and without speaking, on the Malvern road? [2] From that time, I
have prayed for you every day,—except two or three days in the October
of 1828, when the suddenness of a great calamity,[3] stupefied my faculties,
and made me incapable of praying for myself. Once more may God
bless you and make you happy—and me happier by hearing of that
happiness.

I have changed my mind, and will write a few lines to Annie. My
reason for meaning to be silent, was my dislike of entering at all upon
the subject—but if I am *quite* silent she may imagine me to be angry with
her, which I am not. She wrote only in the heat of the moment! When
shall I hear from you?—and how often? Think of me sometimes and
always as your attached friend

E. B. B.

I have written so much my dear Mrs. Boyd, that I have hardly left
myself room to assure you and to beg you to believe, that I do not "think
of you unkindly" from *any* cause. On the contrary I shall retain a grateful
recollection of the kindness and attention you always shewed me when I
was at your house—always and undeviatingly. I am quite aware that in
your late removal I had no right or shadow of right, to be considered—
and I sincerely hope that both you and Annie may gain from it as much
happiness as you expect—and as I have lost. Believe in my remaining
ever

Affectionately yours
E. B. Barrett

2. March 13, 1828.
3. Her mother's death on October 7, 1828.

114.

To Post Office
Bath

Hope End. May 26, 1832

My dearest friend,

I was a little uncomfortable at not hearing from you sooner, but I did not attribute your silence to unkindness. I believed that you would write to me as soon as you could, and I am glad to find that I believed right. I am rather glad too that you are at Bath instead of Frome, and still in *temporary lodgings*. It may make no difference to me at the last,—but at the first, either by fancy or folly, it does a little. I was very sure, and so, from what Henrietta told me, was Papa, that a dull dirty manufacturing town like Frome, would not suit you, or please Mrs. Boyd and Annie even in contradistinction to poor Malvern, and even for a time. Therefore it may be well for you that you could not get a house,—and for me it is well, because Bath is a few miles nearer to this place than Frome is. I hope you will not let Mrs. Boyd make herself unnecessarily uneasy about Annie. That she has been unnecessarily so, is not my opinion only, but the opinion of everybody who has had opportunities of seeing and being with Annie—and I never could apprehend that a person with such breadth of chest and with so little tendency to becoming thin, was of a consumptive habit, and on that account a fit object for the slightest uneasiness. The expression of Dr. Garlike might be applied to *any* case—and his opinion, given in Arabel's hearing, and after the severest attack which Annie has yet had, that "Malvern was as good a place for her as any other place" sufficiently proved how little apprehension he had of *consumption*. Annie was looking fat and well when she left Malvern—and unless she has grown very thin in a very short time, no one can appear farther from a complaint which in this neighbourhood is called not improperly "a wasting away". Mr. Joseph Clarke *has not seen her*. It seems to me and has seemed to me from the first, that the principal cause of her different indispositions, was *fullness* of habit, instead of its contrary,—and indeed Mrs. Boyd herself has observed to me how much better she became after taking a great deal of exercise. I have been very sorry to hear of her having been so unwell, and earnestly hope that the "quite well" may be permanent. If it is not, why does not Mrs. Boyd make her come to Bath, and take some good medical opinion upon her case? That would be the wiser plan, instead of *fearing* oneself into unhappiness.

I am glad that travelling did not annoy you as you feared it would. Who are the ladies whom you knew 13 or 14 years ago, and have now met at Bath? The moral which you have drawn from that circumstance, scarcely makes me feel more comfortable,—for it amounts barely to this —that if I live 13 or 14 years longer I may see you again—or in other words, that I may live 13 or 14 years without seeing you. And with such a prospect in your mind, you can be "sorry" at my having considered it necessary to ask you not to forget me? Why I thought that no one could know less of the world than I do,—and yet *I* should not be surprised at any person's making such a request to any person—even if the possible term of separation were 14 months instead of 14 years. People whom I was acquainted with before I was acquainted with you, and who professed more regard for me than you did, have forgotten me, I assure you, in less time than fourteen months. *That* act of oblivion made me smile,—but I should not smile, if *you,* with or without a reason, could do the same thing. And I am afraid that, for much more than half the world, it is a very easy thing to do— Therefore you should suffer me to ask you not to forget me!

Papa is always talking about what may be the result of the third reading, among the Lords. He says that if they are scoundrels, they may throw out the bill,—and that he has certainly a very bad opinion of them. In my mind, they may be base enough to do it,—but not daring enough to do it. It is clear, it must be clear even to them, that the people will have the bill, and that the king is pledged to the bill,—and that if the Lords brand themselves as traitors with one hand, the bill must nevertheless be wrenched unmutilated from the other. Papa says—"Let them throw it out—Lord Grey will prorogue Parliament for two days, create a hundred peers, introduce the bill into the House of Lords first, and then send it down to be approved by the Commons". You see, it is quite certain that no Tory administration can stand. My only regret is, that Lord Grey cannot immediately create peers, and by such means, infuse a nobler life into that *kakisto*cratical [1] body. He cannot do so—because he is artfully baited with large majorities. Did you ever read more disgusting language than occurs in the speeches of the anti-reform Lords? Lord Kenyon's, for instance? And is not Lord Grey's position morally sublime? The king's treatment of the Duke of Sussex has thrown upon his name a darker shadow, than his simple refusal to create peers ever did.[2] Papa generally reads the newspaper to us in the evening, so that I

1. Word coined from the Greek κάκιστος (worst) on the analogy of aristocratical.
2. After the Duke of Sussex twice presented to the King a reform petition from Bristol, His Majesty wrote angrily on May 15 "forbidding him the Court."

hear a good deal of all that is going on. Do you still take in the Evening Mail? Altho' you are in a temporary lodging, I think you might tell me where it is, and whether you *wish* it to be otherwise than temporary. I have heard nothing more of our leaving Hope End—at least nothing definite,—but my aunt thinks that we cannot drag on our lives in this manner much longer. Another family came to see the house last Thursday. Perhaps I am more impatient than I ought to be for it all to be over, and for us to be gone to some place where we may live more tranquilly than we can do here—but indeed I cannot help it. You will think I dare say, that I am apt to be out of spirits and to look at the gloomy side of everything—and yet it is not so—it is not so by my nature. Not many years ago I was always laughing and joking! I well recollect that when we were in France,[3] and when a wood-fire was smoking in a disagreeable manner, a gentleman observed— "I am very glad about this smoke. Now I can say that I have seen the tears in Mademoiselle Barrett's eyes". How many they have shed since that day! You will not forget to tell me, whom you have found to read Greek to you,—and whether you are likely to know in Bath, persons in whose society you will have pleasure. Tell me too, if you can walk out, without being annoyed by carriages and crowds and hills—and if you are quite well in every respect. Had you been at Malvern the day before yesterday, I should have spent it with you,—for my aunt went to her friends the Miss Uniacks, and did not return until nearly ten o'clock. Of course I did not go with her!—and I sighed to think why I did not. May *you* never have cause to sigh until we meet again, whether we meet,—at the end of *fourteen years!* upon earth, or in that happier place where years are not numbered, and farewells are not said!

Ever yours very affectionately
E. B. Barrett

You mention Miss Sibree, and I believe she resides somewhere near Bath. If you should see her, do not neglect to give her my kind remembrances— Do write when you can!

The petition from Ledbury for reform, which has been just sent to London, had above 700 signatures. The last petition which was sent, had only above 200. The meeting was very numerous,—and I have heard from different quarters that Bro's was the best speech. I am aware

---

3. In a letter to Miss Mitford, March 1844 (unpublished: Wellesley College Library), reference is made to a family sojourn in France: "We were seven months once at Boulogne, for masters, which are excellent there; and for the acquirement of that habit of talking French, which comes at a call."

that I have written you a dull letter,—but you should not reproach me for it. Dull humours will make dull letters. I have read no Greek since I saw you last. When will you bring out your work? Good-bye once more! If I write too long letters, be candid and tell me so! I promise not to be angry.

I believe I have said to Mr. Boyd the principal part my dear Mrs. Boyd of what I intended to say to you about Annie. Do not make yourself so much more uncomfortable than you need be about her. I feel quite certain that your fears are built upon no reasonable foundation, and that she is as likely to live and be strong as any person of your acquaintance. Dr. Garlike is at Malvern. Arabel wrote to Coleford a few days ago, and I wrote a postscript—but we have not heard yet.

Yours affectionately
E. B. B.

115.

To Bath Hampton
Near Bath

Saturday. June 9, 1832

My dearest friend,

So you have taken a house! But I do not begin to write to you, to write about that. I thought from the first, it would be so, altho' Henrietta and Arabel from what Mrs. Boyd had said to them, assured me to the contrary. I do not *always* make mistakes!

As to my going to see you, I spoke plainly to you, when I told you that it was impossible. And now, it *is* impossible. What is done, is done —and may it prove well done for your comfort and happiness! That I should have felt a little extravagantly the loss of society which was valuable to me, has been the fault of my nature, and punishes itself. Therefore every unreasonable expression in my former letters, I hope you will forgive. I have blamed myself for writing each of them, as soon as ever I had parted from each,—and can easily imagine what "damning proofs" you must have considered them—of that weakness in bearing anything adverse, and that much adoing about nothing, of which you once accused me.

To return to your proposal about Bath. Could you seriously suppose that Papa would go so far out of his way with all his family, and remain there, at a great expense, for *days*? And for what object? That *I* might see *you!!* How could I ask or expect or dream of such a thing? And even if I could, what would be the use of going to see you, only to wish you good-bye again, when it is settled, fixed, that we are not to live in the same place and are so very very unlikely ever to say another how do you do? No!—there would be no use or pleasure in it, even if it were possible—and it is *not* possible. As to Papa's leaving me behind, indeed there is no chance of that, for many reasons, some of which I have told you—and I have written too long on this subject already. Writing on it for ever and ever, would do no good. What is done, is done.

It appears probable that we shall soon leave Hope End. A report has reached me, a report which I have no means of doubting, that the place is sold. Papa has not yet spoken to us—he is likely to speak to us soon—and then, everything will be settled. I shall be glad when *anything* is settled—and when we are once gone and in some other less dear home, I must make up my mind to be tranquil and happy. To be either, here, and now, is not possible. The purchaser is said to be the gentleman who came here for the second time, while I was paying one of my last visits to you. Do not repeat to *any person,* what I have said to you. It will soon be known, if it is true enough to be worth knowing.

I have been reading thro' the eight first chapters of Genesis in Hebrew, and after I have read the whole of that book, I mean to begin Job. As I knew the character[s] and something of the grammar before, I have not been fagging hard—or indeed *at all*—for Papa would not let me do so. Instead of fagging, I have read Corinne for the third time, and admired it more than ever. It is an immortal book, and deserves to be read three score and ten times—that is, once every year in the age of man. Lord Byron hated Madame de Stael because she was always prominent in conversation and used to lecture him,—but I believe he estimated her Corinne, and am sure that his writings were the better for his readings. It was as difficult for him to touch fire and not be ignited, as it is generally, to touch pitch and not be defiled—and it is no new observation that Harold has often spoken with the voice of Corinne, and often when he has spoken with the most passion and eloquence.

The Bill has passed.[1] We may be prouder of calling ourselves English, than we were before it passed,—and stand higher among nations, not only as a freer people, but as a people worthy of being free. Lord Grey, on the other hand, may be proud of the gratitude of such a people. He deserves that gratitude. House and lands and golden vases and civic statues are straw given in exchange for brick—*they* cannot repay his

1. The Reform Bill was finally passed June 4, when Tory opponents, at King William's strong urging, absented themselves from the voting; it received royal assent on June 7.

services—nothing can, except the approbation of his own mind, and that gratitude of his country, which is "more lasting than brass".[2] The poor king, I cannot help being sorry for. He has been Cumberlanded and Fitzclarenced out of his popularity—and what will they give him in exchange? Yet we should remember that when he called the Duke of Wellington to office, he did so upon the sole condition of his *passing the bill*. Therefore the charge against him should not be, that he deserted the people, but that he was weak in serving them. The people however were not weak. They have presented a sublime spectacle. Did you read the account of the meeting of the Birmingham union upon the recall of Lord Grey, when a minister of the Gospel returned thanks to God, to whom the first thanks were due,—and the voices of thirty thousand persons, said Amen? It must have been very fine. I do not wonder at the French being surprised at our bill having been passed by the people and without bloodshed. We think before we fight,—and they fight before they think: exempli gratia, what do *you* decide about the fighting which is going on now in Paris, where the fighters are still undetermined as to whether they would be republicans or Carlists? There is to be a great dinner and procession in Ledbury in honor of the people's triumph,— and a giving away of meat amongst the poor. Papa has contributed a very large cow, to the value of £20. There is also to be another public meeting, to vote the thanks of the people to Lord Grey.

If I were to finish my poem just now, I should make *sad* work of it— in every sense of that word. But if I could finish it properly, Papa would not let me do it. He does not know anything of my studying the little Hebrew which I do study, or I should be well scolded for it. Bro teaches Henry and Daisy their Latin, now.[3]

Mr. Curzon was here on Friday, and enquired about you, and seemed very much surprised at your not having settled at Frome, as he had understood that your object in going, was to live near Mr. Clarke. I knew, and therefore could say, nothing about *that*. I suppose you are likely to have his society where you are, and a great deal of other persons' society besides. There are some things in your disposition, which, when I

2. Horace *Odes* 3.30.1.

3. Henry was at this time almost fourteen, Daisy (Alfred) was twelve. On teaching Latin to Sette (Septimus James, two years younger than Daisy) EBB wrote "I used to think in quite the old times when he read Caesar to me—his eyes (after the ubiquitous manner of Caesar himself) holding communion with Punch out of the window,— that I was unfortunate to have no more power in the way of enforcing discipline. It is better as it is. It is better to be loved than feared—or worse word of all!—*respected* . . . You see how we great pedagogues console ourselves!" Letter from Torquay to Miss Mitford; unpublished: Wellesley College Library.

knew you first, I thought to have no existence,—and which, *now,* I am much inclined to envy.

I began a letter to you, and wrote down two pages of it, a week ago,— but second thoughts prevented my sending it. It related chiefly to our leaving this place, and to wishes which are vain. You do not say one word about Annie. I wish you had. Arabel says that she wrote to her as kind a letter as she was capable of writing, of which no notice even by a line or word or message, has been taken. What can be the reason? That she wishes to obliterate even the *recollection* of our past acquaintance? Give our best love to Mrs. Boyd,—and to Annie, thro' her. You will write—will you not?—whenever you can. You do not know what a comfort it is to me, to hear from you!

Ever affectionately yours
E. B. B.

116.

To Bath Hampton
Near Bath

Hope End. Saturday [1832]

My dearest friend,

I do not mean to write a long letter to you; but I am uncomfortable at the idea of having written one about you, without apprizing you of it, —and I wish besides to ask you something. After Mr. Curzon had received the letter from Miss Henrietta Mushet,[1] enclosed by Annie to Arabel, he wrote to me, delivering over to me Miss H. M.'s "kindest and best wishes", and claiming for her my esteem notwithstanding certain charges brought against her by Mr. Boyd. Of you, he said nothing harsh, and little in any way,—while towards myself, he expressed himself with much warmth of kindness and interest. But I knew well that an ex parte statement could not do otherwise than prejudice against you those who were the least inclined to be so prejudiced,—and I could not bear to think that Mr. Curzon or any other person should entertain of you an ill and unjust opinion. Therefore I wrote to him an account of the whole business from the beginning to the end,—explaining to him, what you would not explain to Miss H. Mushet, that you did not mean to bring against her conduct at Margate or elsewhere a serious charge, or indeed a charge of any kind except that of an unmerited severity to-

---

1. Henrietta Mushet had been acting as Boyd's secretary. See Letter 99. The cause of their misunderstanding is nowhere made clear.

wards yourself—and that when you used the word *"indelicate"* in your letter, you did so in the very *uncommon* sense in which she herself had used it—and that in the observation made there, and in your previous one to Mrs. Boyd, you had not intended to speak disrespectfully of Miss H. M., but only to intimate that what was mere nonsense, she had once laughed at as nonsense, without improperly stigmatizing it as indelicacy and immorality.

I rely upon what I know of your nature, for forgiveness, in telling you this. From Miss H. M.'s expressions in her letter to you, it was evident that she considered your observation communicated to her thro' Mrs. Boyd, in a serious light. You would not explain, then, because you thought she was predetermined not to understand. But I am quite sure that you do not wish her to continue to think, and to have it in her power to represent to others, that she is suffering under a charge from you, which is as heavy a one as a man could bring against a woman of delicacy. Because you have been treated with injustice and harshness, there is no reason for your being unjust and harsh. And what I am anxious to request of you is, that, in your next letter to me—whenever it may be written!—you will write a few words to justify yourself from having intended to make any accusation reflecting on Miss H. M.'s propriety of mind and conversation, that I may be able to repeat them to Mr. Curzon, as from yourself. What *I* have said, may be attributed to my *wish* and not to my *ability* of justifying you.

I do not often make requests to you—and you, knowing my regard for you, will not refuse this one, which nothing but that regard has prompted me to make. I feel strongly that after you have granted it, you will stand upon higher ground, and render every harsh expression which has been levelled against you, less excusable than ever. I wish you would say at the same time, that you *forgive* those harsh expressions! Many weeks have passed since they were said,—and life itself is not composed of very many weeks. There are only two classes of human beings,—those to whom we shall be eternally united, and those from whom we shall be eternally severed,—and neither of them can afford a fit object for our anger. The more harshly you have been dealt with, the more generous, and the more according to the spirit of Christ, will your forgiveness be. Say then, "I meant to bring no serious accusation against her, and I forgive her unjust expressions towards myself." If you will say so, I do not promise to think more highly of you, but I shall think as I have always done—that you can act at once with gentleness and with dignity—and with kindness to *me*.

There is another thing. Arabel has told me of her having repeated

to Mrs. Boyd, some words of Annie, with regard to my writing that letter
for you. I beg of you, to take no notice to Annie of anything which she
has said respecting me. I cannot bear to think that you should be displeased with her on my account,—and besides I would rather that the
subject were discussed no more. My feelings towards a child of yours
could never be turned into coldness,—and with regard to hers for me,
the time will come, and may not be far distant, when, having tried and
found wanting, the professions of the world, she may turn with regret
to the recollection of one who has sincerely loved her.

Give my best love to Mrs. Boyd—and believe me

> Ever and very affectionately yours
> E. B. Barrett

I need not entreat of you to write nothing harsh to *anybody*. I have
done you justice with Mr. Curzon. I trust the whole to your kindness.

117.

To Bath Hampton
   Near Bath

[1832]

My dearest friend,

Indeed you are not just. Do you not recollect that I ascertained from
my aunt and told you, that every plan was unsettled? Therefore you are
unjust in making that reproach,—and if my heart were open before you,
together with my words and actions ever since I knew you, you would
agree with me, that from *you* I deserve no reproach. Have I not asked
again and again about going to see you, whenever there seemed the
slightest chance of my receiving a favourable answer? And is it likely, for
my own sake, that I would at any time omit asking any question, if I
had not very strong reasons for believing that the answer would not
bring me nearer to you? Do you not think *in your heart* that I lost more
pleasure, in not going to see you, than *you* did?—and that it gives me
more pain at this moment to feel that I cannot see you, than it gives
you? When you were at Malvern I made it clear to you that if you lived
at a distance from us, I should not be able to go and see you. You immediately take a house at a distance, and ask me to go and see you, and
then because I say "it is impossible", appear more than half displeased
with me. And *you*,—who have, not unwisely, judged that the consideration of which is the cheapest way to take a house, outweighed the con-

sideration of living near me,—expect *me* to displease the person, who
loves me better than any person in the world loves me, for the sake of
visiting you for a week or two!! Indeed this is not just!—and if it were,
I have no "spirit and resolution" for doing it. All that I have of those
qualities, is expended in bearing up against the different deprivations
under which I suffer,—without my having it in my power to give
voluntary and unmerited pain to the few who care for me.

You say that I "appear rather vexed" at your having taken a house. If
rather vexed means *very sorry*, I will not deny that natural feeling—but
if it means *at all angry* I appeared to be what I was not. If you have
taken a house for a year, or more, upon the decision of your judgment
and inclination, and without reference to me, you have done right. I do
assure you, I am *convinced* you have done right and wisely,—and I
ought not even to regret it. I am at least reconciled to it,—and satisfied
that if I am not to see you again, it is for some just and wise reason. I
had a strong impression on my mind before you left Malvern that it
would be so—and I have therefore suffered no disappointment. May you
be only half as happy as I have wished you to be, altho' that happiness
should blot me from your recollection. But if you *do* think of me, be
just in your thoughts,—and do not blame me for occasioning directly
or indirectly, by word or deed, or by neglect of word or deed, a separation, to prevent which, I would have done anything—to prevent which,
I *have* done and said more than I can quite excuse to myself now. Why
should we write one additional word on this subject? There is no use
in it—and there *is* pain in it—at least to *me*. I have written about it
today, because I could not be silent after reading your letter, or even
wait until you answered mine which went to the post only two hours
before yours came from it. Don't forget or refuse to answer that letter in
the way I begged you to do. And recollect! Mr. Curzon has brought no
accusation against you, to me. In my letter to him, I gave him to understand that I did not wish any part of the business to be mentioned to
Papa,—and I believe he is to be trusted. Yet I shall be anxious until you
take the high ground, of *forgiving*—anxious for *your sake*—and that
proves *how* anxious I am!

It may not be of any consequence now, as far as you are concerned,
whether we remain here or go to the other side of England,—yet I do
not like writing another letter without mentioning Hope End. We are
still in the dark. Mr. Heywood [1] gives out at Malvern that *the place
belongs to him*,—and on the other hand, Papa has not heard a word of
it, from London. It is *"absolutely impossible"* to know what to think,—

1. Hope End was bought by Thomas Heywood.

but the general belief in the neighbourhood is, that Mr. Heywood's account is the accurate one. If it is, I am not dissatisfied.

I have read Hebrew regularly every day since I told you of my beginning Genesis,—and I am now more than half thro' Genesis, and begin to relax a little from the lexicon. From its being a primitive language it is very interesting in a philosophical point of view. I like to find the roots of words and ideas at the same time. The syntax seems to be simple; and there is apparently no copiousness in synonyms and expletives, as is the case in Greek—yet it is an expressive language. I am glad I thought of having recourse to it, for if it had no other advantage, it has, at least given a kind of change of air to my mind. I have been reading besides, two Italian novels,—one by Manzoni, entitled the Betrothed, which, tho' heavy enough sometimes, is very well written and very amiably written. The other is a continuation of the story, by a different and an unequal writer. Both works have had a great run on the continent, and are tolerably well-known, I believe, in England.

Poor Sir Walter Scott! Yon have heard that he is dying,[2]—that he has lost even consciousness. The other night Papa read a passage from the Lady of the Lake to me; and I did not like to hear it. It sounded like something unnatural—as if you were looking at a broken instrument, and hearing its sweetest music at the same time. The poetry so glowing and animated—and the poet so silent and insensible! and the idea of each, forced at once upon your mind! You know I am not an admirer of poor Sir Walter's poetry. It never appeared to me as animated as it did the other night, and never gave me as little pleasure—and *contrast* accounts for both circumstances. For a long time after Lord Byron's death, I hated to read his poetry, but then in his case, the poet and his poetry are quite identified, and you could not at any time, read one, without thinking of the other.

It appears now that the House of Commons is not to be actually re-formed until the spring. Mr. Robert Biddulph has come forward for Hereford in the place of Lord *Eastnor resigned,*—so that there will probably be two reform members for that city. In Ledbury there are only three anti-reformers!—in the whole town! Occyta says, he supposes the reform bill has "done away the cholera", but the cholera seems to resist everything, and we have heard so much lately of its ravages, that I cannot help thinking rather anxiously about you. Bath Hampton is quite unconnected with Bath—is it not? I hope that if it is not, or that even if it is, you will go farther into the country for two or three months, in

2. Sir Walter Scott was stricken with apoplexy and paralysis on June 10, 1832, but did not die until September 21.

the case of the disease appearing in Bath. To make use of those means of safety which Providence has placed within our reach, is not flying from Providence, notwithstanding the foolish expressions of some people. Lady Smith an acquaintance of ours, would stay in Dublin, and died there. You know there is no occasion for you to be alarmed *now*. Only be cautious at the proper time. May God bless and preserve you! We have seen the Cliffes lately, oftener than we used to do,—and my aunt and Henrietta were invited to a dinner party of sixteen which Mrs. Cliffe has fixed for next Wednesday. Henry and Daisy and Arabel have had the chicken pox,—but they are all well except Arabel who has not yet shown herself down stairs, tho' a headache is her only unpleasant feeling. I am finishing this letter which I began on Tuesday, on Wednesday morning; and I believe there is not much more to tell you, or room to tell it in. You cannot think how very glad I was to hear, from Mrs. Boyd's letter to Arabel, that you have less heaviness in your head than you used to have at Malvern. Give my love to her.

Ever yours affectionately
E. B. Barrett

Do mention your book.[3] You never do.

118.

To Bath Hampton
   Bath

Hope End. Tuesday
July 10, 1832

My dearest friend,
   You desire me to transcribe and send to Mr. Curzon, a passage in your letter to me, supposing that in my opinion, any disadvantageous statement with regard to you, has been addressed to him from another quarter. Now I have no reason for believing any such thing. Mr. Curzon did not show me Miss H. Mushet's letter to him, nor did he speak of it as if it contained any charge against you. In his letter to me, he considers Miss H. Mushet to be lying under *an accusation of yours,* and pleads in her behalf that she should not "lose the place in my esteem and regard which she is by grace fitted for". If I had *known* of any charge being brought against you, you should have heard of it. Mr. Curzon does not say *one word against you,* in any way.

   3. The translation of Gregory on which Boyd was working and which EBB hoped he would publish in book form.

My reason for writing to him was my fear, not my belief. I did not know what Miss H. M. had said, and I did not choose him to suppose you capable of bringing forward an unjust and unprovoked charge against a woman. I explained everything just as you would have explained it, except that unfortunate word "indelicate" in your letter,— which I imagined you to have used in Miss H. M.'s uncommon sense. But now, *pray* do not make me correct my explanation. My letter did you full justice,—and supposing (a bare supposition) that Mr. Curzon had been prejudiced against you before he read it, he cannot be prejudiced now. When I heard from him first, I felt in such an alarm, that, tho' I was not very equal either to a long drive or even a short controversy, I was on the point of going to Ledbury and speaking to Mr. Curzon myself. I would have done so, but was withheld by another fear. Papa would or at least might have wondered, and asked questions. Three weeks have passed since my letter of reply was received by Mr. Curzon, and indeed it is much better to be quiet and silent and take no more notice on the subject. Now do trust me for once. You may trust me,— for you cannot reasonably believe that I would ask you to be silent, and be silent myself while I supposed that your conduct stood with any person in an unfavourable light.

From your having delayed to write, longer than usual, I had taken it into my head that you thought my letter to you on this subject, presuming and interfering. I am glad I was mistaken. You must,—as I *am* mistaken,—allow me to say in addition, that I don't think you are quite *Mr. Boyd,* in delaying to forgive until amends is made to you for the offence. *Do not even the publicans the same?* [1] I maintain that you ought to forgive at once. If you wait for an apology you may wait for ever,—and even if the apology comes, you will not have the same self-satisfaction, in forgiving *then*. Besides you have expressed to me much esteem for many parts of Miss Mushet's character, and,—until this unfortunate business,—for all parts of her conduct. You have felt and expressed much regard and friendship for her, and she has been useful and attentive to you. On every account therefore, I maintain that you should make an effort,—if an effort is necessary,—and say and feel "I forgive her". It is not right, altho' I am afraid it is natural, to have a so much shorter memory for what has been offensive to us, than for what has been pleasing and valuable to us. Even *I* say this,—and you who profess to feel pleasure more strongly than pain, will be very inconsistent if you do not agree with me. You will write a person's faults whether of conduct or character, "in water", now and then—and in this particu-

1. Matthew 5:46.

lar instance, for the sake of what you must have felt towards Miss H. M. when you wrote to her those flaming letters of which you told me, among other better reasons, you will try to soften down what you feel respecting her now. But I do not wish to preach to you. The impropriety and injustice of Miss H. M.'s letter you cannot be more sensible of than I am,— yet it was written *a long time ago*—and if there were nothing for you to forgive, there would be no need of your forgiving. Do not think that Mr. Curzon has asked me directly or indirectly, or even seemed to wish me, to interfere in Miss H. M.'s behalf. What I have written, has been written entirely and solely, because I was interested in *you*—and perhaps a little in myself—for altho' I never could knowingly offend you, such things as misunderstandings have been heard of, and if I find you quite unbending to those for whom you have felt much regard, what hope can remain to those for whom you have felt a little?

And now with respect to your letter. You did not mean to give me pain. I know you never did. I believe you incapable of *meaning* to give any person pain. You only meant to vindicate yourself. But who brought any charge against you? I do assure you I never *thought* of doing so. Being angry with you for fixing your residence at a distance from me, would be much more flattering to *you* than it would be becoming in *me* —and do not imagine that I had any intention of paying you such a compliment at such an expense. You have of course done what is most likely to make you happy,—and that is all that I wish. As to my asking Papa about going to see you, you think that you have me there in a dilemma—which dilemma appears to me resolvable into some such position as this—that if Papa loves *me,* he must do exactly what *you* think reasonable. Papa certainly does love me, and I believe would make any sacrifice for what, *he* believed, my happiness,—but it would not be reasonable either in you or me, to expect him to take our opinions as the criterion of his conduct. He may think it better for me to remain quietly with him than to go to you or any other person—and indeed tho' you may be angry at my saying so, and tho' I know very well that if I could go to you I would go,—I am not sure that he is not right. I sometimes feel that for the rest of my life, I would barter almost every kind of pleasure for the loss of every kind of pain, and consent to be only tranquil instead of pleased. For a long time my powers of feeling pleasure and pain have been clashing against each other—and neither my body nor mind can bear it any longer. It has been my misfortune to expect to be too happy and too much pleased with everybody,—every string of my imagination has been tuned to happiness, and when first one breaks and then another, the ear of my mind cannot bear, without shrinking, the loss of harmony. We are now expecting every day, to hear of our immediately leaving this place. Supposing Papa consented to my going to you on our way, as you proposed, what would be gained by it? That I should be pleased by seeing you, and sorry again to leave you. Is it worth while? I say, *"is it worth while,"*—to reconcile myself to not visiting you—but my saying so, is not the obstacle to my visiting you. That obstacle I need not dwell upon. I do not think it is to be overcome.

Now do tell me, dear Mr. Boyd, about your book,—and why you have not told me before about it. Have you settled anything with any bookseller? You cannot think how glad I shall be to see the title-page in print, or how much I wish you not to delay the printing. There is one thing at the close of the preface which I have a hundred times resolved to mention to you,—but it always went out of my head. Do you not speak of certain religious persons who would exclude profane literature from their studies, and call them *narrow-minded?* Now I wish you would modify that expression by calling them "narrow-minded in *one* respect", —or else omit it altogether. I do not think it is quite just as it stands— and besides Papa who has, you know, several narrow-minded friends, might not like it. One word for justice, and one word for *me!!*

I was very glad to hear of Mr. Spowers' having been with you. Did he read to you? I supposed [sic] you talked politics most radically together, and threw the THIRD *stone?* [2] After that allusion, I ought to imitate your prudent example, and leave out the signature at the end of this letter, to which you will be so glad to come. But I am safer than you are. No one would think of laying any treasonable charge to *me,* after my poem in the Times newspaper, which you admired so much!! While *you* have nothing but a pun to rely upon, and a palinodia afterwards!

I have read Miss Fanny Kemble's tragedy; [3] and should like you to read it, if it were only to know whether my judgment of it, is a right one or not. It seems to me to be a very clever and indeed surprising production as from the pen of a young person,—but I think that from any other pen, it would not find readers. The dialogue is sometimes very spirited, and ably done—but the poetry is seldom good as poetry,— and scarcely ever original or harmonious. There are however some beautiful passages—and I should like you to find them out for yourself. The play would not cost you much time in reading—and it would certainly interest you.

2. An allusion to John 8:7: "He that is without sin among you, let him cast the first stone."

3. Frances Ann Kemble (1809–93), *Francis the First, an Historical Drama,* London, 1832.

Mr. Croker has lately published an edition of Boswell's Life of John-son.[4] I have been looking over it, and do not think his additions and notes of much value. But he is impartial,—which is a wonderful merit in an editor.

My Hebrew is going on very well. I have done with Genesis, and I shall be in Job tomorrow, where you ought to be the day after, when you receive this letter. Tell me seriously and candidly, dear Mr. Boyd— do you like or dislike such long letters? It is a temptation to me to go on writing, when I am writing to you—it is more like talking to you than anything perhaps which I shall ever do again: and yet if I thought I tired you, my pen would stop very quickly. I wish that when you write, you would tell me more about yourself than you do,—tell me what you are thinking about, and talking about, and making epigrams about. Have you a good place to walk in,—and many new visitors? Do write like Richardson,—and recollect that you never can tell me anything which will not interest me. Therefore fancy that I am sitting near you, —and let your dictation be only conversation.

Mrs. Boyd's headache could not have lasted long, I think, when Annie was with her. I hope Annie looks and is quite well,—and send my love to both of them. How could you think that anyone would bind me to secrecy, and at the same time, make any serious charge against you? I have been—I could not have been otherwise—quite sincere with you. You know I need not have told you at all, of Mr. Curzon's letter to me, or of mine to him, if I could have borne to have concealed anything of the kind from you.

Ever yours affectionately
E. B. Barrett

I must have found a frank for this packet if Eliza did not give me an opportunity of sending it as cheaply.

119.

To Bath Hampton
    Bath

Hope End. Wednesday [1832]

My dearest friend,

If you mean to describe *me* by the lady of sound understanding, I am afraid you pay me an unmerited compliment. At least I have been told so often, and by those who know me best, that I am a mere child in many things, that I cannot help believing it.

4. Ed. John Wilson Croker, 1831.

I am glad you have written. I wished to have one more letter from you while I was at Hope End,—and on this account I tore into pieces a letter which I wrote to you last week, and which might have made the probability of my receiving an answer from you, too uncertain for you to trust to it. Besides I could then tell you nothing certain of Papa's plans. He heard at last from London that the sale of Hope End was finally arranged,—and *immediately,* as I knew he would, he left us to take a house. He went last Wednesday into Devonshire and returned yesterday. He went to all the places which were at all likely to suit him, along the Devonshire coast, and has fixed upon Sidmouth. You cannot be more surprised than I was, at his going into Devonshire. Until he was gone I did not know where he was going. He went away quite suddenly—I did not know that he intended to go anywhere, five minutes before he went,—and his only words to me were, "God bless you my love—I shall be with you again early in the week." He smiled as he said it,—but his voice trembled—and I well knew to what end he was leaving us.

Devonshire is very cheap—and besides as I have a disagreeable cough when I attempt to walk or talk, he fancies that the warmth of the climate may do me good. The situation of Sidmouth is dry as well as warm—myrtles geraniums and hydrangeas grow quite down to the shore —and the country is extremely beautiful, intersected by the most romantic walks, and wooded as picturesquely as if the sea were a thousand miles away. This is Papa's account,—and I hope he may continue to like what he now admires,—for if he pleases himself he will please me. . . .[1]

I wish you had said something about Mr. Mushet, for since hearing from Mrs. Boyd, I have felt rather uncomfortable about him and you. How *could* you do such a foolish thing?—and when I had just wasted so much paper in entreating you to keep the peace? Did not you tell me once that it was the easiest thing in the world to persuade you to do anything? To do anything *you liked*—I suppose you meant. Of the very few persons whom I have known, you seem to me one of the most unpersuadable—but I am far from blaming you on that account. If it is a fault at all, it is a fault on the right side. Yet do not suppose that I consider you on the right side, in making your confidence to Mr. Marsh.

If I said anything in my last letter which sounded disagreeable in your ears, I hope you will forgive my having done so. That letter was written a week before it was sent to you, and I have no very distinct recollection of what it contained. As far as I do recollect, I am sure I did not intend

1. The omitted passage answers two questions from Boyd: it gives Adam Clarke's interpretation of the Greek word *baptizo* and reports a vain search to find the phrase "baptizing beds."

to annoy you by any intimation however remote, that I considered you as wanting in regard towards me. When I described your regard for Miss H. M. as being "great", I spoke merely of what it had been, years ago. I did not intend to oppose it *invidiously* to the degree of regard which I may flatter myself, you entertain for me,—but merely to observe that what you had found possible to withdraw from her, you might find possible *a fortiori* to withdraw from me. This observation was intended as an argument, not as a reproach. But you know, there is not any use in that kind of argument, with unpersuadable people.

I have been interrupted in my letter,—and now I cannot send it today, as I intended. Your letter I received yesterday, and as it desired me to write soon, and you may be anxious to hear about the baptism, I wished you to have my answer by return of post. Since I left off writing, I have heard that we shall probably leave this dear place, next week— and perhaps early in the week. The house at Sidmouth is taken for only a month—because altho' it is the largest vacant house there, it is rather too small for us—and by the expiration of the month, other larger ones may become vacant. I have not yet steeled my heart to think of the hour of going away—but I believe that He who has given the sorrow, will give also the strength. I have found it so, in bitterer sorrows than this— and I cannot doubt that in this sorrow, I shall find it so. Henrietta Arabel and I have been perfectly prepared, by all that we have heard, for many weeks—and we shall go through the painful days which we have to suffer here where we have enjoyed so many happy ones, as calmly and patiently as we can. There is one thing—perhaps a foolish thing—but I cannot bear to think of it. I cannot bear to think that the rooms and walls in which we have not been for so long,[2] because they have become to us, too painfully dear,—will be inhabited and trodden and laughed in, by strangers. But I suppose this is foolish—at any rate it is *very* foolish to teaze you with a dull letter. I shall take a great deal of care of your books. But perhaps you might like to have them returned to you—you might not like me to take them down into Devonshire. Shall I send them to you? In that case you must write by return of post. I am not *certain* that we shall be here after Monday,—but as it is possible that we may, do not write to me at Sidmouth, do not write to me anywhere,— unless you write by return of post,—until you hear again from me. Papa went thro' Bristol in going to Sidmouth, and we must go as near you as he did. I wish it were possible to see you on the road,—but I suppose it is not. I shall take with me some of my books of course: the rest will be

2. Mrs. Barrett's rooms and her possessions were left unaltered and unused after her death.

packed with Papa's library, and left with the furniture, in warehouses in Ledbury. The plate will be sent to London, to the Bank.

Henrietta has been to visit all the cottages on Wellington Heath, on Bible business, and hoping that they knew nothing of ours. The news of our going away, had however reached them by some means—and in every cottage, there were such scenes! The women bursting into tears the moment they saw Henrietta, and calling down blessings upon Papa's head wherever he went, in the most affecting manner—and some of the poorest, entreating Henrietta to *write to them*. I told you how much beloved he was, but I did not know then, how much—and they are as fond of Henrietta as her attention to them deserves. One woman who had been blessing "every hair of Master's head, and all his children from the biggest to the least", fell down in such an agony of grief, that they thought she was in a fit. I almost wonder how Henrietta and Arabel could get through these painful visits—but I suppose they were necessary things. You seem to be fated to receive dull letters from me. I meant to write only a few lines, but in a letter to you I always have so much to say, and even when the sayings are melancholy, a certain pleasure in saying them. My aunt has kindly promised to go with us, and remain with us a little time. Do not think of writing to Papa about my seeing you on the road. It *would not do*. Forgive the vanity of my suspecting you of thinking of it. It came into my head at that moment. Why did you not mention Annie? My best love to her and Mrs. Boyd. God bless you.

Your affectionate friend
E. B. Barrett

120.

To Bath Hampton
　　Bath

Hope End. August 13, 1832

My dearest friend,

It appears to me that I must have managed very badly to be so long without hearing from you,—for I think you would have written to me before today, if I had not asked you not to do so. And yet, how could I have done otherwise? We have expected to go every day for many days,— and on last Tuesday, Papa had actually fixed the following morning for our removal. But we begged him,—thro' my aunt,—to allow us to remain with him until some more packing was done—so he changed his mind and we are now dragging on day after day, not knowing how many hours of Hope End are left to us. After all I am afraid it will be necessary for him to remain a little while behind us—as to break up his establishment here and pack up *all* the furniture, would, until we were gone, be impossible. But by staying longer than he intended us to stay, we shall have considerably abridged the time of his being by himself— and that is something gained, both for his comfort and ours.

Mathews and his men have been packing furniture, a whole fort- night,—and I suppose they will remain in the house at least another week. Five cartloads went to the warehouses on Saturday. Mathews says that by staying more than a day or two longer, we shall be in the way— therefore this is too certainly the last letter I shall write to you from Hope End,—and you may write to me,—if you are inclined to write to me,—at the end of this week or at the beginning of next week, directing your letter to the post office Sidmouth, Devonshire. I will give you a more particular direction, afterwards.

With regard to your books, dear Mr. Boyd, I hope you have not thought that in sending the large ones to Ledbury instead of to Sid- mouth, I was pleasing myself. We have sent to Sidmouth only one box of books, and not a very large one, as Papa particularly desired us to take as few as we could. In this box, are a good many music books,—and all the lesson books, which take up much room, but are necessary for the children. I have sent fewer than I had occasion for,—and would have left Wolf behind, if they had not seen that I was sorry about it, and found out that it would lie flat, and be very little in the way. Besides Wolf, I have sent Gregory, and the first volume of Heyne's Homer, which you gave me—and the first volume of Heyne's Pindar,—and the two plays of Aeschylus which I have, edited by Blomfield,—and two volumes of Sophocles in *8vo*—and six very little volumes of Euripides in duo- decimo—a few duodecimo Latin books—my Hebrew and Greek Bibles —and your Select Passages and Agamemnon. That is nearly, if not quite all, besides your smaller books. The two folios of Chrysostom and two quartos of Dr. Clarke, I have seen carefully packed with my other books, —and they will be placed at the Ledbury warehouse with Papa's. He is packing his own, himself, with the assistance of the boys who dust them and fold them in paper and give them to him. Oh I do wish that all this painful confusion were over! The noise of hammering, and of men walking up and down stairs, from morning till night—and dear Hope End looking so unlike the happy Hope End it used to be! I sometimes sit at the window and wonder if it is a dream. But dreams are dull things to write about, and I must not tire you with mine.

David says of the unrighteous—"Because they have no *changes, there-*

fore, they fear not God".[1] May it please God that the desolating changes which have fallen upon *me* in the course of the last four years, may have fallen not in vain—not without the increase of my fear of Him. In the course of those years, I have lost five relatives. I was attached to four of them—and to have saved the lives of two—I would have laid down my own life and been happier in the sacrifice than, I am likely to be now. From other causes, too, my feelings have been pained! The last stroke— our removal for ever from our dear and happy home—is of course a heavy one,—but I know we ought not to murmur at it, and I hope we do not. Dearest Papa's resolution and cheerfulness are our example and our support. I exert myself in mind and body, as much as either will allow.

I did not mean to say a word to you of all this—but sometimes people cannot help saying more than they mean. We *intend* to be very happy at Sidmouth. Lady Margaret Cocks gave me an agreeable account of it the other day. She is the only person of whom I have taken leave—and she was *so* kind and affectionate in her manner! You ought not to be severe upon her, *indeed.* Mrs. Cliffe and Eliza are much distressed at the prospect of losing us,—and cannot make up their minds to pay us a parting visit. I am glad of it—such a visit would have been painful to everybody. The Martins and the Peytons have also written—*they* will not come—and our more distant acquaintances, we could not admit. Therefore we shall see none of them again. I hope they may all like our successors here,—and that our successors here may not only like but love this place as much as we have loved it.

How often in the day do you walk round your garden? I wish you had some place to walk in, besides your garden,—for more extended exercise must be good for you, even if it is not necessary. I used to think when you were at Malvern that you did not walk enough, or far enough, —and I am *sure* I should think so now. Though you call Bath Hampton a village, I suppose it is only the fag-end of the great town,—and that if you attempt to walk towards Bath, you get into Bath. That there should be no road the other way, is very unfortunate. I liked your last letter better than most of the letters which you have written to me since we parted. Continue to tell me more about yourself, and your publication. Why did you not send your essay with your translations? You disappointed me by not doing so. A very little attention would have removed all the *"immorality"*, and preserved the innocence of the age, —and I should regret your losing an opportunity of publishing what I liked so much. If you have any difficulty about doing it, will you send

1. Psalms 55:19.

it to me at Sidmouth, and let me weed it, and transcribe it, and return it to you? In the meantime the printer will have enough to do, in printing the translations,—and when he is ready for the essay, the essay will be ready for him. Do think about it. I will not *say* that I shall have pleasure in doing this for you, because you *know* that I shall. Give my best love to Mrs. Boyd and Annie, who are, I hope, quite well. I did not think I *could* have written so much—yet you see it is written! Perhaps I may be able soon, to write to you more cheerfully,—and then you will be better able to forgive me for writing too long letters to you sometimes. As you say nothing to the contrary, tho' I have asked you about it twice or thrice, I am obliged to think that you *do* consider them "too long".

Your affectionate friend
E. B. Barrett

121.

To Bath Hampton
   Bath

Raffaral House. Sidmouth
Saturday.
[*postmark* August 26, 1832]

My dearest friend,

Of course you cannot expect me to agree with Mr. Spowers and his bookseller. I would quite as soon admit that Gregory's work is mere declamation, as that your translation is executed in an inferior manner to any of your preceding ones. I am not inclined to do either. I earnestly hope that you will secure justice to yourself and your ms. by applying to another bookseller. And if that other rejects it—which, without casting one shade on the merit of your work, is quite possible—why should you be daunted from applying to another bookseller and another? Why should you say that you cannot be admitted as an impartial judge? Cannot you judge whether Gregory's work is or is not *mere declamation?* And if you determine that it is *not,* may you not safely infer that critics who can err in one material point, may also err in a point not equally material—that a man who cannot estimate an original may be incapable of estimating a copy? Surely you may infer this, and without any degree of partiality to your own performance or your own judgment.

From what you observe in the letter which I have just received, I am afraid you will be angry when I tell you that we slept in Bath the night before last night. Papa determined upon the line of road he wished us to take, only half an hour before we parted from him. We arrived at Bath almost in the dark: and as we were not expected at Sidmouth, it was of course an important point to set off early enough the next morning, to admit of our reaching it before the night closed in. It was therefore fixed that we should set off at eight the next morning. The Landlady of the York Hotel told me that Bath Hampton was three miles from her door. Now if I had gone to you at six in the morning, I might have spent half an hour with you, but not more. Whatever I may have written or thought, I could not have helped going to see you, if it had been in my power, even for that short time. But I was much exhausted by agitation and fatigue,[1] and could scarcely *stand* when the carriage stopped at the hotel—and the next morning, I was obliged to breakfast in my bedroom and go from it, into the carriage. After all we did not leave Bath, until past nine,—the consequence of which, happened just as was feared. We arrived [2] here in the dark, and had some difficulty in finding our house: a crowd of tradespeople followed us up the town, and we were confused and frightened and in an unpleasant situation. I assure you I did not leave Bath, without feeling sorry at not having seen you. But I consoled myself with the reflection, that even if my going to see you had been possible, I might have hurried myself into a coughing fit, and made you wish in your heart that I had stayed away.

This place appears to be very pretty. We have the house [3] which the Grand Duchess Helena had. It is not *grand,*—but it is comfortable and convenient, with a fine view of the sea in front, and green sloping hills, and trees, behind. In the drawing room there are four windows all facing the sea,—and I was lulled to sleep last night by the rolling reverberating solemn sound of its waves. Of course I like this. The warmth and softness of the air are quite peculiar—and are striking to all of us. Myrtles and hydrangeas flowering in our garden! Papa Bro and Sette, whom Papa *could not* part with,—follow us soon by the coach. Now do recollect what I have said to you about your work. I hope I have

1. Eleven years later EBB recalled that she was "too weak and out of health to stir from the hotel window." To Miss Mitford, May 4, 1843; Miller, p. 178.

2. The arrival is described also in a letter to Mrs. Martin; Kenyon, *1,* 12.

3. Numbers 7 and 8 Fortfield Terrace, a three-story Georgian house which still displays on the pediment the Russian imperial eagle put up by the Council in honor of the Grand Duchess Helena. She and her two daughters were in residence there for three months in 1831. The house is in the town, adjoining a row of attached houses, and contrasts strongly with both the isolation and the splendor of Hope End. I can find no record of the name Raffaral (or Rafarel) House, which EBB twice applies to this residence.

pleased *both you and Mrs. Boyd* in this letter. Quantum mutatus a te!!

Yours affectionately

E. B. Barrett

You will not, my dear Mrs. Boyd, think what I am going to say to you, strange, or let others think it rude. Miss Moore does not appear to be a particular friend of yours. I have resolved, that, altho' it may not be possible for me to live as secludedly as I have done, I will have no new acquaintance except by necessity. Besides, Papa might not like my knowing people whom he does not know. I am of course obliged by Miss M.'s wish of being acquainted with me. It is not likely to be a *very* strong one—and if you say nothing more about it to her, she will forget that she ever expressed it. I am very sorry that Annie should have fallen down stairs, and earnestly hope the accident may not occasion any uneasiness to you. My best love to her. Arabel will write soon.

Yours affectionately

E. B. B.

Our journey consisted of 130 not 140 miles. Bath is almost exactly half way.

122.

To Bath Hampton
Bath

Rafarel House
Sidmouth
August 30, 1832

My dearest friend,

When I saw the death of Dr. Adam Clarke [1] mentioned in the paper today, I thought I would write to you. I know that the event is one likely to give you pain and that its suddenness may have startled and agitated you. I should like to know how you feel about it—but I cannot know it now when I am more than sixty miles away from you. The loss of your distinguished friend, to the world as well as to his immediate acquaintances, is a great and peculiar affliction—great, because the loss of no ordinary man can be compared to it,—and peculiar, because it would not be lawful or indeed reasonable, to mourn as for common mortal dust, over one, whose spirit we *know* to be shining as the stars, with those who have turned many to righteousness. He has lived a long life—

1. Dr. Clarke died of cholera on August 26, 1832.

he has fought a good fight, and finished his course—and if it ended abruptly at the last, and no warning hand was extended to his suffering friends to point out their impending affliction, yet it must be their consolation to consider, that the very abruptness of his departure was the means made use of by the God whom he acknowledged in death, to avert from him the common infirmities of age—the weakening of the flesh, and the clouding of the spirit. As it was, the sight of his intellect remained undimmed—and while it was fixed by the light of faith, on the face of his Lord, that face was at once revealed to him in the perfect and immortal light which shines after death. He was not forced to sit down in his Master's vineyard—he could work until the last—and he was about his Father's business until he was called to his Father's house. And in that house, how many happy beings were prepared to welcome him—many whom he had loved in the flesh—more whom he had loved and benefited in the spirit—and among them all, and above them all, the "well done, thou good and faithful servant" from the lips of Jesus. Oh!—who can stand in this world of doubt and sorrow and sin, and weep for those who are here no longer—except from very selfishness? From that very selfishness—for my sake more than for yours—I must hope and pray that *your* years of time may be long. But when they last no longer, may you my dearest friend, be reunited in bonds stronger than earthly friendship, unto *him,* who was among the just, upon earth, and is, in Heaven, among the just made perfect. May this be, for the sake of Christ!—the Justifier!

Reading over the last few sentences, one sentence among them has made me smile. It is the one which begins—"From that very selfishness etc."—as if I were sure of living to see your "long life" *out!* I was thinking of my being younger than you, when I wrote it—but altho' I *am* younger, you are certainly likely enough to outlive me by years and years. It is a happy circumstance for human beings, that the measuring out of human life, is not entrusted to the hands of Time.

Papa has not arrived yet. Yesterday, I walked my donkey into the sea above its knees—and tomorrow I am going to walk it up a very high cliff—that I may try every element by turns, air as well as water. They all climbed it yesterday, by means of a path cut in the rock, and thought the scenery so "exquisite", that I must run the risk of my neck—or *nec* sopor *nec* quies. I have slept better, and been much cooler,—as far as the body goes—within the last few days. My love to Mrs. Boyd and Annie.

Ever yours affectionately
E. B. Barrett

I have received such a very kind letter from Lady Margaret Cocks! Mr. and Mrs. Hering [2] with whom I told you Papa was slightly acquainted, are the only persons who have yet called upon us. They have been as kind and attentive as if they were our near relations. The place is very full—and there is so much quadrilling and cricketing that nobody can doubt its intellectuality.

123.

To Bath Hampton
Bath

Sidmouth. September 4, 1832

My dearest friend,

How could I think that you should be angry at my not going to see you? You certainly don't appear to be in the least angry, and I must own my mistake in thinking anything of the kind.

You acquit *me,* but you lay upon others a heavy weight of blame. You are right in acquitting me, and in believing that had it been in my power I would have remained at Bath for the purpose of seeing you. I would have done so, both because to have seen you once more, would have given me satisfaction, and because I do not like to make you angry, —and I know well that any apparent want of attention, even from persons to whom you are indifferent, is apt to make you angry. You must allow me to say, that in being angry on this occasion with *anybody,* you are not as just, as, with your clear-headedness and power of judging, you always ought to be. Fifteen of us, and two carriages were at the Bath Hotel—and we could not have remained a day longer at it, without some expense. People do not incur expense without an object, and what would have been Papa's? To do me good,—or to do you good? Was he likely to think, that seeing you and wishing you good-bye on the same day, would have done *me* any real good? And had he much reason for thinking that *you* would care enough about seeing me, for him to be justified in increasing by at least eight or nine pounds, his already large expenses, that you *might* see me?

I do not like mentioning the word expense,—but you mentioned it yourself on another occasion, when the object was not, to be in our neighbourhood for merely a few hours—and it is *necessary* for Papa to do everything just now in the cheapest manner, with his large family,

2. "West India people, not very polished, but certainly *very* good-natured." To Mrs. Martin; Kenyon, *1,* 13.

and the call which there has been lately upon him, for ready money. It may seem to you incredible—but a hundred pounds worth of wood, in the bare material,—has been used in making only the rough packing cases for furniture. As to Papa's intending any slight, any want of attention to you, by "directing or permitting" us to pass thro' Bath without seeing you, do not suppose it! We passed my uncle's place at Frocester,[1] *within* three miles,—and yet he had asked us to visit him on the road. We might have gone through Frocester on our way to Bath,—and yet we did not go. You cannot suppose that any want of attention was intended towards Mr. Clarke.

Papa told my aunt that if we had left Hope End earlier in the summer, he might have gone to Tenby for a few months, and spent the winter in Bath.

I did not mean to write to you so soon again. Writing so often will be worse than writing so long, as you have to pay for it. But I don't like the feeling of *your* being angry and of *my* saying nothing—therefore you see you must be patient under the consequences of your injustice. My best love to Mrs. Boyd and Annie.

Yours affectionately
E. B. Barrett

My aunt is still with us,—but I am afraid she thinks of moving soon. Papa is to arrive this week.

124.

To Bath Hampton
     Bath

Sidmouth. Friday
[*postmark* October 20, 1832]

My dearest friend,

I hope that before now you have sent your translations to Mr. Clarke and obtained his opinion. Was I right in understanding from a letter of yours that you had intended to do so, before he lost his father? I think I was—but I am sure it would not be right in *you,* or fair to your own reputation, to make any unnecessary delay in applying to him. Whatever his decision may be, it cannot induce me to alter mine. I am unalterable about it. I *may* be unalterably wrong, of course.

1. John Altham Graham-Clarke had residences at Kinnersley Castle, Herefordshire, and at Frocester, Gloucester, both of which had belonged to his wife's family. Burke's *Landed Gentry.*

The epigram which you sent to me, I forgot to mention when I wrote last. Should I have forgotten to mention it, if I had not forgotten to admire it? I dare say you have written many, which I should admire, since we parted. How pleased I was to hear from Mrs. Boyd of your being quite well. May that pleasure not be as transient as I have found others to be! If I can now, or hereafter do one thing little or great for you, do not refuse to let me hear of it.

I have nothing to say which is likely to interest you—except, May God bless you—and I can say *that* without writing it on paper.

Yours affectionately
E. B. Barrett

Dearest Annie,

I am trying to get some lobsters for you, and will send them when I succeed. They seem to be scarce here, just now. Thank you and Mrs. Boyd for your letter: I will write more to you, by the lobsters. What made you think of our leaving Sidmouth this winter? Did I not tell you that Papa came here, on account of its being warmer during the winter, than other places? Bro and Sam were at a party last night, where there were a hundred and sixty people—which proves how full the place is still! This letter is not full—but I shall end it.

Your affectionate Ba.

There have been only eight cases of suspected cholera in all: and for the last three weeks, not one case. Very few people believe that the disease has been really here, even under the most mitigated form. Your report made us smile.

I hope Mrs. Boyd is quite well. My best love to her! Arabel is expecting to hear from you. Her love—and Henrietta's.

125.

To Bath Hampton
Bath

[postmark November 22, 1832]

My dearest friend,

In not hearing from me immediately on the subject you mentioned, you will not, because you cannot, believe that I was waiting for "leisure". I do not mean to send what I have written until I hear further from Bath.[1] They are incredulous here in my *really thinking* that you

1. The Boyds' house at Bathampton was leased until June 1833, but Mr. Boyd, discontented and unhappy there, had gone to stay in Bath. In less than three weeks

will not come to Sidmouth. But I *do* think so,—and I have two reasons for the thought—and one of them is, that the pleasure would be far greater than any which I now expect.

I was of course sorry to find that you had actually sent your ms. to the Methodists Magazine,[2] where it will probably be read by very few capable of appreciating it. If I had decided upon not publishing in a separate form, I would at least have consigned it, to a publication of a higher literary character. You did not tell me Mr. Clarke's opinion.

Thursday

I cannot wait any longer. What you said of your inability to take exercise and to give your attention to literature as you used to do, made me feel sure that something in Bath did not agree with you. I am very certain you were able to attend to reading last winter as long if not longer than you did when I knew you first. You told me yourself that you had less heaviness in your head and nervousness than you formerly suffered from—and if last winter you could not walk for 8 miles, the evident reason was, your having thrown yourself out of the habit of walking, by not employing a person to walk with you regularly. If I had any influence with you, I would beseech you to leave Bath. The air must be the same as at B. H.; and besides, if it were not, a large town is not a place calculated for, or safe for your residence. I am sure you believe what you say,—but you may mistake your feelings. That a person in tolerable health, should be physically fatigued by listening to English reading for ten minutes once a fortnight, (to take an outside calculation) appears to me difficult to understand; and that a person should be morally so, by this degree of communication from another, and yet preserve a friendship for that other, appears to me still more difficult. You

---

from the time of this letter he followed the Barretts to Sidmouth. On December 14 EBB wrote, "Mr. Boyd arrived here three days ago, and is going to settle himself close to us. Neither Bathampton nor Bath agreed with him,—and altho' his house in the former place is on his hands for six months, he has left it behind, and seems to be quite satisfied with the Sidmouth air and the sound of the sea, and Mr. Russel's rolls. Mrs. Boyd is not satisfied in the *same degree,* but I have no compassion for her. You may suppose how astonished I was to hear of their arrival, not having an idea of its probability. It was a plan to astonish me,—and I had received a letter the very same day from Bath which did not contain a word on the subject." To Mrs. Martin; omitted from Kenyon, *1,* 16.

2. Published *Wesleyan-Methodist Magazine* (December 1832, May 1833), whose readers were "pious people, but not cultivated, nor, for the most part, capable of estimating either the talents of Gregory or his translator's." To Mrs. Martin, December 14, 1832; Kenyon, *1,* 17.

know it *was* not so! I deeply regret having occasioned annoyance to one to whom I always wished to give only pleasure. But it shall never be repeated. I wish I could save you from every other annoyance as easily, tho' at the price of as much pain to myself.

Your affectionate friend
E. B. B.

Burn *this* half of this sheet.

[In Arabel's handwriting]

I shall seize upon this before Ba begins to finish it to write a few lines to you my dearest Annie. Why have you not answered my last letter? Pray do write *immediately* and tell me exactly what you mean to do. Ba is afraid that Mrs. Boyd will think it unkind our not asking *her* at any rate to come here to this house on account of her cough but indeed we are all squeezed in little rooms, two in a bed. The best way is for her to take a house for herself and bring you all with her. Ba is sure it will suit Mr. Boyd. We enquired about two houses the other day on the parade which is close to the sea and the gayest situation and very near us besides. One of them had three sitting rooms and 8 bedrooms, it was at two guineas a week for the whole winter, the other two sitting rooms and 6 bedrooms which was at 1 guinea. How very warm the weather is! it is quite refreshing to bathe which I was obliged to do in the middle of the day today to *cool myself* and it was such a splendid sea. The waves rolling much higher than any hill you can see round Bath—you ought to come if it was only for the sake of seeing me bathe [3]—I know you would enjoy yourself if you were here, but however please yourselves gentlefolks.

Your affectionate Arabel

126.

To Mrs. Boyd
  Bath Hampton
  Bath [1]

Sidmouth. May 3, 1833

My dear Ann,

I hope you received the letter which Jane wrote for me the other night. I advise you to be very careful, with respect to what you say of Dr.

---

3. "Arabel bathes regularly—and this is the fourteenth of December." To Mrs. Martin; omitted from Kenyon, *1*, 16.

1. Written in EBB's hand. Mr. Boyd, attended by their maid Jane, had been board-

Harvey. If you were to say anything actionable, I think there is little
doubt that he would prosecute you. I think you must not send for
more than *fifty pounds*. If you want any more, you must make use of
certain articles in your possession. Do *not* make use of those which Ba
once had in her care.[2] I think that *those* are all new and bright. If you
are well enough, which I hope will be the case, do not delay coming, any
longer than is absolutely necessary. I do not like to run the risk of taking
a house,[3] which you might not like,—and the longer you delay, of course
there may be fewer houses to choose. Love to little Ann.

Yours affectionately

H. S. Boyd

Arabel will be much obliged by your taking care of her parcel, and
bringing it when you come.

I have just received your last letter. You ask me to write directly,—or
it will delay you. I do not know what I am to write about. I have already
told you that I think you cannot write for more than fifty pounds,—
and that you had better use some of the other.

127.

To 27 Brock Street
    Bath [1]

Friday morning [*postmark* May 30, 1834]

My dear Mr. Boyd,

As I am going to write a very impertinent letter, I will in the first
place supplicate your *for*bearance and *for*giveness *for* whatever I may

---

ing in Sidmouth for nearly five months, while his wife and Annie continued to stay
in Bathampton. Three weeks before this letter (April 13), EBB wrote to Mrs. Boyd,
"For me to say, that I have not deeply regretted your not having come *before* your
illness rendered exertion injurious to you, would not be honest in me. I certainly
have been unable to see poor Mr. Boyd so solitary, in this strange place, without wishing you had determined otherwise than you did. I have been unable to help thinking
that as soon as Annie was strong enough to attend the Bath parties, she was strong
enough to come here. . . . From an expression in your letter, you seem to think me
more selfish than I am. Whatever pleasure I have received from Mr. Boyd's being
here, it has not prevented me from wishing more than once, that he had not come
here. But the past is past and I hope, your being able to come soon, will cause him
to forget his four months want of comfort." Typescript deposited by Kenyon in the
British Museum, MSA. 42,229–42,231.

2. In Letter 44 and Weaver, Letter III, mention is made of coins in EBB's care.

3. A house was taken soon after this "not farther than a five minutes' walk" from
the Barretts'. To Mrs. Martin, May 27, 1833; Kenyon, *1*, 20.

1. The Boyds left Sidmouth for Bath in May 1834.

say. The day before yesterday I was in Mr. Harvey's shop, and he—
(you must not be angry with him, for you know he considered me a
corrector of the press and a privileged person) showed me your preface.[2]
The impertinent thing which I am going to say, is, that I do not like
it—(*that* you did not expect me to do, did you?)—and I wish you,
very very much to show the ms. to Mr. Spowers or to some friend in
whose intelligence and freedom from prejudice, you can place full re-
liance, before you actually publish it. I do wish this—and I not only
wish it, but *beseech* you to do it. There is plenty of time for it to be
done, before the poetical portion of the work is out of the press—and
I am very sure that your own reputation and the reputation of your
book will stand, in a safer place, should you be induced to adopt certain
corrections in this preface. The mere composition appears to me *rather
loose and crude:* but it is to the matter that the more important objections attach themselves. Whatever opinion you entertain of the Church
of England, you are not wrong in expressing—but then you might have
expressed it less figuratively and oratorically, and so, with more effect.
It appears to me that the tears of Apollo and the Muses [3] may be considered inappropriate to the downfall of a church, by others than dissenters. I see an objection besides, to the introduction of your prophecy
on the subject of the Roman Catholics [4]—to the detailed account of the
visit and observation of the Bishop of London [5]—(unless you consulted
him in the first place, he might not be pleased at those details) and to
your mention of *Porson* among the sons of the Church of England. There
are some other expressions which I should like to see expunged—but I
read the preface thro' very hurriedly, and they do not occur to me now.
Let me entreat you, dear Mr. Boyd, *do* allow some person *whom you
esteem,* to read it with attention. A preface is an important part of a
book; and if any of your readers should be inclined to ridicule yours, *I*

2. To *The Fathers Not Papists,* London, Samuel Bagster, and Sidmouth, John
Harvey, 1834. The preface, dated May 22, 1834, consists of tirades against "Roman
Catholicks and Popish translators of the Scriptures," with digressions on such diverse
topics as the sins of the Unitarians, Boyd's own "Essay on the Greek Article," and the
errors in typography which will probably result from his blindness.

3. "If she [the Church af England] be doomed to fall, she will descend in a blaze
of glory; and the tears of Apollo and the Muses will be mingled with the more hallowed sorrows of her afflicted offspring!"

4. "Popery is making the most rapid and gigantick strides. Should our national
church be done away, I think there is no doubt (humanly speaking) that in forty
or fifty years, perhaps in a less time, Popery will again be the established religion!
Then will the Dissenters groan in the anguish of their hearts . . . but their repentance and sorrow will be too late."

5. On this one point Boyd took EBB's advice: the reference is omitted.

should be sorry, even if *you* did not care. Now you will forgive me my impertinence—will you not? Were I not interested in the success and character of your work, I should not have courage to write to you so freely.

You will be surprised to hear that Mr. Joseph Biscoe arrived here three weeks ago with his bride, and has taken Myrtle Hall for a year. He met Arabel and me in the lane opposite to our house, and introduced to us—Mrs. Joseph Biscoe! *She is not at all pretty*—and as I did not hear her speak, I had no opportunity of judging of her other attractions. I believe they were married—Mr. Biscoe and Miss Brandling—in Germany, two or three months ago. He does not look well. He told us that he liked very much what he saw of Sidmouth, but that he was afraid of its being too *gay!!* for him,—as it was his intention, in coming here, to live in as secluded a manner as possible. A splendid Mount St. Bernard dog follows them about, and makes them celebrated people at Sidmouth.

What do you think we did last Saturday? Arabel and I and the boys, escorted by Mr. Hunter and Mary,[6] went from hence at ten o'clock in the morning, by the steam packet to Torquay. The packet returned us to Exmouth at about six in the evening,—and there we had tea, and came home upon wheels at nine. It would have been very pleasant indeed, had it not been for a most devastating sea sickness which in consequence of a rough rolling sea, laid prostrate seventy out of ninety passengers. Mr. Hunter and I had to nurse all our party—and, sad to relate, just within a mile of landing I lost my oceanic reputation too—"and universal ruin swallowed all"—except Mr. Hunter. The entrance of Tor bay is very very fine,—and we had a *band*, to throw the right shade of dramatic effect over the scenery. We saw Torquay, Teignmouth, Dawlish, Exmouth: but after all, we saw nothing (at least so some of us agreed) so green and lovely as this valley of Sidmouth.

I suppose you will write to me, some time or other. Yet, I do not mean to be *troublesome*, in saying so. We are going to remain here—at Belle Vue.[7]

Give my love to Mrs. Boyd and Annie, and believe me

Affectionately, tho' so impertinently yours

E. B. Barrett

6. George Barrett Hunter, nonconformist clergyman, and his eight-year-old daughter. Mrs. Betty Miller has written a convincing account of his emotional attachment to EBB, "Miss Barrett and Mr. Hunter," *Cornhill Magazine* (Spring 1951), pp. 83–96.

7. "A thatched cottage, with a green lawn bounded by a Devonshire lane." To Miss Commeline, September 22, 1834; Kenyon, *1*, 26. This was the Barretts' third home in Sidmouth; the second was an ugly "ruin," in imminent danger of collapse

Say how you like Bath.

Harvey would not allow even Papa to see your Preface—only *me;* so you really must not be angry with him.

128.[1]

To Howley Square
Margate, Kent

Sidmouth. September 14, 1834

My dear Mr. Boyd,

I won't ask you to forgive me for not writing before, because I know very well that you would rather have not heard from me immediately. I was glad once again to see your signature, and to hear from yourself where you were. Your being at Margate surprised me,—and it pleased me besides, because I knew how much gladness of heart Miss Boyd must feel in having you with her. Will you give my love to her, and say so? And when you write next, will you say whether you mean to *reside* at Margate—and how your health is—and how you like the old associations around you? You do not mention what interests me most.

You did Mr. Harvey injustice in imagining that he would not show us your letter. He sent it to us on the very evening of its arrival. He was wrong and injudicious to bring forward his application for the £10, as a *claim,*—when his own part of the engagement was not strictly and literally fulfilled. No one acquainted with you as I am, dear Mr. Boyd, could attribute to you the sins of meanness and illiberality. At the same time, will you permit me to say that I was and am very sorry at your not giving the £10? The engagement was *almost* fulfilled on Harvey's side,—and would certainly have been so completely, had not your removal occasioned *some* delay, and the accident about the types, *more.* An attention to different wishes of yours has also appeared to increase the expense to him: and after all this heavy expense, a remuneration can scarcely be among his prospects, as the book *does not seem to sell here at all.* As you mentioned the subject to me, you will forgive me for venturing to say so much.

Mr. Hunter returned a fortnight ago from London where he has been passing several weeks. There, he saw Mr. Arthur Wallis. Do you at any time hear from him? I fear that he is more zealous in the pursuit of

---

(to Mrs. Martin, September 7, 1833; Kenyon, *1,* 22) but still able to harbor them briefly after Belle Vue was sold in the summer of 1835. Weaver, Letter XVI.

1. Published in part in Kenyon, *1,* 24.

the vulgar honors of that society which is at once above him and below him—above him in station, and below him in intellect—than of the classic honors of Oxford. Learning, like "Art", is a "jealous god".

And so, you and Mrs. Mathew [2] have been tearing to pieces, to the very rags, all my elaborate theology! And when Mr. Young is "strong enough," he is to help you at your cruel work!! "The points upon which you and I differed", are so numerous, that if I really *am* wrong upon every one of them, Mrs. Mathew has indeed reason to "punish me with hard thoughts." Well! she can't help my feeling for her, much esteem, altho' I never saw her. And if I were to see her, I would not argue with her,—I would only ask her to let me love her. I am weary of controversy in religion,—and should be so, were I stronger and more successful in it, than I am or care to be. The command is—not, "argue with one another"—but, "love one another." It is better to love than to convince. They who lie on the bosom of Jesus, must lie there *together!*

Not a word about your book!! Don't you mean to tell me anything of it? I saw a review [3] of it—rather a satisfactory one—I think in an *August* number of the Athenaeum. If you will look into Fraser's Magazine for August, at an article entitled "Rogueries of Tom Moore," you will be amused with a notice of the Edinburgh Review's criticism, in the text,—and of yourself, in a note. [4]

We have had a crowded Bible meeting,—and a Church Missionary and London Missionary meeting besides; and I went last Tuesday to the Exmouth Bible meeting with Mrs. Maling, Miss Taylor and Mr. Hunter. We did not return until half past one in the morning. Your beloved friend Mr. Cox, has received his dismissal from the curacy,—and it is supposed that Mr. Bradney will be the new curate. From what I understand and believe however, Mr. B. is not likely to remain long in the Church of England. The Bishop of Barbadoes and the Dean of Winchester were walking together on the beach yesterday, making Sidmouth look quite episcopal. You would not have despised it *half so much,* had you been here.

Do you know any person who would like to send his or her son to

2. *A Malvern Tale* (London, 1827) was dedicated "To her who is pre-eminently the child of religion and virtue; to my esteemed friend, Mrs. Mathew, of Stanwell, Middlesex."

3. *The Fathers Not Papists,* reviewed in the *Athenaeum* (August 9, 1834), p. 593: "The volume is valuable for its specimens of the literature of the early Christians, but as a work of controversy, it possesses a very small portion of merit."

4. One of the "Prout Papers," *Fraser's Magazine, 10* (1834), 200. It refers satirically to a devastating review by Moore of Boyd's *Select Passages.*

Sidmouth, for the sake of the climate, and private instruction: and if you do, will you mention it to me? [5]

I am very sorry to hear of Mrs. Boyd being so unwell. Arabel had a letter two days ago from Annie; and as it mentions Mrs. Boyd's having gone to Dover, I trust that she is well again. Should she be returned, give my love to her.

The black edged paper may make you wonder at its cause. Our dear aunt Mrs. Butler,[6] died last month at Dieppe—and died *in Jesus*. Miss Clarke is going, if she is not gone, to Italy for the winter.

You ought to try to be sorry for poor Mr. Cox. Besides the dismissal, which he takes much to heart,—the lady to whom he is engaged, is dying!

Believe me affectionately yours
E. B. Barrett

Write to me whenever you *dislike it least*—and tell me what your plans are. I hear nothing about our leaving Sidmouth.

129.

Sidmouth. Saturday evening [1834]

My dear friend,

I did not complain even within myself of any unkindness in your silence, and can easily understand that you may have received many letters besides mine,[1] to which you might have a painful reluctance to reply. Therefore, pray *never* think of writing to me because you fancy that you ought to write, instead of, because you feel that you would like to write to me.

I took your letter today to Mr. Harvey, and read the passage which refers to him. He said that he had not received the money transmitted by you to Mr. Bagster,—and that, Mr. Bagster having received it, you should apply to *him* for the receipt. I am so glad to hear of the favourable reviews. Except one in the Athenaeum, I have seen none of them. May the countenance of all your reviewers and readers be bright upon your book,—and (am I not liberal?) I will excuse them from frowning

5. This inquiry was made on behalf of Mr. Hunter.

6. Charlotte Graham-Clarke, wife of Rev. Richard Pierce Butler. Frances Graham-Clarke was married to his elder brother, Sir Thomas Butler.

1. A letter of sympathy November 2, 1834 (Weaver, Letter XIV), on the death of Mrs. Boyd, who died in October at her brother's London home.

even over certain preliminary sentences which I myself once frowned over so blackly. But you have forgiven that frown of mine, have you not my dear friend?

I send the parcel which looks the most like your Select Passages, and you ought to praise me for sending them *instantly. That* will prove, will it not?—that I have not forgotten *you.*

As you have resolved upon remaining at your present house until March, I conclude that you and dear Annie are satisfied with it. Does Mrs. Mathew often go to see you? I hope she does,—and that you have other congenial and comforting society. You do not say how you feel within yourself. May all my wishes respecting you be realities!

I could tell you a great deal about the state of the religious parties here,—and how Mr. Bradney and a new chapel are standing midway between Episcopacy and Dissent. What the ultimate leaning will be I dare not presume to say: but, you know, I always *think as I like!* The Baynes's are at Malvern—poor Harriet, I fear, ill again. But the rod of the Divine Chastener blossoms with His love!

This is a hurried letter, which you will be more glad to read than a longer one. Give my kind love to dear Annie. I thank her for her postscript, and if Arabel had not written so much at length, and if it had not been now so late, she should have had a few lines from me. You will have sympathized in our anxiety respecting our dear Papa.[2] We can't help being still anxious about him, altho' the latter accounts have been very satisfactory. May God bless you both.

Yours affectionately
E. B. Barrett

130.[1]

Sidmouth. Tuesday [1835]

My dear Mr. Boyd,

Perhaps you will be a little surprised to hear of a letter from me again,—when I have [sic] received the signal of its acceptability to you. But it seems to me a long time since I wrote last—and here is Arabel wondering whether Annie is ill or angry that she takes no notice of her! And so you must forgive this intrusion of mine, and pay the penalty of

2. Mr. Barrett was in London, suffering from an illness which he told his family was "of a rheumatic character" but which they were informed by other sources was "water on the lungs." He was being cared for by Miss Trepsack. To Mrs. Martin, December 19, 1834; Kenyon, *1*, 27 (with portions omitted).

1. Published in part in Kenyon, *1*, 29.

those who have true friends, in submitting to be asked how you are at least once in two months. We hear a report of your being about to take and furnish another London house. Of this I shall be glad, I mean in the case of your determining to remain anywhere in London—as from what I have understood, Circus Road cannot be a desirable situation for you. It surprises me that you should prefer London as a residence—but *since* you do prefer it, and dear Annie prefers it, I would not move you—not, if my words were a whirlwind and could do it.

And now I am going to tell you the only good news I know, and you will be glad, I know, to be told what I am going to tell you. Dear Georgie has taken his degree, and very honorably, at Glasgow, and is coming to us in all the dignity of a Bachelor of Arts. He was examined in Logic, Moral philosophy, Greek and Latin, of course publicly: and we have heard from a fellow student of his, that his answers were more pertinent than those of any other of the examined, and elicited much applause. Mr. Groube is the fellow student—but he has ceased to be one, having found the Glasgow studies too heavy for his health. Stormie shrank from the public examination, on account of the hesitation in his speech. He would not go up,—altho' according to report, as well qualified as Georgie. Mr. Groube says that the ladies of Glasgow are preparing to break their hearts for Georgie's departure: and he and Stormie leave Glasgow on the first of May! Now, I am sure you will rejoice with me in the result of the examination. Do you not, dear friend? I was very anxious about it,—and almost resigned to hear of a failure—for Georgie was in great alarm and prepared us for the very worst. Therefore the surprise and pleasure were great.

I can't tell you of our plans,—altho' the Glasgow students come to us in a week and this house will be too small to receive them. We may leave Sidmouth immediately, or not at all. I shall soon be quite qualified to write a poem on the "Pleasures of Doubt" [2]—and a very good subject it will be. The pleasures of certainty are generally far less enjoyable— I mean as pleasures go in this unpleasing world. Papa is in London, and much better when we heard from him last—and we are awaiting his decree.

Do you see Mrs. Mathew often? I hope you do, dear friend! The friendship of such as she,—is it not, as the impress of the seal of the friendship of Jesus? We know that we have passed from death unto life because we love the brethren: and something of the same knowledge seems to come—*because the brethren love us!* The widow of Mr. Sipps of Hereford, of whom you may have heard, has lately spent a fortnight

2. An allusion to Thomas Campbell's poem of this name.

here. In the course of two years she has lost her sister and her husband—
her daughter is dying—and her infant never knew the sight of its father's
face. She is a lovely illustration of that lovely contrast of words in
Scripture—"much affliction, in joy of the Holy Ghost". You will be surprised to hear that Harriet Baynes is—not dead, but about to be married
to Mr. Groves [3] the Persian missionary!— She is of course perfectly well:
and immediately upon her marriage, sails with him to India! Is not this,
very like a miracle?

And now what remains for me to tell you? I believe I have read more
Hebrew than Greek, lately: yet the dear Greek is not less dear than ever.
Who reads Greek to you? Who holds my office? Some one I hope with an
articulation of more congenial slowness!

Give Annie my kind love. May God preserve both of you.

Believe me

Your affectionate friend

E. B. Barrett

131.

To 3 Circus Road
St. John's Wood
London

Sidmouth. Tuesday

[*postmark* July 29, 1835]

My dear Mr. Boyd,

I meant to have written to you very long ago—but when I think of
writing to you, I always think—"perhaps I had better for his own sake,
be silent a little longer". Now however—before I am quite an infidel,
which you apprehend as the awful and somewhat *necessary* consequence
of my reading Collins's [1] treatise,—I will write to you,—but *not* to enter
upon any controversy upon Calvinism. I think it is better not to con-
trovert and dispute about it. If you meet with *no* difficulty on the
subject, and run with your thoughts, with the multitude of your
thoughts, against no hard corners, μακαριος! [2] "happy are you!" And if,
on my humbler part, I am content, amid the difficulties visible to my

3. Anthony Norris Groves (1795–1853), medical missionary in Persia and India,
married at Malvern April 25, 1835, to Harriet, third daughter of General Edward
Baynes of Woolbrook Cottage, Sidmouth.

1. Anthony Collins (1676–1729), deist, author of *Discourse on Freethinking* and
other works attacking orthodox theology.

2. "happy."

eyes, to sit down very stilly and try to hold fast by the right hand of Jesus without prying too closely into the way of his footsteps, μακαρια! happy am I. Pray for me, dear friend,—that so it may be. I do assure you that I did not read Collins with any expectation, any unholy expectation, of finding within him interpretations of Scripture. You know, I like to read everything—a liking which may be dangerous or at least unprofitable—but not indicative, in this particular instance, of the particular evil apprehended by you! I have been reading besides, Lord Brougham's Natural Theology [3]—and have shaken my head over it, altho' critics far taller than I am, have nodded theirs. It seems to me to have its most valuable parts in its notes,—in the observations there upon Hume's philosophy. By the way, I ought not to presume to say a word about Hume's philosophy to you,—having a very humbling recollection of your having once said to me that I was quite incapable of understanding it. But to return to Lord Brougham—he leaves upon me the impression of his being, *not* profound,—*not* original,—not *accustomed* to psychological studies. And very wrong I may be. Only, am I wrong in complaining of his style? Surely there are "hard corners" more than enough, in *that!*

How much I have written without saying a word of dear Annie. It has pleased us with so much pleasure, to have her with us once more, and to see her looking well, and seeming cheerful—and I feel that she is very kind in not being in a repining spirit, in the midst of our dullness. All that she repines about, is not hearing often enough and fully enough from *you.* Do write to her as often as you can,—for whenever you don't write, she begins to fancy that you don't think of her—as we are always apt to do, you know, in the silences of those whom we love. On Saturday, she and every one of us went to dine at Pinney Cliffs,[4] near Lyme,—in scenery too exquisite for England, and immortalized by Lord Chatham, if Nature had not given it a nobler immortality. We shall think of such scenes in Heaven! But I won't describe it to you now, because I know that you eschew all long descriptions when they are not made in Greek.

Miss Boyd is reading Shakespeare again. So shall I, when I stand face to face with Shakespeare,—and that may only be when I see my books

3. Henry Peter Brougham (1778–1868), lord chancellor, *A Discourse on Natural Theology*, 1835.

4. (Pinny, Pinhay.) "The counterpart of Dreamland, on earth. We made an excursion to Lyme for the sake of the vision, when we resided at Sidmouth—and I was obliged to lie in bed almost all the next day from the exercise to which I was quite unequal but which that most surpassing scenery beguiled me into taking." To Miss Mitford, from Torquay; unpublished letter: Wellesley College Library.

again. Has she read the German critics upon Shakespeare? as brought
to light, by some surpassingly beautiful papers in the last numbers of
Blackwood—not the very last. The German critics are the only critics
who criticise as Longinus did. They are poet-critics—and know more of
Shakespeare than any of Shakespeare's compatriots do. Now, don't you
quote Porson against the Germans.[5] Give my love to Miss Boyd instead,
—and tell her from me that I wish her prosperity in Shakespeare—and
that she should always, particularly in your presence, speak most
reverentially of Hermann, just for this very reason, because *"Hermann's
a German"*.

How impertinent I am!—but I have written in a very large hand and
am coming to an end very soon, to make up for it!

Believe me, dear friend,
Yours affectionately
E. B. Barrett

[In Annie Boyd's handwriting]
My dear Papa, I have received the Parcel that Jane sent some time ago,
it has all arrived safely, and please to tell her that the very books that
she has kept back are the very ones I wished for most, and I wish her to
send them down to me at Taunton directly. I am glad that you are quite
well, and I am now much better but when first I came I was very unwell.
Good night.

Yours affectionately
A. H. Boyd

132.[1]

Sidmouth. Friday [1835]

My dear friend,

I don't know how I shall begin to persuade you not to be angry with
me—but perhaps the best plan will be to confess as many sins as would
cover this sheet of paper, and then to go on with my merits. Certainly, I
am altogether guiltless of your charge of not noticing your book's arrival
because no Calvinism arrived with it. I told you the bare truth, when
I told you *why* I did not write immediately. The passages relating to

5. When his *Hecuba* was attacked by Gottfried Hermann, Porson, who did not care
for German scholarship, circulated an epigram (based on Phocylides) which was
widely quoted: "The Germans in Greek are sadly to seek; / Not five in five score, but
ninety-five more; / All, save only Hermann, and Hermann's a German."

1. Published in part in Kenyon, *1*, 23.

Calvinism, I certainly read, and as certainly was sorry for: but as certainly as both those certainties, such reading and such regret had nothing whatever to do with the silence which made you so angry with me.

The other particular thing of which I should have written, is Mr. Barker and my letters.[2] I am more and more sorry that you should have sent them to him at all—not that their loss is any loss to anybody, but that I scarcely like the idea—indeed I don't like it at all—of their remaining, worthless as they are, at Mr. B.'s mercy. As for my writing about them, I should not be able to make up my mind to do *that*. You know I had nothing to do with their being sent to Mr. Barker, and was indeed in complete ignorance of it. Besides, I should be half ashamed to write to him now, on any subject. A very long interregnum took place in our correspondence; which was his own work,—and when he wrote to me the summer before last, I delayed from week to week and then from month to month, answering it. And now I feel ashamed to write at all.

Perhaps you will wonder why I am not ashamed to write to *you!* Indeed I have meant to do it, very very often. Don't be severe upon me. I am always afraid of writing to you too often—and so the opposite fault is apt to be run into—of writing too seldom. *If that* is a *fault.* You see my scepticism is becoming faster and faster developed!

Let me hear from you soon, if you are not angry. I have been reading the Bridgewater treatises,[3]—and am now trying to understand Prout upon chemistry. I shall be worth something at last, shall I not? Who knows but what I may die a glorious death under the pons asinorum after all? Prout (if I succeed in understanding him) does not hold that matter is infinitely divisible: and so I suppose the seeds of matter—the ultimate molecules—are a kind of tertium quid between matter and spirit. Certainly I can't believe that any kind of matter, primal or ultimate, can be *indivisible,* which it must, according to his view.

Chalmers's treatise is, as to eloquence, surpassingly beautiful: as to matter, I could not walk with him all the way—altho' I longed to do it, for he walked on flowers, and under shade—'no tree on which a fine bird did not sit.'[4]

I never look at the newspapers now, but I hear that the House of

2. For Mr. Barker's request to publish EBB's letters to Boyd see Letter 61.

3. Eight treatises on "natural theology," published 1833, provided for in the will of the Duke of Bridgewater. The two referred to here are William Prout's "Chemistry, Meteorology, and the Function of Digestion Considered with Reference to Natural Theology" and Thomas Chalmers' "The Adaptation of External Nature to the Moral and Intellectual Constitution of Man."

4. "No branch whereon a fine bird did not sit," Spenser, *Faerie Queene,* 2.6.13.2.

Lords is dying a *natural* death,—in one sense at least. I hear that a re-
formed House of Commons, and an unreformable House of Lords can't
co-exist. Papa wants to have a new House on a representative system—
and I want the Lords to be content to be merged in the other House,
the reformed House, and make *one* with the people. Of course you
will agree with me. We shall be able to *talk* all this over, besides all the
Greek, soon, I dare say. Dear Annie will have told you of the likelihood
there is, of our removing to London next month. There are just two
faces in London whom I shall care about seeing, exclusive of dear Annie's
—and Miss Trepsack's is one. I will leave the other to your ingenuity
to divine. How I shall ever breathe when I am walled up like a trans-
gressing man, and out of hearing of that sea, requires a somewhat more
profound divination. χρόνος μόνος [5] can instruct. This sounds very much
like joking, but is too sad and sober earnest after all! The next page
belongs to Arabel. Don't you owe her everlasting gratitude? Is Miss Boyd
still with you? Because if she is, my love shall go to her, and to dear
Annie too!

Believe me
Your affectionate friend
E. B. B.

133.

Tuesday [1835]

My dear friend,

Thank you for your very kind invitation. We are like stubble before
the wind—uncertain as to our movements—but if we do go to London,[1]
whether I am able to *stay* with you or not, I shall be *quite able* as well
as *willing* to "drink delicious poison" from your Chinese green tea *tecum*
as you kindly propose, *on many an evening,*—and lose our Chinese con-
traries, in our Greek sympathies. I need not say how very very glad I shall
be to see you, and hear you, and read to you, and perceive how far you
have proceeded in forgetting me since we parted at Sidmouth—*your*
"boat upon the shore", and *my* "barque upon the sea".[2] Don't expect—

---

5. "Time alone."

1. The move to London, to furnished rooms at 74 Gloucester Place, was made
during the summer; Boyd greeted their arrival with a gift of Chinese tea. ("Papa and
I were very much obliged to you for the poison." Kenyon, *1*, 32.)

2. "My boat is on the shore, / And my bark is on the sea; / But before I go, Tom
Moore, / Here's a double health to thee." Byron, "To Thomas Moore."

even if you expect *me*—to find me improved in anything—albeit I *have* read Collins upon necessity. You know, women never *do* improve—after a certain point. I am just as obstinate and fanatical as I used to be, and as uncomprehending of the mathematics—and what is worse, with a vestment of Calvinism—so that, if dear Mr. Boyd has not a great deal of patience besides the green tea, perhaps I had better stay away. The best of me is, that I am intending to read Plato very devotedly when I go to London if I ever go, and procure a Plato, if I ever procure one. Since I saw you, I have read nothing of him—nor of Plotinus. Lately, I have been reading Hebrew, and writing verses—for the most part. But the verses are very miscellaneous (not a poem) and I dare say you would not care much for any of them.

You will have heard of the arrival of my dear Bro.[3] It has been a great joy to me. He looks so well, and is so happy to be back again—almost as happy as I am to see him. On the passage home he nearly died a glorious death by poison. Now, can you guess what poison? Green tea? No!—something more "high fantastical" than even yours from China. *A dolphin which had hung in the moonshine!* The moonshine poisoned the dolphin and the dolphin poisoned Bro—and poor Brozie grew quite black and swollen in the face. Would it not have been a glorious death— to die of a dolphin and moonshine? But I dare say you think the story moonshine altogether. And so did I, before I heard Bro's asseverations. . . .[4]

A few weeks ago Dr. Payne [5] of Exeter,—the academician and metaphysician you know,—called here,—and while we were talking of Stuart's work on the Romans,[6] I observed that he held an opinion not altogether orthodox, of the non-eternity of the Sonship of Christ. "If you call that opinion unorthodox", said Dr. Payne, "I myself am among the heterodox. I feel that a rejection of the doctrine of the eternal Sonship *keeps me from Arianism.*" He then went on to tell me that the opinion was

3. Bro had been in Jamaica for more than a year, helping his Uncle Sam with the supervision of the family estates. On the decision to send him to Jamaica, Mr. Barrett wrote to his brother, "Our beloved Ba upon the colour I put upon the project, namely as being profitable to Bro's interest, has consented in a spirit that has, if possible, raised her still higher in my estimation." Jeanette Marks, *The Family of the Barrett* (New York, 1938), p. 423.

4. The omitted passage refers to *A Dissertation on Infant Baptism* by Ralph Wardlaw (1779–1853) and *Dissent Not Schism* by Thomas Binney (1798–1874), with comment on philological arguments.

5. George Payne (1781–1845), theological tutor in the Western Academy at Exeter.

6. Moses Stuart (1780–1852), American biblical scholar, author of *A Commentary on the Epistle to the Romans*, 2 vols. 1832.

gaining ground—and that he was lately present at a meeting of ministers in London, where the only individual, orthodox according to my view, was Dr. Pye Smith.[7] I am very sorry for it. Have you observed among your friends any similar bending and breaking? Dr. Payne is a delightful man, highly cultivated, and gentle and pleasing in his manners—and dearer, I believe, to the heart of Jesus than even to his human friends. He has within a year, given his two daughters to be wives to missionaries in the East and West Indies—and gladly given them—altho' the parting appears to have weighed his head nearer to the grave. Give my love to dear Annie—and to Miss Boyd. Papa is in London. By this time, you will have wished *me* in New Zealand.

Dear Mr. Boyd's affectionate friend.

134.

74 Gloucester Place. Thursday morning
[January 1836] [1]

My dear Mr. Boyd,

As certainly as that Arabel cannot draw the teacup, I had intended to go to see you today. And I am quite aware that I shall drink a very large overflowing teacup of your wrath, in not going. It is at my lips. I must drink, for I cannot walk. I have such a cough *again!* that I should hasten it to a wrong conclusion, by going out today, particularly to a place so far off as your house. Will you be generous, and forgive me for having a cough? When it goes, I shall be very happy indeed to go too.

In the meantime I am going to tell you that dear Georgie has entered at the Inner Temple, after passing triumphantly a classical examination. A classical examination!—*not* in the Olynthiacs of Demosthenes—*not* in the *school* of Hackney—*not* by a Scotchman—*not*—proh pudor! by a dissenter; but—in the choruses of the Greek tragedies—by a native of England ("Angeli sunt Angli!") [2]—by a member of England's infallible church, and a first class man from the omniscient university of Oxford.

ακουετε λαοι!—[3]

7. John Pye Smith (1774–1851), nonconformist minister, author of *Scripture Testimony to the Messiah*, 2 vols. 1818–21.

1. Dated by a letter to Mrs. Martin, January 1, 1836, saying that George would probably enter at the Inner Temple on the fifth or sixth of the month. Kenyon, *1*, 35.

2. Commonly quoted as "Non Angli sed Angeli" (Gregory the Great).

3. "Hear, ye people!"

The examiner said "very well". What will *you* say? For my part, I am so vain of my brother, that I shall soon begin to think my sister capable of drawing a teacup.

Mr. Newdick paid us a visit yesterday for half an hour,—and I had the satisfaction of hearing that while we were frozen to the fender, in Christmas week, they at Sidmouth only had "a *little* frost every day". What would you give to be there?

Have you heard from Annie, and when?—and when do you expect to have her with you again?

Your affectionate friend
E. B. Barrett

[*In Arabel's handwriting*]
Dear Mr. Boyd, I am much obliged to you for the trouble you have given yourself about the tea cup. I am most anxious to see it, and to copy it— and if I manage to draw it, I suppose I may consider myself very *scientific indeed!* May I not? Annie begged me to write to her, but she neither left me her direction nor has she written to me, at which of course I am very angry—I used all my persuasive endeavours to induce her to postpone her trip to Margate, but it was all in vain.

Yours sincerely
Arabel Barrett

I am rather a dangerous person to invite to your house. Remember my attack upon your cellar the other day!

135.

To 3 Circus Road
St. John's Wood

Tuesday
[postmark March 16, 1836]

My dear friend,

When I am able, I will gladly attend to your request—but at this present moment I am quite *dis*abled by a very bad cold which has kept me in my bedroom all today.

I congratulate you on the incense which seems to be exhaled upon

your Baskett's bible [1] from all sides as well as from the Aedes Althorpianae.[2] May it be *"redolent* of joy" to you.

Forgive me for feeling stupefied. Arabel's kind regards.

Yours affectionately

E. B. Barrett

My excuse for writing is my fear of your thinking me unkind for not
going to you immediately.

136.[1]

To 3 Circus Road
St. John's Wood

Thursday
[*postmark* December 15, 1836]

My dear Mr. Boyd,

Don't be very much frightened when the size of this sheet is described
to you. It does not mean any harm—only to give you a paragraph in
the Morning Chronicle of today—[A letter to the editor from Mr. Barker,
enclosing a Latin poem by his "learned correspondent Dr. Friedemann,"
which ends "Cedite, Romani, Graii quoque,—cedite, Galli; / Daedaleam
laurum Greenius unus habet."]

And so all the Greeks are to yield to Mr. Green! [2] What *you* mean to
do, I don't know, but certainly *I* shall do no such thing. There was such
a glorious admixture of wax and presumption in our Daedalus,—and I
take upon myself to say, that *he* never affronted the sun, by approaching
it with a chicken under one arm, and a coffee pot under the other!! To
think of comparing Mr. Green with Daedalus! And to talk besides of
transferring Daedalus' laurels to Mr. Green!!! Why Daedalus had the
cypress for all *his* laurels, and stood in good need of the shadow of it.

1. John Baskett (*d.* 1742), King's printer, produced the "magnificent" but carelessly
printed "Vinegar Bible."

2. *Aedes Althorpianae* (1822), a description of the famous Althorp library done for
the second Earl Spencer by his librarian Thomas Frognall Dibdin.

1. Published in part in Kenyon, *1*, 44.

2. Charles Green (1785–1870) had since 1821 been making balloon ascents from
various parts of England in a "stupendous, aeronautic machine, composed of nearly
1100 yards of silk in alternate stripes of crimson and gold" (e.g. from the Gas Works,
Hereford, October 23, 1827. "Admission to the yard, 2 shillings"). In the fall of 1836,
his new balloon, said to inflate to eighty feet in height, took intrepid passengers from
the Vauxhall Gardens to destinations (which could not be predetermined) as far
away as Frankfurt, Germany.

Mr. Green's laurels may be as green as *greens*—but let him enjoy the lustre of them in Covent Garden Market,—without their being scorched with the *thought* of our Greeks!

You see, Mr. Barker is in London! or at least *was,* a few days ago! But little recks *he,* of either you or *me!*—which is extemporary, and quite (I dare say you will observe) in *my style.*

Two mornings since, I saw in the paper, under the head of literary news, that a change of Editorship was taking place in the New Monthly Magazine,—and that Theodore Hook [3] was to preside in the room of Mr. Hall.[4] I am so much too modest and too wise to expect the patronage of two Editors in succession, that I expect both my poems in a return cover, by every twopenny post. Besides what has Theodore Hook to do with Seraphim? So, I shall leave that poem of mine to your imagination, —which won't be half as troublesome to you as if I asked you to read it, —begging you to be assured,—to write it down in your critical rubric,— that it is the very finest composition you ever read, *next* (of course) to the beloved *De virginitate* of Gregory Nazianzen.

Mr. Stratten [5] has just been here. I admire him more than I ever did, for his admiration of my doves. By the way, I am sure he thought them the most agreeable of the whole party,—for he said, what he never did before, that he could sit here an hour! Our love to Annie—and forgive me for Baskettiring a letter to you. I mean of course, as to size—not type.

Yours affectionately,
E. B. Barrett

Is your poem printed yet?

3. Theodore Edward Hook (1788–1841), novelist and playwright, editor of the *New Monthly Magazine* during 1836–37.

4. Samuel Carter Hall (1800–89), assistant editor of the *New Monthly Magazine* under Bulwer Lytton, editor 1832–36.

5. Rev. James Stratten, clergyman at Paddington Chapel, which the Barretts attended. For an appreciative account of him see EBB—RB, 2, 489–90. The name is there given as "Stratton." I have checked the original in the Wellesley College Library and although the spelling is not clear, I am inclined to think it should be read Stratten. The spelling "Stratton" is also given in Huxley, p. 18.

137.[1]

To 3 Circus Road
   St. John's Wood

Tuesday [Christmas 1836]

My dear friend,

I am very much obliged to you for the *two* copies of your poem, so beautifully printed, with such "majestical" types, on such "magnifical" paper, as to be almost worthy of Baskett himself. You are too liberal in sending me more than one copy—and pray accept in return a duplicate of gratitude.

I have heard nothing more of Mr. Barker. Perhaps Dr. Friedemann may have inspired him into a balloon, and sent him out of London. Are you quite sure that he *knows* your address?

As to my "Seraphim," they are not returned to me, as in the case of their being unaccepted, I expressly begged they might be. Had the old Editor been the present one, my inference would of course be, that their insertion was a determined matter: but as it is, I don't know what to think. A long list of great names, belonging to *intending* contributors, appeared in the paper a day or two ago—and among them was Miss Mitford's.[2]

Are you wroth with me for not saying a word about going to see you? Arabel and I won't affirm it mathematically—but we are, metaphysically, *talking* of paying our visit to you next Tuesday. Don't expect us, nevertheless.

Yours affectionately
E. B. Barrett

What are my Christmas good wishes to be? That you may hold a Field[3] in your right hand, and a Baskerville[4] in your left,—before the year is out? That degree of happiness will satisfy at least the *bodily* part of you.

You may wish, in return, for *me,* that I may learn to write rather more legibly than "at these presents."

1. Published in part in Kenyon, *1,* 45.
2. Mary Russell Mitford (1787–1855), novelist and dramatist, author of "Our Village." She first met EBB in 1836. See Miller for an account of their friendship.
3. Richard Field (1579–1624), printer of the first three editions of Shakespeare's *Venus and Adonis.*
4. John Baskerville (1706–1775), printer of fine editions of Latin authors and of the Greek New Testament.

Our love to Annie.

Won't you send your new poem to Mr. Barker, to the care of Mr. Valpy, with your Christmas benedictions?

If we go on Tuesday, it will be very early, directly after breakfast, as we are obliged to go away early. Why does not Annie fulfil her promise of coming to dine with us?

138.

To 3 Circus Road
St. John's Wood

Monday morning [1837]

My dear Mr. Boyd,

I do not know if you will think it a "sufficient reason" for not going to see you that I did not feel at all well—all the latter part of last week— and in the case that you do not, I may as well say that I did *not* fix any particular time with Annie for my visit to you—merely telling her that I meant to pay it soon.

Arabel and I had determined to pay it this morning—but last night Papa appeared displeased that we had not been to see some relatives of ours and particular friends of his, who were under affliction. They live at some distance from us, and we are obliged to spend a great part of today in visiting them. Tomorrow brings with it the prayer meeting— but on Wednesday, if it is a fine day, we shall be happy to dine at your house and stay till eight o'clock or a little later—unless it is really your *wish* that we should *"stay away altogether"*. In *that* case, will you write a line or a word? If I do not hear, I will venture to go. Suffer me to say on my side, that your injustice is not always very kind and that *"we* have been served too often in this manner".

I did not receive your note until *late* on Saturday. After all, I remain

Your affectionate friend
E. B. Barrett

139.

To 3 Circus Road
St. John's Wood

[1837]

My dear friend,

I am very much obliged to you for your kindness in mentioning to Mrs. Holmes, my desire of seeing the mss. in the British Museum. But—

do you remember that she is quite a stranger to me and that I have a *xenophobia* as strongly, and perhaps more so than, a *bibliomania;* and that besides, even if I liked it, Papa might not like my troubling so a person with whom I have not any acquaintance. Then will you say nothing more about me to Mrs. Holmes, and let me wait for some other opportunity of seeing the museum?

I will write out two passages from Justin Martyr, the only ones which struck me while I was reading him, on the subject of the Lord's supper. . . .[1]

If you have *Athenaeus,* or any Anthology by Stephans [2] or others, will you lend me either or both? I promise to be careful.

Yours affectionately
E. B. Barrett

Our love to Annie.

140.

To 3 Circus Road
St. John's Wood

[August 2, 1837]

My dear friend,

Papa says that it *is* the custom for the lady's friends to send the notice of the marriage [1] to newspapers—but that there will be no expense to you in consequence, as the editors will be rather glad than otherwise to have anything in this way to print.

Henrietta and Arabel and I were at Marylebone Church yesterday. The bride looked very lovely, and behaved very well—I mean, without *demonstrating* in any unbecoming manner, the agitation which was within her evidently. It seemed to me that she had been shedding many tears, altho' they did not fall in the church—at least not to my observa-

1. Two passages in Greek are omitted: "First Apologia to the Romans" 66 and "Dialogue with Trypho" 70.

2. Henri Étienne (Stephanus) (1528–98), French printer and scholar, publisher of *Thesaurus Graecae linguae,* and of many ancient classics, including the "Planudean Anthology."

1. The Register of Marylebone Church records the marriage without banns on August 1, 1837, of Henry William Hayes, Esq. of 7 Hanover Terrace and Ann Henriette Boyd of 3 Circus Road. "Once indeed I was at a wedding—poor Annie Boyd's—but we met at the church and separated there,—and *that* was enough of it—and too much for *her,* poor thing, who has had reason to sit in ashes ever since." To Miss Mitford, August 1843; Miller, p. 193.

tion. I am sure that you have prayed for her and blessed her—and that none but affectionate thoughts and associations are between you at this moment. She must love you dearly as her father—and you must dearly love your child! I congratulate you my dear friend, on the appearances of happiness which seem to have gathered above her path! May God keep the sunshine there, with His own smile!

I shall be so anxious and glad to hear that your plans are arranged and happily—with regard to your very self!

Ever believe me
Your affectionate friend
E. B. Barrett

141.

To 3 Circus Road
St. John's Wood

Wednesday [1837]

My dear Mr. Boyd,

I don't know what you will say when you hear what the enclosed is. I am ashamed of writing my confession. Miss Harding will divulge the fatal secret,—and I will only observe that Arabel has this instant found the fragment in question on a table, and that it must have taken advantage of my carelessness to escape from a certain book while I folded up a certain parcel. I would send it to Mr. Lowry,[1] but I do not know his address. The cups and saucers, being found neither on the table nor under it, may possibly have reached him.

Your desire was conclusive. I sent mine. Are not my modesty and my exactitude fairly matched? I am going to see you very soon.

Your affectionate incorrigible friend
E. B. Barrett

142.

To 3 Circus Road
St. John's Wood

Monday
[*postmark* September 25, 1837]

My dear Mr. Boyd,

I certainly *did* intend to go to see you last week, notwithstanding your assurance to the contrary!

1. Joseph Wilson Lowry (1803–79), engraver, half brother of Mrs. Boyd.

Yesterday an illness under which our servant William [1] is suffering, was pronounced to be the smallpox. You will not therefore be desirous of having us near you,—neither will the Miss Heards. Will you give my kind remembrances to them, and say to them and yourself that if it should please God to spare ourselves from this disease, I hope it will not be long before we may go to St. John's Wood without danger to any of you.

Believe me

my dear friend

affectionately yours

E. B. Barrett

Mr. Giuseppe is attending William.

143.

[1838]

My dear friend,

I shall be glad to see Mrs. Smith [1] whenever she is kind enough to come—should I be up, and as well as usual. For the last fortnight I have not left my bed until the afternoon, in consequence of the severe weather,—but this being, to my great joy, at an end, I mean tomorrow morning to get up as early as you know I always used to do, to your great admiration! Therefore pray say to Mrs. Smith the message I have already written—together with two things more—my thanks for her caring to see me—and my hope that she won't come *far* out of her way to do so, lest I should happen to be put into prison again by a confluence of cough and frost. But Mr. Murphy [2] the prophet of the almanacks who said that Saturday would contain the pith of the frost, and Sunday the thaw, declareth that we shall have no more until Friday or Saturday and Sunday. Have you heard of him? He is considered the seer of seers, and *sees* all about the weather in the stars.

As to your good counsel dear Mr. Boyd, I assure you that I *do* consider

1. William Treherne, the butler, who was married secretly to EBB's personal maid, Crow. To Miss Mitford, March, 1844; unpublished letter: Wellesley College Library.

1. Daughter of Dr. Adam Clarke. Boyd dedicated *Select Passages* (1813) to her in a poem "To Myra" ("O marvel not, sweet maid, to see / The wreath I fondly wove for thee"), but did not reveal Myra's identity until *The Fathers Not Papists* (1834), when she had become "known both to the literary and religious world."

2. Patrick Murphy (1782–1847), very prominent in 1838 for the exactness of some predictions in his *Weather Almanack*.

myself *better*. Dr. Chambers ³ told me openly that my indisposition would not go, for medicine. He told me that, in his *conviction*, my lungs were without disease—but so *weak,* that they struggle *against* the cold air—which occasions the cough. It is a sensible deduction that until the warm weather comes, I cannot be well. In the meantime, he gives me soothing medicines—to produce as much as possible of quiet and sleep. If it pleases God I shall be better in time.

If you see Mr. Woodforde, do say how obliged I feel by his expression of kind interest, in calling three times here to enquire after me.

[E. B. B.]

144.

To 3 Circus Road
St. John's Wood

Monday morning
[*postmark* February 26, 1838]

My dear friend,

I saw the following advertisement in the Athenaeum of Saturday, and believing that it may interest you, do not delay to send it.

To clergymen etc.—

To be sold by order of the proprietor, a copy of Archbishop Cranmer's Bible, the very rare edition of 1539, folio, black letter, in very fine condition, wanting only the first title, which has been replaced by a facsimile from Lewis's translation.

Apply to Smallfield and Son. 69 Newgate St.

You may have perhaps heard that we have lost a beloved relation, poor Papa's only brother,¹ and one who was once more than uncle to *me*. But we have the only comfort for his absence from us, in the perfect security of his presence with our Lord. May God so comfort us all, in all our griefs—

3. Dr. William Frederick Chambers' medical opinions are mentioned frequently in the published letters.

1. Samuel Moulton-Barrett died in Jamaica December 3, 1837, at the age of fifty. "Papa's only brother, who used to tell me that he loved me better than my own father did, and was jealous when I was not glad. It is through him in part, that I am richer than my sisters—through him and his mother—and a great grief it was and trial, when he died a few years ago in Jamaica, proving by his last act that I was unforgotten." EBB—RB, December 13, 1845.

My cough is quieter since the frost went away,—but I am very weak and far from being well.

Mr. Curzon has been in London for a few days,—or rather at *Fulham*. But in spite of the distance he was so kind as to make his way to see us— and I had great pleasure in seeing him once more, and so little altered that these five long years seem to have passed for nothing with him. He left Mrs. Curzon and his boy at Plymouth, to which place he returns— but with no intention of joining the church there—rather of returning to London,—and even this plan appears to be at present a mere uncertainty. He enquired with great appearance of interest after you, and desired me to give you his very kind remembrances.

I never hear anything of you dear Mr. Boyd! May you be quite well and happy.

Your affectionate friend
E. B. Barrett

Do you know that Mr. Valpy is giving up business?
Remember me—do—to Miss Holliday.
Daisy is quite well again, thank God.

145.

To 3 Circus Road
St. John's Wood

74 Gloucester Place. Friday
[*postmark* March 10, 1838]

I heard last night my dear friend of the grief [1] sent to you by God. I am sure that you will remember its being sent by Him, and receive it resignedly and calmly, and, read upon it the mark of His love—and yet I am so sure besides of the painfulness of that grief, that I must tell you how much and truly I feel with you and for you. Do my dear friend, accept this expression of sympathy from me. Such sympathy always goes to you from me,—and is the deeper in proportion to the depth of your gladness or your sorrow.

If there is anything which you wish to be done for you, Arabel will certainly be glad to do it. Would that there were anything for *me* to do! I am a helpless useless being just now—but your kindness will care to know that I feel better today than I was yesterday.

1. This must be the death of Mr. Boyd's sister.

May God bless you—and then there will be no more need of human actions—or words.

Your affectionate friend
E. B. Barrett

146.

To 3 Circus Road
St. John's Wood

129 Crawford Street.[1] Monday [1838]

My dear friend,

I was thinking of writing to you when your kind enquiry came. In the Athenaeum of Saturday is a notice which is likely, or rather, sure, to interest you. It is to this effect.

"The examination of a m.s. entitled *The Homilies of St. Chrysostom*, which was bequeathed to the Royal Library of Dresden, has discovered five homilies of St. Chrysostom which have been hitherto unedited, and in fact unknown. A copy has been forwarded to Dr. Becken, a distinguished theologian and Greek scholar at Leipsic, with orders for him to make a Latin translation of them."

Thank you for your notices of *seraphical* passages in Gregory,—tho' I had examined them previously and found nothing reflecting any particular light on *my* subject. I have just sent away a proof sheet up to the 216th page.[2]

There can be no question as to your being *perfectly in the right,* with regard to Lady Olivia Sparrow,[3]—so much so, that upon reconsideration it must appear so to whomsoever your view of the subject was displeasing. Do not be angry with me, my dear friend,—but I *would not let* Henrietta apply for an opinion elsewhere. You will at once know my reasons—and after abusing me for a quarter of an hour by the clock, are sure to forgive me in your abundant indulgence—particularly when I tell you that Dr. Chambers condemned me yesterday to two applications of leeches before Wednesday. And so for my sake, you must smooth your frowns away—I mean such as were meant for *others,* as well as for me!

He found me yesterday in a very weak state—with what he calls a

1. The Barretts had left Gloucester Place, and moved to 50 Wimpole Street. While the house was being redecorated, EBB and her sisters stayed with friends at 129 Crawford Street.
2. Of the *Seraphim.*
3. See above, Letter 10, n. 24.

"miserable pulse"—and it could not be expected to be much better today, after "leeches the first" last night. I feel however better this morning in some respects. He says that he hopes to overcome the complaint in time,—and considers it a favourable circumstance that all the warm weather should be before me!

I wish I had a prospect of seeing you! May God bless you dear Mr. Boyd! Mr. Kenyon's [4] book is splendid—I mean as to type and paper— and beautiful, as to composition. You ought to read some of it at least? Will you? Would you, if I were to send it to Circus Road? Give my kind remembrances to Miss Holmes.

Affectionately yours
E. B. Barrett

147.

[1838]

Thank you my dear friend for your kind enquiry. I am better today than I felt yesterday,—and *then*, Dr. Chambers preceived some improvement upon my state some days ago. He thinks that the warm weather, when it comes, will really do much for me—and it will, if God sees fit that this should be.

I want to tell you about the Seraphim.[1] I do not know whether the sheets are completed. I rather believe that they are not. But at any rate, I have a fancy in my head that you should see the whole book instead of a part of it—that you should read the preface before the poem,—in which I mean to teach you exactly how much to admire it!! I have had an affectionate and very pleasing letter from Miss Bordman.[2] She speaks feelingly of your late loss—as being to her the loss of one of her earliest and kindest friends—

Do give my regards to Miss Holmes,

and believe me
Your affectionate friend
E. B. Barrett

4. John Kenyon (1784–1856), poet and benefactor of poets, cousin of EBB, to whom he introduced Robert Browning. The book is *Poems, for the Most Part Occasional*, 1838.

1. Published May 1838, a dramatic poem on the Crucifixion, suggested by the *Prometheus*.

2. Nelly Bordman, gentle orphaned daughter of a clergyman, dependent on the charity of Mr. Jago, a doctor of Hammersmith, whom she later married.

148.

To 3 Circus Road
   St. John's Wood

                                                       Monday [1838]
My dear friend,

I send you the Examiner wherein is a review, which I cannot but consider a favorable and gratifying one, of my book.

And I send to dear Miss Bordman my deep repentance for an omission on Saturday evening which has haunted my conscience ever since. I suffered her to go away without any of Miss Mitford's flowers!! And now, that their petals are frailer, I dare not put them into motion again. Beg her not to think me the most selfish and miserly, but only the most careless person of her acquaintance—for indeed I *did* MEAN to give them to her,—but you know my meanings are apt to be obscured—and for want of any other kind of obscuration, came forgetfulness, on the present occasion.

The *"betterness"* in which she found me has lasted until now,—and Dr. Chambers called me yesterday a most astonishing person for *rallying!* Not for "sneering", mind, whatever the Reviewer may think—and with regard to the Reviewer,—*I* think that if I had said Dr. Johnson *was* Longinus, the saying would be less pardonable (even from "a woman") than the "sneer" itself.[1] It would be as great a mistake as my chronology about Adam—I don't say, as "the stars roll on afar" [2] which indeed I cannot admit to be a mistake at all. The Virgin is sitting in the sunlight, and can therefore discern no stars visible or invisible. But she may infer the vainness of her adjuration, and the consequent calm on-rolling of the bodies she adjured, by the continued darkness, and the uncrownedness of the Infant's brow. Have I spoken clearly? *at last?*

My dear friend, I *cannot* let you have the extract you ask for. If ever I see you again I will explain the why,—and you in the meanwhile must try to forgive me.

Is not this blessed sunshine?—to thank God for? Dr. Chambers thinks that if I try the carriage again while it lasts and while there is a south

1. "For, let us add, notwithstanding the sneer (a thing that never sits well on a woman's face) in Miss Barrett's admirable preface, at the unlucky critic who was *'not* Longinus' (Doctor Johnson, we presume), we venture to be of opinion that religious, or what is exclusively understood by 'sacred subject,' is not fit for poetry, except on very rare and brief occasions." The *Examiner*, June 24, 1838, p. 387.

2. "The Virgin Mary to the Child Jesus." The phrase is changed in later editions to "Each empyreal star / Sits in a sphere afar."

wind, I shall be able to breathe *this time*. And I mean to try—but as to
being able to go to *you*, there seems to be not a hope of it. Even if I went
to your door, and were carried up stairs, there would be no power of
talking for long afterwards. I say this, to prevent your reproaching me in
a thought.

I thank you my dear friend, for all your kind expressions, and if I did
not, should still *feel* them gratefully. Mr. Crosse [3] is staying with Mr.
Kenyon.

Affectionately yours
E. B. Barrett

I *petition* for Miss Bordman to come and see me sometimes! Her parcel
has not arrived *yet!*

149.

[*postmark* January 28, 1839]

[*In Arabel's handwriting*]
My dear Mr. Boyd—

You may fancy our surprise when upon opening the Athenaeum on
Saturday, the first thing Papa saw, was these lines [1] of Ba's,—who had
written them and sent them to the editor, unknown to any one. I supposed that you would care about seeing them, therefore, I have written
them out for you. I dare say you heard of Miss Landon's last letter that
she wrote to some friend in England, a day or two before her death—
Supposing it may not have been in your newspaper, I must tell you, that
the question upon which these lines are written, were the last words of
her letter. I shall be anxious to know what you think of Ba's lines. Papa
returned last Friday, but did not bring an improved account of Ba. He
thinks her much the same as when he last saw her.

When you write to Torquay,[2] do not say anything of what I said to
you about my going there or of what you may think about it. I understand Annie is to return on the 10th of February.

Yours very sincerely
Arabel

3. Andrew Crosse (1784–1855), student of electro-crystallization, gained notoriety
in 1837 when he published a report of the appearance of insect life in metallic solu-
tions supposed to be destructive to organic life. He had recently called on EBB with
Mr. Kenyon. Kenyon, *1*, 72; Miller, p. 30.

1. "L. E. L.'s Last Question (Do you think of me as I think of you?)," *Works*, p. 251.

2. EBB's increasing ill health had led several months before to her removal to
Torquay.

150.

To 3 Circus Road
   St. John's Wood
   London

Torquay. May 21, 1839

My ever dear friend,

I am very very sorry to understand from Arabel that you are not pleased with me for not having noticed even by a message the *"three or four"* letters which you have written to me. When did you write to me three or four letters? I am conscious of having in my possession only one unanswered letter which I was about to reply to at the end of January when the bad attack came on and prevented my writing at all for a very long time. *That* was the last writing project in my head! and if I did not carry it into effect quite as soon as I was able, and as I did write to others, it was because I *do know* that you are not apt to be made uncomfortable by epistolary silences, and that the pleasure of our correspondence is rather more on *my* side than yours, notwithstanding your kindest feelings towards me. Lately I have been waiting for your return from Hampstead—and the cause of my sending no message is to be found in my intention of delivering it myself. You think this explanation dull enough. So be it—but pray don't think *me* ungrateful towards you or forgetful of you,—because, while I am alive, I can never deserve such a reproach,—and there is a degree of painfulness in being *supposed* to deserve it, corresponding to that degree in which I value your regard.

Thank you my dear friend for the very kind opinions you sent me of the stanzas on L. E. L.—and on the care you took to give me pleasure by letting me know Leigh Hunt's of my poetry generally. Did it strike you that his criticism had two faces—one of them far from being as gracious-looking as the other? "Miss B. sits as a queen" etc. etc. *"but* her poetry is too elaborate" etc. Now if "and" were substituted for "but" (and it sounds so much more natural in the place, that I can't help fancying its not being so an "error in the report") the first apparently complimentary clause becomes a mere illustration of the objecting second clause. Is Major Campbell the *Calder* Campbell who is a poet? Arabel did not say.

I have a confusion of poems running about in my head—a chaos of beginnings and endings and little pieces of middles, which are not likely to end in an Iliad, and so help Atheism to an argument. I should be glad to be allowed to get them (not in the character of an Iliad) into some little nutshell of my own [1]—but Dr. Barry [2] insists upon my not writing, and as you taught me passive obedience a long time ago I have been practising it like a St. Aylmer—not that I mean to do so all this summer, if it pleases God to spare me through it. I ought to say with a deep-felt thanksgiving, how much better I am—*wonderfully* better to everybody who saw, and most of all to myself who felt, the manner in which I seemed to hang by a thread between life and death, and for two months at a time, the latter half of the past winter. The weakness was excessive —and indeed I have not even *tried* to stand up, since January—but everything is "in good time" Dr. Barry says,—and it is planned for me to go upon the sea before the present week closes, which would be a "vision of delight" for me if it were not for the fatigue. It was a true kindness in you, my dear friend, to warn me of not suffering my natural affections (so naturally strengthened by the tenderness of some most dearly beloved) to bind me down too closely to the earth.[3] The exercise of love, even of human love, is a suggester of God—and may God forbid, that what He permits as a suggestion should be monstrously transfigured into an intervention by the heart of His creature. Not that my heart has not often so transfigured it! I know that it has! Pray for me that it may not again! It is a foul sin, to sin *by* love, *against* Love! even as if we used the mystic faces of the cherubim which enshadowed the Jewish altar,— the lion's the bull's and the eagle's faces—to bow down before the beast, and blaspheme the altar's God.

Do try to remember that you have not written three or four unan-swered letters to me *yet*—and write *one* as soon as you can. I was glad to hear of your excursion to Hampstead,—and hope that it made you fancy yourself two years old again!—although as to the question of your settling there, it seems pleasanter for us in Wimpole Street that you should not entertain it. You see while *you* are fancying yourself two years old, *my* fancy is suggesting to *me* a renewal of our old inter-course—and how many cups of coffee and pages of Gregory you and I are still likely to discuss. But "all goeth but Goddes' will" according to the ancient verse—and the fulfilment of God's will is better, yes, and happier, than all that goes.

Arabel often mentions you in the long letters her long affection

---

1. "*Iliad* in a nutshell" was a Latin proverb: *in nuce Ilias*.

2. Dr. Robert Fitzwilliam De Barry, who died the following October 2, after a three weeks' illness.

3. Boyd may have referred particularly to Bro, who at EBB's tearful insistence was permitted to devote himself to her in Torquay, even though Mr. Barrett considered it "very wrong in [her] to exact such a thing." EBB—RB, *1,* 176.

makes me so grateful for. It has been very very trying and disappointing to me never to have seen her all these months—and dreary ones they have been to me. But now, being in the summer and the sunshine, I would rather think of pleasures to come than of sadnesses past—and I am willing to believe that no obstacle in the common course of things can keep us apart much longer. My dearest Papa has visited me again and again—but I want Arabel—and I long to be tied fast to him and her and all of them—so that the words *"we"* and "us" may be used in their dear home sense. If I had my own way I should be in London by this time,—before this time. I have not my own way —and everybody fancies that I could not yet bear the removal—and so there is no use in kicking against the goad.

Upon consideration I begin to be of opinion that a gynocracy is the next best thing to a republic—and I do not despair of you, a thinking man, being *at one* with me in this opinion,—notwithstanding your favorite project for the future of which Arabel has told me—the combination-government,—consisting of the Pope's head and Mr. O'Connell's tail.[4] By the way, until I was assisted to it by your ready memory, I never for a moment suspected Dryden of loitering in Mr. O'Connell's verses. Certainly they had been "agitated" enough, to shake Dryden out of them—to say nothing of the "emancipation" from metres and meaning! Do let me ask one more question, notwithstanding this long letter. When Popery becomes the state-religion of England, is it to *stand?*—or may we look forwards to a little Mohammedism and Heathenism? Answer this—and believe that I balance my misfortune of being *"a female and a whig"*, by the abundance of truth with which I remain

Your affectionate friend
E. B. Barrett

Poor Mr. Barker! I felt so very sorry and *memory-struck* in hearing of his death.[5] Have you heard any details?

Not knowing who is with you at present, I can send my remembrances to nobody.

4. "O'Connell's tail" was a nickname given to Daniel O'Connell's parliamentary following.

5. Mr. Barker "became more and more involved in rash adventure, and ultimately died 21 March, 1839 in a mean lodging house near Covent Garden Market." *DNB*.

151.

To 3 Circus Road
   St. John's Wood
   London

Torquay. Monday
[*postmark* June 24, 1839]

My dear friend,

I take the liberty, which I know you will not be angry about, of enclosing to you a letter of *private gossip* for my dear Arabel. Will you be so very kind as to enclose it to her as soon as you conveniently can. Perhaps you would allow a servant to take it to her in the course of the day.

You wrote me a kind and welcome letter to which I mean to reply very soon—more at length than I can this morning, being quite tired with writing. Finden's Tableaux are to be edited again this year by Miss Mitford, and she has sent to me for a ballad,—and I have begun already a wild and wicked ballad.[1] There are so many monks and nuns in the engraving forwarded for me to fit my poetry to it, (think of the very annuals turning papistical!) that I am thinking of introducing you as a St. John's Wood Bard versus Gray's "Welsh judges",[2] taking a grand prophetic view of the Pope's dynasty which is to be in our O'Connellized country.

My dear Mr. Boyd, believe me
   truly and ever affectionately yours
      E. B. Barrett

I am better.

152.[1]

To 21 Downshire Hill
   Hampstead, near London

Torquay. May 29, 1840

My ever dear friend,

It was very pleasant to me to see your seal upon a letter once more, —and although the letter itself left me with a mournful impression

---

1. "The Legend of the Brown Rosarie," *Finden's Tableaux* for 1840, edited by Mary Russell Mitford. The 1839 issue contained "The Romaunt of the Page," which was finished before EBB left London. Kenyon, *1*, 61.

2. Presumably the spirits of the Welsh bards put to death by Edward I; *The Bard*, 1, 3.

1. Published in part in Kenyon, *1*, 79.

of your having passed some time so much less happily than I could wish and pray for you, yet there remains the pleasant thought to me still, that you have not altogether forgotten me. Do receive the expression of my most affectionate sympathy under this and every circumstance,—and I fear that the shock to your nerves and spirits could not be a light one,—however impressed you might be and must be with the surety and verity of God's love working in all His will. Poor poor Patience! Coming to be so happy with you, with that joyous smile I thought so pretty! Do you not remember my telling you so? Well—it is well and better for her,—happier for her, if God in Christ Jesus have received her, than her hopes were of the holiday time with you. The holiday is *for ever* now—

> "Gone from work, and taen her wages" [2]—

I am thinking of Kate—poor Kate! How old is she? Quite a child—is she not?—yet not too young, having felt the "much affliction" to rejoice in the "joy of the Holy Ghost". Do tell me when you write, dear Mr. Boyd, how she is and how her spirits are, and whether you mean to let her return to school. If I were you I would not permit it. Do not, unless you cannot help it, or object to her remaining with you on other grounds than any I am aware of—for indeed that return would be very desolate and distressing to her—that return *alone!*

I heard from Nelly Bordman only a few days before receiving your letter, and so far from preparing me for all this sadness and gloom she pleased me with her account of you whom she had lately seen—dwelling upon your retrograde passage into youth and the delight you were taking in the presence and society of some still more youthful, fair, and gay *monstrum amandum,* some prodigy of intellectual accomplishment, some little Circe who never turned anybodies into pigs. I learnt too from her for the first time that you were settled at Hampstead! Whereabout at Hampstead, and for how long? She didn't tell me *that,* thinking of course that I knew something more about you than I do. Yes indeed! you *do* treat me very shabbily—I agree with you in thinking so. To think that so many hills and woods should interpose between us—that I should be lying here, fast bound by a spell, a Sleeping Beauty in a forest, and that *you* who used to be such a doughty knight should not take the trouble of cutting through even a hazel tree with your good sword, to find out what had become of me!! Now do tell me, the hazel tree being down at last, whether you mean to live at Hampstead, whether you have taken a house there and have

2. "Home art gone and ta'en thy wages." *Cymbeline,* IV.2.261.

carried your books there, and wear Hampstead grasshoppers in your bonnet (as they did at Athens) [3] to prove yourself of the soil!

All this nonsense will make you think I am better—and indeed I am pretty well just now. Quite, however, confined to the bed—except when lifted from it to the sofa baby-wise while they make it,— and even then apt to faint. Bad symptoms too do not leave me, —and I am obliged to be blistered every few days—but I am free from any attack just now, and am a good deal less feverish than I am occasionally. There has been a consultation between an Exeter physician and my own—and they agree exactly—both hoping that with care I shall pass the winter, and rally in the spring—both hoping that I may be able to go about again with some comfort and independence, although I never can be fit again for anything like exertion.

Dr. Scully, the physician who attends me now and has done so since poor Dr. Barry's death (of which you may have heard as affecting me most painfully last October) is a highly intelligent man besides being one of the very kindest in the world. The world calls him a Roman Catholic,—and he calls himself a Whig of the *ob aera*— rather a curious contradiction. The explanatory truth is that he is no more a Roman Catholic than I am. He holds the right of private judgment as firmly with clenched hands as Luther did. I am not able to talk much—indeed my voice has wasted to a whisper,—but he and I talk a *little* every day on the occasion of his daily visit—and he brought me a book last week, a catalogue raisonné of Dr. Parr's library in which, among the *Patres Ecclesiastici* "my heart leaped up to see" the mention of your select passages—by S. Boyd, *1810*. No observation upon it.

Do you know, did you ever hear anything of Mr. Horne [4] who wrote Cosmo de Medici and the Death of Marlowe, and is now desecrating his powers (I beg your pardon) by writing the life of Napoleon? By the way, he is the author of a dramatic sketch in the last Finden.

He is in my mind one of the very first poets of the day,—and has written to me so kindly (offering although I never saw him in my life,

3. Thucydides (1.6) says that the Athenians "bound back their hair in a knot with golden clasps in the form of grasshoppers."

4. Richard Hengist Horne (1803–84), who was highly esteemed by his contemporaries as author and critic, published *Cosmo de Medici* and *Death of Marlowe*, tragedies, in 1837, *The History of Napoleon*, 2 vols., in 1841. He began corresponding with EBB in 1839 and enlisted her as a collaborator in *Chaucer Modernized* (1841) and *A New Spirit of the Age*, 1844.

to cater for me in literature and send me down anything likely to interest me in the periodicals) that I cannot but think his amiability and genius do honor to one another.

Do you remember Mr. Caldicott who used to preach in the infant schoolroom at Sidmouth— He died here the death of a saint, as he had lived a saintly life—about three weeks ago. It affected me a good deal. But he was always so associated in my thoughts more with heaven than earth, that scarcely a transition seems to have passed upon his locality. "Present with the Lord" is true of him now,—even as "having his conversation in heaven" was formerly. There is little difference.

May it be so with us all—with you and with me, my ever and very dear friend! In the meantime do not forget me. I never can forget *you.*

Your affectionate and grateful
Elizabeth B. Barrett

Arabel desires her love to be offered to you.

153.[1]

To 21 Downshire Hill
Hampstead
London

1 Beacon Terrace. Torquay
July 8, 1840

My ever dear friend,

I must write to you, although it is so very long, or at least seems so, since you wrote to me. But you say to Arabel in speaking of me that I *"used* to care for what is poetical"—therefore perhaps you say to yourself sometimes that I *used* to care for *you!* I am anxious to vindicate my identity to you, in that respect above all.

It is a long dreary time since I wrote to you. I admit the pause on my own part, while I charge you with another. But *your* silence has embraced more pleasantness and less suffering to you than mine has to me—and I thank God for a prosperity in which my unchangeable regard for you, causes me to share indirectly. Indeed it is, and always must be very pleasant for me to hear of your being well and appearing well, and enjoying any sort of gladness from Greek to bell-ringing, from the Majores to the Bobs Major—and I perceive that the latter

1. Published in part in Kenyon, *1,* 81.

"bears the bell" just now. I congratulate you on your bell neighbourhood. The *caste* seems excellent. And the *clappers,* according to Swift's
Laputa,[2] augur understanding.

> "Bells on your fingers and rings on your toes
> And you will have music wherever you *goes"*

in your walks round the monastery. May other people have rings on
their *fingers,* to give you the benefit of their marriage bells. I know
your politics, and that you always liked a Peel [3]—excepting those three
weeks when you wore the cap and bells and *wear* a radical "for love
of me." But you don't write to me now—only to Ara*bel.*

You see you have made me write nonsense once more, my dear
friend. Indeed it seems almost time for me to pause from such work,
and that I have had almost enough to wear out my laughters. I have
not rallied this summer, as soon and well as I did last. I was very ill
early in April at the time of our becoming conscious to our great
affliction [4]—so ill, as to believe it utterly improbable, speaking humanly, that I ever should be any better. I am however a very great deal
better, and gain strength by sensible degrees, however slowly—and do
hope for the best—"the best" meaning one sight more of London. In
the meantime I have not yet been able to leave my bed.

To prove to you that I who "used to care" for poetry, do so still, and
that I have not been absolutely idle lately, an Athenaeum shall be
sent to you containing a poem on the subject of the removal of Napoleon's ashes.[5] It is a fitter subject for you than for me. Napoleon is
no idol of *mine. I* never made a "setting sun" of him. But my physician suggested the subject as a noble one,—and then there was something suggestive in the consideration that the Bellerophon [6] lay on
those very bay-waters, opposite to my bed.

Another poem (which you won't like, I dare say) is called "The Lay
of the Rose" [7] and appeared lately in a magazine. Arabel is going to
write it out for you, she desires me to tell you, with her best love.
Indeed I have written lately (as far as manuscript goes) a good deal—
only on all sorts of subjects and in as many shapes.

---

2. Flying island in *Gulliver's Travels;* the attendants who promoted understanding
were "flappers."
3. Sir Robert Peel, conservative statesman, prime minister 1834–35, 1841–46.
4. EBB's brother Sam died in Jamaica February 17, 1840.
5. "Crowned and Buried"; *Works,* pp. 254–6.
6. The British warship to whose Captain Maitland Napoleon surrendered in 1815.
7. "A Lay of the Early Rose"; *Works,* pp. 276–8.

Lazarus would make a fine poem—*wouldn't* he? I lie here, weaving a great many schemes—I am seldom at a loss for thread.

Do write sometimes to me—and tell me if you do anything besides hearing the clocks strike and bells ring. My beloved Papa is with me still. There are so many mercies close around me (and his presence is far from the least)—that God's *Being* seems proved to me, *demonstrated* to me, by His manifested love. May His blessing in the full lovingness, rest upon you always! Never fancy I can forget or think of you coldly.

Your affectionate and grateful
Elizabeth B. Barrett

154.[1]

To 21 Downshire Hill
Hampstead
London

1 Beacon Terrace
May 10, 1841

My very dear friend,

Throughout this long silence, embracing the most afflictive time of my whole life,[2] I hope you have known me better than to believe *any* grief could force me to forget you. I have thought of you on the contrary often, and wished that you might be very happy—and regarded you as truly as if I could smile and say so to you in the light of days gone for ever. But you will understand the shrinking from writing, when one's heart is full—and *that* has been my case often and often—after the *power* of writing had returned to me. Lately I have been impatient with myself about you, lest you should murmur to *your*self "Ah she forgets me"—and thus I wouldn't let Arabel write although she proposed it. So you must forgive her for my sake, and me—for my own sake. There is no help for me otherwise.

Arabel heard from Annie a day ago—and thus I became aware that you had lately been grieved by the loss of your old valued friend Mr. Spowers. Receive my sympathy, dear Mr. Boyd. I fear this event will sadden Hampstead to you as a residence—or perhaps you have other friends there. Will you write to me and tell me a little about yourself —and not as to one who could ever forget you. Bright hours of my life have been spent at your side, and you know the metaphysicians

1. MS in the Library of Harvard University.
2. Bro died ten months before the date of this letter, on July 11, 1840.

say that contrast is a principle of suggestion. So that I couldn't forget *them* now and here.

Do you remember when you told me that I clung too much to human affections? And therefore perhaps it was, that the Divine Hand cast me down in the place of graves and struck me terribly in the very life of my heart. But I cannot write of this even now. Only I know and recognize God's chastening in it, and my own transgression—my God and my sin—eminent in the sweeping agony as causes and interpretations. Presently, and perhaps very soon, all will be calm and smooth in Christ Jesus. Oh dear friend! What an "anarithmon gelasma" [3] *that* will be, in the eternal world!

I have been much better this spring—really better, I think—and am waiting only for some fine days, to remove from my bed to the sofa, as an almost immediately previous step to a removal to London. You *cannot* know how the only strong earthly wish I have left, relative to myself, is set towards being once more *at home*—and my physician hopes that I shall be able to travel quietly and slowly in June. It may please God for you and me to meet again, after all. Storm and Octavius besides my sisters are with me.

Will you write to me when you can conveniently,—and will you speak, *not* of *me,* but of yourself—and let me hear whether you listen still with charmed ears to the charming clocks?—above all, whether you are as well as usual and with good spirits? May God bless you in Christ! I have a counterpart to your clock amusement, in a little spaniel dog which was sent to me by Miss Mitford, for company. Now you wonder at my pastime as I at yours—although Flush doesn't bark I assure you.

I have written very little poetry lately—but I love it as I always did —and shall write on if I live on.

Do try to forgive this letter for not going to you before—believing with how much earnest truth its writer remains

Your affectionate

Elizabeth B. Barrett

Henrietta and Arabel are quite well, thank God. Their kindest regards to you.

---

3. *Prometheus,* line 90. EBB's own translation: "laughter innumerous."

155.[1]

To 21 Downshire Hill
  Hampstead

50 Wimpole Street [2]
October 2, 1841

My very dear friend,

I thank you for the letter and books which crossed the threshold of this house before me, and looked like your welcome to me home. I have read the passages you wished me to read—I have read them *again,*—for I remember reading them under your star (or the greater part of them) a long while ago. You on the other hand, may remember of *me,* that I never could concede to you much admiration for your Gregory as a poet—not even to his grand work *De virginitate.* He is one of those writers of whom there are instances in our own times, who are only poetical in prose.

The passage imitative of Chryses, I cannot think much of. Try to be forgiving. It is toasted dry between the two fires of the Scriptures and Homer—and is as stiff as any dry toast out of the simile. To be sincere,—I like dry toast better.

The Hymns and Prayers I very much prefer; and although I remembered a good deal of them, it has given me a pleasure you will approve of, to go through them in this edition. The one which I like best, which I like far best, which I think worth all the rest (*De virginitate* and all put together) is the *second* upon page 292, beginning *Soi charis.*[3] It is very fine I think—written out of the heart and for the heart—warm with a natural heat, and not toasted dry and brown and stiff at a fire, by any means.

Dear Mr. Boyd, I coveted Arabel's walk to you the other day. I shall often covet my neighbour's walks, I believe, although (and may God be praised for it) I am more happy, that is, nearer to the feeling of happiness now, than a month since I could believe possible to a heart so bruised and crushed as mine has [been]. To be at home is a blessing and a relief beyond what these words can say.

But—dear Mr. Boyd,—you said something in a note to Arabel some little time ago, which I will ask of your kindness to avoid saying

1. Published in part in Kenyon, *1,* 91.
2. EBB made the journey from Torquay to London in September 1841.
3. "To you thanksgiving," *Poemata dogmatica* 1.34.

again. I have been through the whole summer very much better,—
and even if it were not so, I should dread being annoyed by more
medical speculations and consultations. Pray do not suggest any. I
am not in a state to admit of experiments—and my case is a very
clear and simple one. I have not *one symptom* like those of my old
illness—and after more than fifteen years' absolute suspension of
them, their recurrence is scarcely probable. My case is very clear—not
tubercular consumption—not what is called a "decline",—but an affection of the lungs which leans towards it. You know a blood vessel broke three years ago—and I never quite got over it. Mr. Jago not
having seen me, could scarcely be justified in a conjecture of the sort,
when the opinions of four able physicians, two of them particularly
experienced in diseases of the chest, and the other two the most
eminent of the faculty in the east and west of England, were decided
and contrary, while coincident with each other. Besides you see I am
becoming better—and I could not desire more than that. Dear Mr.
Boyd, do not write a word about it any more, either to me or others.
I am sure you would not willingly disturb me. Nelly Bordman is good
and dear, but I can't let her prescribe for me anything except her own
affection.

I hope Arabel expressed for me my thankful sense of Mrs. Smith's
kind intention. But indeed—although I would see *you,* dear Mr. Boyd,
gladly, or an angel or a fairy or any very particular friend, I am not
fit either in body or spirit for general society. I *can't* see people—and
if I could, it would be very bad for me. Is Mrs. Smith writing? Are
you writing? Part of me is worn out; but the poetical part—that is,
the *love* of poetry,—is growing in me as freshly and strongly as if it
were watered every day. Did anybody ever love it and stop in the
middle? I wonder if anybody ever did.

My dear friend, I remember your once telling me that you were at
a loss sometimes for objects of charity—that you would sometimes
gladly give if you knew to whom. I do therefore take the liberty of apprizing you of the melancholy circumstances under which Mrs. Hop-
kins (*Cousins*) is at present. She is very industrious—and unexcep-
tionable as a wife and mother—but her husband is so involved in
debt, that all her struggles cannot rescue herself and her poor little
children from a state of deep poverty. She knows nothing of my resolve
to mention it to you—and I do so, simply as friend to friend, and out
of compassion and sympathy, and because I am sure that if you can
give her anything it will be a gift to the much-afflicted. Nevertheless

you will of course do as you think best—and not through courtesy to me. When do you expect Annie?

> Believe me
> Your affectionate
> E. B. B.

156.

To 21 Downshire Hill
Hampstead

> Friday evening
> [*postmark* January 15, 1842]

Thank you, my dear friend, for all your kindness. It is very welcome to me—and indeed, in spite of it, I am in some straight as to how my business [1] is to be completed. I should not like to be incorrect—to leave out poets and misplace dates—when every fault must become prominent, not merely in black and white, but in *printed black.* Would that I could talk to you for one hour.

I return the paper intended for the Athenaeum, with a very grateful appreciation of the praise you lavish upon me in it. But dear Mr. Boyd, it is too much! You should not have done it. Particularly *that* opposition between *eminent persons,* Rollin *and me!!* [2] particularly *that,* does strike me and will of course strike others, as so extravagant, that I venture to supplicate you to strike it out. People will think you are "making game" of *me!* Do strike it out, I beg of you.

Well—and then, I fear that the Athenaeum, which never will nourish the snake of a controversy in its bosom, may reject your paper altogether. Of course you have a perfect right to object to my note, but the paper you have written might be compressed, shortened—and thus the chances of its appearance would be increased tenfold. Leave out some of *my compliments*—all about my preface, for instance—and let the "lover of literary justice" go upon justice, barely and briefly.

If I can find or make room for more translations from Gregory, I will do your bidding faithfully. Depend upon that. But I have just

1. Four papers on the Greek Christian poets which EBB was preparing for the *Athenaeum* (printed February 26 to March 19, 1842).

2. Mr. Boyd may have compared her to Charles Rollin (1661–1741), French writer on ancient history, whose work was much praised by Voltaire.

finished the *whole* of that immensely long ode to his soul,[3] asking her what she pleased to do. It is too long for my purpose—I was tempted by the variety of its merits,—besides the occasional great beauty, and by some touches of satire which you do not find very often out of his prose writings.

God bless you, my dear friend! Forgive me for suggesting that the Athenaeum paper should be transcribed by somebody who can *spell correctly.*

Yours affectionately
E. B. B.

You shall hear when I have anything in the Athenaeum. I shall not, next Saturday. Thank you about Mr. Clarke's book. I wish very much to see that.

157.

Saturday [1842]

My dear friend,

I send you the Athenaeum, which they have been too long in bringing to me. How will you like it? That is a question I ask myself of you anxiously! Tell me the exact truth of your impressions.

It would have been a great security to my "remarks" and the translations accompanying them, if you could have seen either previous to publication—but what with the obscurity of my handwriting and the briefness of the time, and, to do myself justice, the consideration I have for your *ease,* I could not ask you to do such a thing. The *third* paper is almost going to Mr. Dilke [1]—and I believe now that nothing can save him from a fourth.

Arabel sends her love to you. Next Thursday she is to take you a visitor, —and on Monday she talks of being the visitor to you herself—provided there is fine weather and no obstacle.

Think of my walking to the sofa now! Isn't that an improvement? God bless you dear Mr. Boyd!

Ever your affectionate and grateful
E. B. B.

3. Published complete in the *Greek Christian Poets,* under the title "Soul and Body," *Works,* pp. 606–7. For earlier reference to the beauty of this poem and to Boyd's translation of it see Letter 47 (1829).

1. Charles Wentworth Dilke (1789–1864), noted for his strict impartiality as editor of the *Athenaeum* 1830–46.

Remember! Gregory is in the second paper—which, by the way, is longer than the first.

158.[1]

To 21 Downshire Hill
Hampstead

50 Wimpole Street
April 2, 1842

My very dear friend,

I am sorry I should have omitted to notice any part of your letter— but I did not neglect it really. Mr. Hunter spent an hour or two with us the other day, having come to London upon business, and I did not neglect making the enquiry of him you desired. The enquiry was vain— he did not know of any young person likely to suit you. Arabel will speak about it either to Mr. Stratten or his wife—and take courage, for we shall succeed at last. There must be many young persons who would be delighted to make themselves useful to you. The difficulty is to take knowledge of them.

Arabel is much obliged to you for wishing to see her still oftener— and would I am sure go oftener to you if the distance were not so great and herself engaged much in different ways. She talks of paying you a visit next week.

Is this better writing? I try to make it clear.

In regard to Mr. Burges I mean to repeat what you have said to me to Mr. Kenyon, that, the mistake being cleared away, you may have your visitor again.[2]

As to your kind desire to hear whatever in the way of favorable remark I have gathered for fruit of my papers, I put on a veil and tell you that Mr. Kenyon thought it well done altho' "labor thrown away from the unpopularity of the subject"—that Miss Mitford was very much pleased, with the warmheartedness common to her,—that Mrs. Jameson [3] read them "with great pleasure" unconsciously of the author, —and that Mr. Horne the poet and Mr. Browning the poet were not

---

1. Published in part in Kenyon, *1*, 103.

2. Burges had called on Boyd and been discouraged by what he considered an un-friendly reception. EBB wrote to Mr. Kenyon May 20, 1842 (unpublished letter: Wellesley College Library), " 'What an unhappy manner I must have!' ejaculated poor Mr. Boyd to me—'because I really was *very* GLAD to see him!!' "

3. Anna Brownell Jameson (1794–1860), author of *The Diary of an Ennuyée* (1826) and publications on art; intimate friend of EBB and RB.

behind in approbation! Mr. Browning is said to be learned in Greek, especially in the dramatists—and of Mr. Horne I should suspect something similar. Miss Mitford and Mrs. Jameson altho' very gifted and highly cultivated women are not Grecians, and therefore judge the papers simply as English compositions.

The single unfavorable opinion is Mr. Hunter's who thinks that the criticisms are not given with either sufficient seriousness or diffidence, and that there is a painful sense of effort through the whole. Many more persons may say so whose voices I do not hear. I am glad that yours, my dear indulgent friend, is not one of them.

Believe me
Your ever affectionate
Elizabeth B. Barrett

159.[1]

May 17, 1842

My very dear friend,

Have you thought all unkindness out of my silence? Yet the inference is not a true one, however it may look in logic.

You do not like Silentiarius VERY *much* (that is *my* inference), since you have kept him so short a time. And I quite agree with you that he is not a poet of the same interest as Gregory Nazianzen, however he may appear to me of more lofty cadence in his versification. My own impression is that John of Euchaita is worth two of each of them as a poet. His poems strike me as standing in the very first class of the productions of the Christian centuries. Synesius and John of Euchaita! I shall always think of those two together—not by their similarity but their dignity.

I return you the books you lent me with true thanks—and also those which Mrs. Smith, I believe, left in your hands for me. I thank *you* for them—and *you* must be good enough to thank *her*. They were of use— although of a rather sublime indifference for poets generally.

Arabel will take this packet to your door—but she will not go in to see you because she is only just convalescent from the measles, making the fourth victim within the last few weeks in this house. They are well now,—I thank God! But I have not seen Arabel for nearly a week,—and therefore I leave you to judge whether it would be right to expose *you* to a hazard from which her carefulness has preserved *me*. She had had the measles *before* this attack; and so had Alfred.

1. Published in part in Kenyon, *1*, 104.

I shall send you soon the series of the Greek papers you asked for—
and also perhaps, the first paper of a survey of the English Poets,[2] under
the pretence of a review of "The Book of the Poets" a bookseller-
selection published lately. I begin from Langland of Piers Plowman
and the Malvern Hills. The first paper went to the editor last week, and
I have heard nothing as to whether it will appear on Saturday or not—
and perhaps if it does, you won't care to have it sent to you. Tell me if
you do or don't. I have suffered unpleasantly in the heart lately from
this tyrannous dynasty of east winds, but have been well otherwise, and
am better in *that*. Flushie means to bark the next time he sees you in
revenge for what you say of him.

Good bye dear Mr. Boyd. Think of me as

Your ever affectionate
E. B. B.

160.

To 21 Downshire Hill
Hampstead

July 7, 1842

My very dear friend,

How you praise me! and how almost vain-glorious and quite well-
pleased you make me by such praise! I did not dare to hope that you
would prove half as easily satisfied—and the candour in regard to the
first paper gives to this expression of your satisfaction a full "queen's
head" of additional value—talking sovereigns rather than letter-stamps!
You may imagine how pleased I am, when I assure you that I should not
have been either surprised or offended, though you had thrown me up
from the first paper as *unreadable!*

The fourth did not appear on Saturday, nor is likely to do so for
several Saturdays more. The British Association is rampant just now
in the Athenaeum. In the meanwhile I am turning to my review [1] of
Wordsworth,—the king-poet of our times—and in the meanwhile (only
yesterday) I have received some precious cuttings and leaves out of his
garden, which I commissioned Mr. Kenyon to get for me as for himself,
but which the poetical Majesty was graciously pleased to send me as to
myself.

Arabel hopes to know *your* Maitlands and so complete her knowledge

2. Five papers published in the *Athenaeum* between June 4 and August 13, 1842.
1. Published in the *Athenaeum*, August 27, 1842; included in "The Book of the
Poets," *Works*, pp. 652–8.

of their family—and she desires me to give you her love and her con-gratulations on the safety of Francis.[2] Poor wretch—Norfolk Island is scarcely safety—prolonged agony it certainly is. Do you observe that there has been more shooting?—and that while the tyrants of the earth sit serenely on their thrones, no breath of tobacco pipes turned against them,—our liberal, blameless queen cannot stir abroad without there being shot at her out of pistols! It is a national dishonor. I am very angry, very sorry, and very ashamed—only *not unto death.*

It gave me great pleasure to hear that you permitted your wonderful Memory to minister to you again from the old Greek fountains. As quite an old friend and half a Greek one let *me* too come in for a remembrance,—while I remain dearest Mr. Boyd's unchangeably affectionate and grateful

E. B. Barrett

Yes! I have observed that same trochee-ending monotony in Otway and others of the later dramatists—just as you say!

161.

To 21 Downshire Hill
Hampstead

Friday
[*postmark* July 11, 1842]

My very dear friend,

Of course you will do as you please about showing my note—but my own impression is and Arabel has the same, that Annie would not be pleased and still less *influenced* by a note of mine addressed to *you* on the particular subject in question.[1] She might think that I had no business

2. On May 30, John Francis, 20, son of a stage carpenter at Drury Lane, had fired at the open barouche in which Queen Victoria and Prince Albert were taking their evening drive; this was presumably his second attempt, since on the day before a young man had been seen to aim a pistol at the Queen but had disappeared in the crowd before he could be apprehended. Francis was found guilty, but on July 4 Her Majesty commuted his sentence to "be forthwith transported and subjected to hard labour in the most penal settlement in the Australian colonies [Norfolk Island]." On July 3 another young man, "a youth of deformed appearance," was prevented by a bystander from firing at the royal carriage.

1. "We have heard today that Annie proposes to publish her Miscellany by sub-scription; and although I know it to be the only way, compatible with publication at all, to avoid a pecuniary loss, yet the custom is so entirely abandoned except in the case of persons of a lower condition of life than *your daughter*, that I am sorry to think of the observation it may excite." To Boyd, June 3, 1842; Kenyon, *1,* 106,

to write to *you* upon that subject—and as she already knows my full opinion in relation to it I do not see how we could gain much by running the risk. If she should ever speak to me of it again, I shall try a little more persuasion—and you would do more by speaking your own thoughts from yourself than anybody else could—you must be sure of *that*.

Don't be uneasy about Synesius. Flush didn't swallow it—only I forgot it! You shall have the little book with another I retain of yours, by an early opportunity.

Thank you my dear dear friend for your note. Flushie kissed the harp [2] when it was brought close to him, but he rather eschewed the neighbourhood.

May God bless you!
Your affectionate
E. B. B.

Another paper on Saturday—and another—and perhaps another. I doubt whether to send it or not—because you can get it more quickly at Hampstead than I can here. Still, as quickness is scarcely an object, I *will* send it. Good night again.

162.

Wednesday [1842]

My very dear friend,

You have been so much more in my thoughts for not having been on my paper,—but the intense heat in which most of my good resolutions have evaporated lately, has even up to half an hour, persuaded me that I had far better put off writing to you until "day after day". In the meantime I have received from you at least two notes, both very kind, and beg you to believe how sensibly I felt this kindness through all the burning of the sun, however I might have acknowledged it more quickly and comfortably "sub tegmine fagi" [1]—you and I sitting in an hypothetical coolness like poetical shepherds.

But something is on my conscience and must be written off. Ever since I read your note—the one about the *parentage* of my printed criticism on Milton with the reference to Shakespeare's "Midsummer Night's Dream" [2]—where you tell me that it consists of your own opinion and

2. An Aeolian harp given to EBB by Mr. Barrett. On June 3, 1842, she wrote to Boyd "Flushie is jealous and thinks it is alive." Kenyon, *1*, 106.
1. Vergil *Eclogues* 1.1.
2. ". . . the Midsummer Night's Dream displays more of the fairyhood of fairies

comparison, communicated by yourself to me in conversation,—I have
been pondering and wondering how it was. I quite remember the conversation—the last or almost the last I ever had with you!—but still
my impression resolutely remains that *I* addressed both opinion and
comparison to *you,* and that you agreed with me. Consider it again!
Certainly if you hold fast the claim, I yield mine—for I do not dare to
contend with you on a point of memory.

The reason why I say so much about it, is *not* that I am jealous of my
vanity of authorship—not at all— If I learnt this from you, it would not
be strange, still less unpleasant to confess—considering how much I have
learnt, frankly confessing my obligations, to the same source. But to
learn anything from you and then print it out staringly to the world as
the result of my own reflections and without a word of acknowledgement to its originator—of such an act I should be ashamed, and beg you
to believe that I never *consciously* could commit it.

Saturday

My dear friend (*very* dear!—so do not fancy me unkind again!) these
three pages were written several days ago—and now I have to thank you
for another note and also to retort against it with another article. Mr.
Dilke has proposed to send me any work I pleased for the pleasure of
the dissection—but I sent in my resignation as critical journalist, and
am going to write poetry all the rest of my life! I retire to play at "chuck
farthing"—and whenever I drink with an ostler, I shall do it, be sure, to
your good health— Yet the "sub tegmine fagi" plan would suit me
better; and I would willingly sit there with *thee,* O Menalcas! [3]

As for your blasphemies against such of the gods as dwell near
Helvellyn,[4] it would certainly be prudent not to sit near you under any
sort of *tree* while you utter them—for fear of a thunderbolt. My controversial answer to them all, is here in my "article"—which you are

---

than the *Paradise Lost* does of the angelhood of angels." "The Book of the Poets,"
Works, p. 648.

3. One of the shepherd singers in *Eclogues* 3 and 5. It was Tityrus who sat under
the beech tree's shade ("sub tegmine fagi") in *Eclogue* 1.

4. "Wordsworth upon Helvellyn!" were the opening words of EBB's sonnet "On
a Portrait of Wordsworth by B. R. Haydon"; *Works,* p. 329. On their controversy over
Wordsworth, EBB wrote, "Dear Mr. Boyd has been writing a good deal to me lately,—
and we have been quarreling fiercely upon Wordsworth—and I am pleased, through
all the quarreling, to see him armed with his old iron and energy, exactly as of yore."
To Annie Boyd Hayes, Taunton Castle, Taunton, December 1, 1842; unpublished
letter: Yale University Library.

not obliged to read because I send it. And to claim a like liberty for myself, *I* am not obliged to believe that *you* believe what you say or intimate of the great poet of our times! Pope—Goldsmith! Measure out broad praises to either!—but for genius, for philosophy, for various and expressive language and cadence,—for *poetry,* in brief—you cannot seriously place Wordsworth below *them.* Oh surely, surely not!

They have been praising me at length (with some critical blame) in the North American Review [5]—the chief Review in America—and this is the second time that I have been "taken up" in America—once before by "Arcturus" [6] a critical work published at Boston. The North American Review (if it were my book I would send it to you—and yet you might not care to see it) mentions the "Greek Christian poet" series in the Athenaeum, as mine,—and says that my prose wears "the peculiar characteristics of my poetry". It praises too, extravagantly my "House of Clouds"—the very poem which made you think I was losing the use of my faculties—(didn't you tell Arabel so?) makes quite a wonder of it, and ranks it as the best poem I ever wrote! What do you think of the "art of criticism" in America? You will forgive me for being unkind to Pope and kind to Wordsworth, after *that.*

I have written too much today to overburden you with the extract from Shakespeare.

Arabel has just gone out to walk with Flushie. She said to him in the other room, the door being open—"Go and kiss Miss Barrett first" —and in he came, galloping and prancing, kissed me on my lips, and ran out again. Isn't that *sense?* Couldn't he write a review if he tried? Yes, you will say—and *not* dispraise Pope!

May God bless you! Thank you for being glad that I am better, and for wishing that we may meet. I have hope that we may.

Ever your affectionate
E. B. B.

5. *North American Review, 97* (1842), 200–45. A review of six volumes of poetry, including three by EBB: *Essay on Mind, Prometheus,* and the *Seraphim.*

6. *Arcturus, 1* (1841), 171–6. A review of the *Seraphim,* concentrating especially on "The Poet's Vow."

163.

To 21 Downshire Hill
Hampstead

October 5, 1842

My very dear friend,

I scarcely need assure you that anything in my power to do to benefit Miss Heard's book,[1] should be done for her as your friend without your request, both willingly and gladly—and thus you will not doubt my motive when I say that the attempt to introduce her to the Athenaeum people as a friend of mine, would occasion more harm than good. The Athenaeum is resolutely *honest*—professes *honesty,* and holds to it cruelly sometimes,—stabbing its own contributors with poisoned daggers *"cum privilegio".* It has even been said that whenever Mr. Dilke shakes hands with an author in the street, he runs home crying "Shaken hands with an author?! My honesty is in danger!" and forthwith he exonerates his honesty by killing the author. I am perfectly sure that if I forwarded the book with the introduction you suggest, it would be the sign for a massacre—my friendship would do just so much for it.

Miss Heard's publishers should send her book to each of the different reviews, Literary Gazette, Athenaeum, Magazines etc.—he will best understand where—with a request on a slip of paper, "The publisher desires a notice". But none of these reviewers like the most distant appearance of being interfered with by private tampering of an author or his friends. There is poor Mr. Reade the poet,[2] who wrote one or two civil notes to Fraser,[3] and had the pleasure of seeing them publicly

1. The book was *The Shipwreck of the Dryad,* told in the form of letters to a sister. On April 19, 1843, EBB wrote to Boyd, "I enclose to you back again Miss Heard's letter—and I will also copy out the two notices of her little book which have fallen under my observation. The first is from Tait's Edinburgh Magazine [*10* (1843), 67]— 'The Dryad was wrecked some days after leaving the Mauritius, in the spring of 1841. The crew and passengers, among whom were several ladies, took to the boats, and after enduring great hardships, were so fortunate as to reach Port Dauphin in Madagascar. The narrative which is written in a simple and natural manner, is like that of every shipwreck, interesting.' The next is from the Athenaeum [*12,* (1843), 259]—'This little narrative may pair off with the well known story of the burning of the Kent East Indiaman. In both catastrophes, the gentle but high-toned fortitude of our countrywomen is calculated to arouse our national pride. Here, one of them narrates the perils and sufferings of shipwreck as unaffectedly as she bore them heroically.'" Omitted from Kenyon, *1,* 125.

2. John Edmund Reade (1800–70), whose poems showed a "remarkable capacity for plagiarism." *DNB.*

3. James Fraser (*d.* 1841), publisher of *Fraser's Magazine.*

exposed, printed in the magazine, afterwards, with an insulting notice that such were the means devised by Mr. Reade in order *to be read!*

Thank you for directing me to the reflective passages in Miss Heard's book. But whatever we judge their merit to be, we must not expect that a little book of so slight a structure should be taken up much by the reviews. It is more likely to be read and circulated than it is to be reviewed,—and so far it is happy.

Arabel heard from Annie two days ago,—and there is a message to you about her feeling too unwell to write much,—so you are not to wonder at her silence. It is a pain in her face—she calls it tic dolorous and it seems to be, poor thing, a cause of great suffering to her, altho' by no means dangerous.

Ever your affectionate
E. B. B.

164.[1]

November 26, 1842

My very dear friend,

I have sent your verses as you desired me to do, to the editor of the Athenaeum,—and yet am quite prepared in my own mind for the probability of their not being inserted. The Athenaeum only occasionally receives poetry, and does not profess to do so at all. Therefore you must not be surprised if they neglect yours, more especially as it is of a religious cast.[2] Have I not seen before the second one? and admired to you that idea about the budding of the rod of affliction? [3] I think so—altho' I will not say that these poems appear to me among the best you have written.

You surprised me very much by withholding your applause from the lines I quoted from Coleridge. His intention was to express the idea

1. MS in the Cornell University Library.

2. On December 4 EBB wrote, "Was I wrong too, dearest Mr. Boyd, in sending the poems to the 'Athenaeum'? Well, I meant to be right. I fancied that you would rather they were sent; and as your *name* was not attached, there could be no harm in leaving them to the editor's disposal. They are not inserted, as I anticipated. The religious character was a sufficient objection—their character of *prayer*. Mr. Dilke begged me once, while I was writing for him, to write the name of God and Jesus Christ as little as I could, because those names did not accord with the secular character of the journal!" Kenyon, *1*, 117.

3. EBB herself employed this figure in Letter 129: "But the rod of the Divine Chastener blossoms with His love!"

solitude wholly,—and by excluding the apparent presence of God, to make it solitude not only to the senses, but *to the soul*.

> So lonely 'twas, that God himself
> Scarce seemëd there to be.[4]

Never before, to my apprehension, was imaged so intensely, the fulness of desolation and loneliness.

When I spoke of public, my dearest Mr. Boyd, I *meant* the literary public—the *vox populi* among critics. That voice cried as loudly against Wordsworth once as it cries loudly for him now—and as loudly for Byron once as it does against him now: and I hope never to be led by any sort of public, literary or otherwise. I agree with you warmly that the present fashion of decrying Byron as a poet is pitiable or rather contemptible,—and it was but the other day that I expressed a strong disgust to Mr. Serjt. Talfourd's,[5] the author of Ion's, printed disclaimer of any desire to see Manfred's castle, when he stood at a few yards distance from it among the Alps. You cannot praise Byron as a poet, with warmer words than are always ready for him on my lips: he was a great and wonderful poet—passionate—eloquent—witty—with all powers of swift allusion and sarcasm and satire—full and rapid in the mechanical resources of his art, and capable of a sufficient and brilliant conveyance of philosophic thought and argument. In many, in most of these points he is superior beyond all comparison to Wordsworth—who is not passionate—nor witty—nor sarcastic—nor satirical—nor brilliant—nor peculiarly flexible and facile in rhyme and rhythm. Still I am not, in my own view, guilty of inconsistency, when I hold that Wordsworth is the greater poet in the proper sense of greatness, the profounder thinker, the nearer to the poetic secrets of nature, more universal, more elevated, more full and consistent in his own poetic individuality,—and more influential for good upon the literature of his country and age.

The expression you allude to in Coleridge is not quite as you repeat it. It is not "white and red," but "large and red" or "round and red" [6]— I don't exactly remember which. It may be an extravagance,—and I don't pretend to admire it—but it belongs to a poem which is one of its kind,—most singular and supreme in dauntless originality and sublime conception—the work of a soul more intensely poetical (in the apprecia-

---

4. *The Rime of the Ancient Mariner*, Pt. 7, lines 599–600.

5. Thomas Noon Talfourd (1795–1854), jurist and writer, became sergeant-at-law in 1835. *Ion*, a tragedy, was privately printed in 1835 and produced at Covent Garden in 1836.

6. Or perhaps "nor dim nor red," *Ancient Mariner*, Pt. 2, line 97.

tion of mind) than either the author of the Excursion or he of Childe Harold.

My very dear friend, if it should please God to permit me once again to go to see you, I shall welcome it as one of the pleasures left to me of many taken. But I would rather read anything with you than the epistle to the Romans, just because it is probable that we might not come precisely to the same results in our review of it. I have been to my own conviction very near death since I saw you last, and have suffered the bitterness of death without attaining to its calm,—and the effect upon my mind is a complete state of antagonism to anything like religious controversy. I believe that the particular points agitated between Calvinists and Arminians are of no importance, and are not intended to be rendered clear in the present aspect of the church—and that the aspiration of Christians should simply be to *love more* rather than to *learn more.* "Knowledge puffeth up" says the apostle—"but Love buildeth up." [7] We shall be right in loving—and safe in loving Christ—and happy in loving each other,—and glorified in love in Heaven. Into the counsels of God we have no right to enter (it seems to me) as the Calvinists are fond of doing, with definitions and classifications,—nor do the Arminians appear to me justified in much which they assume. In almost every religious controversy, there are two wrong sides,—and one bad spirit which is common to both,—and whether we do or not increase our knowledge by controversy, we are sure to diminish our love.

Therefore, if you please my very dear friend, we won't read the Romans until we have done all the other reading and subjects of talk remaining to us to explore. Thank you from my heart for caring to see me again!

Ever your affectionate
Elizabeth B. Barrett

You shall hear of the Athenaeum.

165.[1]

To 21 Downshire Hill
  Hampstead

December 24, 1842

My very dear friend,

I am afraid that you will infer from my silence that you have affronted me into ill temper by your parody upon my sonnet. Yet "lucus

7. 1 Cor. 8:1.
1. Published in part in Kenyon, *1,* 117.

a non lucendo" [2] were a truer derivation. I laughed and thanked you over the parody,—and put off writing to you until I had the headache which forced me to put it off again.

The extreme difficulty, nay, the impossibility of advising you in respect to Mary Hunter, had something moreover, to do,—I won't deny it,—with my silence. I cannot wish to prevent you from inviting her to your house—and I cannot wish to persuade you into the same. I have much affection for Mary Hunter, as you are aware—and yet, she might not suit you as a companion, *I* am aware. If intelligence and kindheartedness and good and upright principles were all you needed, I should say—*take her*. But you are particular in respect to manners and voice and gentleness,—and altho' Mary is ladylike, she is apt to be a little hasty and abrupt, and to walk and talk too little according to your music; and I am in great difficulty how to give counsel about her.

My very dear friend, if you should determine upon making the trial, the proposition should certainly go directly from you to Mr. Hunter.[3] I mentioned to him that you had thoughts in your head which referred to Mary,—and he will be prepared to reply to the very few lines it would be necessary for you to address to him. Decide, then, yourself—and write yourself!—and let Mr. Hunter on the other side act upon his own opinion. I am afraid of saying "yes" or "no" for fear I should say wrong—I am afraid of making a mistake and a gesture at the same time. And then, perhaps after all, Mr. Hunter would find it impossible to spare her at present—but I don't know how this may be.

May God bless you my dear Mr. Boyd. Mr. Savage Landor once said that anybody who could write a parody deserved to be shot—but as he has written one himself since saying so, he has probably changed his mind. Arabel sends her love.

Ever your affectionate and grateful
Elizabeth B. Barrett

2. "A grove [is named] from having no light": proverbial for a misnomer.

3. The proposition was made through Arabel. "Arabel has written according to your desire, about Mary Hunter—and if she can go to you, you must not fancy that I was not always persuaded of your being pleased with her in certain respects. You could not fail to estimate her quickness of intelligence and affectionateness of character. I was rendered overcautious perhaps in what I have said on this subject, by the affection I feel towards both of you—both yourself and *her*." To Boyd, January 5, 1843; passage omitted, Kenyon, *1*, 118. Apparently the invitation was not accepted.

166.

December 28, 1842

My very dear friend,

I am the worst riddle-guesser in the world. If I had been in Oedi-pus's case the Sphinx would have put an abrupt end to me. Some poet whom I never praised—never spoke of to you!!! Why who can *he* be? Did you never hear me praise *Shelley?* Can it be *Shelley?* What you say of the cadencial music might perfectly apply to him—and he was very capable of the pathetic, altho' he did not keep near enough to Humanity to communicate largely and warmly with its emotions. Can it be Shelley—or Keats even? Suppose it to be either, my not having recognized them as poets in your presence, was a mere ac-cident of omission—I love and admire them as poets.

Who else can this poet be? [1] And I missed him from my papers on the English poets—did I indeed? And he deserves all you say of him? —does he really? Behold me puzzled.

Earnestly praying for your solution I remain most affectionately and ignorantly

Your *She-Davus* [2]
E. B. B.

I hope you received my letter acknowledging the parody?

167.

Friday, February 1843

My very dear friend,

I snatch eagerly at the next post to assure you that I am not "an-noyed" by your candour,—altho' I can by no means accept your in-vitation to "despise your stupidity". Oh no! I am sorry of course to have missed your approbation which is always most pleasant to me— and to have missed it by that want of clearness which I struggle against so vainly. For I am used to be told that nobody can under-stand me—*that* is my destiny—I was probably "built in an eclipse

1. The answer to the riddle was "Ossian." "I never, never should have guessed the name; not though I had guessed to Doomsday." To Boyd, January 5, 1843; Kenyon, *1*, 118.

2. "Davus sum, non Oedipus," i.e. "I am a plain man and do not understand rid-dles." Terence *Andria* 1.223.

and rigged with curses dark"! [1] My wonder is simply, that you should be the first to complain to me of the unintelligibility of these particular poems.[2] The Americans must have fancied they understood them, or they would not talk of their "successfulness"—unless indeed they take me for a right down riddle maker, and take the hardest riddles for the best ones. Well! If I am as dark as the Archbishop of Canterbury whose charade is past guessing, forgive me for his sake.

And now my dearest Mr. Boyd, instead of reproaching you, who are always as kind as your incorruptible truth will let you be,—let me thank you for being sincere with me on this occasion as always. You speak of me (and therefore think) far too well in general. *That* I know, knowing what is in me.

> Gratefully and affectionately yours
> Elizabeth Barrett B.

168.

To 21 Downshire Hill
Hampstead

March 31, 1843

My very dear friend,

I feel guilty before you, since your last letter has remained too long unanswered—but I have had a great deal of necessary writing to do,—and I thought it necessary also to read "Cuthullin" [1] steadily through as a preliminary to replying to your remarks upon it. This has been achieved at last,—and of course I admit the great beauty of certain things in the poem, although the image which struck me first, still strikes me most,—and although I preserve my opinion upon the general monotony and defective individuality. To my ear, upon *the whole,* even the rhythm is monotonous. Detached passages have an exquisite rhythm—but as you go on reading page after page you (nay, but I should rather say *I*) grow sensible of a sameness which is fatiguing. It is

"Those evening bells, those evening bells" [2]

1. Milton, *Lycidas,* line 101.
2. Probably the "Cry of the Human" and four sonnets, which EBB was sure Boyd would not "abide." To Boyd, February 21, 1843; Kenyon, *1,* 124.
1. By Ossian (James Macpherson). The debate on this subject continued briskly through the winter and spring. See published letters.
2. Thomas Moore, "Those Evening Bells."

ringing throughout the four and twenty hours. It is your melodious clocks striking the minutes. It is my doves cooing without interval. It is, in literal fact, *melody,* without the intricacies, the varieties, the light and shade of *harmony*—and therefore, is it, in long continuousness, fatiguing to the ear and ungrateful to the sense of music.

Another defect I must allude to in your Ossian—he wants perspective—you see everything equally and on a level—through a mist indeed, but through a mist spread over everything alike and in a like degree. Is it not so? Are you not sensible of this yourself? *I speak as to a wise man.* You once replied to me with a justice which I confessed at once, that Dr. Johnson's opinion against the authenticity of Ossian was of no weight whatever. I refer now to another authority which, whether in point of national attachments or familiarity with the antique in Scottish poetry, must be considered the highest and weightiest of all—Sir Walter Scott's. Sir Walter Scott was decided in his opinion against the authenticity of Ossian—and as far as any authority may influence the decision of any question, this authority seems to me to affect this question.

Well!—we shall never, I suppose, agree upon it! Remember however that we have noble poets in England, and that you should not give away all your admiration to these vague mist-bound glories.

Poor Southey is gone at last.[3] For three years his great intellect was shrunken and misshapen,—and he stood an idiot with the laurel on his brow. A few weeks ago he had an apoplectic fit—and passed finally from the world by an attack of typhus fever. Never for a moment, did the light of his mind return. The transition was immediate, without twilight or dawn, from the thick darkness of moral insensibility, to the radiance before the Throne.

May God bless you, dearest Mr. Boyd!

I thank you for permitting me to see Miss Heard's letter which is here returned to you. No! it isn't returned—it is mislaid. I will look for it and let you have it.

Ever affectionately yours
Elizabeth B. Barrett

3. Southey died March 21, 1843.

169.

To 24a Grove End Road

Friday, 1843

My very dear friend,

I write in haste to thank you for the additional stanzas to Flush's poem.[1] They amused me very much, but are not, I beg to explain, so strictly historical as the rest,—Flush being the most disinterested as well as the most faithful of friends. If he consents, he says, ever to go out of doors, it is because it is necessary to his health, or perhaps to leave his mistress's homage at the feet of Mr. Boyd.

I must observe however that the new stanzas are very spirited—and better-spirited than mine,—and that the conclusion of the last one is all the more in my style, that it is densely obscure.

Most affectionately yours

E. B. B.

170.[1]

April 3, 1844

My very dear friend,

You are to understand, if you please, that if Occy finds it possible to go to see you tomorrow and goes, his intention is not to take a lesson in architecture from you, but to show his sense of your kindness in desiring to be the means of his instruction.[2] It was very kind in *you*,—and it is only right that he should acknowledge the value of the kindness. And now, to go on to my poor "Pan". [3]

He has come to life again. My critic would not accept any compromise; and said so much of the pain I should give him by keeping to my resolution, that I was forced to give way. So "Pan" will be published, either in the first or second volume;—and without his horns being broken off in the first place. I cannot accede to the breaking of the horns—although perhaps, after all, the critic would

1. "To Flush, my Dog"; *Works,* p. 257. Boyd had criticized the original verses and EBB had expressed herself as humbled "by your hard criticism of my soft rhymes about Flush." To Boyd; Kenyon, *1,* 152.

1. MS in the Henry W. and Albert A. Berg Collection of the New York Public Library.

2. Boyd had expressed a desire for conversation with Octavius on the subject of architecture. Letter to Boyd; Kenyon, *1,* 173.

3. "The Dead Pan." EBB had carried on a long discussion of this poem with Kenyon the year before.

appear to you right, and the poet wrong. Only the poet is obstinate on this one point—no, these *two points*—of the *horns.*

In relation to Mrs. Smith,[4] I am embarrassed how to express myself. She is very good and kind in taking any interest in me, and in caring to hear either of my health or my poetry—and, having a sincere personal respect for *her,* I should be exceedingly loath to have the appearance of responding coldly or indifferently to a proposition coming from her. Still, it is out of my power to enter upon unnecessary correspondences on indefinite subjects;—*I,* who have so much more to do already, than I *can* do without fatigue. I have been thinking only today, that I am either busy, or tired, from morning to night—and really there is no exaggeration in this. There is the writing for literature's sake—and then, there is the writing growing up from *that,*—in answer to letters from persons known or unknown in relation to literature,—and then there is the writing to my personal friends whom I could not forget for all the Muses. Often and often, have I been obliged to neglect somebody dear to me,—nevertheless,—for many a post,—just because I was so tired that I could not write any more. Think how feeble I am—and how (apart from opium) I am feebler still—incompetent, in fact, to anything—and agree with me, my dearest Mr. Boyd, that it would be wrong in me, not to say out of the question, to attempt the sort of correspondence suggested by Mrs. Smith's courtesy. Miss Martineau [5] wrote to me six weeks ago, begging me to send her a minute account of this, and this, and this, —naming such and such things. I acknowledged her letter by a brief note, and promised to write at length soon. Well—*I have not written yet —I,* with my earnest admiration of Harriet Martineau, and with a full heart for her kindness to me! I could not write—I have not had time! Now, you see how it is! You will make apologies for me to Mrs. Smith! —explaining that if she has, at any time, anything definite to ask of me, I shall be happy always to receive a letter from her, and also to answer it. It is only the entering upon a correspondence with indefinite objects and therefore without end, that I am forced to decline—thanking her, however, for the honor she proposed to confer on me.

And now my very dear friend, I have passed my bounds in writing a letter to you. No wonder that you wished to establish a conduit for my epistolary superfluities, under the name of Mrs. Smith!

Most affectionately yours
Elizabeth B. Barrett

4. Probably the daughter of Rev. Adam Clarke.

5. Harriet Martineau (1802–76), popular writer, authority on social and economic problems.

171.[1]

To 24a Grove End Road
   St. John's Wood

[*postmark* August 14, 1844]

My dearest Mr. Boyd,

I must thank you for the great, great pleasure with which I have this moment read your note [2]—the more welcome, as (without hypocrisy!) I had worked myself up into a nervous apprehension, from your former one, that I should seem so "rudis atque incomposita" to you, in consequence of certain licences, as to end by being intolerable. I know what an ear you have!—and how you can hear the dust on the wheel as it goes on! Well—I wrote to you yesterday, to beg you to be patient and considerate.

But you are always given to surprise me with abundant kindness,—with supererogatory kindness. I believe in *that*, certainly.

I am very, very glad that you think me stronger and more perspicuous. For the perspicuity, I have struggled hard.

And I am very grateful to you for drinking my health—it is doing me only too much honour! and in such wine!—and from your high classical lips,—and from Miss Heard's high heroic lips,—and from Miss Kate Heard's right roseate ones!!! I thank you all,—wishing, for my own part, to be worthier.

But how can it be, that Miss Heard has not her copy?—and you would have mentioned it, I think, if she had received it. It was sent to her on Monday, together with the vial.

Your affectionate and grateful
Elzbeth [3]

172.[1]

Tuesday, September 22, 1844

Thank you my dearest friend for your song called the "Force of Truth," which had force enough to make me laugh, although by no

1. Published in part, Kenyon, *1*, 184.
2. A letter of congratulation on *Poems*, 2 vols., published August 1844.
3. In a letter dated August 6, 1844, EBB asked Boyd to "promise never to call me Miss Barrett again. You have often quite vexed me by it. There is Ba—Elizabeth—Elzbeth—Ellie—any modification of my name you may call me by—but I won't be called Miss Barrett by *you*." Kenyon, *1*, 180.
1. MS in the Huntington Library.

means with its truth. If you praise me on the same sheet on which you make epigrams on Wordsworth, people will say that there is as little ground for one as the other, and that you mean it to be understood so. Is it possible that you were in earnest as to ground-work of this song? —that, like wits in general, you did not think more of your flower than of your root? I will try to believe that you *did,* in any case,—and so, I thank you for the flower! I like the first stanza best—*"but the pity of it, Iago!"* [2]

Arabel should have told you that I had a letter the other day, and a most kind letter, from Mr. Serjeant Talfourd, who has taken a cottage at the Lakes to be near Mr. Wordsworth, whom he calls his "illustrious neighbour." He (Mr. Serjeant Talfourd) after speaking very kindly of the "Drama of Exile" and the "Vision of Poets", singles out as one of his especial favorites among the minor poems, "Cyprus Wine", and does me the honour of imagining that *Mr. Boyd must be pleased with it.*[3] He says besides, that my books have been the companions of his pleasantest walks in that romantic country,—and I am glad that the mountains and lakes had not power to put the poems to shame. And oh, such a letter as I have had from Harriet Martineau! She had bound herself by a promise to tell me the full truth about the books,—let it be pleasant or unpleasant truth—and because her letter was long in coming, I began to fear that it would be unpleasant. But there never was a more delightful generous letter, or one fuller of fervent sympathy. She tells me that every day she has had the volumes open before her, and that their power over her is of the deepest. What particularly pleases me, is, that her predominant impression, she says, is of their entire *"originality"*. Also she observes upon what she calls the "immense advance" on the former work —being of opinion, nevertheless, that "a few of the pieces" of that former work, might be considered "worthy of a place in this." I was very much delighted by this letter from such a person, who unites to high logic, a deep sensibility to poetry—certainly the most manlike woman (in the best sense of man) in the three Kingdoms.

I should tell you however that she complains of a general impression of monotony, after reading the "Drama of Exile,"—and that she prefers upon the whole, the smaller poems. "Lady Geraldine's Courtship" she singles out for praise, and says of it that she felt herself *"swept through it."* Now it is curious, that people in general are pleased with "Lady Geraldine"—and it is true that I always hear of their being pleased

2. *Othello* IV.1.206.

3. "Wine of Cyprus" was inscribed, "Given to me by H. S. Boyd, author of 'Select Passages from the Greek Fathers,' etc., to whom these stanzas are addressed."

with it, with a feeling like a *sense of escape,*—seeing that some peculiar circumstances attended its composition. Do not tell anybody—people might and would immediately call me a careless, hasty writer,—but the last *thirteen* of those printed pages were written,—composed and written—in one day. It was dangerous and might have been fatal speed. When people praise the poem, I always think, "What stuff it *might* have been!"—and *that* is very natural.

Dearest Mr. Boyd, I hear of your talking of more generosity about the Cyprus wine. Now I do beseech you not to think of such a thing any more. When I go to see you, you shall give me a whole glass of it,— only if you won't see Flush, you won't be able to see me. He and I are inseparable companions, and I have vowed him my perpetual society in exchange for his devotion. Why if he were to bite you even, it would do you no harm, unless he were mad—and if he were mad, I would not send him to see you. Consider this logic, and believe me always

Your very affectionate
Elibet

173.

To 24a Grove End Road
St. John's Wood

[*postmark* September 25, 1844]

I thank you, dearest Mr. Boyd, for the coffee, and would have written immediately to thank you, but I thought I ought to appreciate it properly before I began to thank you for giving me the opportunity. It is very good, I think, but inferior to my recollection of what I used to find at your house. Perhaps it would seem better, if you were sitting by—and, to try the experiment, I am thinking, musing, dreaming, of going to see you some day. Oh—it is not a joke, indeed! I am coming,— and am not so far off as the end of the world, however you may consider of it. In the meantime, while I take your coffee apart from you, I thank you, and am quite aware of its being better than most sublunary coffee besides.

Dearest Mr. Boyd, when I go to see you,[1] I will not ask you to meet me on the stairs, or in the drawing room—I would not run the risk of doing you any harm,—but I will ask you, on the other hand, to let it all pass quietly, and with as little retrospection as may be—I shall feel a good deal in seeing you, and being weak still in soul and body, would try

1. The projected visit was not paid until July 1, 1846. See Letter 185 and n. 2.

to keep as calm as possible. Believe that I have the truest affection for you, and that if sorrow has not changed me in this respect, still less can any manner of joy.

As to Ossian, I have endeavoured vainly to procure the book you spoke of by purchase,—but as soon as Mr. Kenyon returns, I will teaze him into teazing his friends until we get it somehow. My infinite generosity, or else desperate despondency, in so loading the pistols which are to shoot my head off, is therefore most "aspectable"—to use an old favorite word of yours.

May God bless you, dearest Mr. Boyd.

I am ever your affectionate and grateful

Elibet

174.[1]

To 24a Grove End Road
St. John's Wood

October 4, 1844

My dearest Mr. Boyd,

I must not delay longer in telling you that I was much moved by Miss Heard's letter, and that I appreciated your kindness in sending it to me. Such testimonies are of course far dearer and more welcome to me than critical compliments from reviewers,—and I feel, in receiving them, that with all my faults and deficiencies, I may not perhaps have written nor lived quite in vain.

Perhaps you are right respecting the scriptural question,—but I have certainly heard from pulpits such an application of the "dyed garments" as I ventured on. Sin was an enemy like the rest, and conquered by the Great Victor. Still it is true that the idea of triumph rather than of suffering, is, under any aspect, conveyed by the image—and therefore I kiss your sword or rod.

As to the "Lost Bower," I am penitent about having caused you so much disturbance. I sometimes fancy that a little varying of the accents, though at the obvious expense of injuring the smoothness of every line considered separately, gives variety of cadence and fuller harmony to the general effect. But I do not question that I deserve a great deal of blame on this point as on others. Many lines in "Isobel's Child" are very slovenly and weak, from a multitude of causes. I hope you will like the "Lost Bower" better when you try it again than you did at first, though

1. Published in part in Kenyon, *1*, 200.

I do not, of course, expect, that you will not see much to cry out against. The subject of the poem, was an actual fact of my childhood.

Oh—and I think I told you, when giving you the history of "Lady Geraldine's Courtship," that I wrote the *thirteen* last pages of it in one day. I ought to have said *nineteen* pages instead. But don't tell anybody. Only keep the circumstance in your mind when you read it and see the faults. Nobody knows of it except you and Mr. Kenyon and my own family, for the reason I told you. I sent off that poem to the press piecemeal, as I never in my life did before with any poem. And since I wrote to you, I have heard of Mr. Eagles,[2]—one of the first writers in Blackwood and a man of very refined taste,—adding another name to the many of those who have preferred it to anything in the two volumes. He says that he has read it at least six times aloud to various persons, and calls it a "beautiful *sui generis* drama." On which Mr. Kenyon observes that I am "ruined for life, and shall be sure never to take pains with any poem again."

The American edition (did Arabel tell you?) was to be out in New York a week ago,—and was to consist of fifteen hundred copies, in two volumes, as in England.[3]

She sends you the verses, and asks you to make allowances for the delay in doing so. I cannot help believing that if you were better read in Wordsworth, you would appreciate him better. Ever since I knew what poetry is, I have believed in him as a great poet—and I do not understand how reasonably there can be a doubt of it. Will you remember that nearly all the first minds of the age have admitted his power, (without going to intrinsic evidence) and then say that he *can* be a mere Grub Street writer? It is not that he is only or chiefly admired by the "profanum vulgus"[4]—that he is a mere popular and fashionable poet,— but that men of genius in this and other countries, unite in confessing his genius. And is not this a significant circumstance? significant, at least!

With regard to Miss Martineau, as Arabel has been telling me what you say, I must say something again. As far as she is a political economist, I can judge no more of her ability than I can judge of Mrs. Somerville's [5] in mathematicks. But as an eloquent writer and lucid thinker,—as

---

2. John Eagles (1783–1855), contributor of articles on art to *Blackwood's Magazine.*
3. Published in America as *A Drama of Exile: and Other Poems,* New York, 1845.
4. "Odi profanum vulgus." Horace *Odes* 3.1.1.
5. Mary Somerville (1780–1872), writer on science. "Her grasp of scientific truth in all branches of knowledge, combined with an exceptional power of exposition, made her the most remarkable woman of her generation." *DNB.*

possessing singular powers of description and pathos,—and as the possessor of an original and originating mind endowed with high logic and imaginative sensibility, I consider her very superior to Mrs. Somerville, according to my limited knowledge of what Mrs. Somerville is. In my creed, an *originating* mind must always be greater than a *receiving* mind—always!—whatever the learning may be which is received. Surely you will agree with me in this. For the rest, I have a very high respect for Mrs. Somerville, and shall always be ready to express it.

I have had a letter from Mrs. Jameson too—you have heard of *her* of course. She is a very gifted and eloquent woman. May God bless you my dearest friend. Assure Miss Heard when you write to her or see her next, of my deep sympathy with an affliction I can understand.

Believe me, yourself,
Your affectionate and grateful
Elibet B. B.

How kind you are,—far too kind,—about the Cyprus wine! I thank you very much.

175.

To 24a Grove End Road
St. John's Wood

November 21, 1844

My very dear friend,

Forgive me for whatever may have borne the appearance of negligence! I could not determinately neglect any request of yours,—and the truth is in the present case, that I fancied I had either written to you or sent you a message on the subject of the Cyprus wine, and that, so far from imagining myself to be your debtor in the way of writing, I was every day expecting a letter from you which seemed to me to loiter. See how it is with me! Thought is so much to me what action is to people in general, that when I think of doing a thing, it remains doubtful to my mind often, whether I have not done it in the thinking.

As to the magazines, if I had told you of the reviews directly, I knew that you would have been impatient, and bought them, and I wanted to send them to you, so as to spare you that expense,—and then they were detained here by loitering readers, longer than I expected in the first instance. Be sure, I did not forget *you* in reading them. How could I? Whenever I read a review that pleases me, the thought of you comes instantly and naturally with the assurance of your sympathy. Did Arabel tell you that the Westminster Review has announced a criticism? The poems have been well reviewed,—have they not? Blackwood has treated them better than he has been known to treat poetry for years and years.[1] And yet you see, these gentlemen of the press appear "agreed" to throw over the "Drama of Exile" as a failure, before they admit any good in what follows. I suppose, as you say with sufficient niceness of distinction, they take one to be warm in the mouth, and the other, warm in the stomach.

And this warns me to return to the unfinished theme of Cyprus wine. I pause to thank you for your generosity in sending me another bottle (indeed it is too kind of you!) and then I proceed to try and answer your question. But how am I to answer it? I am afraid that I did not analyze my sensations with definitiveness enough to distinguish between the mouth-warmth and the stomachic warmth, in my recollection of the first wine I had from you and its effects. I thought and still think that first wine a little superior to what you have had the kindness to send me lately,—but the only point of difference I can perceive strongly enough to describe is the point of *flavour*. The first wine had more of the flavour of oranges and was sweeter, I think. There is assuredly a difference, and perhaps it may consist in something *more* than what I have mentioned —but I cannot analyze or describe the degree. My palate has not been educated with regard to wines—and this is the only wine of the gods I ever tasted. Therefore you should not expect too much from me.

The lady who gave her heart in exchange for a vial of Cyprus wine, must have been like the gentleman in the song

"Fond of love but fonder of the bottle".

For my own part and in matters of sentiment, I decidedly prefer Ben Jonson's cellarage—

"Drink to me only with thine eyes,
And I will pledge with mine".

So,—to shift the question between you [*word torn away*] I beg you to consider (analyzing your sensations) what is the difference to your imagination, between a cup of Cyprus and a pair of the brightest of

1. "Miss Barrett is a person gifted with very extraordinary powers of mind, and very rare sensibilities of heart. She must surely be allowed to take her place among the female writers of England as a poetess of no ordinary rank." From review in *Blackwood's Edinburgh Magazine*, 56 (1844), 621–39.

eyes—say Miss Caroline Marcus's! Which is the warmest in the mouth?
—and which, the warmest in the stomach?

Ever most affectionately yours
Elizabeth B. Barrett

176.

To 24a Grove End Road
St. John's Wood

Thursday morning
[*postmark* November 28, 1844]

My dearest friend,

I should thank you gratefully for the kind words you say to me about
the "Drama of Exile", if I could speak or think of anything just now,—
except of your being unwell. Arabel assures me that you look very well,
—but still it is impossible for me to hear of your suffering under any
kind of indisposition, without pain and anxiety. I have been thinking
my dearest friend, that if you had a sofa in your room, and were to lie
on it now and then, in order to change your position, it might be found
pleasant and useful. Will you try it? Arabel says there is a comfortable
sofa in your drawing room, which might be removed to your room without the least difficulty. Nothing appears to me more certain than the
fact of your retaining one position, as you sit on that chair, far too undeviatingly. Think of the sofa when you think of me. There should be
plenty of pillows on it, so as to keep your head raised—and, in this way,
you would obtain repose, without the debilitating effects of a bed.

Yes!—I well remember and always bear in mind your "zeal *with*
knowledge" [1] concerning Aeschylus.

May God bless you, dearest Mr. Boyd! Will you direct Jane to write
me a short note just to say how you are. Send me a message by her just
to say so, without taking the trouble of regularly dictating. If there is
anything which I or *mine* can do for you,—if there is anything which I
can get for you in any way, do please me by speaking.

Am I not always
Your affectionate and grateful
Elibet

---

1. "Zeal without knowledge is sister of folly," John Davies of Hereford, *The
Scourge of Folly* (1611), p. 42.

Mr. Burges applies to me through Mr. Kenyon to know whether you would like to have a copy of a treatise of Apuleius "De Deo Socratis", edited by a young man of promising ability and attainments, called Mr. Buckley.² Answer at your leisure.

177.

To 24a Grove End Road
St. John's Wood

Wednesday morning
[*postmark* December 4, 1844]

My dearest friend,

I cannot let today pass without thanking you for your most kind note, and for your consideration in sending Jane to talk to me of you. Everytime the post comes I hope to have a line, just to say that you think yourself better, and, so, to add to the gladness with which I have heard that others think you better. Surely you could not doubt of my true and tender interest in your health and sickness, your pleasure and pain? Everything in the past comes back warmly as I write your name—and the tears stand in my eyes. I would have your companionship in almost all things—except in any sorrow. May God bless you, my dearest friend.

I have fancied that you might hear with interest Miss Martineau's letters on mesmerism,¹ as printed in the Athenaeum,—and therefore I shall send them to you, together with the Westminster Review which contains a notice of the poems. Keep the Athenaeums altogether, if you like, and keep the Westminster *as long as* you like. Do not hurry yourself in the reading of it. I was pleased with Jane, and liked her countenance, and her feeling manner of speaking of you. I think of you now more than ever of course,—but I will not write a long letter for fear of fatiguing you.

Your ever affectionate and grateful
Elibet

2. Theodore William Alois Buckley (1825–56), translator of classical works. His schooling had stopped at the age of twelve, but this edition of Apuleius' treatise led friends to send him to Oxford.

1. Miss Martineau, who had recovered from an "incurable" illness by the use of mesmerism, described her cure in six letters to the *Athenaeum* from March 23 to December 21, 1844. These aroused prolonged discussion, in which Miss Martineau was accused of fraud and credulity.

The medical press (for instance, the *"Lancet"* I understand) attacks poor Miss Martineau most cruelly on account of her statement in the Athenaeum.

178.

To 24a Grove End Road
St. John's Wood

Saturday
[*postmark* December 14, 1844]

My dearest friend,

If I have not written, there has been a great deal of thought of you through all my silence,—and I have been thankful to think from Arabel's account as from your own, that if you continue to suffer pain and sleeplessness, there is every hope of its being a transient affection,— and not at all like *my affection for you.* The weather is very hard to bear,—and nobody, I should fancy, can help feeling that they should feel better for thaw and sunshine instead of frost and east wind, supposing the power of bartering one for the other, to be within reach.

And now I am going to give you Arabel's opinion of the chair. At the Baker Street Bazaar she found one which she considers suitable to you. It is not quite new, but is quite as good as new,—and from the fact of its not being actually so, you have it for four guineas, and not for six. It is handsome-looking and covered with leather, and has *low arms,* which will be no obstacle but an assistance to your rising up and sitting down. All the easy chairs have arms of some kind—and although she saw a chair without them, it was inferior to the others, and too narrow in the seat for you. But what can be your objection, my dearest Mr. Boyd, to the arms? You will find the arms to be a comfort to you, to keep you warmer than you would otherwise be, and to assist you in moving. I venture to urge upon you the desirableness of *trying the arms. Now do.* I wish too that you would lose no time about the chair, but send for it directly. The comfort will be very great—and the advantage in other respects, still greater than the comfort.

I hope Arabel told you how well the poems are selling,—and how half the edition is sold already, after little more than three months. I agree with you that the Westminster Review article is inferior as a critique and a composition, although I thought it very kind.

May God bless and keep you. To know that He blesses you, must always be a blessing to

Your most affectionate
Elibet

179.[1]

To 24a Grove End Road
   St. John's Wood

Monday

[*postmark* December 24, 1844]

My dearest Mr. Boyd,

I wish I had a note from you today—which optative aorist, I am not sure of being either grammatical or reasonable! Perhaps you have expected to hear from *me* with more reason. Your last note I have turned over and over in my thoughts, feeling almost as uncomfortable in it as I am afraid *you* do in your new chair. I was sorry that the lumbago should haunt you so pertinaciously; and I was sorry too, that you should have been "evil-entreated" to give four guineas for a piece of furniture which did not suit you. For the first, we must, I believe, wait for the passing of the east wind and of the cold belonging to it. Nobody can flourish much in this weather, I know by experience. But for the chair, —it is different,—and I am not a little vexed with my own part in persuading you to your destruction. Dearest friend,—why did you *take* the chair, if, upon trial, you felt that it would not suit you? I agree at once that you must know what is most comfortable to yourself. I do not talk in favor of your chair, "ex cathedra"—I submit like a chairwoman. And I suggest moreover that you should allow Arabel to ask the people to take it back and *make you another according to your own direction,* which they could not object to do. My individual opinion, perhaps, is that if you would lean your head backward instead of forward upon your chest, your general health would very much profit by it,—and that any slanting back of the chair which permitted this change, would be desirable on account of it. You are not aware how much you *droop,* in sitting, and how the circulation and the digestion may both be impeded by this continued position. You *are,* however, aware, that I am infinitely impertinent, and that I ought to sit on the stool of repentance for it, instead of on any chair whatsoever.

I fancied that you would be struck by Miss Martineau's lucid and able style. She is a very admirable woman—and the most logical intellect of the age, for a woman. On this account it is, that the men throw stones at her, and that many of her own sex throw dirt—but if I begin on this subject I shall end by gnashing my teeth. A righteous indignation fastens on me. I had a note from her the other day, written in a noble

1. Published in part in Kenyon, *1,* 225.

spirit, and saying, in reference to the insults lavished on her, that she was prepared from the first, for *publicity,* and ventured it all, for the sake of what she considered the truth—she was sustained, she said, by the recollection of Godiva.

Do you remember who Godiva was—or shall I tell you? Think of it— Godiva of Coventry, and peeping Tom.[2] The worst and basest is, that in this nineteenth century there are thousands of Toms to one.

I think, however, myself, and with all my admiration for Miss Martineau, that her statement and her reasonings on it are not free from vagueness and apparent contradictions. She writes in a state of enthusiasm, and some of her expressions are naturally coloured by her mood of mind and nerve.

May this Christmas give you ease and pleasantness, in various ways, my dearest friend! My Christmas wish for myself is, to hear that you are well! I cannot bear to think of your suffering. Are the nights better? May God bless you. Shall you not think it a great thing if the poems go into a second edition within the twelvemonth? I am surprised at your not being satisfied. Consider what poetry is,—and that four months have not passed since the publication of mine,—and that, where poems have to make their way by force of *themselves,* and not of name nor of fashion, the first three months cannot present the period of the quickest sale. *That* must be for afterwards. Think of me on Christmas Day, as of one who gratefully loves you.

Elibet

180.

To 24a Grove End Road
  St. John's Wood

Christmas Eve 1844

My dearest friend,

Your letter reached me half an hour after mine left me to go to you,— and now I must write to assure you of my regret and pain in thinking of your being worse for having acceded to the wish of your friends to call in a physician. My only comfort is, that perhaps, when the immediate effect of the strong medicine has passed, you may be the better essentially for the temporary depression—I hope in *this.* Tell me how you continue to feel, my dearest Mr. Boyd! And what physician, did you call in? And

---

2. The name given to the tailor of Coventry who was struck blind when he tried to catch a glimpse of Lady Godiva's ride.

what *did he say of you?* I do wish you had told me *that.* I agree with you absolutely that a medical man acquainted with your constitution, has immense advantages over a stranger,—which I know by myself,—for, whenever I have had a new doctor, I have been worse for several weeks. If indeed Mr. Giuseppe were in difficulty,—if your case be an obscure one, and he doubt how to proceed in it,—*then,* it would be right to have further advice. But can this be the case? I hope not. I have been saying to myself lately, that if you continued to be troubled by these lumbago pains, the reason was to be looked for in the severe weather,—and that presently you would revive like the snowdrops. Dearest friend, let me know by a line, how you feel. Perhaps today you are stronger again. Give me my Christmas wish,—or rather may God give it,—and let me hear of your being better.

My thoughts are very near to you—and my affections still nearer.

I will take the liberty of sending Arabel's love, though she is not in the house,—and, as for mine, I beg Jane to put it up with the holly tomorrow, in the nearest place to your chair.

Your affectionate and grateful
Elibet

You are suffering like Job among your friends. Miserable comforters are we all!—are we not?

181.

To 24a Grove End Road
   St. John's Wood

Saturday
[*postmark* January 6, 1845]

My dearest friend,

I have just received your note, after a good deal of anxiety which is not relieved by it. Do you know that you have written this note with all the obscurity which Elizabeth Barrett could put into a poem? I can't make out what you mean by "the thing being as you were told"—Do you mean the telling of Mr. Jago or of Mr. Giuseppe? I have been anxious about you,—expecting to hear Mr. Travers's opinion—and now I hear it, it is like Confucius to me—and I entreat of you, if Jane cannot come, to write just a word of clear meaning in explanation.

Mr. Jago's account of you through Nelly Bordman, made me quite happy—only if he was right in his particular view, Mr. G. has been so *very wrong* that I do not think you should retain him as a medical attendant.

My present comfort through all the darkness, is, that you feel yourself to be easier and better! May God increase all the good!

You will understand me when I say briefly, in reference to the opinion asked from Papa and myself, that an oath of so grave a nature as the one described to and repeated by Arabel, should, according to our impression, be either *kept,* or absolved by the person to whom you made it. You should write to that person, and state that you regret your oath and desire to be released from it. If the person have any honour at all, you will be released instantly, and then you may act freely. This is our opinion.

I am going to send you the New Quarterly, which, in an article on the "poetesses of England",[1] praises me very kindly,—and also some American criticisms which may amuse you.

May God bless you. My thoughts are with you most affectionately—
Your Elibet

182.[1]

To 24a Grove End Road
St. John's Wood

April 3, 1845

My very dear friend,

I have been intending every day to write and tell you that the Cyprus wine is as nectareous as possible,—so fit for the gods, in fact, that I have been forced to leave it off as unfit for *me*,—it made me so feverish. But I keep it until the sun shall have made me a little less mortal,—and in the meantime, recognize thankfully both its high qualities, and *your* kind ones. How delightful it is to have this sense of a summer at hand. *Shall* I see you this summer, I wonder! That is a question among my dreams.

By the last American packet I had two letters, one from a poet in Massachusetts and another from a poetess,—the *he*, Mr. Lowell,[2]—and

1. By Henry Fothergill Chorley (1808–72), to whom EBB wrote a letter of appreciation January 3, 1845; Kenyon, *1*, 229.
1. Published in part in Kenyon, *1*, 250.
2. James Russell Lowell (1819–91).

the *she,* Mrs. Sigourney.[3] She says that the sound of my poetry is stirring the "deep green forests of the New World"—which sounds pleasantly, —does it not? And I understand from Mr. Moxon [4] that a new edition will be called for before very long—only not immediately.

You will be delighted to hear that Wordsworth is in London,—having been "commanded" up to attend the queen's ball. The majesty of England, when she saw him, was quite *"fluttered"*, Mrs. Jameson heard from one of the maids of honour—and I am well contented that it should be so.

Also I hear that a learned Greek of my acquaintance sees more virtue in the cutting of throats, than in mending the ragged stockings of the ragged Maynooth priests.[5] I humbly hope that he is eclectic in his philosophy about the throats,—and does not mean throats in general, or even the throats of his own friends in particular.

Seriously and without a jest, if there cannot be love among Christians —as this loud party-cry through England disproves,—I think there ought to be a sense of equal justice, at least. Not that I discuss the point with you, my dearest friend! I would rather say that I affectionately think of you every day, and that I beg you to think of *me* as

Your affectionate and grateful friend
Elibet

Arabel and Mr. Hunter talk of paying you a visit some day.

183.

To 24a Grove End Road
  St. John's Wood

[postmark May 12, 1845]

My dearest Mr. Boyd,

Papa is delicate about giving an opinion as to the necessity of the appointment of another trustee,—but he thinks that if (as he believes) Mr. Williams's death leaves him *sole trustee,* there certainly should be a second. George says decidedly that there should be *two trustees capable of acting, according to law.*

---

3. Lydia Huntley Sigourney (1791–1865). Her poems set the standard for American sentimental poetry for at least fifty years.

4. Edward Moxon (1801–58), publisher.

5. In a letter to Mrs. Martin of the same date (Kenyon, *1,* 252) EBB reports more fully on the Queen's reaction to Wordsworth and on the proposed grant to Maynooth, the Catholic seminary in Ireland.

After all, Papa's impression is that the new trustee is already appointed, in the person of Mr. Lethbridge.

My experience in respect to the Cyprian nectar, is no mistake,—although I can easily and fully believe of it, that it is much less exciting than Port or Madeira, or even sherry. But you are not aware, perhaps, that two teaspoonfuls of the latter wines will always make me feverish. I am made of dry chips, and shall die some day of spontaneous combustion. Well!—wait a little while! Wait till the east wind has done with us and the summer has fairly begun,—and then, my heart may take to lying very quiet, and let me return to the Cyprus. In the meantime I shall send you (in a day or two) a review or two from America. They never will have done reviewing me,—will they? It is as everlasting as the east wind.

May God bless you!

Your ever affectionate
Elibet

184.

To 24a Grove End Road
St. John's Wood

[*postmark* September 17, 1845]

My dearest friend,

I am going to be very impertinent and very meddling, and therefore I do invoke your *patience* to be the Muse of my letter. Now listen to me.

I understand from all my enquiries of you, that you still are inclined to what I call the *iniquity* of getting out of bed in the night, and sitting in your chair. That you are easier in the chair and prefer the posture altogether, I understand also,—and yet it is so clear to me that you must ultimately suffer from this habit, that I cannot help entreating you to consider the subject under some particular aspects of it. I might beg you for love of me, to grant my request and remain in bed—I might say that it would be kind of you to relieve the anxiety of such of your friends as cannot bear to think of your sitting up all the night through—but I would rather lay before you the exact reasons which make me anxious.

In the first place, then,—there is the *exposure*. The body is more sensitive to cold during the night, and the atmosphere is more inclined towards chilling,—and therefore (supposing your pains to be rheumatic) you exchange for momentary ease, many of the probabilities of progress and essential improvement. This is one reason—but I think still more of the next.

In the second place, then, according to the constitution of our bodies, *rest* is necessary to their well-being: and by rest I do not mean sleep,— but the repose which is produced by *posture and stillness.* Anatomists tell us that the horizontal posture relieves the spinal process from its burden,—and that it is *necessary,* in order to the due relaxation of the muscles and nerves and of the frame in general. In any other position than the horizontal, there are pressures throughout the frame, which if they are perpetual, are likely to produce disease. You see I speak generally. I might say that you have always had the habit of stooping rather too much,—and that therefore, in your case, the general observation acquires a new emphasis,—and the fact grows clearer and clearer, that you will be sure to suffer hereafter from your present disinclination to the horizontal posture. You will suffer in your digestion— in your chest,—or wherever you are the weakest in body. The weakest part will feel the fatigue first. Is not this reasonable? And is it not natural that I should shrink and fear before the pain of seeing you incur new diseases? Forgive me for speaking. You will grant that it is natural for me to fear!—and fear sometimes gives courage,—which is natural too! and, so, I speak.

When I speak of the horizontal posture, of course I do not mean it quite literally. If the posture gives you pain, it should be modified to the degree necessary to escaping the pain. But I think that it should be sufficiently horizontal, to give rest to the body by opposing a new posture to the posture of sitting up in the chair. The legs should be laid up— and the head (above all) laid back. Also, if you should consent to a little propping by pillows,—why should you not allow Jane to make for you a loose flannel bedgown reaching to the hips, or a little below,—lined with very thick wadding or, as I should prefer, with *fur? Coloured flannel lined with fur and made very loosely* would last long,—and you would find it as warm as the blankets,—or warmer. Will you for my sake, my dearest friend, think of these things, and weigh my reasons well—and be sure that if I did not feel them to be strong reasons, I would not run the risk of teazing you or perhaps of displeasing you. And even with these strong reasons, I might be afraid of running this risk, if I did not hold you in so much affection that I would rather be scolded than see you suffer. May God bless you, dearest Mr. Boyd! I will not tire you with too long a note, whatever else I may do—that is, if you are not tired already.

Your attached and grateful friend
Elibet

185.

To 24a Grove End Road
St. John's Wood

[*postmark* July 7, 1846]

Is it true, dearest Mr. Boyd, that I appear to you so guilty? The intention, at least, has clean hands.

I waited to be able to tell you, together with my gratitude about the Cyprus, on what day I could hope to see you again—and I have been again shaken and saddened by more details of poor Mr. Haydon,[1]—besides the excitement, from the arrival, in the house, of my aunt and cousin. Do try to forgive me,—because I never could *intend* an unkindness towards you—think if I could. Your affectionate words sink deeply, —and affectionately and gratefully I feel towards *you,* beyond what words could say on that day of my visit,[2] and beyond what they will attempt to say now. May God bless you.

As to the Cyprus, I almost think that I will ask you to keep for me the bottle you speak of, and let me drink it with the gods, when I go to see you. It will be doing the right honour to the nectar. And I will drink, if you please, to Ossian's immortal memory!—which you, on the other side, shall set against all my faults!

Your ever affectionate
Elibet

186.

[1846]

Believe of me, my very and ever dear friend, that I am deeply touched and moved by the kindness and affectionateness of your letter, and that I thank you for it heart to heart. From my heart I may say to you, that, looking back to that early time, the hours spent with you, appear to me some of the happiest of my life—a life in which the "happiest part has

1. Benjamin Robert Haydon, the artist, took his own life June 22, 1846. EBB's correspondence with him has been published by Martha Hale Shackford, *Letters from Elizabeth Barrett to B. R. Haydon,* New York, 1939.

2. July 1, 1846. This first visit "after seven heavy, changeful years" had been planned by Arabel in a preliminary call at Mr. Boyd's on June 21, during which Elizabeth stayed in the garden. EBB—RB, June 22, 1846, and July 1, 1846.

not prevailed",[1] as in the chorus of Agamemnon. A prophet said to me (by the way) a week since, that God intended me compensation, even in the world, and that the latter time would be better for me than the beginning.[2] And if this oracle were fulfilled, I should still look back, from the new happiness, as from the accustomed sorrow, to the hours spent with you, and call them, gratefully, very happy hours, just as I call *you* my very dear friend. May God bless you, dearest Mr. Boyd! Pray do not talk of dying, when I am returning to life. You look as well as ever, I am delighted to have seen with my own eyes,—and I will hope that we shall spend together still, many hours out of many years—the winter not killing *me,* nor any other cause, *you,*—and your goodness continuing to forgive me my various sins, whether in or out of bad verses.

In the meanwhile I intend to go to see you during this summer as long as I can and as often. You will have me near you in a day or two again.

Here is an epitaph written by a wit on a great talker— *Hic tacet.*
With which, appropriately, I end—
Your ever affectionate and grateful
Elibet

187.

To 24a Grove End Road
St. John's Wood

Pisa. November 19 [1846]

My dearest Mr. Boyd, I do not know whether you have expected to hear from me, but certainly I expected to write to you long before this. Silent or speaking however, I have borne with me a constant remembrance of and gratitude for your sympathy and goodness to me,—and in looking back through all these thick vapours of dreamland, to the friends whom I best love in England, your name stands among the very first— Indeed I seem to be living in a dream—life is so different to me from what it ever was. Can it be possible, I think to myself, that creatures on this side the grave, can be so happy? I am very happy, very strangely

---

1. "Sing woe, woe, but let the good prevail," choral refrain of the *Agamemnon.*
2. Boyd, turning over this phrase in his mind and probing into it on successive visits, finally elicited from Elizabeth the secret of her plan to marry Robert Browning. See EBB—RB, August 18, 1846. Her old friend was drawn into the conspiracy and on September 12, after her wedding at Marylebone Church, EBB went directly to Mr. Boyd's home before returning to 50 Wimpole Street. EBB—RB, September 12, 1846.

happy, in every possible respect except in the anger left behind where I do not like to think of it—but *here,* the constant companionship and tenderness of the best and most gifted of human beings, has transfigured life to me. No woman was happier in her choice—no woman— And after above two months of uninterrupted intercourse, there is still more and more cause for thankfulness;—and more and more affection on his side— He loves me better every day, he says—and indeed I believe—Thank God for me that He should let me be so happy,—and "according to Lowth's version" *"smile a little,* before I go hence to be no more seen." [1] If the world ended for me at this moment, I may now say the grace of life with satisfied lips, having tasted so much of its sweetness. It was worth the endurance and even the *survival* of all my trials, to have lived these last two months—so much do I thank God for them. My health improves still, too.

We saw Notre Dame in Paris, and the wonderful cathedral at Bourges, where the painted glass windows (of which the secret is lost) torture the sun into giving out solemn and glorious oracles. We had a delightful journey through Provence, in the very steps of the Troubadours, to Marseilles—and made a pilgrimage from Avignon, to the fountain of Vaucluse where Petrarch *lives still,* through the strong memory of the great scholar and poet. The fountain, shut up in everlasting walls of rock, is full of beauty—the little river flashing from it like a green singing-bird,—and we sate upon stones in the middle of the water till Flush dashed through it to look for me. As to Pisa, it is a majestic, silent city, built of marble and backed by purple mountains. We like it very much, and have rooms in an ancient college built by Vasari, and close to the gorgeous Duomo, the Campo Santo, and Leaning Tower. I am able to walk out every day through the mildness of the climate, and to sit in the sun to watch the lizards—and the other morning Robert caught me a gigantic grasshopper, exactly like Anacreon's.[2] For the rest, we see nobody, but read and write and talk and never are tired of those three things. Sometimes too, we talk of you, and I teach my husband my affection for you, which cannot be a difficult lesson— Do think of us together as of two persons who have reason to love you gratefully. For me, the last sympathy you gave me, did not touch me least, of all you have given me in the course of my life. May God bless you my dearest friend —Shall I have a word from you sometimes? Say how you are. I am

Your grateful and most affectionate
Elibet

1. Psalms 39:13.
2. See *Anacreontic* 32, quoted in Letter 105.

Will you have the enclosed put into an envelope and send it to Arabel? I hope you will see much of my dearest Arabel— How I miss her, for all the happiness!

188.[1]

To 24a Grove End Road
St. John's Wood

December 21 [1846]

You must let me tell you, my dearest Mr. Boyd, that I dreamed of you last night and that you were looking very well in my dream, and that you told me to break a crust from a loaf of bread which lay by you on the table—which I accept on recollection as a sacramental sign between us, of peace and affection. Wasn't it strange that I should dream so of you? Yet no!—thinking awake of you the sleeping thoughts come naturally. Believe of me this Christmas-time as indeed at every time, that I do not forget you, and that all the distance and change of country can make no difference. Understand too (for *that* will give pleasure to your goodness) that I am very happy, and not unwell, though it is almost Christmas. It is a little cold just now—but, until these few days, I have been walking out every morning, and sitting out of doors in the sun, and I hope not to lose much strength by the temporary change of weather. Even now, the sun shines so hotly, as to inconvenience the walkers in it,—and I thankfully admit that the climate, upon the whole, is more qualified to do me good, than I had been led to hope.

Does Arabel go to see you properly,—that is, frequently? It is a grief to me that she should be treated coldly on my account,—and the injustice is *rampant,* as she knew nothing, you know, of the marriage. For myself, I am wounded,—yet feel myself *justified,* both by the hardness *there,* and the tenderness *here.* Completely spoilt and happy, I may write myself down. Now, everything I ever said to you of my husband, seems cold and inadequate! He is my compensation for the bitterness of life, as God knows and you *knew.*

Dearest friend, are you well and in good spirits? Think of me over the Cyprus, between the cup and the lip—though bad things are said to fall out so. We have, instead of Cyprus, *Montepulciano,* the famous "King of Wine," crowned king, you remember, by the grace of a poet! [2] Your Cyprus, however, keeps supremacy over me, and will not abdicate the

1. Published in part in Kenyon, *1,* 314.

2. Montepulciano in Tuscany, famous for its wine, was the birthplace of the poet Poliziano (1454–94).

divine right of being associated with you. I speak of wine—but we live here the most secluded, quiet life possible,—reading and writing and talking of all things in Heaven and earth and a little besides,—and sometimes even laughing as if we had twenty people to laugh with us— or rather—*hadn't*. We know not a creature, I am happy to say,—except an Italian professor (of the university here) who called on us the other evening and praised aloud the scholars of England. "English Latin was best" he said, "and English Greek foremost." Do you clap your hands?

The new pope [3] is more liberal than popes in general, and people write odes to him in consequence.

Robert is going to bring out a new edition of his collected poems, and you are not to read any more, if you please, till this is done. I heard of Carlyle's saying the other day "that he hoped more from Robert Browning, for the people of England, than from any living English writer"— which pleased me of course. I am just sending off an anti-slavery poem [4] for America—too ferocious, perhaps, for the Americans to publish: but they asked for a poem and shall have it.

If I ask for a letter, shall I have it, I wonder? Remember me and love me a little—and pray for me, dearest friend, and believe how gratefully and ever affectionately

I am
Your Elibet

—Though Robert always calls me *Ba,* and thinks it the prettiest name in the world!!! Which is a proof, you will say, not only of blind love but of deaf love.

I hope Jane is well—and your Toby besides. Flush has grown insolent, and barks when he wants a door opened. Do you see Nelly Bordman? She has been very affectionate to me.

189.[1]

To 24a Grove End Road
St. John's Wood, Regent's Park

Florence. May 26 [1847] [2]

I should have answered your letter, my dearest friend, more quickly, but when it came I was ill, as you may have heard, and afterwards I

3. Pope Pius IX.
4. "The Runaway Slave at Pilgrim's Point," *Works,* pp. 228–31.
1. Published in part in Kenyon, *1,* 330.
2. This last letter to Boyd was written a year before his death, May 10, 1848.

wished to wait until I could send you information about the Leaning
Tower and the bells. The book you required, about the cathedral,
Robert has tried in vain to procure for you. Plenty of such books, but
not in English. In London such things are to be found, I should think,
without difficulty, for instance, "Murray's Handbook to Northern Italy,"
though rather dear (12s) would give you sufficiently full information
upon the ecclesiastical glories both of Pisa and of this beautiful Florence
from whence I write to you. He says of the Leaning Tower—"On the
summit are seven bells, so arranged that the heavier metal is on the side
where the weight counteracts the slope of the building. These bells, of
which the largest weighs upwards of twelve thousand pounds, are re-
markably sonorous and harmonious. The best-toned is the fourth—
called the Pasquareccia—it was this bell which was tolled when criminals
were taken to execution. It was cast in 1252 and has many ornaments,
a figure of the Virgin, and the devices of Pisa. The Bell-founders of this
city enjoyed great reputation." So far, Murray! I will answer for the
harmony of the bells, as we lived within a stone's throw of them, and
they began at four o'clock every morning and rang my dreams apart.
The Pasquareccia (the fourth) especially, has a profound note in it,
which may well have thrilled horror to the criminal's heart. It was
ghastly in its effects,—dropt into the deep of night like a thought of
death. Often I have said "Oh, how ghastly," and then turned on my
pillow and dreamed a bad dream. But if the bell-founders at Pisa have
a merited reputation, let no one say as much for the bell-ringers. The
manner in which all the bells of all the churches in the city are shaken
together sometimes, would certainly make you groan in despair of your
ears. The discord is fortunately indescribable. Well—but here we are at
Florence, the most beautiful of the cities devised by man! I was too weak
when I came, to see anything, and had to lie on the sofa and grow strong,
while the Venus of Medici stood two or three streets off—think how
tantalizing!—but my poor dearest Robert had suffered great anxiety
about me, and it was only just to him to run no risks. Now I am well
and beginning to go out and see all the glories. I am really quite well
and look better than I have done for years, and we have ever so many
wild schemes— Here is one! We talk of spending the heat of the summer
in Vallombrosa ³ with the monks—yes, indeed, we almost have settled it.

3. Their stay was shortened to five days when the new Abbot resolutely refused
to relax further the rules which excluded women from the monastery. Back in the
heat of Florence, the Brownings searched for a cool apartment, and found spacious
rooms in the Palazzo Guidi (Casa Guidi) which was to be EBB's home until her death
on June 29, 1861.

We shall enjoy so infinitely the sublime solitude of the mountains, rocks, cascades, and chestnut forests. There is not a carriage road—so much the happier! Oxen will drag us in baskets up the precipitous mountain-sides. Then we shall sit out in the forests and write poetry which you shall read, and the poems will be as wild as the poets. One difficulty we apprehend, from my sex, as the monks have vowed "their holy sod shall ne'er by woman's foot be trod"—but if I promise to behave well and do nobody in the confraternity any manner of harm, it is supposed that the Archbishop of Florence will let me go in with my husband. What do you think? Will it not be delightful? Flush wags his tail when we consult him on the subject, and seems to draw a rapid conclusion that liberty and coolness in the woods, will be clear gain after this intense Florentine heat, of eighty four degrees of Fahrenheit. Always it is cool at Vallombrosa— Oh, the cool, green, lonely, deep chestnut forests! How pleasant they will be to me and Flush!

In the meanwhile I have seen the Venus—I have seen the divine Raphaels—I have stood by Michael Angelo's tomb in Santa Croce—I have looked at the wonderful Duomo! This cathedral!! After all, the elaborate grace of the Pisan cathedral is one thing, and the massive grandeur of this of Florence is another and better thing—it struck me with a sense of the sublime in architecture. At Pisa we say, "How beautiful,"—here we say nothing—it is enough if we can breathe. The mountainous marble masses overcome us as we look up—we feel the weight of them on the soul. Tesselated marbles (the green treading its elaborate pattern into the dim yellow, which seems the general hue of the structure) climb against the sky, self-crowned with that prodigy of marble domes. It struck me as a wonder in architecture. I had neither seen nor imagined the like of it in any way. It seemed to carry its theology out with it—it signified more than a mere building. Tell me everything you want to know—I shall like to answer a thousand questions. Florence is beautiful as I have said before, and must say again and again, most beautiful. The river rushes through the midst of its palaces like a crystal arrow; and it is hard to tell, when you see all by the clear sunset, whether those churches and houses and windows and bridges and people walking,—in the water or out of the water,—are the real walls and windows and bridges and people and churches. The only difference is that, down below, there is a double movement,—the movement of the stream besides the movement of life. For the rest, the distinctness to the eye is as great in one as in the other.

My dearest friend, I was much pleased to have your account of yourself, as it was better than I had feared. Let me entreat you, now that the summer has come, to take the opportunity and the advice of the wise, and change the air—ah, if I dared say *for my sake!* A little exercise—consider how necessary it must be to your health. I hear on all sides that *you have it in your power* to recover habits of healthful activity and to prolong your life *with enjoyment.* Dearest Mr. Boyd, I excommunicate that chair of yours,—I beseech you to take courage and to remember the duty of self preservation. Robert and I drank your health two evenings ago in wine of Cyprus. It is good wine, brought straight from Cyprus, at sixteen pence a bottle—but for some reason or other I thought it inferior to yours—yes, certainly it is inferior. Tell me whether drinking your health did you good. Do you see Mrs. Smith? Do you see my dearest Arabel? and Nelly Bordman? Remember me to such of my friends as remember me kindly when unreminded by me. I am very happy—happier and happier. My late indisposition had nothing to do with former illnesses, but it prevented, no less, my ascent to the top of the Leaning Tower—a disappointment, notwithstanding your exhortations. Is Jane still a comfort to you? If so, thank her from *me*—who never cease to be

Your grateful and most affectionate
Elibet

Robert's best regards to you always.

CHRONOLOGICAL ARRANGEMENT OF THE KNOWN LETTERS OF EBB TO HSB*

MCCARTHY	WEAVER	KENYON
1–27 (Mar. 11, 1827–[1828])		
	IV [1828]	
28–33 ([1828]–Nov. 18, 1828)		
	VIII [Dec. 1828]	
34–38 (Jan. 10–May 16, 1829)		
	II [1829]	
39–42 (June 26, 1829–[1829])		
	I (August 8 [1829?])	
43–46 [1829]		
	VI [1829?]	
47–73 ([1829]–[1831])		
	VII [1831]	
74–77 (Mar. 8, 1831–[April, 1831])		
	III [1831]	
78 [1831]		
	X (April 29, 1831)	
79–93 (May 4, 1831–Sept. 7 [1831])		
	V, XI(?) [1831]	
94–124 ([Oct. 22, 1831]– Oct. 20, 1832)		
	XII (Nov. 3, 1832)	
125–127 (Nov. 22, 1832– May 30, 1834)		
	XIII (July 20, 1834)	
128 (Sept. 14, 1834)		*I*, 24
	XIV (Nov. 2, 1834)	
129 [1834]		
	XV (Feb. 4, 1835)	
130 [1835]		*I*, 29
	XVI (July 25, 1835)	
131 (July 29, 1835)		

* Since some letters lack sufficient evidence for accurate dating, this placing has occasionally had to be somewhat arbitrary. The present editor assumes responsibility for the conjectural dates in square brackets.

MCCARTHY	WEAVER	KENYON
132 [1835]		*1*, 23
133 [1835]		
		1, 32 [1835]
134–135 ([Jan. 1836]–Mar. 16, 1836)		
		1, 37, 38, 39 (Oct. 14 [1836]–Nov. 26, 1836)
136 (Dec. 15, 1836)		*1*, 44
137 [Christmas, 1836]		*1*, 45
	IX [1836]	
138–141 [1837]		
	XVIII, XVII [1837]	
142–145 (Sept. 25, 1837–Mar. 10, 1838)		
		1, 57 (Mar. 27, 1838)
146–147 [1838]		
		1, 60, 61, 62, 68, 69, 70, 72 ([May, 1838]–[June, 1838])
148 [1838]		
	XIX [1838]	
		1, 73 [1838]
	XX [1838]	
149–151 (Jan. 28–June 24, 1839)		
		1, 77 (Nov. 27, 1839)
152 (May 29, 1840)		*1*, 79
153 (July 8, 1840)		*1*, 81
154 (May 10, 1841)		
		1, 88, 89 (Aug. 28–31, 1841)
155 (Oct. 2, 1841)		*1*, 91
		1, 93, 95, 96 (Dec. 29, 1841–Jan. 13, 1842)
156 (Jan. 15, 1842)		
		1, 98 (Feb. 4, 1842)
157 [1842]		
		1, 99, 101 (two letters), 102 (Mar. 2–29, 1842)
158 (April 2, 1842)		*1*, 103
159 (May 17, 1842)		*1*, 104
		1, 105, 106 (June 3–22, 1842)

MCCARTHY	WEAVER	KENYON
160–162 (July 7, 1842–[1842])		
		1, 109 (Sept. 14, 1842)
163 (Oct. 5, 1842)		
		1, 113 (Oct. 31, 1842)
164 (Nov. 26, 1842)		
		1, 115 (Dec. 4, 1842)
165 (Dec. 24, 1842)		*1*, 117
166 (Dec. 28, 1842)		
		1, 118, 119, 124 (Jan. 5–Feb. 21, 1843)
167–168 (Feb.–Mar. 31, 1843)		
		1, 125, 138, 139, 141, 152 (Apr. 19–Sept. 8, 1843)
169 (1843)		
		1, 154, 171, 173 (Sept. 19, 1843–Apr. 1, 1844)
170 (April 3, 1844)		
		1, 175, 176, 179, 183 (June 18–Aug. 13, 1844)
171 (Aug. 14, 1844)		*1*, 184
		1, 192 (Sept. 1, 1844)
172 (Sept. 22, 1844)		
173 (Sept. 25, 1844)		
174 (Oct. 4, 1844)		*1*, 200
175–178 (Nov. 21–Dec. 14, 1844)		
179 (Dec. 24, 1844)		*1*, 225
180–181 (Dec. 24, 1844– Jan. 6, 1845)		
		1, 242, 246 (Mar. 3–29, 1845)
182 (April 3, 1845)		*1*, 250
183 (May 12, 1845)		
		1, 264 (July 21, 1845)
184 (Sept. 17, 1845)		
		1, 270, 279 (Oct. 27, 1845–June 27, 1846)
185–187 (July 7, 1846– Nov. 19 [1846])		
188 (Dec. 21, [1846])		*1*, 314
189 (May 26, 1847)		*1*, 330

INDEX